AMERICAN POLITICAL, ECONOMIC, AND SECURITY ISSUES

U.S. VISA POLICIES, PROGRAMS AND CONSIDERATIONS

AMERICAN POLITICAL, ECONOMIC, AND SECURITY ISSUES

Additional books in this series can be found on Nova's website under the Series tab.

Additional E-books in this series can be found on Nova's website under the E-books tab.

AMERICAN POLITICAL, ECONOMIC, AND SECURITY ISSUES

U.S. VISA POLICIES, PROGRAMS AND CONSIDERATIONS

AARON R. MILLER
EDITOR

Nova Science Publishers, Inc.
New York

For permission to use material from this book please contact us:
Telephone 631-231-7269; Fax 631-231-8175
Web Site: http://www.novapublishers.com

Library of Congress Cataloging-in-Publication Data

U.S. visa policies, programs and considerations / editors, Aaron R. Miller.
p. cm.
Includes index.
Includes reports to Congress from the Congressional Research Service and the Government Accountability Office.
ISBN 978-1-61470-333-4 (hardcover)
1. United States--Emigration and immigration--Government policy. 2. Emigration and immigration law--United States. 3. Visas--United States. I. Miller, Aaron R. II. Library of Congress. Congressional Research Service. III. United States. Government Accountability Office. IV. Title: United States visa policies, programs and considerations.
JV6483.U34 2011
325.73--dc23

2011022497

Published by Nova Science Publishers, Inc. † New York

CONTENTS

Preface		**vii**
Chapter 1	Immigration Visa Issuances and Grounds for Exclusion: Policy and Trends *Ruth Ellen Wasem*	**1**
Chapter 2	Visa Security Policy: Roles of the Departments of State and Homeland Security *Ruth Ellen Wasem*	**27**
Chapter 3	Diversity Immigrant Visa Lottery Issues *Ruth Ellen Wasem*	**49**
Chapter 4	Visa Waiver Program *Alison Siskin*	**61**
Chapter 5	Foreign Investor Visas: Policies and Issues *Alison Siskin and Chad C. Haddal*	**83**
Chapter 6	DHS's Visa Security Program Needs to Improve Performance Evaluation and Better Address Visa Risk Worldwide *United States Government Accountability Office*	**113**
Chapter 7	H-1B Visa Program: Reforms Are Needed to Minimize the Risks and Costs of Current Program *United States Government Accountability Office*	**141**
Chapter 8	H-2B Visa Program: Closed Civil and Criminal Cases Illustrate Instances of H-2B Workers Being Targets of Fraud and Abuse *United States Government Accountability Office*	**229**
Index		**243**

PREFACE

The conventional wisdom is that the terrorist attacks on September 11th 2001 prompted a substantive change in U.S. immigration policy on visa issuances and the grounds for excluding foreign nationals from the United States. A series of laws enacted in the 1990s, however, may have done as much or more to set current U.S. visa policy and the legal grounds for exclusion. This book reviews the legislative developments in visa policy over the past 20 years and analysis of the statistical trends in visa issuances and denials provide a nuanced study of U.S. visa policy and the grounds for exclusion.

Chapter 1- The conventional wisdom is that the terrorist attacks on September 11, 2001, prompted a substantive change in U.S. immigration policy on visa issuances and the grounds for excluding foreign nationals from the United States. A series of laws enacted in the 1990s, however, may have done as much or more to set current U.S. visa policy and the legal grounds for exclusion. This report's review of the legislative developments in visa policy over the past 20 years and analysis of the statistical trends in visa issuances and denials provide a nuanced study of U.S. visa policy and the grounds for exclusion.

Chapter 2- Foreign nationals (i.e., aliens) not already legally residing in the United States who wish to come to the United States generally must obtain a visa to be admitted, with certain exceptions noted in law. The Departments of State (DOS) and Homeland Security (DHS) each play key roles in administering the law and policies on the admission of aliens. Although the DOS's Consular Affairs is responsible for issuing visas, the U.S. Citizenship and Immigrant Services (USCIS) in DHS approves immigrant petitions, the Immigration and Customs Enforcement (ICE) in DHS operates the Visa Security Program in selected embassies abroad, and the Customs and Border Protection (CBP) in DHS inspects all people who enter the United States. In addition, the Executive Office for Immigration Review (EOIR) in the U.S. Department of Justice (DOJ) has a significant policy role through its adjudicatory decisions on specific immigration cases.

Chapter 3- The purpose of the diversity immigrant visa lottery is, as the name suggests, to encourage legal immigration from countries other than the major sending countries of current immigrants to the United States. Current law weights the allocation of immigrant visas heavily toward aliens with close family in the United States and, to a lesser extent, toward aliens who meet particular employment needs. The diversity immigrant category was added to the Immigration and Nationality Act (INA) by the Immigration Act of 1990 (P.L. 101-649) to stimulate "new seed" immigration (i.e., to foster new, more varied migration from other parts of the world).

Chapter 4- Since the events of September 11, 2001, concerns have been raised about the ability of terrorists to enter the United States under the visa waiver program (VWP), because the VWP bypasses the first step by which foreign visitors are screened for admissibility to enter the United States. Nonetheless, the inclusion of countries in the VWP may help foster positive relations between the United States and those countries, promote tourism and commerce, facilitate information sharing, and ease consular office workloads abroad. The VWP allows nationals from certain countries to enter the United States as temporary visitors (nonimmigrants) for business or pleasure without first obtaining a visa from a U.S. consulate abroad. Temporary visitors for business or pleasure from non-VWP countries must obtain a visa from Department of State (DOS) officers at a consular post abroad before coming to the United States. As of January 2011, 36 countries participate in the VWP.

Chapter 5- With the current economic downturn, Members of the 111th Congress are likely to be faced with many policy options aimed at economic improvement, including the possible consideration of amending visa categories for foreign investors. Foreign investors are often viewed as providing employment opportunities for U.S. citizens rather than displacing native workers. Yet, extending foreign investor visas provides several potential risks as well, such as visa abuses and security concerns. Thus, a potential policy question for Congress—and particularly legal permanent resident (LPR) investors—is whether the benefits reaped from allocating visas to foreign investors outweigh the costs of denying visas to other employment-based groups.

Chapter 6- Since 2003, the Department of Homeland Security's (DHS) Visa Security Program (VSP) has participated in the visa process by reviewing applications at some embassies and consulates, with the intention of preventing individuals who pose a threat from entering the United States. The attempted bombing of an airline on December 25, 2009, renewed concerns about the security of the visa process and the effectiveness of the VSP. For this report GAO assessed (1) the ability of DHS's Immigration and Customs Enforcement (ICE) to measure the program's objectives and performance, (2) challenges to VSP operations, and (3) ICE efforts to expand the VSP program. To evaluate the VSP, the authors reviewed VSP data, guidance, and the ICE's 5-year expansion plan. The authors also interviewed ICE officials, and observed VSP operations at 6 posts overseas.

Chapter 7- Congress created the H-1B program in 1990 to enable U.S. employers to hire temporary, foreign workers in specialty occupations. The law capped the number of H-1B visas issued per fiscal year at 65,000. Since then, the cap has fluctuated with legislative changes. Congress asked GAO to assess the impact of the cap on the ability of domestic companies to innovate, while ensuring that U.S. workers are not disadvantaged. In response, GAO examined what is known about (1) employer demand for H-1B workers; (2) how the cap affects employer costs and decisions to move operations overseas; (3) H-1B worker characteristics and the potential impact of raising the cap; and (4) how well requirements of the H-1B program protect U.S. workers. GAO analyzed data from 4 federal agencies; interviewed agency officials, experts, and H-1B employers; and reviewed agency documents and literature.

Chapter 8- The H-2B visa program assists U.S. employers anticipating a shortage of domestic nonagricultural workers by permitting them to hire nonimmigrant foreign workers temporarily. The program is overseen by several agencies, including the Department of Labor

(Labor), the Department of Homeland Security's United States Citizenship and Immigration Services (USCIS), and the Department of State. Employers often hire labor recruiters or other intermediaries to assist with the process of obtaining labor certifications and finding foreign workers. GAO was asked to determine if there were examples of recruiters and employers engaging in illegal or fraudulent activity within the H-2B visa program.

In: U.S. Visa Policies, Programs and Considerations
Editor: Aaron R. Miller
ISBN: 978-1-61470-333-4

Chapter 1

IMMIGRATION VISA ISSUANCES AND GROUNDS FOR EXCLUSION: POLICY AND TRENDS*

Ruth Ellen Wasem

SUMMARY

The conventional wisdom is that the terrorist attacks on September 11, 2001, prompted a substantive change in U.S. immigration policy on visa issuances and the grounds for excluding foreign nationals from the United States. A series of laws enacted in the 1990s, however, may have done as much or more to set current U.S. visa policy and the legal grounds for exclusion. This report's review of the legislative developments in visa policy over the past 20 years and analysis of the statistical trends in visa issuances and denials provide a nuanced study of U.S. visa policy and the grounds for exclusion.

Foreign nationals not already legally residing in the United States who wish to come to the United States generally must obtain a visa to be admitted. Those admitted on a permanent basis are known as immigrants or legal permanent residents (LPRs), while those admitted on a temporary basis are known as nonimmigrants (such as tourists, foreign students, diplomats, temporary agricultural workers, and exchange visitors). They must first meet a set of criteria specified in the Immigration and Nationality Act (INA) that determine whether they are eligible for admission. The burden of proof is on the foreign national to establish eligibility for a visa. Conversely, foreign nationals also must not be deemed inadmissible according to other specified grounds in §212(a) of the INA. These §212(a) inadmissibility criteria are health-related grounds; criminal history; security and terrorist concerns; public charge (e.g., indigence); seeking to work without proper labor certification; illegal entrants and immigration law violations; ineligible for citizenship; and aliens illegally present or previously removed.

The number of aliens excluded on the basis of §212(a) of the INA has fluctuated over the years. In FY2008, §212(a) exclusions of prospective nonimmigrants hit 35,403 and surpassed the prior high point of 34,750 in FY1998. For prospective LPRs, §212(a) exclusions peaked in FY1998 and FY1999, reaching over 89,000 in both years. The

---

* This is an edited, reformatted and augmented version of a Congressional Research Service publication, CRS Report for Congress R41104, from www.crs.gov, dated March 10, 2010.

§212(a) exclusions of prospective LPRs fell from FY2000 through FY2003, then began climbing to reach 77,080 in FY2008.

Most LPR petitioners who were excluded on §212(a) grounds from FY1994 through FY2004 were rejected because the Department of State (DOS) determined that the aliens were inadmissible as likely public charges. By FY2004, the proportion of public charge exclusions had fallen but remained the top basis for denial. The lack of proper labor certification was another leading ground for exclusion from FY1994 through FY2004. By FY2008, however, illegal presence and previous orders of removal from the United States was the leading ground.

Exclusions of *nonimmigrant* petitions have a somewhat different pattern than that of immigrant petitions. Violations of immigration law were the leading category from FY1994 through FY2006, but fell to the second ranking by FY2008. Illegal presence and prior removal became the leading ground in FY2008. Over time, criminal activity has become a more common ground for refusal, and has represented a larger portion of exclusions among nonimmigrant petitioners than it was for immigrant petitioners.

Legislation aimed at comprehensive immigration reform may take a fresh look at the grounds for excluding foreign nationals enacted over the past two decades. Expanding the grounds for inadmissibility, conversely, might be part of the legislative agenda among those who support more restrictive immigration reform policies. More specifically, the case of Umar Farouk Abdulmutallab, who allegedly attempted to ignite an explosive device on Northwest Airlines Flight 253 on December 25, 2009, has heightened scrutiny of the visa process and grounds for exclusion.

INTRODUCTION

Policy Context

The conventional wisdom is that the terrorist attacks on September 11, 2001, prompted a substantive change in U.S. immigration policy on visa issuances and the grounds for excluding foreign nationals.[1] A series of laws enacted in the 1990s, however, may have done as much or more to set current U.S. visa policy and the legal grounds for exclusion. This report's review of the legislative developments in visa policy over the past 20 years and analysis of the statistical trends in visa issuances and denials provide a nuanced study of U.S. visa policy and the grounds for exclusion.

Legislation aimed at comprehensive immigration reform may take a fresh look at the grounds for excluding foreign nationals that were enacted over the past two decades. While advocacy of sweeping changes to the grounds for inadmissibility has not emerged, proponents of comprehensive immigration reform might seek to ease a few of these provisions as part of the legislative proposals. Waiving the provision that makes an alien who is unlawfully present in the United States for longer than 180 days inadmissible is often raised as an option within a legislative package that includes legalization provisions. Expanding the grounds for inadmissibility, conversely, might be part of the legislative agenda among those who support more restrictive immigration reform policies. Regardless of which legislative path Congress may take, the case of Umar Farouk Abdulmutallab, who allegedly attempted to ignite an explosive device on Northwest Airlines Flight 253 on December 25, 2009, has heightened scrutiny of the visa process and grounds for exclusion.[2]

Background

Foreign nationals may be admitted to the United States temporarily or may come to live permanently. Those admitted on a permanent basis are known as immigrants or legal permanent residents (LPRs), while those admitted on a temporary basis are known as nonimmigrants (such as tourists, foreign students, diplomats, temporary agricultural workers, and exchange visitors). Humanitarian admissions, such as asylees, refugees, parolees, and other aliens granted relief from deportation, are handled separately under the Immigration and Nationality Act (INA).

Foreign nationals not already legally residing in the United States who wish to come to the United States generally must obtain a visa to be admitted.[3] They must first meet a set of criteria specified in the INA that determine whether they are eligible for admission. Conversely, foreign nationals also must not be deemed inadmissible according to other specified grounds in the INA.

Under current law, three departments—the Department of State (DOS), the Department of Homeland Security (DHS), and the Department of Justice (DOJ)—play key roles in administering the law and policies on the admission of aliens.[4] DOS's Bureau of Consular Affairs (Consular Affairs) is the agency responsible for issuing visas, DHS's Citizenship and Immigration Services (USCIS) is charged with approving immigrant petitions, and DHS's Bureau of Customs and Border Protection (CBP) is tasked with inspecting all people who enter the United States. The Attorney General and DOJ's Executive Office for Immigration Review (EOIR) play a significant policy role through the adjudication of specific immigration cases and ruling on questions of immigration law.

VISA ISSUANCE POLICY

The documentary requirements for visas are stated in §§221-222 of the INA, with some discretion for further specifications or exceptions by regulation (as discussed below). Generally, the application requirements are more extensive for aliens who wish to permanently live in the United States than those coming for visits. The amount of paperwork required and the length of adjudication process to obtain a visa to come to the United States are analogous to that of the Internal Revenue Service's (IRS's) tax forms and review procedures. Just as persons with uncomplicated earnings and expenses may file an IRS "short form" while those whose financial circumstances are more complex may file a series of IRS forms, so too an alien whose situation is straightforward and whose reason for seeking a visa is easily documented generally has fewer forms and procedural hurdles than an alien whose circumstances are more complex. The visa application files must be stored in an electronic database that is available to immigration adjudicators and immigration officers in DHS. There are over 70 U.S. Citizenship and Immigration Services (USCIS) forms as well as DOS forms that pertain to the visa issuance process.

The visa issuance procedures delineated in the statute require the petitioner to submit his or her photograph, as well as full name (and any other name used or by which he or she has been known), age, gender, and the date and place of birth. Depending on the visa category, certain documents must be certified by the proper government authorities (e.g., birth certificates and marriage licenses). All prospective LPRs must submit to physical and mental examinations, and prospective nonimmigrants also may be required to have physical and mental examinations.

§221(g) Disqualification

The statutory provision that gives the consular officer the authority to disqualify a visa applicant is broad and straightforward:

> No visa or other documentation shall be issued to an alien if (1) it appears to the consular officer, from statements in the application, or in the papers submitted therewith, that such alien is ineligible to receive a visa or such other documentation under section 212 [8 USC §1182], or any other provision of law, (2) the application fails to comply with the provisions of this Act, or the regulations issued there under, or (3) the consular officer knows or has reason to believe that such alien is ineligible to receive a visa or such other documentation under section 212 [8 USC §1182], or any other provision of law....[5]

These determinations are based on the eligibility criteria of the various and numerous visa categories.[6] The shorthand reference for these disqualifications is §221(g), which is the subsection of the INA that provides the authority.

§212(a) Exclusion

In addition to the determination that a foreign national is qualified for a visa, a decision must be made as to whether the foreign national is admissible or excludable under the INA. The grounds for inadmissibility are spelled out in §212(a) of the INA. These criteria are health-related grounds; criminal history; security and terrorist concerns; public charge (e.g., indigence); seeking to work without proper labor certification; illegal entrants and immigration law violations; ineligible for citizenship; and aliens previously removed. These grounds for exclusion or inadmissibility are discussed extensively later in the report.

In some cases, the foreign national may be successful in overcoming the §212(a) exclusion if new or additional information comes forward. The decision of the consular officer, however, is not subject to judicial appeals.

PERMANENT ADMISSIONS (IMMIGRANT VISAS)

Foreign nationals who wish to live permanently in the United States must meet a set of criteria specified in the INA.[7] To qualify as a family-based LPR, the foreign national must be a spouse or minor child of a U.S. citizen; a parent, adult child, or sibling of an adult U.S. citizen; or a spouse or minor child of a legal permanent resident. To qualify as an employment-based LPR, the foreign national must be an employee for whom a U.S. employer has received approval from the Department of Labor to hire; a person of extraordinary or exceptional ability in specified areas; an investor who will start a business that creates at least 10 new jobs;[8] or someone who meets the narrow definition of the "special immigrant" category. The INA also provides LPR visas to aliens who are selected in the diversity lottery for low-immigrant sending countries.

Procedures

Petitions for immigrant (i.e., LPR) status are first filed with USCIS by a sponsoring relative or employer in the United States. If the prospective immigrant already resides in the United States, the USCIS handles the entire process, which is called "adjustment of status." If the prospective LPR does not have legal residence in the United States, the petition is forwarded to Consular Affairs in his or her home country after USCIS has reviewed the petition. The Consular Affairs officer (when the alien is coming from abroad) and USCIS adjudicator (when the alien is adjusting status in the United States) must be satisfied that the alien is entitled to the immigrant status. Many LPRs are adjusting status from within the United States rather than receiving visas issued abroad by Consular Affairs. Although over 1 million aliens became LPRs in FY2008, for example, only 42% of immigrant visas were issued abroad that year.

A personal interview is required for all prospective LPRs.[9] The burden of proof is on the applicant to establish eligibility for the type of visa for which the application is made. Consular Affairs officers (when the alien is coming from abroad) and USCIS adjudicators (when the alien is adjusting status in the United States) must confirm that the alien is qualified for the visa under the category he or she is applying, as well as is not ineligible for a visa under the grounds for inadmissibility of the INA, which include criminal, terrorist, and public health grounds for exclusion, discussed below.[10]

Trends

The number of immigrant visas issued each year by consular officers abroad has held steady at about 0.4 to 0.5 million in the past 15 years. The trend analysis of the FY1994-FY2008 period, however, reveals an interesting pattern (Figure 1). FY1998 and FY2003 emerge as the years in which the fewest visas were issued in absolute numbers, 375,684 and 364,768 respectively. In terms of the percentage of visas approved, FY1998 was the lowest year (51.9%).

Disqualifications on the basis of INA §221(g) as discussed above exhibit a trend line that is somewhat complementary to the trend line of those who were issued a visa from FY1994 through FY2008. FY1998 was one of the peak years with 256,706 disqualifications (35.4%), but fell short of FY2005 and FY2006 with 270,590 disqualifications (37.9%) and 269,608 disqualifications (34.8%) respectively.

In terms of INA §212(a) exclusions, FY1998 along with FY1999 had the largest portion of prospective immigrants excluded, 12.3% and 12.4% respectively. In absolute numbers, FY1998 led with 89,848 determinations that were §212(a) exclusions, followed closely by FY1999 with 89,641 exclusions. Although FY1998 and FY1999 were the only years analyzed in which the percentages of §212(a) exclusions were in double digits, exclusions trended upward in FY2008 with 9.6% or 77,080 denials.

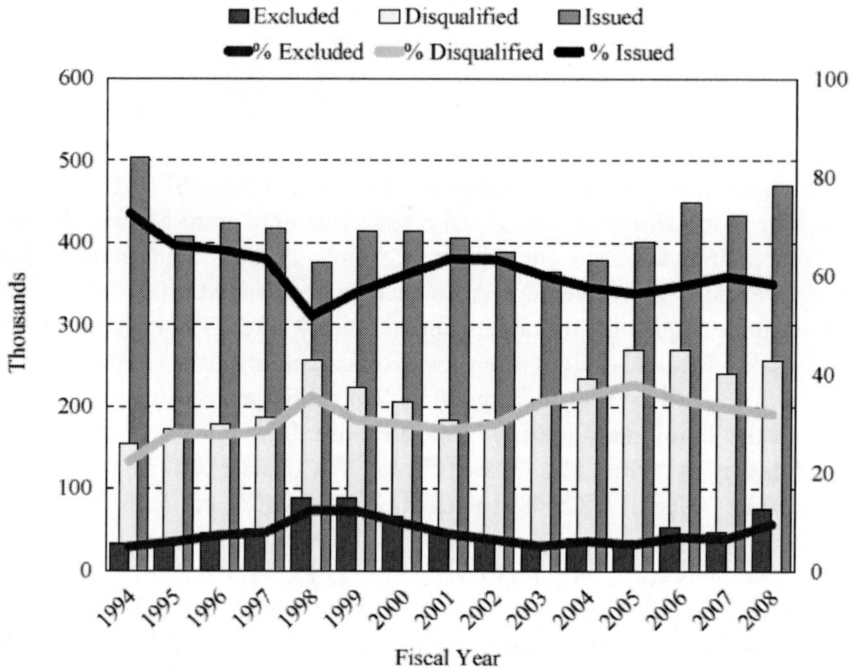

Source: Report of the Visa Office, U.S. Department of State, Bureau of Consular Affairs (multiple years).

Figure 1. Initial Determinations on Immigrants Excluded, Disqualified, or Issued Visas, FY1994-FY2008.

TEMPORARY ADMISSIONS (NONIMMIGRANT VISAS)

Aliens seeking to come to the United States temporarily rather than permanently are known as nonimmigrants.[11] These aliens are admitted to the United States for a temporary period of time and an expressed reason. There are 24 major nonimmigrant visa categories, and over 70 specific types of nonimmigrant visas are issued currently. Most of these nonimmigrant visa categories are defined in §101(a)(15) of the INA. These visa categories are commonly referred to by the letter and numeral that denotes their subsection in §101(a)(15); for example, B-2 tourists, E-2 treaty investors, F-1 foreign students, H-1B temporary professional workers, J-1 cultural exchange participants, and S-4 terrorist informants.

Procedures

Nonimmigrants must demonstrate that they are coming for a limited period and for a specific purpose. As with immigrant visas, the burden of proof is on the applicant to establish eligibility for nonimmigrant status and the type of nonimmigrant visa for which the application is made. The Consular Affairs officer, at the time of application for a visa, as well as the Customs and Border Protection Bureau (CBP) inspectors, at the time of application for admission, must be satisfied that the alien is entitled to a nonimmigrant status.[12]

Personal interviews are generally required for foreign nationals seeking nonimmigrant visas. Interviews, however, may be waived in certain cases; [13] prior to the September 11, 2001, terrorist attacks, personal interviews for applicants for B visitor visas reportedly were often waived. After September 11, 2001, the number of personal interviews rose significantly as part of broader efforts to meet national security goals. DOS issued interim regulations on July 7, 2003, that officially tightened up the requirements for personal interviews and substantially narrowed the class of nonimmigrants eligible for the waiver of a personal interview. Congress then enacted provisions requiring an in-person consular interview of most applicants for nonimmigrant visas between the ages of 14 and 79 as part of the Intelligence Reform and Terrorism Prevention Act of 2004 (P.L. 108-458).[14] Prior to implementation of P.L. 108-458, personal interview waivers could have been granted only to children under age 16, persons 60 years or older, diplomats and representatives of international organizations, aliens who were renewing a visa they obtained within the prior 12 months, and individual cases for whom a waiver was warranted for national security or unusual circumstances.[15]

§214(b) Presumption

Specifically, §214(b) of the INA generally presumes that all aliens seeking admission to the United States are coming to live permanently; as a result, most aliens seeking to qualify for a nonimmigrant visa must demonstrate that they are not coming to reside permanently. There are three nonimmigrant visas that might be considered provisional in that the visaholder may simultaneously seek LPR status. As a result, the law exempts nonimmigrants seeking any one of these three visas (i.e., H-1 professional workers, L intracompany transfers, and V accompanying family members) from the requirement that they prove they are not coming to live permanently.[16]

USCIS and CBP play a role in determining eligibility for certain nonimmigrant visas, notably H workers and L intracompany transfers. Also, if a nonimmigrant in the United States wishes to change from one nonimmigrant category to another, such as from a tourist visa to a student visa, the alien must file a change of status application with the USCIS. If the alien leaves the United States while the change of status is pending, the alien is presumed to have relinquished the application.

Trends

DOS typically issues about 5 to 6 million nonimmigrant visas annually. Depending on the visa category and the country the alien is coming from, the nonimmigrant visa may be valid for several years and may permit multiple entries. The 15-year trend analysis for nonimmigrant visa determinations in Figure 2 reveals a different pattern than that in Figure 1 for LPRs. Foremost, FY2001 is noteworthy because more visas were issued in that year (7,588,778) and more applicants were ineligible for a visa in that year (2,276,611) on the basis of §214(b) presumed immigrants than in any other year during the 15-year period. In terms of the percentage of nonimmigrant visas issued, FY1996 was the top year with 80.0%. By FY2008, there were 6,603,073 nonimmigrant visas issued, yielding a percent of 75.8%, which was the first time the percentage surpassed FY1999.

The growth in nonimmigrant visas issued in the 1998-2001 period was largely attributable to the issuances of new border crossing cards to residents of Canada and Mexico and a periodic lifting of the ceilings on temporary worker visas. The largest percentages of nonimmigrant visa applicants that were presumed immigrants, excluded or otherwise disqualified were in FY2002 and FY2003, when just under 70% of nonimmigrant visas were approved. Of that increase visa denials, much of it came not from §212(a) exclusions, which some might have expected following the September 11 terrorist attacks, but from disqualifications under §221(g), meaning that the visa applications did not comply with the INA or regulations. Throughout the 15-year span, §214(b) presumption was the most common basis to reject a nonimmigrant visa applicant. Never rising above one-half of one percent over this period, §212(a) exclusions were too few to depict in Figure 2.

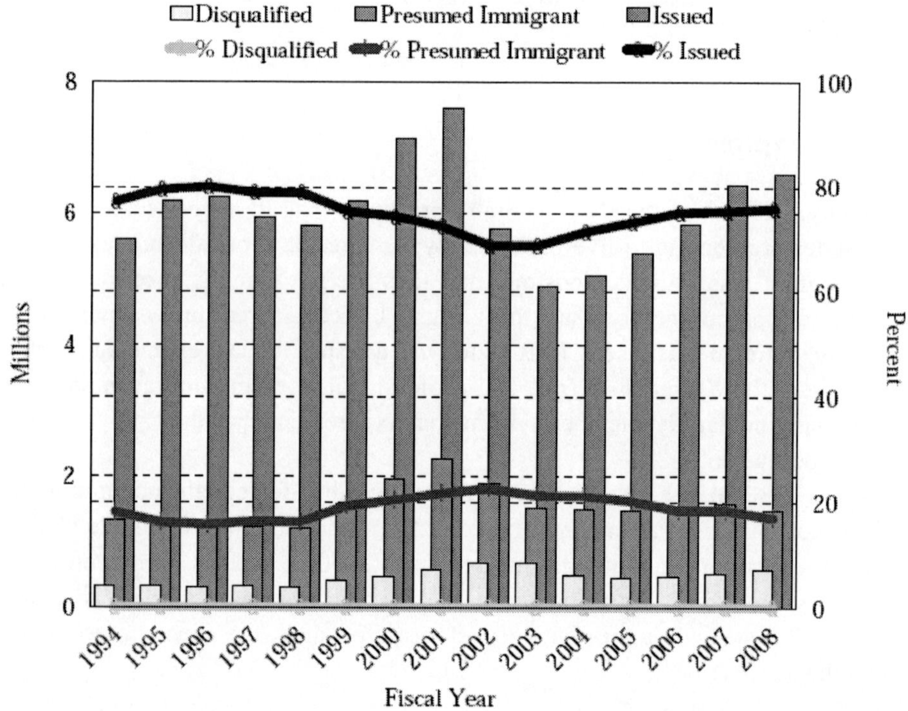

Source: Report of the Visa Office, U.S. Department of State, Bureau of Consular Affairs (multiple years).

Notes: Exclusions on the basis of INA §212(a) are too few to depict.

Figure 2. Initial Determinations on Nonimmigrants Disqualified, Presumed Immigrant, or Issued Visas, FY1994-FY2008.

Although the §212(a) exclusions represent a small portion of nonimmigrant visa determinations, their number is not trivial. Because Figure 3 is scaled in thousands in comparison to Figure 2, which is scaled in millions, the ups and downs in the §212(a) exclusion trends become apparent. In FY2008, §212(a) exclusions of nonimmigrant visas hit 35,403 and surpassed the prior high point of 34,750 in FY1998. For prospective LPRs, §212(a) exclusions peaked in FY1998 and FY1999, reaching over 89,000 in both years. The §212(a) exclusions of prospective LPRs fell from FY2000 through FY2003, then began climbing to reach 77,080 in FY2008.

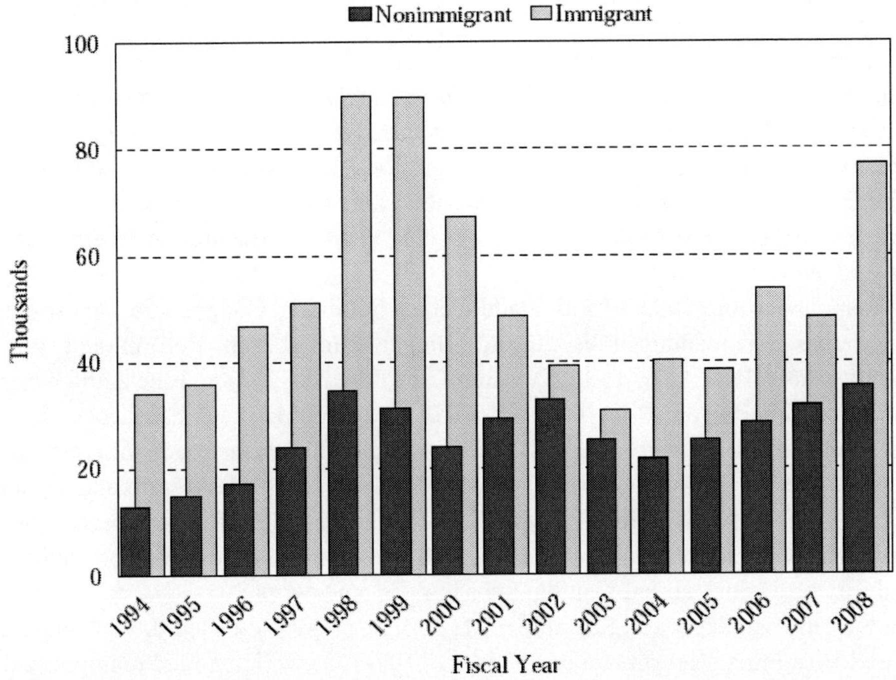

Source: CRS presentation of DOS Bureau of Consular Affairs data from Report of the Visa Office, U.S. Department of State, Bureau of Consular Affairs.

Figure 3. Trends in Initial Determinations of §212(a) Ineligibility for LPR and Nonimmigrant Visa Applicants, FY1994-FY2008.

The ebbs and flows depicted in Figure 3 challenge the commonly held assumption that the terrorist attacks of September 11, 2001, were the watershed moment for U.S. visa policy and the exclusion of foreign nationals.[17] These 15-year trends also invite a more detailed study of the grounds for exclusion, as well as a more nuanced analysis of these trends over time.

GROUNDS FOR EXCLUSION

All aliens seeking visas must undergo admissibility reviews performed by DOS consular officers abroad.[18] These reviews are intended to ensure that aliens are not ineligible for visas or admission under the grounds for inadmissibility spelled out in the INA.[19] Consular decisions are not appealable or reviewable; however, some of those seeking visas are able to bring additional information that may be used to overcome an initial refusal.[20] As previously mentioned, these criteria are health-related grounds; criminal history; security and terrorist concerns; public charge (e.g., indigence); seeking to work without proper labor certification; illegal entrants and immigration law violations; ineligible for citizenship; and aliens previously removed. Each of these grounds is explained more fully following a brief legislative history of the provisions.

Brief Legislative History

When the various immigration and citizenship laws were unified and codified as the Immigration and Nationality Act of 1952 (INA), there were 31 grounds for exclusion of aliens specified in §212(a) of the Act. The Immigration Amendments Act of 1990 streamlined and modernized all of the grounds for inadmissibility into nine broad categories. These nine categories, as amended, remain the basis for denying visas and excluding the entry of foreign nationals into the United States.[21]

As a response to the 1993 World Trade Center bombing, Congress revised the national security grounds for inadmissibility in the Illegal Immigration Reform and Immigrant Responsibility Act (IIRIRA) of 1996 (Division C of P.L. 104-208) and the Antiterrorism and Effective Death Penalty Act (P.L. 104-132). IIRIRA ramped up the consequences for foreign nationals attempting to return to the United States if they had prior orders of removal or had been illegally present in the United States. IIRIRA also revised the criminal grounds for exclusion. Along with the IIRIRA, Title IV of the Personal Responsibility and Work Opportunity Reconciliation Act of 1996 (P.L. 104-193) strengthened the enforceability of the inadmissibility provisions aimed at indigent or low-income people.

After the terrorist attacks on September 11, 2001, Congress enacted the Enhanced Border Security and Visa Entry Reform Act of 2002 (P.L. 107-173), which aimed to improve the visa issuance process abroad, as well as immigration inspections at the border. It expressly required that, beginning in October 2004, all newly issued visas have biometric identifiers. In addition to increasing consular officers' access to electronic information needed for alien screening, it expanded the training requirements for consular officers who issue visas. Congress passed the REAL ID Act (P.L. 109-13, Division B) in 2005, which expanded the terror-related grounds for inadmissiblity and deportability, and amended the definitions of "terrorist organization" and "engage in terrorist activity" used by the INA.

Over the past two years, Congress has incrementally revised the grounds for inadmissibility. Two laws enacted in the 110th Congress altered longstanding policies on exclusion of aliens due to membership in organizations deemed terrorist.[22] The 110th Congress also revisited the health-related grounds of inadmissibility for those who were diagnosed with HIV/AIDS.[23] Questions about the public charge ground of inadmissibility arose in the context of Medicaid and the state Children's Health Insurance Program (CHIP) in the 111th Congress.[24]

Communicable Diseases §212(a)(1)

The statutory language permitting the exclusion of aliens on the basis of health or communicable diseases dates back to the Immigration Act of 1891, when "persons suffering from a loathsome or a dangerous contagious disease" were added to the grounds of exclusion.[25] Since the Immigration Amendments of 1990, the INA authorizes the exclusion of any alien "who is determined (in accordance with regulations prescribed by the Secretary of Health and Human Services) to have a communicable disease of public health significance."[26] While the INA does not define "communicable disease of public health significance" directly, it does task the Secretary of Health and Human Services (HHS) to define the term by regulation.[27] The relevant regulation's definition expressly lists eight diseases as a "communicable disease of public health significance": chancroid, gonorrhea, granuloma inguinale, infectious leprosy, lymphogranuloma venereum, active tuberculosis,[28] and infectious syphilis.[29] However, this list is neither exclusive nor exhaustive, because the regulatory definition also includes other diseases incorporated by reference to a Presidential executive order.[30] The relevant executive order lists cholera; diphtheria; infectious tuberculosis; plague; smallpox; yellow fever; viral hemorrhagic fevers (Lassa, Marburg, Ebola, Crimean-Congo, South American, and others not yet isolated or named); severe acute respiratory syndrome (SARS); and "[i]nfluenza caused by novel or reemergent influenza viruses that are causing, or have the potential to cause, a pandemic."[31]

Furthermore, the regulatory definition also includes communicable diseases that may pose a "public health emergency of international concern."[32] A disease rises to this level, and thus qualifies as a "communicable disease of public significance," if the Centers for Disease Control (CDC) Director, after evaluating (1) the seriousness of the disease, (2) whether the emergence of the disease was unusual or unexpected, (3) the risk of the spread of the disease in the United States, and (4) the transmissibility and virulence of the disease,[33] determines that "a threat exists for [the disease's] importation into the United States" and the disease "may potentially affect the health of the American public."[34]

Foreign nationals who are applying for visas at U.S. consulates are tested by in-country physicians who have been designated by the State Department. The physicians enter into written agreements with the consular posts to perform the examinations according to HHS regulations and guidance. A medical examination is required of all foreign nationals seeking to come as legal permanent residents and refugees, and may be required of any alien seeking a nonimmigrant visa or admission at the port of entry. Foreign nationals are generally tested at their own expense, though the costs for refugees are covered by the U.S. government. If there is reason to suspect an infection, applicants for temporary admission as nonimmigrants (such as tourists, business travelers, temporary workers, and foreign students) are tested at the discretion of the consular officer or admitting CBP inspector. Children under 15 years of age are required to have a general physical examination and provide proof of immunizations, but they are not required to have the chest x-rays, blood tests, or HIV anti-body test.[35]

The Secretary of Homeland Security[36] has discretionary authority to waive some of the health-related grounds for inadmissibility under certain circumstances.[37] For example, foreign nationals infected with a communicable disease of public health significance can still be issued a waiver and admitted into the country if they are the spouse, unmarried son, unmarried daughter, minor unmarried lawfully adopted child, father or mother of a U.S. citizen, alien lawfully admitted for permanent residence, or an alien issued an immigrant visa.[38] Waivers are also available, under certain circumstances, for those who are inadmissible because they lack proper vaccination[39] and for those who have a physical or mental disorder.[40] The Secretary may also waive the application of any of the health-related grounds for inadmissibility if she finds it in "the national interest" to do so.[41]

Criminal History §212(a)(2)

Criminal offenses in the context of immigration law cover violations of federal, state, and, in some cases, foreign criminal law. Most crimes affecting immigration status fall under a broad category of crimes defined in the INA, notably those involving moral turpitude or aggravated felonies. It does not cover violations of the INA that are not defined as crimes, such as working without employment authorization, overstaying a nonimmigrant visa, or unauthorized presence in the United States.[42]

Criminal history as a grounds for exclusion under the INA applies to the following foreign nationals:

- Those who have been convicted of, admit having committed, or admit to acts comprising essential elements of a crime involving moral turpitude.[43]
- Those who have been convicted of or admit having committed a federal, state, or foreign law violation relating to a controlled substance.
- Based on the knowledge or reasonable belief of a consular officer or immigration officer, either (1) an alien who is or has been an illicit trafficker in a controlled substance, or knowingly is or has been an aider or abettor of a controlled substance, or (2) an alien who is the spouse, son, or daughter of an alien as described above and who received any financial or other benefit from the illicit activity and who reasonably should have known that the financial or other benefit resulted from illicit activity.
- Those who have been convicted of two or more offenses (other than purely political offenses) for which the aggregate sentence imposed was at least five years.
- Those who are coming to the United States to engage in (or within 10 years of applying for admission have engaged in) prostitution (including procurement and receipt of proceeds) or are coming to the United States to engage in another form of unlawful commercialized vice.
- Those who have committed a serious crime for which diplomatic immunity or other form of immunity was claimed.
- Those who have committed or have conspired to commit a human trafficking offense or who are known or reasonably believed to have aided or otherwise furthered severe forms of human trafficking, or are known or reasonably believed to be the adult child or spouse of such an alien and knowingly benefitted from the proceeds of illicit activity while an adult in the past five years. [44]

Also, the INA gives authority to consular officers or immigration officers, based on their knowledge or reasonable belief, to exclude a foreign national who they think is engaging in, or seeks to enter the United States to engage in, a federal offense of money laundering, or who is or has been a knowing aider, abettor, assister, conspirator, or colluder with others in such an offense.

There is authority in §212(h) of the INA to waive certain criminal grounds of inadmissibility, if certain criteria are met.[45] No waiver is permitted for aliens who have been convicted of murder or criminal acts involving torture, as well as attempts or conspiracies to commit murder or a criminal act involving torture.[46]

Security and Terrorist Concerns §212(a)(3)

A foreign national may be deemed inadmissible if he or she has engaged in or intends to engage in any activity a purpose of which is the opposition to, or the control or overthrow of, the government of the United States by force, violence, or other unlawful means. If the Secretary of State has reasonable grounds to believe an alien's entry, presence, or activities in the United States would have potentially serious adverse foreign policy consequences for the United States, that alien may be deemed inadmissible or deportable. However, an alien generally may not be deported or denied entry into the United States on account of the alien's past, current, or expected beliefs, statements, or associations, if such beliefs, statements, or associations would be lawful within the United States, unless the Secretary of State personally determines that the alien's admission would compromise a compelling United States foreign policy interest. Additionally, aliens who are foreign officials or candidates cannot be denied entry or deported solely because of past, current, or expected beliefs, statements, or associations that would be lawful in the United States.

Engaging in specified, terror-related activity has direct consequences concerning an alien's ability to lawfully enter or remain in the United States. Since 1990, the INA has expressly provided that aliens who have engaged or intend to engage in terrorist activity either as an individual or as a member of a terrorist organization are inadmissible and deportable. Over the years, the INA has been amended to lower the threshold for how substantial, apparent, and immediate an alien's support for a terrorist activity must be for the alien to be rendered inadmissible, removable, and ineligible for most forms of relief from removal.[47]

The Secretary of State or Secretary of Homeland Security, in consultation with the other and the Attorney General, has the general authority to waive INA §212(a)(3)(B) concerning terrorist activity. However, §212(a)(3) of the INA may not be waived for aliens who are engaged or are likely to engage in terrorist activity after entering the United States; voluntarily and knowingly engage or have engaged in terrorist activity on behalf of a designated terrorist organization; voluntarily and knowingly have received military training from a designated organization; are members or representatives of designated terrorist organizations; or voluntarily and knowingly endorse or espouse the terrorist activity of a designated organization, or convince others to support the group's terrorist activities.[48]

Public Charge §212(a)(4)

Opposition to the entry of foreign paupers and aliens "likely at any time to become a public charge"—language found in the INA today—dates from colonial times.[49] Over time, a policy developed in which applicants for immigrant status can overcome the public charge ground for exclusion based on their own funds, prearranged or prospective employment, or an *affidavit of support* from someone in the United States. For most prospective immigrants, this exclusion is implemented by provisions on deeming sponsors' income and binding affidavits of support.[50]

The affidavit of support is a legally binding contract that requires the sponsor to ensure that the new immigrant will not become a public charge and makes the sponsor financially responsible for the new immigrant, as codified in INA §213A.[51] Sponsors must demonstrate the ability to maintain an annual income of at least 125% of the federal poverty line (100% for sponsors who are on active duty in U.S. Armed Forces), or share liability with one or more joint sponsors, each of whom must independently meet the income requirement. Current law also directed the federal government to include "appropriate information" regarding affidavits of support in the Systematic Alien Verification for Entitlements (SAVE) system.[52] Congress has required the establishment of an automated record of the sponsors' social security numbers (SSN) in order to implement this policy. [53]

Employment-based LPRs are rarely required to have an affidavit of support because they meet the public charge ground by means of the job offer. Employment-based LPRs only need an affidavit of support if the prospective employer is a relative. All family-based immigrants must have binding affidavits of support signed by U.S. sponsors in order to show that they will not become public charges. The INA waives the public charge ground for refugees and asylees and for other special cases.[54]

Labor Market Protections §212(a)(5)

The INA bars the admission of any immigrant who seeks to enter the United States to perform skilled or unskilled labor, unless the Secretary of Labor provides a certification to the Secretary of State and the Attorney General.[55] Specifically, the Secretary of Labor must determine that there are not sufficient U.S. workers who are able, willing, qualified, and available at the time of the alien's application for a visa and admission to the United States and at the place where the alien is to perform such skilled or unskilled labor. The Secretary of Labor must further certify that the employment of the alien will not adversely affect the wages and working conditions of similarly employed workers in the United States.[56]

The foreign labor certification program in the U.S. Department of Labor (DOL) is responsible for ensuring that foreign workers do not displace or adversely affect working conditions of U.S. workers. Under current law, DOL adjudicates *labor certification* applications (LCAs) for permanent employment-based immigrants, temporary agricultural workers, and temporary nonagricultural workers, as well as the streamlined LCA known as *labor attestations* for temporary professional workers.[57]

The labor market protections of §212(a)(5) do not apply to most foreign nationals seeking to immigrate to the United States. Only employers of certain employment-based LPRs and certain temporary workers seeking H visas are required to be certified by the DOL. LPRs entering as priority workers who are persons of extraordinary ability in the arts, sciences, education, business, or athletics; outstanding professors and researchers; and certain multinational executives and managers are exempt from labor certification. A waiver is available for those members of the professions holding advanced degrees or persons of exceptional ability who are deemed to be "in the national interest." [58]

There are also specific provisions that bar the admission of unqualified physicians and uncertified health care workers.[59]

Illegal Entrants and Immigration Law Violations §212(a)(6&7)

Any foreign national who is present in the United States without being legally admitted or paroled, or who arrives in the United States at any time or place other than as designated, is inadmissible. There are exceptions to this ground for certain battered spouses and children. As currently constructed, this §212(a) basis for exclusion is relatively new and dates back to the IIRIRA of 1996.

Foreign nationals who "without reasonable cause" fail to attend their removal proceedings or remain in attendance at a hearing are inadmissible for a period of five years following their subsequent departure. If the alien can establish a reasonable cause for the failure to attend the removal proceedings, he or she might not be deemed inadmissible; however, the burden of proof in demonstrating reasonable cause is on the alien.

Since the 1952 act, any foreign national who has, by fraud or willful misrepresentation of a material fact, sought to procure or has procured either admission into the United States or a benefit under the INA is inadmissible. [60] An alien who falsely represents himself or herself to be a U.S. citizen for any purpose or benefit under the INA or any other federal or state law is also inadmissible for life, except under narrow circumstances.[61] There is no immigrant waiver available for inadmissibility on the ground of knowingly making false citizenship claims.

Ineligible for Citizenship §212(a)(8)

Although the ground "ineligible for citizenship" suggests a range of criteria linked to the naturalization provisions in Title III of the INA, its actual effect is to bar the entry of individuals who deserted their military service or evaded the military draft. It grows out of applications for exemption or discharge from military training or service based on alienage. Since World War I, Congress has enacted various statutes exempting certain aliens within the United States from military service upon the condition that those taking advantage of such relief would thereafter be ineligible for citizenship.[62] If a foreign national takes advantage of this exemption from military service, he or she becomes excludable. There are no waivers from the military-related exclusion grounds.

Illegal Presence or Previously Removed §212(a)(9)

Foreign nationals who have been deported (i.e., removed) from the United States are barred from re-entry for periods of time dependent on the reasons for the removal. The specific instances in which foreign nationals are deported from the United States are found in §237 of the INA.[63] The procedures for removal are detailed in INA §240, and the procedures for expedited removal are found in INA §235. There are also provisions for the "expedited removal" of removable aliens serving criminal sentences in INA §238. In removal proceedings an immigration judge from the Department of Justice's Executive Office for Immigration Review (EOIR) determines whether an alien is admissible or removable. A final order of removal is not necessary to make such an inadmissibility determination, though a final removal order is also a specific ground for inadmissibility.[64]

The INA specifically states that any alien who has been ordered removed (either under §235(b)(1) pertaining to expedited removal or at the end of general removal proceedings under §240 initiated upon the alien's arrival in the United States) and who again seeks admission within 5 years of the date of such removal (or within 20 years in the case of a second or subsequent removal or at any time in the case of an alien convicted of an aggravated felony) is inadmissible. The INA also specifies that any alien who was ordered removed under §240 or any other provision of law, or departed the United States while an order of removal was outstanding, and who seeks admission within 10 years of the date of such alien's departure or removal (or within 20 years of such date in the case of a second or subsequent removal or at any time in the case of an alien convicted of an aggravated felony) is inadmissible.

As a result of the enactment of IIRIRA in 1996, an alien who is unlawfully present in the United States for longer than 180 days but less than a year is inadmissible for three years after the alien's departure. An alien who is unlawfully present for at least a year is inadmissible for 10 years after the alien's departure. Not counted under these rules are periods during which the alien (1) is a minor, (2) has a pending claim for asylum (unless the alien is working without authorization), (3) is a battered wife or child, or (4) qualifies under family unity provisions of the Immigration Act of 1990 as a long-term (generally pre-1989) spouse or unmarried child of an alien who legalized under the Immigration Reform and Control Act of 1986. Also not counted is a period of up to 120 days in the case of a previously paroled or lawfully admitted alien whose authorized stay has expired but who before expiration of authorized status filed a nonfrivolous application for a change or extension of status (unless the alien works without authorization). Additionally, the INA gives the Attorney General authority to waive inadmissibility for a spouse or a son or daughter of a citizen or permanent resident if refusal of admission would result in extreme hardship to the citizen or permanent resident.

The INA makes indefinitely inadmissible an alien who (1) has been ordered removed or has been unlawfully present for an aggregate period of longer than a year and (2) enters or attempts to reenter without being formally admitted. There is no express exception under this rule for acts occurring prior to April 1997. The sole exception to this bar is a discretionary waiver by the Attorney General for an alien who has been outside the United States for at least 10 years.

The IIRIRA increases from one year to five years the period during which an alien who was previously removed on arrival is inadmissible. The INA sets a 20-year period of inadmissibility for aliens who have been removed on arrival more than once. Separately, the inadmissibility period for aliens ordered removed under other provisions (i.e., ordered removed after arrival other than under expedited removal provisions) is increased to 10 years, with a 20-year period set for aliens removed more than once and an indefinite period of inadmissibility set for aliens who have been convicted of an aggravated felony. The INA gives the Attorney General authority to waive the foregoing provisions.

The INA also gives the Attorney General the authority to grants exceptions to the bars on aliens previously removed in certain instances.[65]

ANALYSIS OF VISA INADMISSIBILITY DETERMINATIONS

To better understand these grounds for inadmissibility, CRS has analyzed DOS data on all visa determinations from two perspectives. One approach analyzes all the grounds of inadmissibility for four selected years : FY1996, FY2000, FY2004, and FY2008. The other approach analyzes the top grounds for exclusion over a 15-year period. As in the discussions above, the immigrant determinations are treated separately from the nonimmigrant determinations. All of these analyses are based on the initial decision and do not take into account initial refusals that might have been overcome with subsequent information.[66]

Inadmissible Immigrants

As Figure 4 makes clear, most LPR petitioners who were excluded on §212(a) grounds in FY1996 and FY2000 were rejected because the DOS determined that the aliens were inadmissible as likely public charges. In FY2004, the proportion of public charge exclusions had fallen, but remained the top basis for denial. The lack of proper labor certification was another leading ground for exclusion in FY1996, FY2000, FY2004, and FY2008. By FY2008, however, illegal presence and previous orders of removal from the United States had become the leading ground. What Figure 4 does not depict is the considerable shifting of trend lines in the late 1990s as well as the late 2000s.

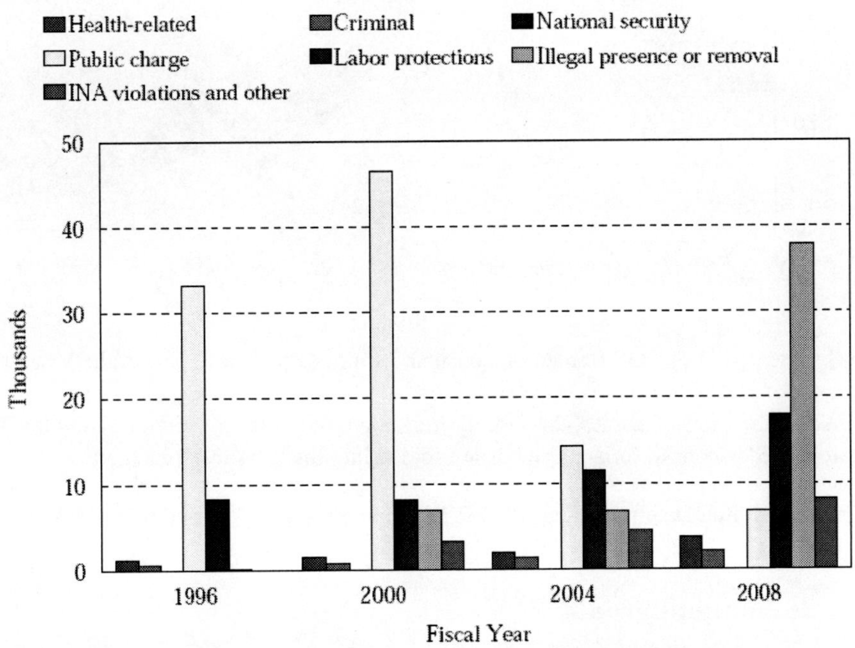

Source: CRS presentation of DOS Bureau of Consular Affairs data from Report of the Visa Office, U.S. Department of State, Bureau of Consular Affairs.

Figure 4. Initial Determinations of LPRs Excluded by Grounds in FY1996, FY2000, FY2004, and FY2008.

The trends in public charge exclusions dominate the 15-year trend analysis, as **Figure 5** illustrates. The importance of public charge as a grounds of inadmissibility is evidenced in the fact that over one-half (53.3%) of all 790,685 exclusions over this 15-year period were on this basis, suggesting an effect of the changes in 1996 to the INA provisions on affidavits of support.[67] Labor market protections and illegal presence and prior removals came in distant second and third, with 18.5% and 14.8% of exclusions, respectively.

The proportion of public charge exclusions had fallen by FY2004, but remained the top basis for denial. By FY2008, however, illegal presence and previous orders of removal from the United States was the leading ground, and public charge was less than 10% of the §212(a) exclusions.

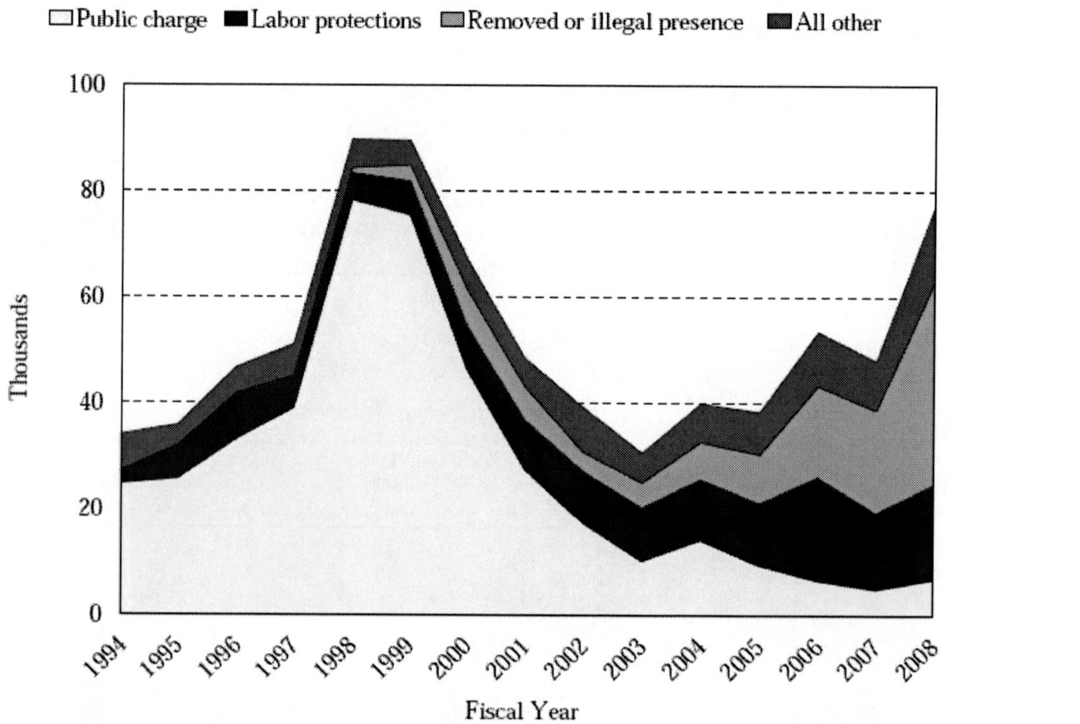

Source: CRS presentation of DOS Bureau of Consular Affairs data from Report of the Visa Office, U.S. Department of State, Bureau of Consular Affairs.

Notes: Denials on the basis of crimes, disease, draft evasion, miscellaneous immigration law violations, and national security or terrorism grounds are folded into the "all other" category.

Figure 5. Trends in Initial Determinations of LPR Exclusions for Top 3 Grounds, FY1994-FY2008.

Inadmissible Nonimmigrants

Refusals of *nonimmigrant* petitions presented have a somewhat different pattern than that of immigrant petitions. Violations of immigration law was the leading category in FY1996, FY2000, and FY2004, but fell to the second ranking in FY2008. Similar to the analysis of immigrant data, illegal presence and prior removal became the leading ground for nonimmigrant visas in FY2008. Over the four points in time, the criminal grounds grew as a more common ground for refusal, and represented a larger portion of exclusions among nonimmigrant petitioners than it was for immigrant petitioners.

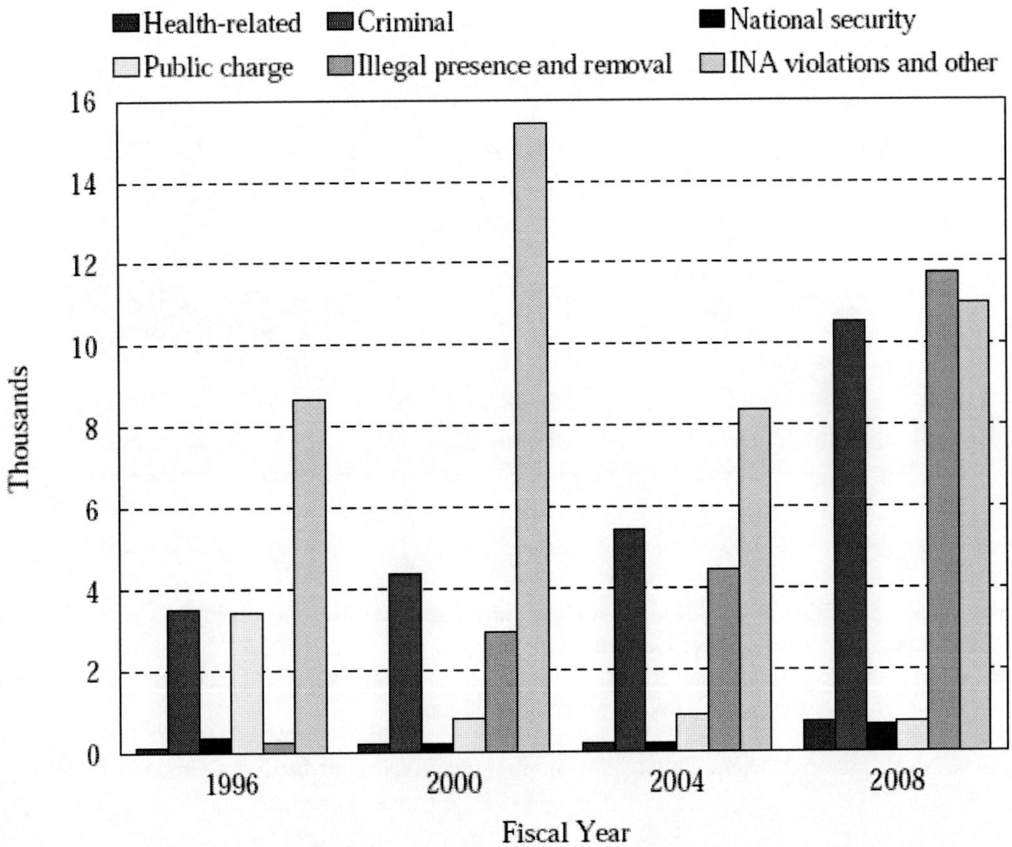

Source: CRS presentation of DOS Bureau of Consular Affairs data from Report of the Visa Office, U.S. Department of State, Bureau of Consular Affairs.

Notes: Denials on the basis of draft evasion, labor certification and miscellaneous grounds are too few to depict.

Figure 6. Initial Determinations of Nonimmigrants Excluded by Grounds in FY1996, FY2000, FY2004 and FY2008.

Violations of immigration law was the leading basis for §212(a) exclusions over the 15-year period, making up 47.7% of all exclusions. It was the top basis from FY1994 through FY2006, but fell to the second ranking by FY2008 (31.0%). Illegal presence and prior removal became the leading ground in FY2007 (38.7%) and FY2008 (33.2%). The criminal grounds have grown as more common basis for §212(a) exclusions, and represented a much larger portion of exclusions among nonimmigrant petitioners (29.8% in FY2008) than among immigrant petitioners (2.8% in FY2008).

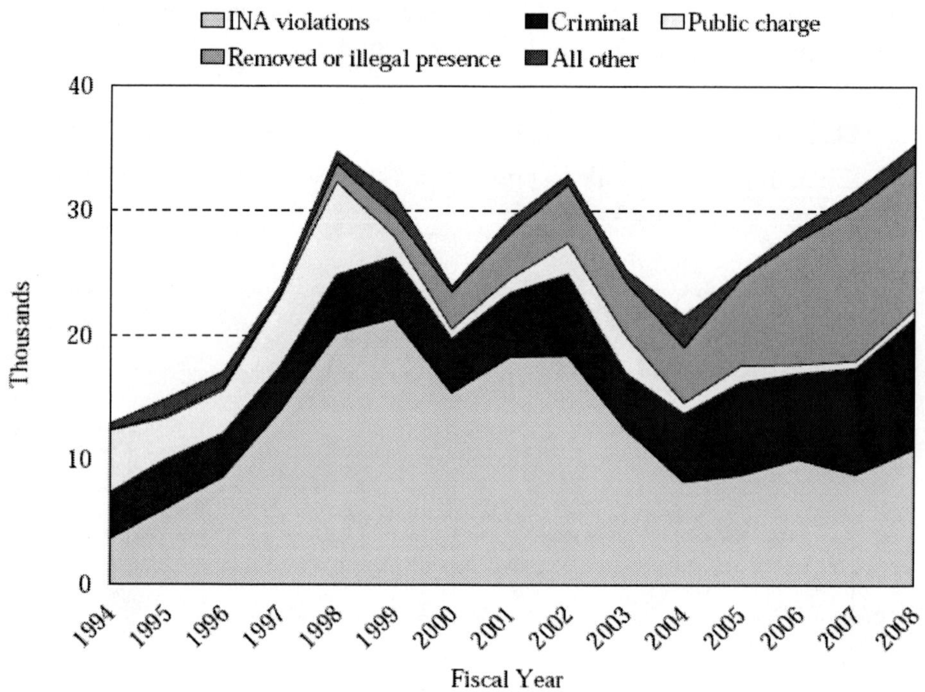

Source: CRS presentation of DOS Bureau of Consular Affairs data from Report of the Visa Office, U.S. Department of State, Bureau of Consular Affairs.

Notes: Denials on the basis of health, draft evasion, labor market protections, and national security or terrorism grounds are folded into the "all other" category.

Figure 7. Trends in Initial Determinations of Nonimmigrant Exclusions for Top 4 Grounds, FY1994-FY2008.

Concluding Observations

The rise and fall of the public charge ground is the most striking feature of the 15-year trend analysis. Foremost, many applicants filed affidavits of support that were insufficient in the first few years after IIRIRA went into effect. As the legal community and the prospective LPRs gained a better understanding of the requirement that the affidavit of support must demonstrate the ability to maintain an annual income of at least 125% of the federal poverty line, they may have submitted more complete financial data to support the affidavit. The statutory change in IIRIRA that made the affidavits of support legally binding may have changed behavior over time as well. Potential sponsors may have become less likely to petition for family members if they lacked adequate resources to support them.

The steady rise in exclusions based on past illegal presence and prior removal is likewise largely due to the statutory change in IIRIRA. Since 1996, foreign nationals who were unlawfully present in the United States for longer than 180 days but less than a year are inadmissible for three years after their departure. Foreign nationals who were unlawfully present for at least a year are inadmissible for 10 years after their departure. When these changes were coupled with database improvements and access to databases across agencies, consular officers became better able to identify visa applicants who are inadmissible on these grounds. The improvements in immigration-related databases as well as the expansion of access to law enforcement databases offer similar explanations for the uptick in criminal grounds of exclusion.[68]

Finally, the increase in immigrant exclusions based upon labor market protections may reflect the growth in demand for foreign workers and the competition for these scarce visas.[69] As of November 1, 2009, there were 3,499,964 employment-based LPRs visa applications pending.[70]

APPENDIX A. CONSULAR DATABASES FOR SCREENING

Consular officers use the Consular Consolidated Database (CCD) to screen visa applicants. Records of all visa applications are now automated in the CCD, with some records dating back to the mid-1990s. Since February 2001, the CCD has stored photographs of all visa applicants in electronic form, and more recently the CCD has begun storing 10-finger scans. In addition to indicating the outcome of any prior visa application of the alien in the CCD and comments by consular officers, the system links with other databases to flag problems that may have an impact on the issuance of the visa. These databases linked with CCD include DHS's Automated Biometric Identification System (IDENT) and FBI's Integrated Automated Fingerprint Identification System (IAFIS) results, and supporting documents.

The CCD also links to the DHS's Traveler Enforcement Compliance System (TECS) for use by CBP officers at ports of entry. A limited number of consular officers have recently been granted access to DHS'Arrival Departure Information System (ADIS). ADIS tracks foreign nationals' entries into and most exits out of the United States. DOS credits access to ADIS with its ability to identify previously undetected cases of illegal overstays in the United States.

For some years, consular officers have been required to check the background of all aliens in the "lookout" databases, specifically the Consular Lookout and Support System (CLASS) database, which contained over 26 million records in 2009.[71] According to Janice Jacobs, Assistant Secretary of State for Consular Affairs, the CLASS database grew by approximately 400% after September 11, 2001.

> This increase in the quantity and quality of CLASS records is largely the result of improved data sharing between the Department of State and the law enforcement and intelligence communities. In 2001, only 25 percent of records in CLASS came from other government agencies. Now, almost 70 percent of CLASS records come from other agencies.[72]

The Security Advisory Opinion (SAO) system requires a consular officer abroad to refer selected visa cases for greater review by intelligence and law enforcement agencies.[73] The current interagency procedures for alerting officials about foreign nationals who may be suspected terrorists, referred to in State Department nomenclature as Visa Viper, began after the 1993 World Trade Center bombing and were institutionalized by enactment of the Enhanced Border Security and Visa Entry Reform Act of 2002. If consular officials receive information about a foreign national that causes concern, they send a Visa Viper cable (which is a dedicated and secure communication) to the NCTC. In 2009, consular posts sent approximately 3,000 Visa Viper communications to NCTC.[74]

In a similar set of SAO procedures, consular officers send suspect names, identified by law enforcement and intelligence information (originally certain visa applicants from 26 predominantly Muslim countries), to the Federal Bureau of Investigation (FBI) for a name check program called Visa Condor.[75] There is also the "Terrorist Exclusion List" (TEL), which lists organizations designated as terrorist-supporting and includes the names of individuals associated with these organizations.[76]

APPENDIX B. EXCEPTIONS TO THE VISA REQUIREMENTS

Not all aliens are required to have a visa to visit the United States. Indeed, most visitors enter the United States without nonimmigrant visas through the Visa Waiver Program (VWP). This provision of the INA allows the visa documentary requirements to be waived for aliens coming as visitors from 35 countries (e.g., Australia, France, Germany, Italy, Japan, New Zealand, and Switzerland). Thus, visitors from these countries are not required to obtain a visa from a U.S. consulate abroad. Since aliens entering through VWP do not have visas, CBP inspectors at the port of entry are responsible for performing the background checks and making the determination of whether the alien is admissible.[77]

P.L. 110-53 created a waiver allowing the Secretary of Homeland Security (Secretary) to admit countries with refusal rates under 10% to the VWP. This waiver authority became available in October 2008, when the Secretary certified that (1) an air exit system was in place that verifies the departure of not less than 97% of foreign nationals that exit through U.S. airports, and (2) the electronic system for travel authorization (ESTA) was operational. The ESTA is a system through which each foreign national electronically provides, in advance of travel, the biographical information necessary to check the relevant databases and "watch lists" to see whether the foreign national poses a law enforcement or security risk.[78] As in all VWP cases, CBP inspectors at the port of entry perform the initial admissibility screening.

In addition to the Visa Waiver Program, a number of exceptions to documentary requirements for a visa have been established by law, treaty, or regulation. The INA also authorizes the Attorney General and the Secretary of State acting jointly to waive the documentary requirements of INA §212(a)(7)(B)(i), including the passport requirement, on the basis of unforeseen emergency in individual cases.[79] In 2003, the Administration scaled back the circumstances in which the visa and passport requirements are waived.[80] In 2004, Congress enacted a provision, now known as the Western Hemisphere Travel Initiative, in §7209 of P.L. 108-458, that affected all citizens and categories of individuals for whom documentation requirements had previously been waived under §212(d)(4)(B) of INA. The Secretary of Homeland Security, in consultation with the Secretary of State, was required to develop and implement a plan as expeditiously as possible to require a passport or other document, or combination of documents, "deemed by the Secretary of Homeland Security to be sufficient to denote identity and citizenship," for all travelers entering the United States. The law expressly states in §7209(c)(2) that "the President may not exercise discretion under § 215(b) of such Act[81] to waive documentary requirements for U.S. citizens departing from or entering, or attempting to depart from or enter, the United States except—(A) where the Secretary of Homeland Security determines that the alternative documentation that is the basis for the waiver of the documentary requirement is sufficient to denote identity and citizenship; (B) in the case of an unforeseen emergency in individual cases; or (C) in the case of humanitarian or national interest reasons in individual cases."

End Notes

[1] For example, see Edward Alden, The Closing of the American Border: Terrorism, Immigration, and Security Since 9/11 (Harper, 2008); and Bay Area Council Economic Institute , Visas for Higher Education and Scientific Exchanges: Balancing Security and Economic Competitiveness, Bay Area Science and Innovation Consortium (BASIC), April 2005, http://www.bayeconfor.org/media

[2] For analysis and discussion of the issues raised by this case, see CRS Report RL32564, *Immigration: Terrorist Grounds for Exclusion and Removal of Aliens*, by Michael John Garcia and Ruth Ellen Wasem, and CRS Report R41093, *Visa Security Policy: Roles of the Departments of State and Homeland Security*, by Ruth Ellen Wasem.

[3] Authorities to except or to waive visa requirements are specified in law, such as the broad parole authority of the Attorney General under §212(d)(5) of the Immigration and Nationality Act (INA) and the specific authority of the Visa Waiver Program in §217 of the INA.

[4] Other departments, notably the Department of Labor (DOL), and the Department of Agriculture (USDA), play roles in the approval process depending on the category or type of visa sought, and the Department of Health and Human Services (HHS) sets policy on the health-related grounds for inadmissibility, as discussed below.

[5] Section 221(g) of the INA. 8 USC 1201.

[6] For further information and analysis of these numerous visa categories, see CRS Report RL32235, *U.S. Immigration Policy on Permanent Admissions*, by Ruth Ellen Wasem, and CRS Report RL31381, *U.S. Immigration Policy on Temporary Admissions*, by Chad C. Haddal and Ruth Ellen Wasem. (Hereafter cited as CRS Report RL31381, *Temporary Admissions*.)

[7] For a full discussion of these policies, see CRS Report RL32235, *U.S. Immigration Policy on Permanent Admissions*, by Ruth Ellen Wasem.

[8] CRS Report RL33844, *Foreign Investor Visas: Policies and Issues*, by Alison Siskin and Chad C. Haddal.

[9] 22 C.F.R. §42.62.

[10] For a recent review of the Bureau of Consular Affair's role in visa processing, see U.S. General Accounting Office, *Border Security: Visa Process Should Be Strengthened as an Antiterrorism Tool*, GAO-03-132NI, October 21, 2002.

[11] For a full discussion and analysis of nonimmigrant visas, see CRS Report RL31381, *Temporary Admissions*.

[12] 22 C.F.R. §41.11(a).

[13] 22 C.F.R. §41.102.

[14] For further discussion, see CRS Report RL32616, *9/11 Commission: Legislative Action Concerning U.S. Immigration Law and Policy in the 108th Congress*, by Michael John Garcia and Ruth Ellen Wasem.

[15] *Federal Register*, vol. 68, no. 129, July 7, 2003, pp. 40127-40129.

[16] §214(b) of the INA; 8 U.S.C. §1184(b).

[17] For example, see Edward Alden, The Closing of the American Border: Terrorism, Immigration, and Security Since 9/11 (Harper, 2008), and Bay Area Council Economic Institute , Visas for Higher Education and Scientific Exchanges: Balancing Security and Economic Competitiveness, Bay Area Science and Innovation Consortium (BASIC), April 2005, http://www.bayeconfor.org/media

[18] USCIS adjudicators also conduct admissibility reviews for petitions filed within the United States, and CBP inspectors do so when aliens seek entry to the United States. Within the United States, however, the immigration judges in Department of Justice's Executive Office for Immigration Review (EOIR) determine whether an alien is admissible.

[19] §212(a) of the INA.

[20] Some of these grounds for exclusion may be waived for aliens seeking admission on immigrant visas if certain criteria are met. Immigration authorities have broader authority to waive these grounds with respect to aliens seeking admission as nonimmigrants (INA section 212(d)(3)).

[21] For a complete analysis of the pre-1990 laws and policies, see U.S. Congress. House of Representatives. *Grounds for Exclusion of Aliens under the Immigration and Nationality Act: Historical Background and Analysis.* Committee print prepared by the Congressional Research Service at the request of the Committee on the Judiciary. September 1988.

[22] P.L. 110-257 expressly excluded the African National Congress from being considered a terrorist organization and P.L. 110-161 exempted 10 groups from being considered as terrorist organizations for INA purposes.

[23] P.L. 110-293 amended the INA to strike the reference to HIV/AIDS from the health-related grounds for exclusion.

[24] CRS Report R40144, *State Medicaid and CHIP Coverage of Noncitizens*, by Ruth Ellen Wasem.

[25] Act of March 3, 1891; 26 Stat. 1084.

[26] Section 305 of P.L. 110-293, the Tom Lantos and Henry J. Hyde United States Global Leadership Against HIV/AIDS, Tuberculosis, and Malaria Reauthorization Act of 2008, eliminated the language in the INA that statutorily barred foreign nationals with HIV/AIDS from entering the United States.

[27] For a thorough discussion, see CRS Report R40570, *Immigration Policies and Issues on Health-Related Grounds for Exclusion*, by Chad C. Haddal and Ruth Ellen Wasem.

[28] The prevalence of active tuberculosis among foreign nationals has been a concern for many years. On January 23, 1991, HHS published a proposed rule in which infectious tuberculosis would have been the only communicable disease listed. That rule was suspended May 29, 1991, largely because of the controversies of leaving HIV/AIDS off the list.

[29] 42 C.F.R. § 34.2(b).

[30] 42 C.F.R. § 34.2(b)(2).

[31] Exec. Order. No. 13295, 68 FR 17255 (April 4, 2003) *as amended by* Exec. Order. No. 13375, 70 FR 17299 (April 1, 2005).

[32] 42 C.F.R. § 34.2(b)(3).

[33] *See* 42 C.F.R. §34.3(d)(2) (factors used to determine whether a communicable disease poses a public health emergency of international concern).

[34] 42 C.F.R. § 34.2(b)(3). *See also* Annex 2 of the revised International Health Regulations http://www.who.int/csr/ihr/ en.

[35] U.S. Department of State Bureau of Consular Affairs, *Frequently Asked Questions—Immigrant Visa Interview Medical Examination.*

[36] INA § 212(g), 8 U.S.C. § 1182(g). The text actually names the Attorney General, but as a result of the Homeland Security Act of 2002 the waiver authority is exercised by the Secretary of Homeland Security.

[37] INA § 212(g), 8 U.S.C. § 1182(g).

[38] INA § 212(g)(1), 8 U.S.C. § 1182(g)(1).

[39] INA § 212(g)(2), 8 U.S.C. § 1182(g)(2).

[40] INA § 212(g)(3). 8 U.S.C. § 1182(g)(3).

[41] INA, § 212(d)(13)(B)(i).

[42] For further discussion, see CRS Report RL32480, *Immigration Consequences of Criminal Activity*, by Yule Kim and Michael John Garcia.

[43] Exceptions include aliens whose crime is considered a purely political offense, and cases in which the alien committed a single offense (1) while the alien was under the age of 18 and the crime was committed (and any related incarceration ended) more than five years prior to the application for admission or for a visa; or (2) where the maximum penalty for the crime at issue did not exceed one year's imprisonment and, if convicted, the alien was not sentenced to more than six months.

[44] INA § 212(a); 8 U.S.C. § 1182(a).

[45] 8 U.S.C. § 1182(h). Criminal grounds also may be waived for aliens seeking temporary admission as nonimmigrants. 8 U.S.C. § 1182(d)(3).

[46] For a complete discussion, see CRS Report RL32480, *Immigration Consequences of Criminal Activity*, by Yule Kim and Michael John Garcia, p. 8.

[47] For further discussion, see CRS Report RL32564, *Immigration: Terrorist Grounds for Exclusion and Removal of Aliens*, by Michael John Garcia and Ruth Ellen Wasem.

[48] The Consolidated Appropriations Act, FY2008, (P.L. 110-161) modified certain terrorism-related provisions of the INA, including exempting specified groups from the INA's definition of "terrorist organization" and

expanding immigration authorities' waiver authority over the terrorism-related grounds for exclusion. For further discussion, see CRS Report RL32564, *Immigration: Terrorist Grounds for Exclusion and Removal of Aliens*, by Michael John Garcia and Ruth Ellen Wasem.

[49] The colony of Massachusetts enacted legislation in 1645 prohibiting the entry of paupers, and in 1700 excluding the infirm unless security was given against their becoming public charges. New York adopted a similar practice. A bar against the admission of "any person unable to take care of himself or herself without becoming a public charge" was included in the act of August 3, 1882, the first general federal immigration law. It is now §212 (a)(4) of the INA; 8 U.S.C. 1182.

[50] 8 C.F.R. § 213a.1.

[51] § 213A of INA; 8 U.S.C. 1631. *Fed. Reg.*, v, pp. 54346-56. Oct. 20, 1997.

[52] The Systematic Alien Verification for Entitlements (SAVE) system provides federal, state, and local government agencies access to data on immigration status that are necessary to determine noncitizen eligibility for public benefits. SAVE's statutory authority dates back to the Immigration Reform and Control Act of 1986. §1137 of the SSA, as amended by P.L. 99-603.

[53] § 213A of INA; 8 U.S.C. 1631.

[54] For additional analysis, see CRS Report RL33809, *Noncitizen Eligibility for Federal Public Assistance: Policy Overview and Trends*, by Ruth Ellen Wasem.

[55] The administration of immigration and citizenship policy was reorganized by Homeland Security Act of 2002 (P.L. 107-296), and the Secretary of Homeland Security now oversees this function that the INA assigns to the Attorney General.

[56] INA §212(a)(5).

[57] For further background and analysis, see CRS Report RL33977, *Immigration of Foreign Workers: Labor Market Tests and Protections*, by Ruth Ellen Wasem.

[58] For a fuller analysis of these requirements and exceptions, see CRS Report RL33977, *Immigration of Foreign Workers: Labor Market Tests and Protections*, by Ruth Ellen Wasem.

[59] INA § 212(a)(5)(B) and (C).

[60] INA § 212(a)(6)(C)(i), 8 U.S.C. § 1182(a)(6)(C)(i). Similar language was in the Displaced Persons Act of 1946.

[61] INA § 212(a)(6)(C)(ii), 8 U.S.C. § 1182(a)(6)(C)(ii). An alien will not be deemed inadmissible if each parent of the alien is or was a U.S. citizen, the alien permanently resided in the United States prior to attaining the age of 16, and the alien reasonably believed at the time of making a representation of U.S. citizenship that he or she was a citizen.

[62] For example, an individual who is, or was at any time, permanently debarred from becoming a citizen of the United States under §3(a) of the Selective Training and Service Act of 1940, as amended (54 Stat. 885; 55 Stat. 844), or under §4(a) of the Selective Service Act of 1948, as amended (62 Stat. 605; 65 Stat. 76) [50 USC Appx. §454(a)], or under any section of this Act, or any other Act, or under any law amendatory of, supplementary to, or in substitution for, any of such sections or Acts, is ineligible for citizenship. INA § 101(a)(19), 8 U.S.C. § 1101(a)(19). INA § 325, 8 U.S.C. § 1101(a)(19)..

[63] These include foreign nationals who (1) are inadmissible at time of entry or violate their immigration status; (2) commit certain criminal offenses (e.g., crimes of moral turpitude, aggravated felonies, alien smuggling, high speed flight); (3) fail to register (if required under law) or commit document fraud; (4) are security risks (such as aliens who violate any law relating to espionage, engage in criminal activity which endangers public safety, partake in terrorist activities, or assisted in Nazi persecution or genocide); (5) become a public charge within five years of entry; or (6) vote unlawfully. The "permanent bar to admissibility" is applicable to aliens who enter or attempt to reenter the U.S. without having been admitted and who have been previously removed. This inadmissibility can only be excused if the alien seeks and is granted permission from the government more than 10 years after the alien's last date of departure from the country.

[64] INA § 212(a)(6)(F), 8 U.S.C. § 1182(a)(6)(F).

[65] INA § 212(a)(6).

[66] As noted earlier, consular decisions are not appealable or reviewable; however, some aliens are able to bring additional information that may be used to overcome an initial refusal. Although the DOS Bureau of Consular Affairs Report of the Visa Office presents data on initial refusals that are subsequently overcome, the data are not matched to the individual nor to the year of initial refusal. As a result, the rates of visa refusals that were overcome cannot be calculated.

[67] § 213A of INA; 8 U.S.C. 1631. *Fed. Reg.*, v, pp. 54346-56. Oct. 20, 1997.

[68] For a discussion of databases and screening procedures, see Appendix A.

[69] From 1994 through 2000, the United States approved 657,570 employment-based LPRs. From 2002 through 2008, the United States approved 1,145,516 employment-based LPRs. In other words, during the seven-year period after September 11, 2001, there were twice as many employment-based LPRs as were admitted in the seven years prior to 2001.

[70] U.S. Department of State, Annual Report of Immigrant Visa Applicants in the Family-sponsored and Employment-based preferences Registered at the National Visa Center as of November 1, 2009, http://www.travel.state WaitingListItem.pdf.

[71] For information on other watchlists, see CRS Report RL33645, *Terrorist Watchlist Checks and Air Passenger Prescreening*, by William J. Krouse and Bart Elias.

[72] U.S. Congress, Senate Committee on Homeland Security and Governmental Affairs, *Five Years After the Intelligence Reform and Terrorism Act: Stopping Terrorist Travel*, 111th Cong., 1st sess., December 9, 2009.

[73] U.S. Congress, Senate Committee on Foreign Relations, Subcommittee on International Operations and Terrorism, *The Post 9/11 Visa Reforms and New Technology: Achieving the Necessary Security Improvements in a Global Environment*, hearing, October 23, 2003.

[74] Unclassified congressional staff briefing by Assistant Secretary of State Janice Jacobs, January 11, 2010.

[75] U.S. Congress, Senate Committee on Foreign Relations, Subcommittee on International Operations and Terrorism, *The Post 9/11 Visa Reforms and New Technology: Achieving the Necessary Security Improvements in a Global Environment*, hearing, October 23, 2003.

[76] For further discussion of terrorist screening, see CRS Report RL32564, *Immigration: Terrorist Grounds for Exclusion and Removal of Aliens*, by Michael John Garcia and Ruth Ellen Wasem.

[77] See CRS Report RL32221, *Visa Waiver Program*, by Alison Siskin.

[78] Section 711(h)(3) of P.L. 110-53 provides: "A determination by the Secretary of Homeland Security that an alien is eligible to travel to the United States under the program is not a determination that the alien is admissible to the United States." That subsection further provides: "A determination by the Secretary of Homeland Security that an alien who applied for authorization to travel to the United States through the System is not eligible to travel under the program is not a determination of eligibility for a visa to travel to the United States and shall not preclude the alien from applying for a visa."

[79] INA §212(d)(4)(A). The Homeland Security Act (P.L. 107-296) transferred most immigration-related functions from DOJ to DHS. It is uncertain as of this writing whether this waiver authority remains, in whole or in part, with DOJ and the Attorney General or with the Secretary of DHS.

[80] For additional information about these exceptions, see 8 C.F.R. §212.1; 22 C.F.R. §41.1; and 22 C.F.R. §41.2.

[81] 8 U.S.C. 1185(b).

In: U.S. Visa Policies, Programs and Considerations
Editor: Aaron R. Miller
ISBN: 978-1-61470-333-4

Chapter 2

Visa Security Policy: Roles of the Departments of State and Homeland Security*

Ruth Ellen Wasem

Summary

Foreign nationals (i.e., aliens) not already legally residing in the United States who wish to come to the United States generally must obtain a visa to be admitted, with certain exceptions noted in law. The Departments of State (DOS) and Homeland Security (DHS) each play key roles in administering the law and policies on the admission of aliens. Although the DOS's Consular Affairs is responsible for issuing visas, the U.S. Citizenship and Immigrant Services (USCIS) in DHS approves immigrant petitions, the Immigration and Customs Enforcement (ICE) in DHS operates the Visa Security Program in selected embassies abroad, and the Customs and Border Protection (CBP) in DHS inspects all people who enter the United States. In addition, the Executive Office for Immigration Review (EOIR) in the U.S. Department of Justice (DOJ) has a significant policy role through its adjudicatory decisions on specific immigration cases.

Although there was a discussion of assigning all visa issuance responsibilities to DHS when the department was being created, the Homeland Security Act of 2002 (P.L. 107-296) opted not to do so. Rather, P.L. 107-296 drew on compromise language stating that DHS issues regulations regarding visa issuances and assigns staff to consular posts abroad to advise, review, and conduct investigations, and that DOS's Consular Affairs continues to issue visas.

The case of Umar Farouk Abdulmutallab, who allegedly attempted to ignite an explosive device on Northwest Airlines Flight 253 on December 25, 2009, refocused attention on the responsibilities of the Departments of State and Homeland Security for the visa process. He was traveling on a multi-year, multiple-entry tourist visa issued to him in June 2008. State Department officials have acknowledged that Abdulmutallab's father came into the Embassy in Abuja, Nigeria, on November 19, 2009, to express his concerns about his son, and that those officials at the Embassy in Abuja sent a cable to

* This is an edited, reformatted and augmented version of a Congressional Research Service publication, CRS Report for Congress R41093, from www.crs.gov, dated December 16, 2010.

the National Counterterrorism Center. State Department officials maintain they had insufficient information to revoke his visa at that time. In the aftermath of the Abdulmutallab case, policymakers explored what went wrong and whether statutory and procedural revisions were needed.

Some have expressed the view that DOS has too much control over visas, maintaining that the Homeland Security Act intended DHS to be the lead department and DOS to merely administer the visa process. Proponents of DOS playing the principal role in visa issuances assert that only consular officers in the field have the country-specific knowledge to make decisions about whether an alien is admissible and that staffing 250 diplomatic and consular posts around the world would stretch DHS beyond its capacity. Whether the visa security roles and procedures are adequately funded may arise as the budget issues are considered.

Introduction

Foreign nationals (i.e., aliens) not already legally residing in the United States who wish to come to the United States generally must obtain a visa to be admitted.[1] Under current law, three departments—the Department of State (DOS), the Department of Homeland Security (DHS) and the Department of Justice (DOJ)—play key roles in administering the law and policies on the admission of aliens.[2] DOS's Bureau of Consular Affairs (Consular Affairs) is responsible for issuing visas, DHS's Citizenship and Immigration Services Bureau (USCIS) is charged with approving immigrant petitions, DHS's Immigration and Customs Enforcement (ICE) operates the Visa Security Program in selected embassies abroad, and DHS's Customs and Border Protection Bureau (CBP) is tasked with inspecting all people who enter the United States. DOJ's Executive Office for Immigration Review (EOIR) has a significant policy role through its adjudicatory decisions on specific immigration cases.[3]

The case of Umar Farouk Abdulmutallab, who allegedly attempted to ignite an explosive device on Northwest Airlines Flight 253 on December 25, 2009, refocused attention on the responsibilities of the Departments of State and Homeland Security for the visa process. He was traveling on a multi-year, multiple-entry tourist visa issued to him in June 2008. State Department officials have acknowledged that Abdulmutallab's father came into the Embassy in Abuja, Nigeria, on November 19, 2009, to express his concerns about his son, and that those officials at the Embassy in Abuja sent a cable to the National Counterterrorism Center. State Department officials maintain they had insufficient information to revoke his visa at that time. In the aftermath of the Abdulmutallab case, policymakers explored what went wrong and whether statutory and procedural revisions were needed.

Overview on Visa Issuances

There are two broad classes of aliens that are issued visas: immigrants and nonimmigrants. Humanitarian admissions, such as asylees, refugees, parolees and other aliens granted relief from deportation, are handled separately under the Immigration and Nationality Act (INA). Those aliens granted asylum or refugee status ultimately are eligible to become legal permanent residents (LPRs).[4] Illegal aliens or unauthorized aliens include those noncitizens who entered the United States without an official inspection at a port of entry, entered with fraudulent documents, or who violated the terms of their visas after entering the United States.

Immigrant Visas

Aliens who wish to come to live permanently in the United States must meet a set of criteria specified in the INA. They must qualify as

- a spouse or minor child of a U.S. citizen;
- a parent, adult child, or sibling of an adult U.S. citizen;
- a spouse or minor child of a legal permanent resident;
- an employee that a U.S. employer has gotten approval from the Department of Labor to hire;
- a person of extraordinary or exceptional ability in specified areas;
- a refugee or asylee determined to be fleeing persecution;
- winner of a visa in the diversity lottery; or
- having met other specialized provisions of law.[5]

Petitions for immigrant (i.e., LPR) status are first filed with USCIS by the sponsoring relative or employer in the United States. If the prospective immigrant is already residing in the United States, the USCIS handles the entire process, which is called "adjustment of status." If the prospective LPR does not have legal residence in the United States, the petition is forwarded to Consular Affairs in their home country after USCIS has reviewed it. The Consular Affairs officer (when the alien is coming from abroad) and USCIS adjudicator (when the alien is adjusting status in the United States) must be satisfied that the alien is entitled to the immigrant status.

Nonimmigrant Visas

Aliens seeking to come to the United States temporarily rather than to live permanently are known as nonimmigrants.[6] These aliens are admitted to the United States for a temporary period of time and an expressed reason. There are 24 major nonimmigrant visa categories, and over 70 specific types of nonimmigrant visas are issued currently. Most of these nonimmigrant visa categories are defined in §101(a)(15) of the INA. These visa categories are commonly referred to by the letter and numeral that denotes their subparagraph in §101(a)(15), e.g., B-2 tourists, F-1 foreign students, H-1B temporary professional workers, or J-1 cultural exchange participants.

Most visitors, however, enter the United States without nonimmigrant visas through the Visa Waiver Program (VWP). This provision of INA allows the Attorney General to waive the visa documentary requirements for aliens coming as visitors from 35 countries (e.g., Australia, France, Germany, Italy, Japan, New Zealand, and Switzerland). Since aliens entering through VWP do not have visas, CBP inspectors at the port of entry perform the background checks and admissibility reviews.[7]

STATUTORY BASIS OF CURRENT VISA POLICY

Today's visa issuance policy dates back to 1924, when Congress first passed legislation assigning consular officers with the responsibility to approve or deny visas.[8] The Immigration Act of 1924 codified a decree in 1917 as a consequence of World War I that proclaimed aliens must present certain documents as a prerequisite to entering the United States. When the Senate Committee on the Judiciary was tasked with investigating the immigration system in 1947,[9] their report offered the following observation:

> After a study of this problem, the Congress provided in the Immigration Act of 1924 for a double check of aliens by separate independent agencies of the Government, first by consular officers before the visas were issued, and by immigration officers after the aliens reached the port of entry. If a double check was essential 25 years ago to protect the United States against criminals or other undesirables, it is the opinion of the subcommittee that it is even more necessary in the present critical condition of the world to use the double check to screen aliens seeking to enter the United States.[10]

This view prevailed in 1952 when Congress codified the various statutes on immigration and nationality into the Immigration and Nationality Act of 1952 (P.L. 82-414), which remains the basis of governing law.

Immigration and Nationality Act

The powers and duties of the Secretary of State are delineated in §104 of the INA. Most significantly, §104 (a) states: "The Secretary of State shall be charged with the administration and the enforcement of the provisions of this Act and all other immigration and nationality laws relating to (1) the powers, duties and functions of diplomatic and consular officers of the United States, *except those powers, duties and functions conferred upon the consular officers relating to the granting or refusal of visas;....*"[11] The INA specifically gives consular officers the sole authority to issue visas in §221 of the act.[12] Over the years, the courts have held that consular decisions are not appealable.[13] Under proscribed circumstances, the Secretary of State may direct a consular officer to deny a visa to a particular inadmissible alien.[14]

Enhanced Border Security and Visa Entry Reform Act of 2002

After the terrorist attacks on September 11, 2001, Congress enacted the Enhanced Border Security and Visa Entry Reform Act of 2002 (P.L. 107-173), which aimed to improve the visa issuance process abroad, as well as immigration inspections at the border. It expressly increased consular officers' access to electronic information needed for alien screening. Specifically, it required the development of an interoperable electronic data system to be used to share information relevant to alien admissibility and removability and the implementation of an integrated entry-exit data system. It also required that all visas issued by October 2004 have biometric identifiers, and DOS met that deadline for biometric visas. In addition to increasing consular officers' access to electronic information needed for visa issuances, it expanded the training requirements for consular officers who issue visas.

§428 of the Homeland Security Act of 2002

The Homeland Security Act of 2002 (HSA) contained language stating that DHS is responsible for formulating regulations on visa issuances. In §428, the Secretary of DHS is expressly tasked as follows:

> ...shall be vested exclusively with all authorities to issue regulations with respect to, administer, and enforce the provisions of such Act, and of all other immigration and nationality laws, relating to the functions of consular officers of the United States in connection with the granting or refusal of visas, and shall have the authority to refuse visas in accordance with law and to develop programs of homeland security training for consular officers (in addition to consular training provided by the Secretary of State), which authorities shall be exercised through the Secretary of State, *except that the Secretary shall not have authority to alter or reverse the decision of a consular officer to refuse a visa to an alien ...*[15]

The HSA also enabled DHS to assign staff to consular posts abroad to advise, review, and conduct investigations, which is discussed more fully below. It further stated that DOS's Consular Affairs continued to be responsible for issuing visas. The HSA required DHS and DOS to reach an understanding on how the details of this division of responsibilities would be implemented.[16]

On September 28, 2003, then-Secretary of State Colin Powell and then-Secretary of Homeland Security Thomas Ridge signed the memorandum of understanding (MOU) implementing §428 of the HSA.[17] The MOU described each department's responsibilities in the area of visa issuances. Among its major elements, the MOU stated that DOS may propose and issue visa regulations subject to DHS consultation and final approval. It further stated that DHS shall assign personnel to diplomatic posts, but that DOS will determine who, how many, and the scope of their functions.

Then-Assistant Secretary of State for Consular Affairs Maura Harty described several key responsibilities that remain with the DOS.

> The Secretary of State will have responsibility over certain visa decisions, including decisions of a foreign policy nature.... He will also be responsible for establishing visa validity periods and fees based on reciprocity. In the case of visa validity periods, however, he will consult with Homeland Security before lengthening them, and Homeland Security will have authority to determine that certain persons or classes of persons cannot benefit from the maximum validity period for security reasons. The Secretary of State will also exercise all the foreign policy-related grounds of visa denial enumerated in Section 428 and the additional provision, not specifically enumerated, under which we deny visas to persons who have confiscated the property of American citizens without just compensation.[18]

She emphasized that the MOU "recognizes that the Secretary of State must have control over officers in his chain of command." She further stated that "DHS officers assigned visa duties abroad may provide input related to the evaluations of consular officers doing visa work, but the evaluations themselves will be written by State Department consular supervisors," and that "direction to consular officers will come from their State Department supervisors, and all officers assigned abroad, including DHS, come under the authority of the Chief of Mission."[19]

In congressional testimony during October 2003, C. Stewart Verdery, Jr., as then-DHS Assistant Secretary for Border and Transportation Security Policy and Planning, discussed DHS' role in visa security. Verdery reported that DHS officers were already in Saudi Arabia reviewing all visa applications prior to adjudication (as required by §428(i) of P.L. 107-296). He indicated that officers in Riyadh and Jeddah also provided assistance, expert advice and training to consular officers on fraudulent documents, fingerprinting techniques and identity fraud. More specifically, he stated:

> As part of the review process, DHS officers at home and abroad have full access to a variety of law enforcement databases, including the National Crime Information Center (NCIC); Treasury Enforcement Communication System (TECS); Interagency Border Inspections System (IBIS); National Security Entry Exit System (NSEERS); Student Exchange and Visitor Information System (SEVIS); Biometric 2-print fingerprint system (IDENT); and Advanced Passenger Information System (APIS). They also have access to selected legacy-INS automated adjudications data and certain commercial databases.[20]

Intelligence Reform and Terrorism Prevention Act of 2004

Congress also relied on recommendations made by the National Commission on Terrorist Attacks Upon the United States (also known as the 9/11 Commission) to revise visa security policies. The Intelligence Reform and Terrorism Prevention Act of 2004 (P.L. 108-458) mandated improvements in technology and training to assist consular and immigration officers in detecting and combating terrorist travel. Among other provisions, it required the Secretary of Homeland Security, in consultation with the Director of the National Counter Terrorism Center, to establish a program to oversee DHS's responsibilities with respect to terrorist travel and required the Secretary of State to establish a Visa and Passport Security Program within the Bureau of Diplomatic Security at the Department of State.

The Intelligence Reform and Terrorism Prevention Act added requirements for an in-person consular interview of most applicants for nonimmigrant visas between the ages of 14 and 79. It further mandated that an alien applying for a nonimmigrant visa must completely and accurately respond to any request for information contained in his or her application.

CONSULAR SCREENING PROCEDURES

Foreign nationals seeking visas must undergo admissibility reviews performed by DOS consular officers abroad.[21] The visa applicant is required to submit his or her photograph and fingerprints, as well as full name (and any other name used or by which he or she has been known), age, gender, and the date and place of birth. Depending on the visa category, certain documents must be certified by the proper government authorities (e.g., birth certificates and marriage licenses). All prospective LPRs must submit to physical and mental examinations, and prospective nonimmigrants also may be required to have physical and mental examinations.

These reviews are intended to ensure that aliens are not ineligible for visas or admission under the grounds for inadmissibility spelled out in the INA.[22] These INA §212(a) inadmissibility criteria are

- health-related grounds,
- criminal history,
- security and terrorist concerns,
- public charge (e.g., indigence),
- seeking to work without proper labor certification,
- illegal entrants and immigration law violations,
- ineligible for citizenship, and
- aliens previously removed.

Consular officers use the Consular Consolidated Database (CCD) to screen visa applicants. Records of all visa applications are now automated in the CCD, with some records dating back to the mid-1990s. Since February 2001, the CCD has stored photographs of all visa applicants in electronic form; since 2007, the CCD has begun storing 10-finger scans. In addition to indicating the outcome of any prior visa application of the alien in the CCD and comments by consular officers, the system links with other databases to flag problems that may have an impact on the issuance of the visa. These databases linked with the CCD include DHS's Automated Biometric Identification System (IDENT) and FBI's Integrated Automated Fingerprint Identification System (IAFIS) results, and supporting documents.

The CCD also links to the DHS's Traveler Enforcement Compliance System (TECS), which enables CBP officers at ports of entry to have access to CCD.[23] A limited number of consular officers have recently been granted access to DHS'Arrival Departure Information System (ADIS). [24] ADIS tracks foreign nationals' entries into and most exits out of the United States. DOS credits access to ADIS with its ability to identify previously undetected cases of illegal overstays in the United States.

For some years, consular officers have been required to check the background of all aliens in the "lookout" databases, specifically the Consular Lookout and Support System (CLASS) database, which contained over 26 million records in 2009.[25] According to Janice Jacobs, Assistant Secretary of State for Consular Affairs, the CLASS database grew by approximately 400% after September 11, 2001.

> This increase in the quantity and quality of CLASS records is largely the result of improved data sharing between the Department of State and the law enforcement and intelligence communities. In 2001, only 25 percent of records in CLASS came from other government agencies. Now, almost 70 percent of CLASS records come from other agencies.[26]

The Security Advisory Opinion (SAO) system requires a consular officer abroad to refer selected visa cases for greater review by intelligence and law enforcement agencies.[27] The current interagency procedures for alerting officials about foreign nationals who may be suspected terrorists, referred to in State Department nomenclature as Visa Viper, began after the 1993 World Trade Center bombing and were institutionalized by enactment of the Enhanced Border Security and Visa Entry Reform Act of 2002. If consular officials receive information about a foreign national that causes concern, they send a Visa Viper cable (which is a dedicated and secure communication) to the NCTC. In 2009, consular posts sent approximately 3,000 Visa Viper communications to NCTC.[28]

In a similar set of SAO procedures, consular officers send suspect names, identified by law enforcement and intelligence information (originally certain visa applicants from 26 predominantly Muslim countries), to the Federal Bureau of Investigation (FBI) for a name check program called Visa Condor.[29] There is also the "Terrorist Exclusion List" (TEL), which lists organizations designated as terrorist-supporting and includes the names of individuals associated with these organizations.[30]

VISA REVOCATION

After a visa has been issued, the consular officer as well as the Secretary of State has the discretionary authority to revoke a visa at any time.[31] A consular officer must revoke a visa if

- the alien is ineligible under the INA §212(a) grounds of inadmissibility to receive such a visa, or was issued a visa and overstayed the time limits of the visa;
- the alien is not entitled to the nonimmigrant visa classification under INA §101(a)(15) definitions specified in such visa;
- the visa has been physically removed from the passport in which it was issued; or
- the alien has been issued an immigrant visa.[32]

The Foreign Affairs Manual (FAM) instructs: "in making any new determination of ineligibility as a result of information which may come to light after issuance of a visa, the consular officer must seek and obtain any required advisory opinion." This applies, for example, to findings of ineligibility under "misrepresentation," "terrorist activity" or "foreign policy." FAM further instructs: "pending receipt of the Department's advisory opinion, the consular officer must enter the alien's name in the CLASS under a quasi-refusal code, if warranted."[33] According to DOS officials, they sometimes prudentially revoke visas (i.e., they revoke a visa as a safety precaution).[34]

When a consular officer suspects that a visa revocation may involve U.S. law enforcement interests, FAM instructs the consular officer to consult with law enforcement agencies at post and inform the State officials of the case, to permit consultations with potentially interested entities before a revocation is made.[35] The rationale for this consultation is that there may be legal or intelligence investigations that would be compromised if the visa were revoked and that law enforcement and intelligence officials may prefer to monitor the individual to further investigate their actions and associates.

Visa revocation has been a ground for removal in the INA §237(a)(1)(B) since enactment of P.L. 108-458 in December 2004. That provision (§5304 of P.L. 108-458) permits limited judicial review of removal if visa revocation is the sole basis of the removal.

DHS VISA SECURITY PROGRAM

As mentioned above, §428 of the HSA gave the Secretary of DHS the authority to assign DHS employees to diplomatic and consular posts. The duties of these DHS employees were delineated in §428 as

- provide expert advice and training to consular officers regarding specific security threats relating to the adjudication of individual visa applications or classes of applications;
- review any such applications, either on the initiative of DHS or upon request by a consular officer or other person charged with adjudicating such applications; and,
- conduct investigations with respect to consular matters under the jurisdiction of the Secretary of DHS.

This statutory language established what is currently known as the Visa Security Program (VSP). The ICE Office of International Affairs (OIA) operates the VSP in high-risk consular posts. As described by DHS, the VSP sends ICE special agents with expertise in immigration law and counterterrorism to diplomatic posts overseas to perform visa security activities, which aim to complement the DOS visa screening process with law enforcement resources not available to consular officers.

The first VSP units were established in Saudi Arabia, as required by §428. In October 2005, VSP units were set up in: Manila, Philippines; Abu Dhabi and Dubai in the United Arab Emirates; and Islamabad, Pakistan. By the end of 2007, there were VSP units in: Cairo, Egypt; Caracas, Venezuela; Montreal, Canada; Hong Kong, China; and Casablanca, Morocco. That year, the VSP proposed a five-year expansion plan, which proposed to concentrate expansion to the highest risk posts with the goal of covering 75% of the highest risk visa activity by 2013.[36]

One of the major tasks of the VSP agents is to screen visa applicants to determine the applicant's risk profile. Unlike consular officers, VSP agents have access to DHS's Traveler Enforcement Compliance System (TECS), a substantial database of law enforcement and border inspection information. The ICE agent further vets visa applicants who are possible matches, performing additional research and investigation of the visa applicant (e.g., in-depth searches in law enforcement databases and other information systems, examining documents, and consulting with consular, law enforcement, or other officials).[37]

VSP agents engage in informal discussions with consular officers, as well as develop formal, targeted training and briefings to inform consular officers and others about threats to the visa process. They "identify and monitor the threat environment and trends in the visa applicant pool specific to their post and host country... Examples of topics covered in these briefings include fraud trends in specific visa categories and how to identify fraudulent documents and imposters."[38] Aimed at improving VSP integration in the SAO process, Congress appropriated $5 million to establish an SAO review unit within VSP headquarters in FY2007, which is more fully discussed below.[39]

CURRENT ISSUES

The case of Umar Farouk Abdulmutallab, who allegedly tried to take down Northwest Airlines Flight 253 on December 25, 2009, refocused attention on the assignment of roles and responsibilities to ensure visa security. The 23 year-old Nigerian national allegedly tried unsuccessfully to ignite an explosive device on an incoming flight to Detroit. U.S. consular officers in London, where Abdulmutallab was a student at the University College London, had issued him a multi-year, multiple-visit tourist visa in June 2008.[40] The suspect's father had reportedly contacted U.S. officials to indicate his concern about his son's welfare and involvement in Islamic fanaticism. State Department officials reported that the father came into the Embassy in Abuja, Nigeria, on November 19, 2009, to express his concerns about his son and that the consular officials at the Embassy in Abuja sent a cable to the National Counterterrorism Center (NCTC).[41] They relied on the standard interagency procedures for screening suspected terrorists, referred to as Visa Viper.[42] In the aftermath of the Abdulmutallab case, policymakers explored what went wrong and whether statutory and procedural revisions were needed.

Competing Interests

Some have expressed the view that DOS retains too much power and control over visa issuances. They maintain the Homeland Security Act intended DHS to be the lead department and that DOS was to merely administer the visa process. They warn that consular officers are too concerned about facilitating tourism and trade to scrutinize visa applicants thoroughly.[43] Some argue that visa issuance is the real "front line" of homeland security against terrorists and that the principal responsibility should be in DHS, which does not have competing priorities of diplomatic relations and reciprocity with foreign governments.

Not long after the attempted bombing of Flight 253, the Chairman of the Senate Committee on Homeland Security and Governmental Affairs, Senator Joseph Lieberman, stated: "I believe, incidentally, that we ought to take a look at taking the visa application and admission responsibility from the State Department. It doesn't really fit with foreign policy anymore." The Chairman continued, "And in an age of terrorism, I think the Department of Homeland Security ought to be handling visas abroad."[44]

Others are recommending further deliberation before changing the law, observing that today's visa security policies grew out of lessons learned from the September 11, 2001, terrorist attacks.[45] The Chairman of the Senate Committee on the Judiciary, Senator Patrick Leahy, stated "After Congress passed major legislation in 2004 to implement the 9/11 Commission's recommendations, and after the country invested significant resources to upgrade security systems and reorganize our intelligence agencies, the near tragedy on Christmas Day compels us to ask what went wrong and what additional reforms are needed."[46]

Proponents of the current division of responsibilities argue that it strikes the proper balance between the two departments and reflects the bifurcation envisioned in the Homeland Security Act. They maintain that it plays off the strengths of the two departments and allows for refinement of the implementation in the future.[47] Proponents of DOS playing the lead role in visa issuances assert that only consular officers in the field have the country-specific knowledge to make decisions about whether an alien is admissible and that staffing approximately 250 diplomatic and consular posts around the world would stretch DHS beyond its capacity.[48]

Acceptance of VSP in Consular Posts

The statutory language of §428(d) of P.L. 107-296 makes clear that authority of the chief of mission remained intact despite the added authorities given to DHS.[49] It states that nothing in that provision may be construed to alter or affect the authority of a chief of mission under §207 of the Foreign Service Act of 1980.[50] Ultimately, it is the DOS chief of mission at a particular consular post who determines whether to accept a VSP unit.[51] A 2008 report of the DHS Office of Inspector General discussed tensions between DOS and DHS in establishing VSP units abroad.

> Some DOS headquarters officials have said that ICE special agents do not need to be posted overseas to conduct their visa security activities. The DOS officials said ICE special agents are able to access the law enforcement databases and information systems used in the screening and vetting process remotely. VSP managers said that experienced law enforcement agents assigned overseas provide unique added value at overseas posts. ICE special agents assigned to VSUs [shorthand for VSP units] use their expertise in immigration and nationality law, investigations, document examination, intelligence research, and counterterrorism to complement the consular visa adjudication process with law enforcement vetting and investigation. In addition, ICE special agents assigned to VSUs at post focus on identifying "not yet known" terrorists and criminal suspects....[52]

More recently, top-level DOS leadership has stated they are fully supportive of the VSP and are coordinating with DHS to expand the units to additional consular posts. [53]

DOS Visa Processing and Security Funding

The adjudication and issuance of visas are largely fee-based, rather than a government service funded by direct appropriations. For the most part, prospective immigrants and nonimmigrants cover the costs of visa processing. The Consular Affairs immigrant visa application processing fee is $355, and the nonimmigrant processing fee is $131.[54] Moreover, the 107th Congress permanently authorized the collection of Machine-Readable Visa (MRV) fees at $65—or the cost of the machine-readable visa service if higher—and a $10 surcharge for machine-readable visas in nonmachine-readable passports. These MRV fees are credited as an offsetting collection used by DOS to recover costs of providing consular services.[55]

Table 1. Department of State Border Security Program Resource Summary (dollars in thousands)

Category	FY2009 Actual	FY2010 Enacted	FY2011 Request
Machine Readable Visa (MRV) Fees	830,948	974,817	975,000
Western Hemisphere Travel Surcharge	248,889	315,000	315,000
Enhanced Border Security Program Fees	257,600	454,254	629,000
Other Consular Fees	0	0	634,000
Fraud Prevention Fee	40,000	40,000	40,000
Affidavit of Support Fee	10,000	0	0
Total Border Security Program Expenses	$1,387,437	$1,784,071	$2,593,000

Source: Secretary of State, *FY2011 Congressional Budget Justifications*, Vol. 1, Department of State Operations (2010).

In the FY2011 Budget Request of the President, DOS presents the Consular Affairs visa operations as part of its Border Security Program. As Table 1 indicates, DOS requested an increase in its Border Security Program from $1.8 billion in FY2010 to $2.6 billion in FY2011, and would rely on the use of additional fee receipts to increase the overall funding. "The FY 2011 budget request includes a proposal that would allow the Department to retain all user fees collected from the provision of consular services for FY 2011 and all future years to cover the full cost of immigration, passport, and other consular services."[56] The question of whether DOS is adequately funded to process visas expeditiously while maintaining visa security procedures may arise as the budget is debated.[57]

Meanwhile, the Full-Year Continuing Appropriations Act, 2011 (H.R. 3082), which the House passed on December 8, 2010, would freeze FY2011 discretionary appropriations at the FY2010 level.

DHS Visa Security Program Funding

The VSP has been growing in terms of funding as well as units located abroad. The FY2009 budget request (the final year of President George W. Bush's Administration) was $11.8 million for the VSP, with $3.4 million to create two additional overseas VSP units in high-risk locations.[58] Congress almost doubled President Bush request of $11.8 million to $22.4 million in FY2009. Funding in FY2010 fell short of President Barrack Obama's Administration request of $32.2 million, as Congress appropriated $30.7 million for the VSP.[59]

DHS has reported expanding the number of VSP units in high-risk consular posts by two each year in FY2009 and in FY2010, but acknowledges that Congress has required DHS to use the remaining two-year enhancement funds of $3.4 million it received for expansion by the close of FY2010 pursuant to its five-year expansion plan (discussed above) or the funds will be lost.[60] DHS also stated that 63 ICE special agents were trained to become Visa Security Officers in FY2009.[61]

Table 2. Department of Homeland Security Visa Security Program Budget Estimates (dollars in thousands)

	FY2009 Actual	FY2010 Enacted	FY2011 Request
Salaries and Expenses	$22,354	$30,686	$30,686
FTEs	36	67	67

Source: Department of Homeland Security, U.S. Immigration and Customs Enforcement, *Fiscal Year 2011 Overview Congressional Justification,* (2010).

The Obama Administration requested that the VSP be funded at the same level in FY2011 as Congress funded it in FY2010—$30.7 million.[62] The modest size of the VSP with 67 full-time equivalent staff (FTEs) has led some to question how many VSP units DHS will be able to realistically staff. Some members of Congress are questioning how long it will take DHS to staff the 40 consular posts it deemed "high-risk" locations with the current level of funding. Congressman Gus Bilirakis, the Ranking Member of the House Homeland Security Subcommittee on Management, Investigations, and Oversight, has called for Congress to shift funding from DHS administrative functions to the VSP.[63] As discussed above, however, others note that the expansion of the VSP has been stymied as much by questions of how much added-value it brings and the inter-department negotiations, as it has been by funding.[64] For example, several Republican Senators reported that the application for Yemen has been pending since September 2008, and applications for Tel Aviv, Jerusalem, Frankfurt and Amman have been waiting for approval since September 2009.[65]

As noted above, the Full-Year Continuing Appropriations Act, 2011 (H.R. 3082), which the House passed on December 8, 2010, would freeze FY2011 discretionary appropriations at the FY2010 level.

APPENDIX A. LEGISLATIVE HISTORY OF THE VISA FUNCTIONS IN THE HOMELAND SECURITY ACT OF 2002

When the 107th Congress weighed the creation of the Department of Homeland Security, considerable debate surfaced about whether or not any or all visa issuance functions should be located in the new department. Enactment of P.L. 107-296 addressed most of these issues, but a few concerns remained after the implementation of the act. Varied viewpoints are discussed below.

As announced on June 6, 2002, the Administration's proposal for a homeland security department would have included Immigration and Naturalization Service (INS) among the agencies transferred to a new homeland security department. The stated goal of the Administration's proposal was to consolidate into a single federal department many of the homeland security functions performed by units within various federal agencies and departments. The Administration would have placed all functions of INS under the border and transportation security division of the proposed department. The narrative of the June 6, 2002, plan did not go into details, however, it appeared that under the plan Consular Affairs in the Department of State would have retained its visa issuance responsibilities. This proposal precipitated considerable discussion on where the visa issuance should be located.

Option: Locating all Functions in DHS

Voices in support of moving Consular Affairs's visa issuance responsibilities to the proposed DHS asserted that consular officers emphasize the promotion of tourism, commerce, and cultural exchange and are lax in screening foreign nationals who want to come the United States. Media reports of the "Visa Express" that DOS established in Saudi Arabia to allow travel agents to prescreen nonimmigrants raised considerable concern, especially reports that several of the September 11 terrorists allegedly entered through "Visa Express." Critics argued that visa issuance was the real "front line" of homeland security against terrorists and that the responsibility for this function should be in a department that did not have competing priorities of diplomatic relations and reciprocity with foreign governments.

Some argued that keeping the INS adjudications and Consular Affairs visa issuances in different departments would perpetuate the types of mistakes and oversights that stem from inadequate coordination and competing chains of command. Most importantly, they emphasized the need for immigration adjudications and visa issuances—as well as immigration law enforcement and inspections activities—to be under one central authority that has border security as its primary mission.

Option: Locating Functions in Different Agencies

Proponents of retaining visa issuances in Consular Affairs asserted that only consular officers in the field would have the country-specific knowledge to make decisions about whether an alien was admissible and that staffing 250 diplomatic and consular posts around the world would stretch the proposed homeland security department beyond its capacity. They also pointed out that under current law, consular decisions are not appealable and warned that transferring this adjudication to homeland security might make it subject to judicial appeals or other due process considerations. The MRV fees, as some point out, have become an important funding stream, contributing almost 10% of DOS total budget. They maintained that the problems Consular Affairs evidenced in visa issuances have already been addressed by strengthening provisions in the USA PATRIOT Act (P.L. 107-56) and the Enhanced Border Security and Visa Reform Act (P.L. 107-173).

Those who supported retained immigrant adjudications and services in DOJ and visa issuances in DOS point to the specializations that each department brings to the functions. They asserted that the "dual check" system in which both INS and Consular Affairs make their own determinations on whether an alien ultimately enters the United States provides greater security. Proponents of the joint DOJ-DOS responsibilities argued that failures in intelligence gathering and analysis, not lax enforcement of immigration law, were the principal factors that enabled terrorists to obtain visas. Others opposing the transfer of INS adjudications and Consular Affairs visa issuances to DHS maintained that DHS would be less likely to balance the more generous elements of immigration law (e.g., the reunification of families, the admission of immigrants with needed skills, the protection of refugees, opportunities for cultural exchange, the facilitation of trade, commerce, and diplomacy) with the more restrictive elements of the law (e.g., protection of public health and welfare, national security, public safety, and labor markets).

Homeland Security Act

Representative Dick Armey, Majority Leader and Chair of the Select Committee on Homeland Security, introduced the President's proposal as H.R. 5005, the Homeland Security Act of 2002. H.R. 5005 would have transferred all of the functions of INS to the newly created department under its Border Security and Transportation Division. As introduced, H.R. 5005 would have bifurcated visa issuances so that DHS would set the policies and DOS would retain responsibility for implementation.

During the week of July 8, 2002, the House Committees on Judiciary, International Relations, and Government all approved language on visa issuances that retained DOS's administrative role in issuing visas, but added specific language to address many of the policy and national security concerns raised during their respective hearings. Breaking with the Administration, the House Judiciary Committee approved language that would have placed much of INS's adjudication and service responsibilities—including its role in approving immigrant petitions—with a new Bureau of Citizenship and Immigration Services headed by an Assistant Attorney General at DOJ.

When the House Select Committee on Homeland Security marked up H.R. 5005 on July 19, 2002, it approved language on immigrant processing and visa issuances consistent with the House Judiciary Committee recommendations. As reported, H.R. 5005 clarified that the Secretary of DHS would have issued regulations regarding visa issuances and would have assigned staff to consular posts abroad to provide advice and review and to conduct investigations, and that Consular Affairs would have continued to issue visas. It would have further expanded the exclusion authority of the Secretary of State by permitting the Secretary to exclude an alien when necessary or advisable in the foreign policy or security interests of the U.S., giving the Secretary of State an authority even broader than that in law before the 1990 Immigration Amendments reformed the grounds for exclusion. It also would have clarified that decisions of the consular officers are not reviewable.

During the floor debate on H.R. 5005, only one immigration-related amendment was considered, and it would have moved the consular visa function to DHS. The amendment offered by Representative David Weldon failed, and the House went on to pass H.R. 5005 on July 26, 2002.

Table A-1 summarizes what department would be responsible for visa issuance activities under the various bills.[66]

The National Homeland Security and Combating Terrorism Act of 2002 reported by the Senate Governmental Affairs Committee (S. 2452) on June 24, 2002, included the immigration enforcement functions of INS and the Office of International Affairs but did not transfer any of the other immigration services and visa issuance functions. Representative Mac Thornberry sponsored H.R. 4660, a bill similar to S. 2452 as introduced, that would have created a homeland security department but also did not transfer any of the immigration adjudications and visa issuances functions.

Table A-1. Visa Issuance Policy Roles and Tasks: Comparison of Major Homeland Security Proposals

Task/Role	INA	S. 2452	S.Amdt. 4471	H.R. 5005 Introduced	H.R. 5005 Passed	P.L. 107-296
Issuing nonimmigrant visas abroad	State	State	Homeland regulates; State issues	Homeland sets policy; State administers	Homeland regulates; State issues	Homeland regulates; State issues
Changing nonimmigrant visas	Justice	Justice	Homeland	Homeland	Justice	Homeland
Approving immigrant (LPR) petitions	Justice	Justice	Homeland	Homeland	Justice	Homeland
Issuing immigrant visas	State	State	Homeland regulates; State issues	Homeland sets policy; State administers	Homeland regulates; State issues	Homeland regulates; State issues
Adjusting immigrant (LPR) status	Justice	Justice	Homeland	Homeland	Justice	Homeland

The Senate Government Reform Committee acted on a substitute for S. 2452 on July 24, 2002, and that language became S.Amdt. 4471. S.Amdt. 4471 differed somewhat on the issues of immigration adjudications and visa issuances from the Administration's proposal and H.R. 5005 as passed. The Senate amendment would have transferred all of INS to a newly created DHS under two new bureaus (the Bureau of Immigration Services and the Bureau of Enforcement and Border Affairs) in a Directorate of Immigration Affairs. Similarly to H.R. 5005 as passed, the Senate amendment would have given the Secretary of DHS authority to issue regulations on visa policy; however, it would have permitted the Secretary of the new department to delegate the authority to the Secretary of State. In contrast to the House-passed bill and S. 2452 as introduced, S.Amdt. 4471 would have established an Under Secretary for Immigration Affairs in DHS who would have handled immigration and naturalization functions as well as immigration enforcement and border functions.

On November 13, 2002, Majority Leader Armey introduced and the House passed H.R. 5710 as a compromise bill to establish a Department of Homeland Security. Among its many provisions, H.R. 5710 retained the language clarifying that—although DOS's Consular Affairs would continue to issue visas—the Secretary of DHS would issue regulations regarding visa issuances and would assign staff to consular posts abroad to advise, review, and conduct investigations. It also would permit the Secretary of the new department to delegate the authority to the Secretary of State. H.R. 5710 would transfer all of INS to two new bureaus in DHS: the Bureau of Citizenship and Immigration Services and the Bureau of Border Security. The former would report directly to the Deputy Secretary for Homeland Security, while the latter would report to the Under Secretary for Border and Transportation Security. Language similar to H.R. 5710 passed the Senate on November 19, 2002, as

S.Amdt. 4901 to H.R. 5005. The House agreed to the Senate amendment on November 22, and the President signed it as P.L. 107-296 on November 25, 2002.

APPENDIX B. LEGISLATION ON THE 9/11 COMMISSION RECOMMENDATIONS PERTAINING TO VISA SECURITY

The report of the National Commission on Terrorist Attacks Upon the United States (also known as the 9/11 Commission) offered its assessment of how visa and immigration inspection failures contributed to the terrorist attacks. The 9/11 Commission contended that "(t)here were opportunities for intelligence and law enforcement to exploit al Qaeda's travel vulnerabilities." The report went on to state: "Considered collectively, the 9/11 hijackers

- included known al Qaeda operatives who could have been watchlisted;
- presented fraudulent passports;
- presented passports with suspicious indicators of extremism;
- made detectable false statements on visa applications;
- made false statements to border officials to gain entry into the United States; and
- violated immigration laws while in the United States."[67]

The report maintained that border security was not considered to be a national security matter prior to 9/11, and as a result neither the State Department's consular officers nor the former Immigration and Naturalization Service's inspectors and officers were considered full partners in national counterterrorism efforts.[68]

The 9/11 Commission made several recommendations that underscore the urgency of implementing legislative provisions on visa policy and immigration control that Congress enacted several years ago. They also suggested areas in which Congress could take further action. The specific recommendations were as follows:

- Targeting travel is at least as powerful a weapon against terrorists as targeting their money. The United States should combine terrorist travel intelligence, operations, and law enforcement in a strategy to intercept terrorists, find terrorist travel facilitators, and constrain terrorist mobility.
- The U.S. border security system should be integrated into a larger network of screening points that includes our transportation system and access to vital facilities, such as nuclear reactors.
- The Department of Homeland Security, properly supported by the Congress, should complete, as quickly as possible, a biometric entry-exit screening system, including a single system for speeding qualified travelers.
- The U.S. government cannot meet its own obligations to the American people to prevent the entry of terrorists without a major effort to collaborate with other governments.[69]

Other 9/11 Commission recommendations, notably those related to intelligence policy and structures, have been the focus thus far of congressional consideration and media attention. The 9/11 Commission prepared a subsequent report that deals expressly with immigration issues.[70]

During the 108th Congress, legislation implementing the 9/11 Commission recommendations (S. 2845, H.R. 10, S. 2774/H.R. 5040 and H.R. 5024) had various provisions that would affect visa issuances. The Intelligence Reform and Terrorism Prevention Act of 2004 (P.L. 108-458), a compromise version of these bills that included some—but not all—of the immigration provisions under consideration, was signed on December 17, 2004.

Most notably, House-passed S. 2845 would have expanded the terror-related grounds for inadmissibility and deportability to include additional activities, such as receiving military-type training by or on behalf of a terrorist organization.[71] P.L. 108-458 would make deportable any alien who has received military training from or on behalf of an organization that, at the time of training, was a designated terrorist organization.

Among the other provisions in the 9/11 Commission implementation bills were: acquire and deploy technologies (e.g., biometrics) to detect potential terrorist indicators on travel documents; establish an Office of Visa and Passport Security; and train consular officers in the detection of terrorist travel patterns. H.R. 10 (as reported by the House Judiciary Committee on September 27 and passed by the House as S. 2845 on October 8, 2004) included provisions to establish an Office of Visa and Passport Security in the Bureau of Diplomatic Security of the Department of State to target and disrupt individuals and organizations at home and in foreign countries that are involved in the fraudulent production, distribution, or use of visas, passports and other documents used to gain entry to the United States. It also would have clarified that all nonimmigrant visa applications are reviewed and adjudicated by a consular officer, and would assign anti-fraud specialists to the top 100 posts that experience the greatest frequency of fraudulent documents. P.L. 108-458 establishes a Visa and Passport Security Program within the Bureau of Diplomatic Security at the Department of State.

As passed by the Senate on October 8, 2004, S. 2845—as well as House-passed H.R. 10—would increase the number of consular officers by 150 over the preceding year, annually FY2006 through FY2009. Both bills also had provisions aimed at improving the security of the visa issuance process by providing consular officers and immigration inspectors greater training in detecting terrorist indicators, terrorist travel patterns and fraudulent documents.[72] These provision were retained by the conferees in P.L. 108-458.

End Notes

[1] Authorities to except or to waive visa requirements are specified in law, such as the broad parole authority of the Attorney General under §212(d)(5) of Immigration and Nationality Act (INA) and the specific authority of the Visa Waiver Program in §217 of INA.

[2] Other departments, notably the Department of Labor (DOL), and the Department of Agriculture (USDA), play roles in the approval process depending on the category or type of visa sought, and the Department of Health and Human Services (DHHS) sets policy on the health-related grounds for inadmissibility discussed below.

[3] For an analysis of the transfer of immigration functions and activities to the Department of Homeland Security, see CRS Report RL31560, *Homeland Security Proposals: Issues Regarding Transfer of Immigration Agencies and Functions*; and CRS Report RL31584, *A Comparative Analysis of the Immigration Functions in the Major Homeland Security Bills*, both by Lisa M. Seghetti and Ruth Ellen Wasem. (Archived reports available upon request.)

[4] For background and further discussion of humanitarian cases, see CRS Report RL31269, *Refugee Admissions and Resettlement Policy*, by Andorra Bruno, and CRS Report RS20844, *Temporary Protected Status: Current Immigration Policy and Issues*, by Ruth Ellen Wasem and Karma Ester.

[5] For a more complete discussion of LPR categories and a statistical analysis of admissions trends, see CRS Report RL32235, *U.S. Immigration Policy on Permanent Admissions*, by Ruth Ellen Wasem.

[6] For a full discussion and analysis of nonimmigrant visas, see CRS Report RL31381, *U.S. Immigration Policy on Temporary Admissions*, by Ruth Ellen Wasem. (Hereafter cited as RL31381, *Temporary Admissions*.)

[7] CRS Report RL32221, *Visa Waiver Program*, by Alison Siskin.

[8] Immigration Act of May 26, 1924; 43 Stat. 153.

[9] During the 80th Congress, Senate Resolution 137 directed the Senate Committee on the Judiciary to make a full and complete investigation of the entire immigration system, which passed on July 26, 1947.

[10] U.S. Congress, Senate Committee on the Judiciary, *The Immigration and Naturalization Systems of the United States, report pursuant to S. Res.137.*, committee print, 81st Cong., 2nd sess., April 20, 1950.

[11] 8 U.S.C. 1104.

[12] 8 U.S.C. 1201.

[13] Some critics of transferring the visa function to DHS warned that visa issuance "adjudication" might become subject to judicial appeals or other due process considerations if a stateside agency, such as DHS, assumed responsibility. As a result, §428(f) of the HSA stated: "Nothing in this section shall be construed to create or authorize a private right of action to challenge a decision of a consular officer or other United States official or employee to grant or deny a visa."

[14] §428(c) of the Homeland Security Act of 2002 (P.L. 107-296)

[15] §428 (b)(1) of the Homeland Security Act (P.L. 107-296).

[16] For a complete account of this debate, see Appendix A.

[17] The text of the MOU can be found at http://www.travel.state

[18] U.S. Congress, Senate Committee on the Judiciary, Subcommittee On Immigration, Border Security and Citizenship, *Visa Issuance: Our First Line of Defense for Homeland Security*, hearing, Sept. 30, 2003.

[19] Ibid.

[20] U.S. Congress, Senate Committee on Foreign Relations, Subcommittee on International Operations and Terrorism, *The Post 9/11 Visa Reforms and New Technology: Achieving the Necessary Security Improvements in a Global Environment*, hearing, Oct. 23, 2003.

[21] USCIS adjudicators also conduct admissibility reviews for petitions filed within the United States, and CBP inspectors do so when aliens seek entry to the United States.

[22] §212(a) of the INA.

[23] Consular officers do not have direct access to the TECS database.

[24] Unclassified congressional staff briefing by Assistant Secretary of State Janice Jacobs, January 11, 2010.

[25] For information on other watchlists, see CRS Report RL33645, *Terrorist Watchlist Checks and Air Passenger Prescreening*, by William J. Krouse and Bart Elias. (Hereafter cited as RL33645, *Terrorist Watchlist Checks and Air Passenger Prescreening.*)

[26] U.S. Congress, Senate Committee on Homeland Security and Governmental Affairs, *Five Years After the Intelligence Reform and Terrorism Act: Stopping Terrorist Travel*, 111th Cong., 1st sess., December 9, 2009.

[27] U.S. Congress, Senate Committee on Foreign Relations, Subcommittee on International Operations and Terrorism, *The Post 9/11 Visa Reforms and New Technology: Achieving the Necessary Security Improvements in a Global Environment*, hearing, October 23, 2003.

[28] Unclassified congressional staff briefing by Assistant Secretary of State Janice Jacobs, January 11, 2010.

[29] U.S. Congress, Senate Committee on Foreign Relations, Subcommittee on International Operations and Terrorism, *The Post 9/11 Visa Reforms and New Technology: Achieving the Necessary Security Improvements in a Global Environment*, hearing, October 23, 2003.

[30] For further discussion of terrorist screening, see CRS Report RL32564, *Immigration: Terrorist Grounds for Exclusion and Removal of Aliens*, by Michael John Garcia and Ruth Ellen Wasem.

[31] §221(i) of the INA; 8 U.S.C. §1201(i).

[32] 22 C.F.R. §41.122 Notes N1.

[33] 22 C.F.R. §41.122 Notes PN3.

[34] Testimony of Janice L. Jacobs, Deputy Assistant Secretary of State for Visa Services, in U.S. Congress, Senate Committee on the Judiciary, Subcommittee on Immigration, Border Security and Citizenship, *Visa Issuance, Information Sharing and Enforcement in a Post-9/11 Environment: Are We Ready Yet?* hearing, July 15, 2003.

[35] 22 C.F.R. §41.122 Notes PN9.2-1.

[36] Office of Inspector General, *U.S. Immigration and Customs Enforcement Visa Security Program*, U.S. Department of Homeland Security, July 2008. (Hereafter OIG, *Visa Security Program,* July 2008.)
[37] OIG, *Visa Security Program,* July 2008.
[38] OIG, *Visa Security Program,* July 2008.
[39] House and Senate Committees on Appropriations, "Summary of the Fiscal 2007 Supplemental Funding Legislation," press release, April 23, 2007.
[40] Ian Kelly, *On-the-Record Briefing*, U.S. Department of State, Washington, DC, December 28, 2009.
[41] Ian Kelly, *On-the-Record Briefing*, U.S. Department of State, Washington, DC, December 28, 2009.
[42] For a more complete discussion of terrorist watch lists and the role of the National Counterterrorism Center, see CRS Report RL33645, *Terrorist Watchlist Checks and Air Passenger Prescreening.*
[43] Proponents of this view often cite: Office of Inspector Genderal, *Review of Nonimmigrant Visa Issuance Policy and Procedures*, U.S. Department of State, Memorandum Report ISP-I-03-26, December 2002, http://oig.state.gov/ documents/organization/16215.pdf.
[44] Senator Joseph Lieberman appearing on ABC's "This Week", January 3, 2010.
[45] U.S. Congress, Senate Committee on the Judiciary, *Securing America's Safety: Improving The Effectiveness of Anti-Terrorism Tools and Inter-Agency Communication*, Statements of DOS Under Secretary Patrick Kennedy and DHS Assistant Secretary David Heyman, 111th Cong., 2nd sess., January 20, 2010.
[46] U.S. Congress, Senate Committee on the Judiciary, *Securing America's Safety: Improving The Effectiveness of Anti-Terrorism Tools and Inter-Agency Communication*, Statement of Senator Patrick Leahy, 111th Cong., 2nd sess., January 20, 2010.
[47] U.S. Congress, Senate Committee on the Judiciary Subcommittee On Immigration, Border Security and Citizenship, *Visa Issuance: Our First Line of Defense for Homeland Security*, hearing, Sept. 30, 2003.
[48] Proponents of this view often cite the conclusions of this report: U.S. Government Accountability Office, *Strengthened Visa Process Would Benefit from Improvements in Staffing and Information Sharing*, GAO-05-859, September, 2005, http://www.gao.gov/new.items/d05859.pdf.
[49] The chief of mission is defined as the principal officer in charge of a diplomatic facility of the United States, including any individual assigned to be temporarily in charge of such a facility. This person, normally the ambassador, is the personal representative of the President to the country of accreditation. He or she is responsible for the direction, coordination, and supervision of all US Government executive branch employees in that country (except those under the command of a United States military commander).
[50] 22 U.S.C. 3927.
[51] For more on this process, see National Security Decision Directive–38.
[52] OIG, *Visa Security Program,* July 2008.
[53] Unclassified congressional staff briefing by Assistant Secretary of State Janice Jacobs, January 11, 2010; and, U.S. Congress, Senate Committee on the Judiciary, *Securing America's Safety: Improving the Effectiveness of Antiterrorism Tools and Interagency Communication*, 111th Cong., 2nd sess., January 20, 2010.
[54] DOS lists its fees at http://travel.state
[55] §103 of the Enhanced Border Security and Visa Reform Act (P.L. 107-173)
[57] For legislative tracking of the FY2011 State Department appropriations, see CRS Report R41228, *State, Foreign Operations, and Related Programs: FY2011 Budget and Appropriations*, by Marian Leonardo Lawson, Susan B. Epstein, and Tamara J. Resler.
[58] U.S. Congress, House Committee on Appropriations, Subcommittee on Homeland Security, *President's Fiscal Year (FY) 2009 budget request for U.S. Immigration and Customs Enforcement (ICE),* Testimony of Assistant Secretary Julie Myers, 110th Cong., 1st sess., February 2008.
[59] U.S. Department of Homeland Security, *Congressional Budget Justifications, FY2010*, February 2009. http://www.dhs.gov/xlibrary/assets
[60] In the FY2007 Supplemental Appropriations Act, Congress appropriated $5 million to the VSP to enhance its Security Advisory Opinion Unit. House and Senate Committees on Appropriations, "Summary of the Fiscal 2007 Supplemental Funding Legislation," press release, April 23, 2007.
[61] U.S. Department of Homeland Security Immigration and Customs Enforcement, *Fiscal Year 2011 Overview Congressional Justification*, February 2010.
[56] Secretary of State, *FY2011Congressional Budget Justifications* , Vol. 1 Department of State Operations, February 2010, http://www.state .
[57] For legislative tracking of the FY2011 State Department appropriations, see CRS Report R41228, *State, Foreign Operations, and Related Programs: FY2011 Budget and Appropriations*, by Marian Leonardo Lawson, Susan B. Epstein, and Tamara J. Resler.

[58] U.S. Congress, House Committee on Appropriations, Subcommittee on Homeland Security, *President's Fiscal Year (FY) 2009 budget request for U.S. Immigration and Customs Enforcement (ICE),* Testimony of Assistant Secretary Julie Myers, 110th Cong., 1st sess., February 2008.

[59] U.S. Department of Homeland Security, *Congressional Budget Justifications, FY2010*, February 2009. http://www.dhs.gov/xlibrary/assets

[60] In the FY2007 Supplemental Appropriations Act, Congress appropriated $5 million to the VSP to enhance its Security Advisory Opinion Unit. House and Senate Committees on Appropriations, "Summary of the Fiscal 2007 Supplemental Funding Legislation," press release, April 23, 2007.

[61] U.S. Department of Homeland Security Immigration and Customs Enforcement, *Fiscal Year 2011 Overview Congressional Justification*, February 2010.

[62] For legislative tracking of the FY2011 Department of Homeland Security appropriations, see CRS Report R41189, *Homeland Security Department: FY2011 Appropriations*, coordinated by Chad C. Haddal.

[63] Mickey McCarter, "Bilirakis Demands Funding for More Visa Security Units," *Homeland Security Today*, March 3, 2010.

[64] OIG, *Visa Security Program,* July 2008.

[65] Letter from Charles Grassley, Senator, Jeff Sessions, Senator, and Orin Hatch, Senator, et al. to Janet Napolitano, Secretary of Homeland Security, January 14, 2010.

[66] For discussion of the issues and options for transfering immigration functions and activities to DHS, see CRS Report RL31560, *Homeland Security Proposals: Issues Regarding Transfer of Immigration Agencies and Functions*; and CRS Report RL31584, *A Comparative Analysis of the Immigration Functions in the Major Homeland Security Bills*, both by Lisa M. Seghetti and Ruth Ellen Wasem. (Archived reports available upon request.)

[67] U.S. National Commission on Terrorist Attacks Upon the United States, *The 9/11 Commission Report*, Executive Summary, pp. 13-14, July 2004.

[68] *The 9/11 Commission Report*, Executive Summary, p. 14, July 2004.

[69] For a discussion of these recommendations, see *The 9/11 Commission Report*, Chapter 12.4, pp. 383-389, July 2004.

[70] U.S. National Commission on Terrorist Attacks Upon the United States, *Monograph on 9/11 and Terrorist Travel,* August 2004.

[71] CRS Report RL32564, *Immigration: Terrorist Grounds for Exclusion and Removal of Aliens*, by Michael John Garcia and Ruth Ellen Wasem.

[72] CRS Report RL32616, *9/11 Commission: Legislative Action Concerning U.S. Immigration Law and Policy in the 108th Congress*, by Michael John Garcia and Ruth Ellen Wasem.

In: U.S. Visa Policies, Programs and Considerations
Editor: Aaron R. Miller
ISBN: 978-1-61470-333-4

Chapter 3

DIVERSITY IMMIGRANT VISA LOTTERY ISSUES*

Ruth Ellen Wasem

SUMMARY

The purpose of the diversity immigrant visa lottery is, as the name suggests, to encourage legal immigration from countries other than the major sending countries of current immigrants to the United States. Current law weights the allocation of immigrant visas heavily toward aliens with close family in the United States and, to a lesser extent, toward aliens who meet particular employment needs. The diversity immigrant category was added to the Immigration and Nationality Act (INA) by the Immigration Act of 1990 (P.L. 101-649) to stimulate "new seed" immigration (i.e., to foster new, more varied migration from other parts of the world).

To be eligible for a diversity visa, the INA requires that the foreign national must have a high school education or the equivalent, or two years experience in an occupation that requires at least two years of training or experience. The foreign national or the foreign national's spouse must be a native of one of the countries listed as a foreign state qualified for the diversity visa lottery. Diversity lottery winners, like all other aliens wishing to come to the United States, must undergo reviews performed by Department of State consular officers abroad and Department of Homeland Security immigration officers upon entry to the United States. These reviews are intended to ensure that the aliens are not ineligible for visas or admission under the grounds for inadmissibility spelled out in the INA.

The diversity lottery currently makes 50,000 visas available annually to natives of countries from which immigrant admissions were lower than a total of 50,000 over the preceding five years. The formula for allocating visas is based upon the statutory specifications; visas are divided among six global geographic regions according to the relative populations of the regions, with their allocation weighted in favor of countries in regions that were under-represented among immigrant admissions to the United States during the past five years. The INA limits each country to 7%, or 3,850, of the total and provides that Northern Ireland be treated as a separate foreign state.

* This is an edited, reformatted and augmented version of a Congressional Research Service publication, CRS Report for Congress R41747, from www.crs.gov, dated April 1, 2011.

The regional distribution of the source countries for diversity immigrants has shifted over time in the four years selected for comparison (FY1994, FY1999, FY2004, and FY2009). Foreign nationals from Europe garnered the overwhelming share of the diversity visas in FY1994 and maintained a plurality share in FY1999. By FY2004, foreign nationals from Africa received a share comparable to those from Europe. In FY2009, foreign nationals from Africa gained the plurality share.

Some argue that the diversity lottery should be eliminated and its visas used for backlog reduction in other visa categories. Supporters of the diversity visa, however, argue that the diversity visa provides “new seed” immigrants for an immigration system weighted disproportionately to family-based immigrants from a handful of countries. Critics of the diversity lottery warn that it is vulnerable to fraud and misuse and is potentially an avenue for terrorists, citing the difficulties of performing background checks in many of the countries eligible for the diversity lottery. Supporters respond that background checks for criminal and national security matters are performed on all prospective immigrants seeking to come to the United States, including those winning diversity visas.

BACKGROUND

The purpose of the diversity immigrant visa lottery is, as the name suggests, to encourage legal immigration from countries other than the major sending countries of current immigrants to the United States. Current law weights the allocation of immigrant visas heavily toward aliens with close family in the United States and, to a lesser extent, toward aliens who meet particular employment needs. The diversity immigrant category was added to the Immigration and Nationality Act (INA) by the Immigration Act of 1990 (P.L. 101-649) to stimulate “new seed” immigration (i.e., to foster new, more varied, migration from other parts of the world).[1] The diversity visas are allocated to natives of countries from which immigrant admissions were lower than a grand total of 50,000 over the preceding five years. The term “immigrant” is synonymous with the phrase legal permanent resident (LPR), both of which are used interchangeably in this report.[2]

Legislative Origins

The Immigration Amendments of 1965 replaced the national origins quota system, which prioritized European source countries, with equally distributed per-country ceilings.[3] In the 1980s, some Members of Congress began expressing concern that the U.S. legal immigration admissions were skewed in favor of immigrants from Asia and Latin America after the 1965 amendments.[4] The first legislative response occurred in §314 of the Immigration Reform and Control Act of 1986 (IRCA), which allowed an extra 5,000 immigrant visas a year for FY1987 and FY1988 to natives of 36 countries that had been "adversely affected" by the 1965 changes to the INA. Over one million people applied for what was then called the NP-5 visa lottery. Natives of Ireland were the big winners in the random lottery. In 1988, Congress extended the NP-5 visa lottery for two more years, making 15,000 immigrant visas available each year in FY1989 and FY1990.[5]

What is now known as the diversity immigrant category was added to the INA by the Immigration Act of 1990 (P.L. 101-649) and went fully into effect in FY1995.[6] The 1990 Act established temporary or "transition" diversity visas for FY1992-1994. Most notably, §132 of P.L. 101-649 provided 40,000 visas a year for a transitional program during FY1992-1994 for certain natives of foreign states that were "adversely affected" by the 1965 changes to the INA. At least 40% of these visas were earmarked for natives of Ireland. The current diversity visa category has had an allocation of 55,000 visas annually since FY1995.

While the diversity visa category has not been directly amended since its enactment, P.L. 105- 100, the Nicaraguan Adjustment and Central American Relief Act of 1997 (NACARA) temporarily decreases the 55,000 annual ceiling. Beginning in FY1999, this ceiling has been reduced by up to 5,000 annually to offset immigrant numbers made available to certain unsuccessful asylum seekers from El Salvador, Guatemala, and formerly communist countries in Europe who are being granted immigrant status under special rules established by NACARA. The 5,000 offset is temporary, but it is not clear how many years it will be in effect to handle these adjustments of status.

Eligibility Criteria

To be eligible for a diversity visa, the INA requires that an alien must have a high school education or the equivalent, or two years experience in an occupation which requires at least two years of training or experience. The alien or the aliens spouse must be a native of one of the countries listed as a foreign state qualified for the diversity visa lottery. Minor children of the qualifying diversity immigrant, as well as the spouse, may accompany as legal permanent residents (LPRs).

The registration for the FY2012 Diversity Lottery began on October 5, 2010 and closed on November 3, 2010.[7] On May 1, 2011, those who registered will be able to find out if they have been selected or not.[8] While there is no cost to apply for the diversity lottery, the funding for the diversity visa lottery is covered by the fees that the lottery winners pay. The $305 immigrant visa fee and the $440 diversity visa fee go to the Department of State. There is also a $985 fee (plus $85 biometric fee, if applicable) paid to the U.S. Citizenship and Immigration Services (USCIS) in the Department of Homeland Security (DHS) to process the I-485 petition to adjust diversity visa holders to LPR status.[9]

Diversity lottery winners, like all other aliens wishing to come to the United States, must undergo reviews performed by Department of State consular officers abroad and DHS inspectors upon entry to the United States. These reviews are intended to ensure that they are not ineligible for visas or admission under the grounds for inadmissibility spelled out in the INA.[10] These criteria for exclusion include the following categories: health-related grounds; criminal history; security and terrorist concerns; public charge (e.g., indigence); illegal entrants; and aliens previously removed. [11] Those who are ultimately approved for diversity visas become LPRs of the United States.

TRENDS IN SOURCE COUNTRIES

The diversity lottery makes 50,000 visas available annually to natives of countries from which immigrant admissions were lower than a total of 50,000 over the preceding five years.

USCIS generates the formula for allocating visas according to the statutory specifications; visas are divided among six global geographic regions according to the relative populations of the regions, with their allocation weighted in favor of countries in regions that were under-represented among immigrant admissions to the United States during the past five years. The INA limits each country to 7%, or 3,850, of the total and provides that Northern Ireland be treated as a separate foreign state.

As Figure 1 depicts, the regional distribution of the source countries for diversity immigrants has shifted over time in the four years selected for comparison (FY1994, FY1999, FY2004 and FY2009). Foreign nationals from Europe garnered the overwhelming share of the diversity visas in FY1994 and maintained a plurality share in FY1999. By FY2004, foreign nationals from Africa received a share comparable to those from Europe. In FY2009, the latest year for which we have data, foreign nationals from Africa gained the plurality share. These trends are consistent with the statutory formula Congress outlined to allocate diversity visas.

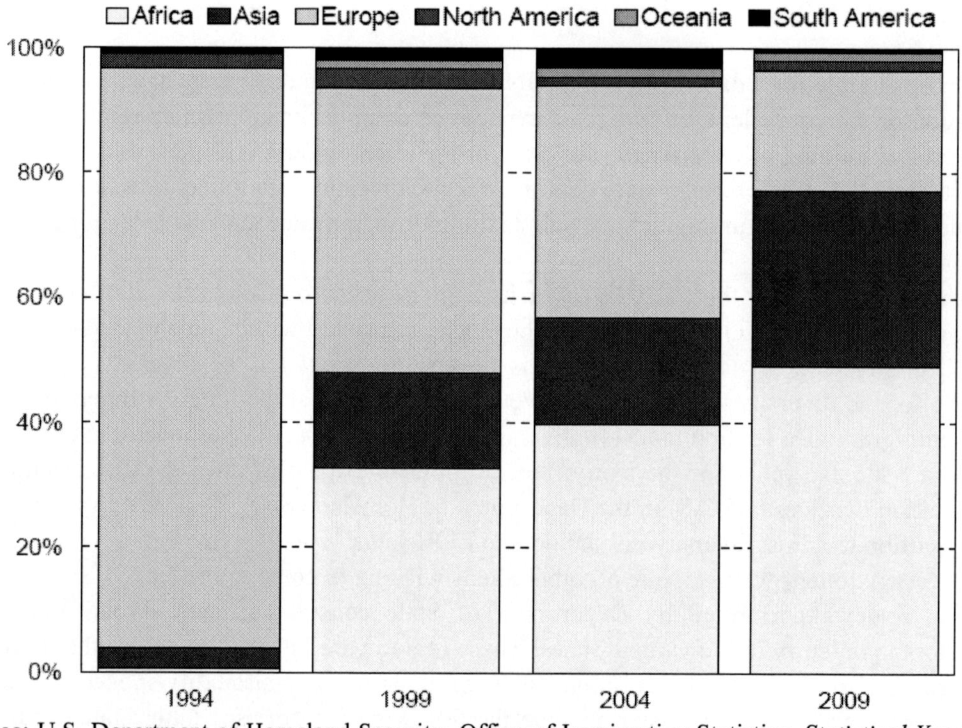

Source: U.S. Department of Homeland Security, Office of Immigration Statistics, *Statistical Yearbook of Immigration*, multiple fiscal years.

Notes: FY1994 was the final year of the transitional lottery, which set aside 40% of these visas for natives of Ireland. North America includes the Caribbean and Central America.

Figure 1. World Region of Source Countries for Diversity Immigrants, FY1994, FY1999, FY2004, and FY2009.

Germany is the only country that ranked among top diversity immigrant source countries in FY1994 that also appears in the top 20 countries for FY2009. There are 11 source countries in the top 20 for FY1999, FY2004 and FY2009: Bulgaria, Nigeria, Albania, Ukraine, Ethiopia, Morocco, Ghana, Bangladesh, Egypt, Turkey and Kenya. Table 1 presents the top source countries in rank-order and the number of diversity visas issued for FY1994, FY1999, FY2004 and FY2009. Bangladesh, Ethiopia and Nigeria were also among the top 20 source countries for total LPRs in FY2009, sending a total of 16,651, 15,462 and 15,253 LPRs respectively.[12]

Table 1. Top 20 Diversity Immigrant Source Countries FY1994, FY1999, FY2004, and FY2009

1994		1999		2004		2009	
Poland	17,396	Bulgaria	3,390	Ethiopia	4,405	Ethiopia	3,829
Ireland	15,659	Nigeria	3,118	Ukraine	2,972	Nigeria	3,720
United Kingdon	3,174	Albania	3,117	Nigeria	2,856	Egypt	3,336
Canada	1,511	Ukraine	3,093	Poland	2,802	Bangladesh	2,928
Japan	797	Romania	2,866	Kenya	2,763	Uzbekistan	2,492
Indonesia	411	Ethiopia	2,191	Bulgaria	2,298	Kenya	2,324
Argentina	286	Morocco	1,940	Morocco	2,223	Morocco	2,100
Germany	220	Russia	1,930	Albania	1,972	Albania	1,948
Australia	148	Ghana	1,734	Nepal	1,859	Ghana	1,819
France	141	Bangladesh	1,697	Togo	1,694	Nepal	1,778
		Pakistan	1,693	Bangladesh	1,692	Ukraine	1,579
		Egypt	1,536	Egypt	1,621	Cameroon	1,386
		Germany	1,250	Lithuania	1,404	Iran	1,057
		Turkey	1,008	Turkey	1,100	Turkey	1,036
		Sudan	987	Ghana	1,095	Armenia	911
		Cuba	975	Romania	1,075	Germany	908
		Lithuania	796	Russia	882	Algeria	837
		Kenya	601	Peru	779	Bulgaria	765
		Algeria	518	Israel	734	Liberia	751
		Armenia	508	Uzbekistan	693	Belarus	664

Source: U.S. Department of Homeland Security, Office of Immigration Statistics, *Statistical Yearbook of Immigration*, multiple fiscal years.

Notes: In FY1994, only the 10 countries listed were the sending country of 100 or more diversity immigrants. FY1994 was the final year of the transitional lottery, which set aside 40% of these visas for natives of Ireland.

DEMOGRAPHIC FEATURES[13]

As one would expect, diversity immigrants come from parts of the world that differ from the leading immigrant sending regions. Figure 2 depicts that almost half (49%) of the 47,879 diversity immigrants came from Africa, which contributed only 11% of the total number of 1.1 million LPRs in FY2009. Europe sent 10% of all LPRs in FY2009, but made up 28% of all diversity immigrants. In contrast, North America is the sending region for 33% of all LPRs (e.g., Mexico, the Caribbean and Central America), but comprised only 1% of the diversity immigrants (e.g., Canada) in FY2009.

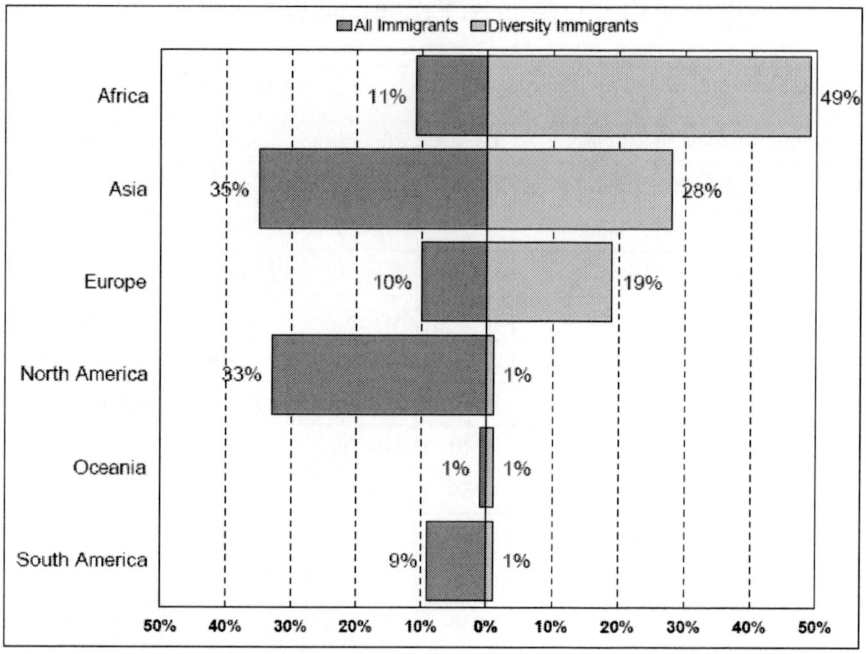

Source: CRS presentation of FY2009 data from the DHS Office of Immigration Statistics.

Notes: In FY2009, there were 1.1 million LPRs, of which 47,879 were diversity immigrants. North America includes the Caribbean and Central America.

Figure 2. World Region of Source Countries for LPRs in FY2009, Diversity immigrants compared with all immigrants.

The distribution for Asia in FY2009 is interesting because it epitomizes the complexities of the two-step formula (e.g., regional population and each country's past immigration total), which is used to allocate diversity visas. Asia included many top sending countries for LPRs, such as the People's Republic of China, India and the Philippines. Yet it also included nations that qualified for diversity visas, such as Bangladesh, Nepal and Turkey. As Figure 2 illustrates, Asia represented a somewhat more comparable portion of the 1.1 million LPRs (35%) in relation to its portion of the 47,879 diversity immigrants (28%) in contrast to the other world regions.

Although the diversity immigrants are required to have only a high school education (or the equivalent) or two years experience in an occupation which requires at least two years of training or experience, they were more likely to report managerial and professional occupations than LPRs generally. Specifically, almost of quarter (24%) of diversity immigrants reported managerial and professional occupations in contrast to 10% of the 1.1 million LPRs in FY2009 (Figure 3).

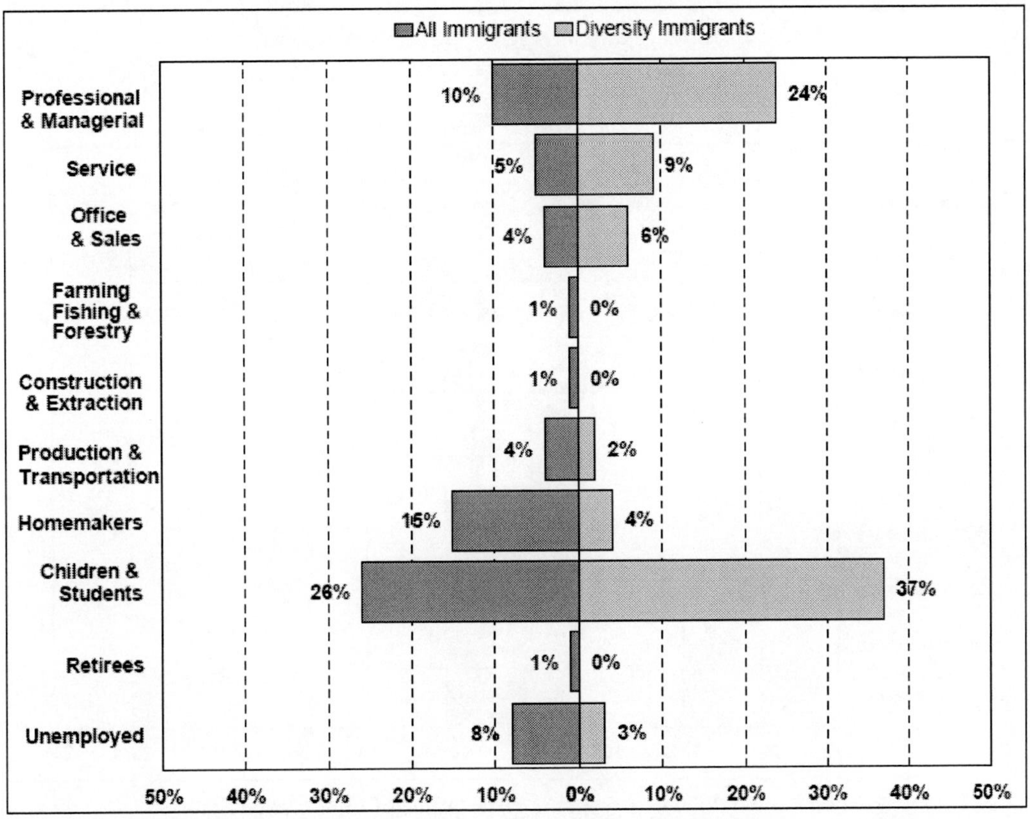

Source: CRS presentation of FY2009 data from the DHS Office of Immigration Statistics.
Notes: In FY2009, there were 1.1 million LPRs, of which 47,879 were diversity immigrants.

Figure 3. Occupations Reported by LPRs in FY2009, Diversity immigrants compared with all immigrants.

Data presented in both P.L. 105-100 and Figure 4 indicate that diversity immigrants included more children and youth than did LPRs generally in FY2009.[14] Indeed, Figure 4 shows that diversity immigrants were more likely to obtain LPR status as they begin their working years than were LPRs overall. The immigrant population of the United States is typically more likely to be in the prime working age group than the native-born population, and the youthful skew of the diversity immigrants' age distribution in FY2009 is even more striking.[15]

Diversity immigrants were somewhat less likely to be married than LPRs generally in FY2009, perhaps a function of their relative youth. Over half (54%) of diversity immigrants were single, in contrast to 37% of LPRs overall. Few of either group were likely to be widowed, divorced or separated. In addition, 57% of diversity immigrants were males while only 45% of all LPRs were males in FY2009.

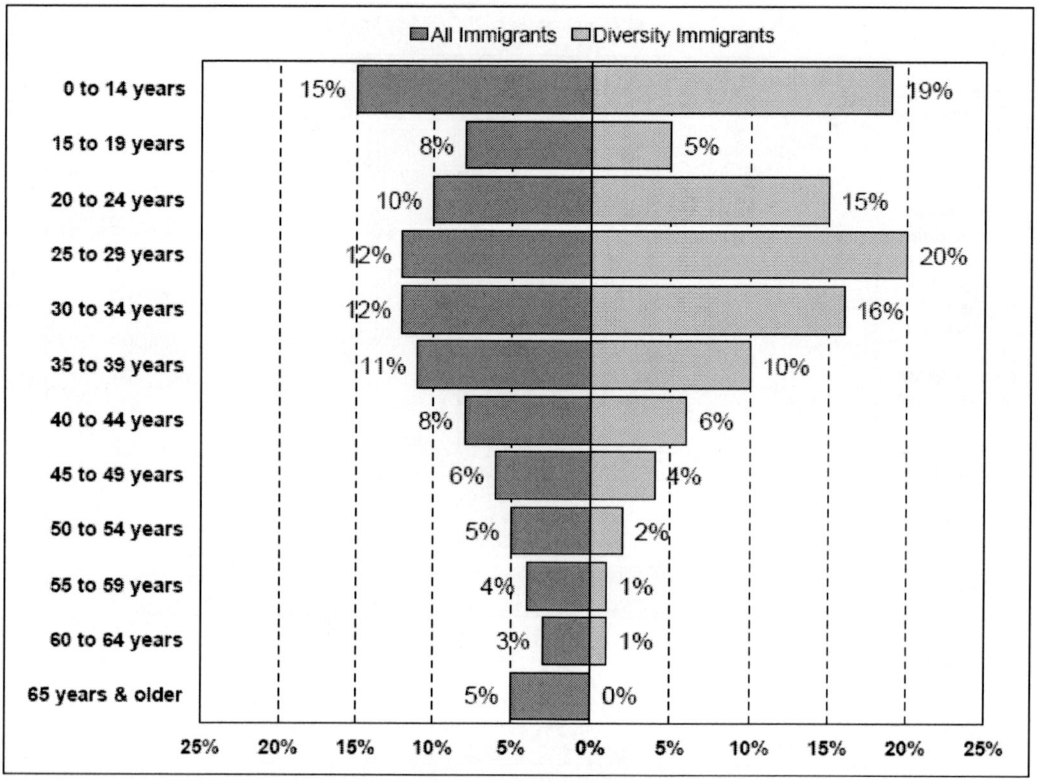

Source: CRS presentation of FY2009 data from the DHS Office of Immigration Statistics.
Notes: In FY2009, there were 1.1 million LPRs, of which 47,879 were diversity immigrants.

Figure 4. Age Distribution of LPRs in FY2009, Diversity immigrants compared with all immigrants.

LEGISLATIVE ISSUES

Legislation to eliminate the diversity visa category, the Security and Fairness Enhancement for America Act of 2011 or SAFE for America Act (H.R. 704), has been introduced in the 112th Congress. In the Senate, §4(c) of the Strengthening Our Commitment to Legal Immigration and America's Security Act (S. 332) would also eliminate the diversity visa category. During the 109th Congress, provisions eliminating the diversity visa lottery comparable to H.R. 704 and those in S. 332 were incorporated into H.R. 4437, which the House passed on December 16, 2005.[16] At that time, there were two themes that characterized the debate over the diversity visa lottery: fairness and security. These issues of fairness and security are likely to arise again when or if the 112th Congress considers H.R. 704. The policy questions discussed below are framed in terms of issues that might arise if debate occurs.

Policy Questions

As Congress weighs whether to eliminate or revise the diversity visa category, various aspects of the diversity visa might be considered. This report concludes with four policy questions that would be pertinent to this discussion. These selected questions are illustrative of an issue that is nested in the broader immigration debate—a debate often characterized as a "zero-sum game."

Is it fair to have the diversity visa category when there are family members and prospective employees who are waiting in queues for visas to become available?

Some might cite the latest National Visa Center data, which indicated there were 4.7 million approved family-based and employment-based petitions waiting for a visa to become available at the close of FY2010.[17] They might advocate that the 50,000 diversity visas would be better used for backlog reduction of the other visa categories. Others might observe that the family-based, employment-based, and diversity visa categories are statutorily designed as independent pathways to LPR status and that the problems of the family-based and employment-based backlogs could only be addressed through comprehensive immigration reform.[18]

Is the diversity visa lottery more vulnerable to fraud and misuse than other immigration pathways?

Some might reference the 2009 arrests of Lassissi Afolabi and Akouavi Kpade Afolabi, who coerced foreign nationals into human trafficking and forced labor rings by paying for the diversity visas if they listed the trafficked young women as their own family on the visa application.[19] They also might cite the U.S. Government Accountability Office (GAO) which found pervasive fraud reported by some consular posts.[20] Others might refer to the numerous fraud investigations and arrests of immigrants who used other visa categories.[21] Others might also point out that DOS and DHS have revised the diversity lottery procedures to address these fraud vulnerabilities. [22] For example, DOS maintains that the electronic registration process increases its ability to screen duplicate and fraudulent entries as well as enables the use of facial recognition software to detect fraud.[23]

Are there national security reasons to eliminate the diversity visa?

Some might cite the case of Hesham Mohamed Ali Hedayet, the Egyptian immigrant who shot and killed two people at Los Angeles International Airport on July 4, 2002, and who had obtained LPR status as the spouse of diversity immigrant.[24] Some might assert that the difficulties of performing background checks in many of the countries currently qualifying for the diversity lottery, as well as broader concerns about terrorism, justify the elimination of the category. Some might cite the 2004 warning of the DOS Deputy Inspector General that the diversity visa lottery "contains significant vulnerabilities to national security" from state sponsors of terrorism.[25] Others might point out that immigrants coming to the United States in the other LPR visa categories are not restricted if they come from these same countries and further argue that background checks for national security risks are performed on all prospective immigrants seeking to come to the United States. Others might reference the broader reform to visa security that Congress has enacted since the early 2000s,[26] or cite the 2007 GAO report stating: "We found no documented evidence that DV immigrants from these, or other, countries posed a terrorist or other threat." [27]

Are the reasons that led to establishment of the diversity visa category (e.g., to stimulate "new seed" immigration) still germane today?

Some might point to the immigration dominance of nationals from a handful of countries and argue that the diversity visa fosters new and more varied migration to counterbalance an immigration system weighted disproportionately to family-based immigrants.

- If diversity of immigration is still a goal of U.S. immigration policy, is a visa lottery the best method to achieve that goal?
- If not a lottery, are there other mechanisms, such as a point system, that could be used to allocate the visas?[28]

Others might argue that, after 20 years, the diversity visa category has run its course. They might cite the overlap between countries that qualified for the diversity lottery and the top immigrant source countries as an indication that the need for "new seed" immigration has been met.

End Notes

[1] §203(c) of INA.

[2] Both terms refer to foreign nationals who are legally admitted to the United States, as defined in the INA, and who come to live permanently in the United States.

[3] P.L. 89-23679 Stat. 911 (1965).

[4] Legal permanent residents from Ireland, for example, fell from 6,307 in FY1964 to 1,836 in FY1986. CRS Report 91-141, *A Brief History of U.S. Immigration Policy*, Joyce C. Vialet, January 25, 1991 (archived report, available upon request).

[5] "State Dept. Advises on New NP-5 Program," *Interpreter Releases*, vol. 65, no. 45 (November 22, 1988).

[6] §203(c) of INA.

[7] U.S. Department of State Bureau of Consular Affairs , "Registration for the Diversity Immigrant (DV-2012) Visa Program," 75 *Federal Register* 60846-60854, October 1, 2010.

[8] The DOS instructs registrants to log onto "Entry Status Check" at dvlottery.state to see if they have been selected. Between May 1 and October 1, 2011, the selected applicants fill out their application forms for the visa, submit information to the Kentucky Consular Center. The Kentucky Consular Center will then schedule the interviews. For more information, see http://www.america.gov/st/texttransenglish/2010/September/20100928165617su0.400932.html#ixzz1I8pvFyxQ.

[9] For further discussion of the fees, see CRS Report RL34040, *U.S. Citizenship and Immigration Services' Immigration Fees and Adjudication Costs: Proposed Adjustments and Historical Context*, by William A. Kandel. For the State Department fees, go to: http://travel.state. For the USCIS fees go to: http://www.uscis.gov/portal/site/uscis/menuitem.eb1d4c2a3e5b9ac89243c6a7543f6d1a/?vgnextoid=db029c7755cb9010VgnVCM10000045f3d6a1RCRD&vgnextchannel=db029c7755cb9010VgnVCM10000045f3d6a1RCRD

[10] §212(a) of INA.

[11] For a full discussion of the grounds for exclusion, see CRS Report R41104, *Immigration Visa Issuances and Grounds for Exclusion: Policy and Trends*, by Ruth Ellen Wasem.

[12] These numbers are modest in contrast to the total number of LPRs admitted to the United States each year. For example, Mexico led all countries with 164,920 foreign nationals who became LPRs in FY2009. The People's Republic of China followed at a distant second with 64,238 LPRs. The Philippines came in third with 60,029 LPRs. India followed with 57,304 LPRs. To compare diversity admissions with the top countries for LPR admissions in FY2009, see Figure 6 and Appendix A in CRS Report RL32235, *U.S. Immigration Policy on Permanent Admissions*, by Ruth Ellen Wasem.

[13] All of the data analyses presented in this section are based on: Office of Immigration Statistics, *Yearbook of Immigration Statistics: 2009*, U.S. Department of Homeland Security, 2010.

[14] Bear in mind that most of the children are accompanying family of the principle LPR who qualifies for the visa.

[15] For further analysis of the foreign-born populations, see CRS Report R41592, *The U.S. Foreign-Born Population: Trends and Selected Characteristics*, by William A. Kandel.

[16] No further action on this legislation occurred in the 109th Congress. CRS Report RL33125, *Immigration Legislation and Issues in the 109th Congress*, coordinated by Andorra Bruno.

[17] U.S. Department of State, *Annual Report of Immigrant Visa Applicants in the Family-sponsored and Employment-based preferences Registered at the National Visa Center as of November 1, 2010*, http://www.travel.stateWaitingListItem.pdf. The USCIS has not reported how many petitions it has approved for aliens adjusting to LPR status within the United States.

[18] For more on the legal immigration issues, see CRS Report RL32235, *U.S. Immigration Policy on Permanent Admissions*, by Ruth Ellen Wasem.

[19] U.S. Attorney District of New Jersey, "Togolese Woman Sentenced To 27 Years In Prison For Forced Labor," press release, September 20, 2010, http://www.justice.gov/usao/nj/Press/files/pdffiles/2010/Afolabi,%20Akouavi%20Kpade%20Sentencing%20PR.pdf.

[20] U.S. Government Accountability Office, *Border Security: Fraud Risks Complicate State's Ability to Manage Diversity Visa Program*, GAO-07-1174, September 21, 2007, http://www.gao.gov/products/GAO-07-1174.

[21] For recent examples, see U.S. Government Accountability Office, *H-2B Visa Program: Closed Civil Criminal Cases Illustrate Instances of H-2B Workers Being Targets of Fraud and Abuse*, GAO-10-1053, September 30, 2010; U.S. Government Accountability Office, *H-1B Visa Program: Reforms Are Needed to Minimize the Risks and Costs of Current Program*, GAO-11-26, January 14, 2011; U.S. Government Accountability Office, *Export Controls: Improvements Needed to Prevent Unauthorized Technology Releases to Foreign Nationals in the United States*, GAO-11-354, February 2, 2011; and Office of Inspecter General, *The Special Immigrant Nonminister Religious Worker Program*, U.S. Department of Homeland Security, OG-09-79, June 2009.

[22] U.S. Department of State, "Diversity Visa Program Scammers Sending Fraudulent Emails and Letters," press release, 2011, http://travel.state

[23] "DOS Announces 2011 Diversity Lottery Program Registration and Instructions," *Interpreter Releases*, vol. 86, no. 38 (October 5, 2009); and "2008 Diversity Visa Registrations," *Interpreter Releases*, vol. 84, no. 1 (January 2, 2007).

[24] U.S. Congress, House Committee on the Judiciary, Subcommittee on Immigration and Claims, *Immigration And Naturalization Service's (INS's) Interactions With Hesham Mohamed Ali Hedayet*, hearing, 107th Cong., 2nd sess., October 2, 2002, Serial No. 110.

[25] U.S. Congress, House Committee on the Judiciary, Subcommittee on Immigration, Border Security, and Claims, *The Diversity Visa Program, and Its Susceptibility to Fraud and Abuse*, 108th Cong., 2nd sess., April 29, 2004.

[26] For more on the reforms of visa security, see CRS Report R41093, *Visa Security Policy: Roles of the Departments of State and Homeland Security*, by Ruth Ellen Wasem.

[27] U.S. Government Accountability Office, *Border Security: Fraud Risks Complicate State's Ability to Manage Diversity Visa Program*, GAO-07-1174, September 21, 2007, http://www.gao.gov/products/GAO-07-1174.

[28] CRS Report RL34030, *Point Systems for Immigrant Selection: Options and Issues*, by Ruth Ellen Wasem.

In: U.S. Visa Policies, Programs and Considerations
Editor: Aaron R. Miller ISBN: 978-1-61470-333-4

Chapter 4

VISA WAIVER PROGRAM*

Alison Siskin

SUMMARY

Since the events of September 11, 2001, concerns have been raised about the ability of terrorists to enter the United States under the visa waiver program (VWP), because the VWP bypasses the first step by which foreign visitors are screened for admissibility to enter the United States. Nonetheless, the inclusion of countries in the VWP may help foster positive relations between the United States and those countries, promote tourism and commerce, facilitate information sharing, and ease consular office workloads abroad. The VWP allows nationals from certain countries to enter the United States as temporary visitors (nonimmigrants) for business or pleasure without first obtaining a visa from a U.S. consulate abroad. Temporary visitors for business or pleasure from non-VWP countries must obtain a visa from Department of State (DOS) officers at a consular post abroad before coming to the United States. As of January 2011, 36 countries participate in the VWP.

In FY2009, 16.2 million visitors entered the United States under this program, constituting 50.5% of all overseas visitors. To qualify for the VWP, statute specifies that a country must offer reciprocal privileges to U.S. citizens; have had a nonimmigrant refusal rate of less than 3% for the previous year or an average of no more than 2% over the past two fiscal years with neither year going above 2.5%; issue their nationals machine-readable passports that incorporate *biometric identifiers;* certify that it is developing a program to issue tamper-resident, machine-readable visa documents that incorporate biometric identifiers which are verifiable at the country's port of entry; and not compromise the law enforcement or security interests of the United States by its inclusion in the program. Countries can be terminated from the VWP if an emergency occurs that threatens the United States' security interests.

P.L. 110-53 added new requirements to participate in the VWP, and provided the Secretary of the Department of Homeland Security (DHS) the authority to waive the nonimmigrant refusal rate requirement. The waiver became available in October 2008; however, it was suspended on July 1, 2009.

---

* This is an edited, reformatted and augmented version of a Congressional Research Service publication, CRS Report for Congress RL32221, from www.crs.gov, dated January 4, 2011.

All aliens entering under the VWP must present machine-readable passports. In addition, passports issued between October 26, 2005, and October 25, 2006, must have a digitized photo on the data page, while passports issued after October 25, 2006, must contained electronic data chips (e-passports). Under DHS regulations, travelers who seek to enter the United States through the VWP are subject to the biometric requirements of the US-VISIT program. In addition, aliens entering under the VWP must get an approval from the Electronic System for Travel Authorization (ESTA), a web-based system that checks the alien's information against relevant law enforcement and security databases, before they can board a plane to the United States. ESTA became operational for all VWP countries on January 12, 2009.

In 2008, eight new countries were added to the VWP who needed the nonimmigrant refusal rate waiver to be part of the program. There are other countries (e.g., Poland, Romania, Taiwan) that have expressed interest in being a part of the VWP. The nonimmigrant refusal rate waiver authority was suspended on June 30, 2009, because DHS did not implement an air-exit system that incorporates biometric identifiers. It is unknown when a biometric exit system will be implemented.

CURRENT POLICY

Under the visa waiver program (VWP), the Secretary of Homeland Security,[1] in consultation with the Secretary of State, may waive the "B" nonimmigrant visa requirement for aliens traveling from certain countries as temporary visitors for business or pleasure (tourists).[2] Nationals from participating countries must use the web-based Electronic System for Travel Authorization (ESTA) to get an approved electronic travel authorization before embarking to the United States, and are admitted into the United States for up to 90 days.[3] The VWP constitutes one of a few exceptions under the Immigration and Nationality Act (INA) in which foreign nationals are admitted into the United States without a valid visa. As of October 2010, 36 countries participate in the VWP.[4]

Temporary foreign visitors for business or pleasure from most countries must obtain a visa from Department of State (DOS) offices at a consular post abroad before coming to the United States.[5] Personal interviews are generally required, and consular officers use the Consular Consolidated Database (CCD) to screen visa applicants. In addition to indicating the outcome of any prior visa application of the alien in the CCD, the system links with other databases to flag problems that may make the alien ineligible for a visa under the so-called "grounds for inadmissibility" of the INA, which include criminal, terrorist, and public health grounds for exclusion. Consular officers are required to check the background of all aliens in the "lookout" databases, including the Consular Lookout and Support System (CLASS) and TIPOFF databases.[6]

Although the VWP greatly eases the documentary requirements for nationals from participating countries, it has important restrictions. Aliens entering with a B visa may petition to extend their length of stay in the United States or may petition to change to another nonimmigrant or immigrant status. Aliens entering through the VWP are not permitted to extend their stays except for emergency reasons and then for only 30 days.[7] Additionally, with some limited exceptions, aliens entering through VWP are not permitted to adjust status. An alien entering through the VWP who violates the terms of admission becomes deportable without any judicial recourse or review (except in asylum cases).

VWP Qualifying Criteria

Currently, to qualify for the VWP a country must

- offer reciprocal privileges to United States citizens;
- have had a nonimmigrant refusal rate of less than 3% for the previous year or an average of no more than 2% over the past two fiscal years with neither year going above 2.5%;
- issue machine-readable passports (all aliens entering under the VWP must possess a machine-readable passport);
- certify that it has established a program to issue to its nationals machine-readable passports that are tamper-resistant and incorporate a biometric identifier (all passports issued after October 26, 2006, presented by aliens entering under the VWP have to be machine-readable and contain a biometric identifier);
- certify that it is developing a program to issue tamper-resident, machine-readable visa documents that incorporate biometric identifiers which are verifiable at the country's port of entry;
- enter into an agreement with the United States to report or make available through International Criminal Police Organization (INTERPOL)[8] information about the theft or loss of passports;[9]
- accept the repatriation of any citizen, former citizen, or national against whom a final order of removal is issued no later than three weeks after the order is issued;
- enter into an agreement with the United States to share information regarding whether a national of that country traveling to the United States represents a threat to U.S. security or welfare; and
- be determined, by the Secretary of Homeland Security, in consultation with the Secretary of State, not to compromise the law enforcement or security interests of the United States by its inclusion in the program.

Countries can be immediately terminated from the VWP if an emergency occurs in the country that the Secretary of Homeland Security in consultation with the Secretary of State determines threatens the law enforcement or security interest of the United States.[10] For example, because of Argentina's economic collapse in December 2001,[11] and the increase in the number of Argentine nationals attempting to use the VWP to enter the United States and remain illegally past the 90-day period of admission,[12] that country was removed from the VWP in February 2002.[13] Similarly, on April 15, 2003, Uruguay was terminated from the VWP because Uruguay's participation in the VWP was determined to be inconsistent with the U.S. interest in enforcing immigration laws.[14]

Additionally, there is probationary status for VWP countries that do not maintain a low visa refusal rate. Countries on probation are determined by a formula based on a disqualification rate of 2%-3.5%.[15] Probationary countries with a disqualification rate less than 2% over a period not to exceed three years may remain VWP countries.[16] Countries may also be placed on probation if more time is necessary to determine whether the continued participation of the country in the VWP is in the security interest of the United States. For example, in April 2003, Belgium was placed on provisional status because of concerns about the integrity of non-machine-readable Belgian passports and the reporting of lost or stolen passports.[17] DHS completed another country review of Belgium in 2005, and removed the country from probationary status.

Nonimmigrant Refusal Rate Waiver

Section 711 of the Implementing the 9/11 Commission Recommendations Act of 2007 (P.L. 110- 53)[18] allows the Secretary of DHS, in consultation with the Secretary of DOS, to waive the nonimmigrant refusal rate requirement for admission to the VWP after the Secretary of DHS certifies to Congress that

- an air exit system is in place that can verify the departure of not less than 97% of foreign nationals that exit through U.S. airports,[19] and
- the electronic travel authorization system (ESTA discussed below) is operational.[20]

The waiver became available in October 2008, and was suspended on July 1, 2009. Under statute, the Secretary of DHS's authority to waive the nonimmigrant refusal rate has been suspended until the air exit system is able to match an alien's biometric information with relevant watch lists and manifest information. It is unclear when DHS will implement an exit system with the specified biometric capacity.[21]

To participate in the program a country who receives a refusal rate waiver also has to

- meet all the security requirements of the program;
- be determined by the Secretary of DHS to have a totality of security risk mitigation measures that provide assurances that the country's participation in the program would not compromise U.S. law enforcement and security interests, or the enforcement of U.S. immigration laws;
- have had a sustained reduction in visa refusal rates, and have existing conditions for the rates to continue to decline;
- have cooperated with the United States on counterterrorism initiatives and information sharing before the date of its designation, and be expected to continue such cooperation; and
- during the previous fiscal year, the nonimmigrant visas refusal rate was not more than 10%, or the overstay rate did not exceed the maximum overstay rate established by the Secretaries of DHS and DOS for countries receiving waivers of the nonimmigrant refusal rate to participate in the VWP the program.

P.L. 110-53 also specified that in determining whether to waive the nonimmigrant refusal rate requirement, the Secretary of DHS, in consultation with the Secretary of DOS, may take into consideration other factors affecting U.S. security, such as the country's airport security and passport standards, whether the country has an effective air marshal program, and the estimated overstay rate for nationals from the country.

Electronic Travel Authorization System (ESTA)

As previously mentioned, P.L. 110-53 mandated that the Secretary of DHS, in consultation with the Secretary of DOS, develop and implement an electronic travel authorization system (ESTA), through which each alien electronically provides, in advance of travel, the biographical information necessary to determine whether the alien is eligible to travel to the United States and enter under the VWP.[22] ESTA became fully operational for all VWP visitors traveling to the United States by airplane or cruise ship on January 12, 2009.[23] There is a $14 fee for travelers who use ESTA.[24]

In advance of departing for the United States by airplane or cruise ship,[25] aliens traveling under the VWP are required to use ESTA to electronically provide biographical information to make the eligibility determinations.[26] Through the Treasury Enforcement Communications System (TECS), ESTA applications are queried against law enforcement databases, including the greater set of watch lists integrated and consolidated in the Terrorist Screening Database, and against databases on lost and stolen passports (including Interpol's Stolen and Lost Travel Documents database), and visa revocations.[27]

ESTA alerts the alien that he or she has been approved to travel, and if not approved that the alien needs to obtain a visa prior to coming to the United States.[28] The information required by ESTA is the same that is currently required on the I-94W form, which aliens arriving in the United States under the VWP are required to complete to be admitted.[29] ESTA also screens applicant responses to the same VWP eligibility questions that are currently collected on the Form I-94W.[30] Eventually, ESTA will replace the I-94W form.[31]

Eligibility to travel, which is determined by ESTA, is valid for two years or until the person's passport expires, is valid for multiple entries, and can be revoked at any time. Notably, a determination under ESTA that an alien is eligible to travel to the United States does not constitute a determination that the alien is admissible. Admissibility determinations are made by Customs and Border Protection (CBP) inspectors at the ports of entry.

Arrival and Departure Inspections

Unlike other nonimmigrants, those entering under the VWP do not have to get a visa and thus, have no contact with U.S. governmental officials until they arrive at a port of entry and are inspected by CBP officers. Nonetheless, in addition to getting authorization through ESTA, prior to the alien's arrival, an electronic passenger manifest is sent from the airline or commercial vessel to immigration inspectors at the port of entry which is checked against security databases.

Since October 1, 2002, passenger arrival and departure information on individuals entering and leaving the U.S. under the VWP has been electronically collected from airlines and cruise lines, through CBP's Advanced Passenger Information System (APIS) system. If the carrier fails to submit the information, an alien may not enter under the VWP. APIS sends the data to the DHS's Immigration and Customs Enforcement's (ICE) Arrival and Departure Information System (ADIS) for matching arrivals and departures and reporting purposes. APIS collects carrier information such as flight number, airport of departure and other data.

At ports of entry, immigration inspectors observe and question applicants, examine passports, and conduct checks against a computerized system to determine whether the applicant is admissible to the United States.[32] CBP inspects aliens who seek to enter the United States. Primary inspection consists of a brief interview with an immigration inspector, a cursory check of the traveler's documents, and a query of the Interagency Border Inspection System (IBIS),[33] and entry of the traveler into the US-VISIT system. The US-VISIT system uses biometric identification (finger scans) to check identity.[34] Currently, inspectors at the border collect the following information on aliens entering under the VWP: name, date of birth, nationality, gender, passport number, country of issuance, a digital photograph, and prints for both index finders. Primary inspections are quick (usually lasting no longer than a minute); however, if the inspector is suspicious that the traveler may be inadmissible under the INA or in violation of other U.S. laws, the traveler is referred to a secondary inspection. Those travelers sent to secondary inspections are questioned extensively, travel documents are further examined, and additional databases are queried.[35]

Additionally, P.L. 110-53 required that the Secretary of DHS, no later than one year after enactment (i.e., by August 3, 2008), establish an exit system that records the departure of every alien who entered under the VWP and left the United States by air. The exit system is required to match the alien's biometric information against relevant watch lists and immigration information, and compare such biographical information against manifest information collected by airlines to confirm that the alien left the United States.

In April 2008, DHS published a Notice of Proposed Rulemaking in the *Federal Register* that would create biometric exit procedures at airports and seaports for international visitors.[36] DHS was expected to publish the final rule for this system by October 15, 2008.[37] However, in legislation that became law on September 30, 2008,[38] Congress required DHS to complete and report on at least two pilots testing biometric exit procedures at airports.[39] DHS has completed the pilot programs, but according to the Government Accountability Office (GAO), "DHS cannot reliably commit to when and how the work will be accomplished to deliver a comprehensive exit solution to its almost 300 ports of entry."[40]

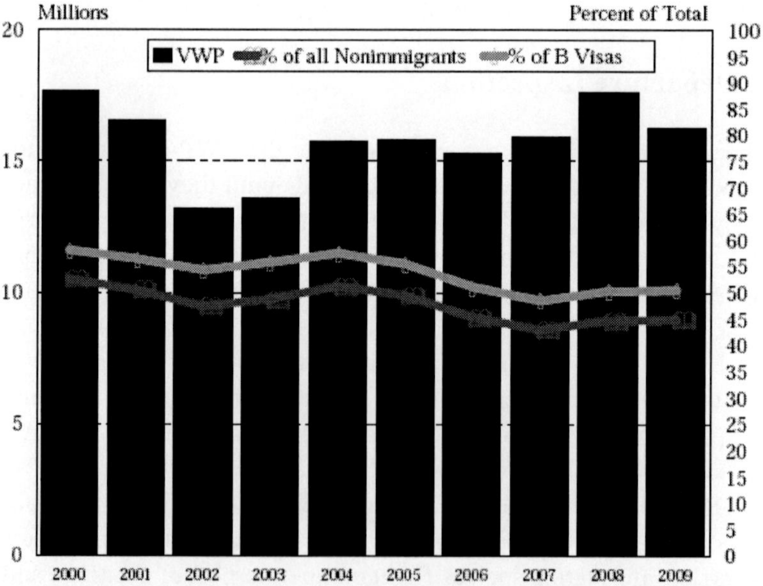

Source: Department of Homeland Security, *FY2006: Yearbook of Immigration Statistics*. Department of Homeland Security, *FY2009: Yearbook of Immigration Statistics,* August 10, 2010.

Note: Number of countries participating in the VWP at the end of the fiscal year: FY1999-FY2001, 29; FY2002, 28; FY2003-FY2008, 27; and FY2009, 35.

Figure 1. Number of Entrants under the VWP for FY1999-FY2009, Percentage of All Nonimmigrant Entrants Who Are VWP Entrants, and Percentage of All B Visa Entrants Who Are VWP Entrants.

Trends in Use of the VWP

The number of people entering under the VWP grew steadily as countries were added to the program, and reached a peak of 17.7 million in FY2000. In FY2009, 16.2 million people entered under the VWP, a decrease from the number of entrants in FY2008 (17.6 million), which was slightly less than the all-time largest number of entrants under the program. The number of visitors entering under the VWP declined by 3.4 million, or 20%, between FY2001 and FY2002. The number of all nonimmigrants entering the United States declined by 4.9 million, or 14.9%, during the same period, but the number of nonimmigrants who were not from VWP countries declined by 1.6 million (9.6%). Similarly, the number of foreign nationals entering the United States with B visas between FY2001 and FY2002 declined by 13.4%, or 1.7 million, which is a smaller decline than the decline in the percent of visitors entering under the VWP.

Between FY2002 and FY2005, the number of people entering under the VWP increased 16.4%, from 13.2 to 15.8 million. The number of people entering under the VWP declined slightly between FY2005 and FY2006, from 15.8 million to 15.3 million; increased to 17.6 million in FY2008; and decreased to 16.2 million in FY2009. The number of people entering as nonimmigrants decreased slightly between FY2002 and FY2003, from 27.9 to 27.8 million; increased from 27.8 to 39.4 million (41.7%) between FY2003 and FY2008; and then decreased to 36.2 million in FY2009, an 8% decrease. The number of aliens entering as temporary visitors for business or pleasure increased 44%, from 24.3 to 35 million, between FY2002 and FY2008, and then decreased to 31.2 million in FY2009.[41] In FY2009, almost identical to FY2008, visitors entering under the VWP constituted 44.9% of all nonimmigrant admissions, and 50.5% of all temporary visitors.

During the most recent years, the majority of the growth in nonimmigrant and temporary visitor admittances came from aliens from countries not in the VWP. Between FY2002 and FY2004, the percent increase of the number of aliens entering under the VWP was *larger* than the increase in both the number of nonimmigrant and temporary visitor entrants. However, between FY2004 and FY2007, the increase in the number of aliens entering under the VWP was *smaller* than the increase in both the number of nonimmigrant and temporary visitor entrants. Conversely, in FY2008, the percent increase in the number of aliens entering under the VWP (9.6%) was *larger* than the increase in both the number of nonimmigrant (5.7%) and temporary visitor entrants (6.1%). For FY2009, the percent decrease in the number of people entering under the VWP (8%) was equivalent to the percent decrease in the total number of visitors and in the number of nonimmigrants admitted.

Policy Issues

The VWP is supported by the U.S. travel and tourism industry, the business community, and DOS. The travel and tourism industry views the VWP as a tool to facilitate and encourage foreign visitors for business and pleasure, which results in increased economic growth generated by foreign tourism and commerce for the United States.[42] DOS argues that by waiving the visa requirement for high-volume/low-risk countries, consular workloads are significantly reduced, allowing for streamlined operations, cost savings, and concentration of resources on greater-risk nations in the visa process. Additionally, some contend that currently DOS does not have the resources to resume issuing visas to all the visitors from VWP countries.[43]

Nonetheless, while the program has significantly reduced the consular workload and facilitated travel to the United States, it has increased the workload of immigration inspectors at ports of entry by shifting all background checks to ports of entry. Furthermore, others contend that the relaxed documentary requirements of the VWP increase immigration fraud and decrease border security. Immigration inspectors have stated that terrorists and criminals believed they would receive less scrutiny during the immigration inspection process if they applied for admission into the United States under the VWP.[44] Another concern has been the lack of information on aliens from VWP countries who overstay the terms of their admittance. Furthermore, some contend that since terrorism does not have national boundaries, the VWP should not be based on particular countries, but should allow visa-free travel for low-risk individuals (e.g., a trusted traveler program).[45]

On September 6, 2006, the Senate Judiciary Committee's Terrorism, Technology, and Homeland Security Subcommittee held a hearing entitled "Keeping Terrorists Off The Plane: Strategies For Pre-Screening International Passengers Before Takeoff." During that hearing, testimony by Jess T. Ford of the Government Accountability Office (GAO) noted that the VWP has many benefits as well as some inherent risks. For example, GAO noted that stolen passports from VWP countries, especially since they are prized travel documents among those attempting to illegally enter the United States, were an issue of particular concern with the safety of the program.[46]

Security

There is debate about whether the VWP increases or decreases national security. As discussed above, travelers under the VWP do not undergo the screening required to receive a visa. While the ESTA system has increased the security of the VWP, it is a name-based system and cannot be used to run checks against databases that use biometrics such as DHS's Automated Biometric Identification System (IDENT) and FBI's Integrated Automated Fingerprint Identification System (IAFIS).[47] (Travelers are checked against these systems through US-VISIT when they enter the United States.)[48]

Nonetheless, others argue that the VWP enhances security by setting standards for travel documents and information sharing, and that the program promotes economic growth and cultural ties.[49] For example, travelers under the VWP have to present machine-readable passports or e-passports, and eventually, all travelers entering under the VWP will present e-passports, which tend to be more difficult to alter than other types of passports.[50] In addition, many B visas are valid for 10 years,[51] and it is possible that a person's circumstances or allegiances could change during that time.

Adding Countries to the VWP

As discussed above, while some view the VWP as a security risk, others contend that the inclusion of countries in the VWP actually increases U.S. security, and argue that increasing membership in the VWP could be used as an incentive to get other countries to share information with the United States.[52] DHS admitted eight new countries into the program in 2008 and one (Greece) in 2010, but there are other countries that have expressed a desire to be included in the VWP. These countries want to be in the VWP because of the possible economic benefits (e.g., increasing commerce and tourism), making it easier and cheaper for their populace to travel to the United States (i.e., since their citizens do not have to get a visa before traveling temporarily to the United States), and because membership in the program is often perceived as evidence of close ties with the United States. In 2005, the administration began providing countries interested in joining the VWP with “road maps” to aid the countries in meeting the program’s criteria.[53] However, some of the countries have complained that since the “road maps” do not contain milestones or time tables, it is difficult to measure the amount of progress made towards fulfilling the criteria for VWP membership.[54] Moreover, others contend that since U.S. consular officers are the ones that approve or disapprove applications for visas, it is extremely difficult for countries to affect their visa refusal rates, limiting the ability of a country to follow a defined set of steps to meet the required VWP criteria.

EU Countries

Five of the current road map countries are members in the EU,[55] which may also raise another issue concerning the VWP. EU rules require that all member states be treated equally (solidarity clause). In addition, a visa is required for all citizens from non-VWP EU countries wishing to travel to the United States, whereas under EU law, these countries do not require visas of U.S. citizens for stays up to 90 days. Presently, any of the EU Member States not participating in the VWP could invoke the EU solidarity clause[56] and visa reciprocity clause,[57] with the result that the other EU countries may have to decline to be members of the VWP, or place visa requirements on United States citizens traveling to EU countries unless the other countries are allowed to enter the VWP.[58] Nonetheless, the other EU countries may put pressure on the non-VWP EU countries not to file a formal complaint which could strain EU-U.S. relations. Also, some of the countries may not have raised this issue yet because they are not full members of the Schengen area.[59] Notably, Greece, a full member of the EU that only became a VWP country in 2010, did not file a complaint about unequal treatment.[60]

Moreover, leaders and publics in many new EU members, such as Poland, are extremely unhappy with their exclusion from the VWP given their support of controversial U.S. policies in Iraq and in the fight against terrorism. They bristle at the time-consuming and expensive requirements their citizens incur when seeking to obtain U.S. visas.[61] For example, there is a $140 nonrefundable application processing fee for tourist visas.[62] Analysts suggest that the VWP issue has contributed to a sense in some central and eastern European states that they have gotten little in return for their efforts to be U.S. allies, and that it is part of the reason for a decline in public support for the United States in some of these countries. Some U.S. officials acknowledge privately that the VWP is the biggest irritant in bilateral U.S. relations with the countries of central and eastern Europe.[63]

The Commission on European Communities has stated that it believes that the road map process could be “an adequate means for ensuring visa exemption for all EU citizens in the medium term.” However, the Commission noted that to make the process fully effective there needs to be more consistency in setting the goals and measures for road map countries. The Commission also stated that the United States had not shown any willingness to consider interim facilitation measures such as providing a fee exemption for tourist visas, and that the EU should continue to press the United States to streamline at least some aspects of the visa application process.[64]

Reportedly, President Obama said in December 2010 that he was going to make it a priority to get Poland into the VWP. [65] Nonetheless, Poland's FY2010 nonimmigrant visa refusal rate was above 3%, and thus, Congress would have to amend the INA to allow Poland into the program.[66]

GAO Report

A September 2008 report by the Government Accountability Office (GAO) noted that the executive branch moved aggressively to expand the VWP by the end of 2008, but that the process was not transparent leading to confusion among interagency partners and aspiring program countries. The Department of State reported difficulties explaining to certain countries with FY2007 refusal rates below 10% and that have interest in joining the program (e.g., Croatia, Israel, and Tawain) why DHS had not negotiated Memorandums of Understanding (MOUs) with them, but had negotiated MOUs with several countries with refusal rates over 10% (e.g., Hungary, Latvia, Lithuania, and Slovakia).[67] GAO also found that DHS had achieved some security enhancements to the program during the negotiations with aspiring VWP countries (e.g., sharing of information on lost and stolen passports), but concluded that DHS had not fully developed the tools to access and mitigate the risks of the VWP.[68]

Lost and Stolen Passports

Currently, all VWP countries provide data on lost and stolen passports (LASP) to the United States. However, concerns have been raised about information sharing on LASP: both the mechanism for sharing the information and whether countries are reporting data in a timely manner.[69] The mechanisms to secure data on LASP have differed over time (e.g., reporting to the U.S. Embassy, access to a common database) and by country (e.g., MOUs, Diplomatic Notes).[70] While DHS receives a few countries' LASP data via direct links to those countries' databases, most data on LASP comes from INTERPOL's Stolen and Lost Travel Documents database[71]— DHS' preferred method of data sharing.[72] Notably, ESTA screens passport information using the INTERPOL database. CBP also accesses LASP data via INTERPOL, but it is unclear if this information is checked during primary inspection.[73]

Overstays

Some maintain that the nonimmigrant visa refusal rate is an unobjective and arbitrary standard, because it is based on decisions made by consular officers rather than the actual behavior of nonimmigrants. In addition, refusal rates are calculated by application, not by person, so if a person applies for the same visa multiple times and is refused, all the refusals are calculated in the refusal rate.[74] When the program was conceived, it was expected that the number of nonimmigrants who overstay the terms of their entry under this program would be a better standard for future program participation. Reportedly, since December 2002, DHS has been matching the entry and exit portions of the I-94 forms for participants in the VWP to create an entry/exit system for VWP nationals. Some question whether this system can produce accurate counts of those who overstay the terms of their entry. Until an automated entry-exit system is fully operational and the data produced are trusted and easily accessible, it is difficult for immigration agents to identify those who have overstayed their 90-day admission periods. Thus, aliens could enter under the VWP and stay indefinitely.[75]

Importantly, although the refusal rate was seen as a proxy for the overstay rate when the program was conceived, people are denied visas for reasons other than being unable to prove that they will not remain illegally in the United States (i.e., they are "intending immigrants").[76] During the visa application process, consular officers[77] must confirm that an alien is not ineligible for a visa under any of the so-called "grounds for inadmissibility" of the INA, such as having a criminal history, engaging in terrorist activity, or having previously violated U.S. immigration law.[78] Although most B visa denials are because the alien cannot prove that they are not an "intending immigrant," there are other reasons a person could be denied a visa that are captured as part of a country's visa refusal rate.

LEGISLATION IN THE 111TH CONGRESS

S. 16

Introduced by Senator George Voinovich on September 29, 2010, S. 16 would have reinstated the nonimmigrant refusal rate waiver by removing the requirement that DHS implement a biometric air exit system before the waiver is reinstituted.

S. 203

Senators Diane Feinstein and Jon Kyl introduced S. 203 on January 12, 2009. S. 203 contained several provisions that aimed to increase the security of the VWP. The bill would have required that within 180 days of enactment every country in the VWP have in effect an agreement to share data on lost and stolen passports. (The requirement to enter into these agreements was included in P.L. 110-53.) Countries that refused to enter into the agreement within the specified time period would have been suspended from the program until an agreement was reached. In addition, S. 203 would have prohibited new countries from being admitted to the VWP until all current countries had agreements. The bill also would have required within a year after enactment that DHS evaluate every country admitted to the VWP prior to January 1, 2009, including calculating the country's overstay rate.[79] Furthermore, S. 203 would have established the maximum overstay rate as 2%, and required that countries with higher overstay rates be suspended from the VWP.

S. 203 also would have changed the language regarding the exit system requirement for the nonimmigrant refusal waiver. In order to have the nonimmigrant refusal rate authority, DHS would have had to certify to Congress that an air entry and exit system was in place that verified the arrival and departure of 97% of all foreign nationals who exit through airports.[80]

Once the Secretary of DHS made such a certification, the U.S. Comptroller would have been required within 180 days to conduct a study of the entry-exit system.

H.R. 1439/S. 1704

Representative Steve Israel introduced H.R. 1439 on March 11, 2009, and Senator Bill Nelson introduced S. 1704 on September 24, 2009. The bills would have required the Attorney General to consider as a part of a country's evaluation for continuation in the VWP the country's cooperation in the extradition and prosecution of Nazi war criminals.

S. 3544

S. 3544, which was introduced by Senator Barbara Mikulski on June 29, 2010, would have mandated the use of overstay rates instead of refusal rates for participation in the VWP. Countries would have had to have an overstay rate of no more than 3% to participate in the VWP. The bill also would have created a probationary period for countries in the program if they did not maintain an overstay rate under 3% or failed to comply with any of the other program requirements. In addition, S. 3544 would have required DHS to report annually to Congress on countries' compliance with the program's requirements. Like S. 203, the bill would have required that within 180 days of enactment, every country in the VWP have in effect an agreement to share data on lost and stolen passports. Moreover, S. 3544 would have required the Secretary of DHS to make information on any aliens who overstayed the term of their admission to the United States available to state and local law enforcement agencies.

H.R. 2954/H.R. 4321

Introduced by Representative Mike Quigley, H.R. 2954 would have delayed from June 30, 2009, to June 30, 2011, the requirement that the air exit system incorporate biometric identifiers as a condition of the Secretary of DHS's authority to waive the nonimmigrant refusal rate. The same provision was included in H.R. 4321 (§306), which was introduced by Representative Solomon Ortiz on December 15, 2009.

Appendix. Legislative History

Visa Waiver Pilot Program

The Visa Waiver Program was established as a temporary program (Visa Waiver Pilot Program) by the Immigration Reform and Control Act of 1986 (P.L. 99-603). Participation in the pilot program was originally limited to eight countries. Congress periodically passed legislation to extend the program's authorization, expand the number of countries allowed to participate in the program, and modify the qualifying criteria. Between 1986 and 1997, Congress passed the following five laws that made changes to the Visa Waiver Pilot Program:

- the Immigration Technical Corrections Act of 1988 (P.L. 100-525);
- the Immigration Act of 1990 (P.L. 101-649), which inserted further requirements for the program and removed the limit on the number of countries that could participate in the program;
- the Miscellaneous and Technical Immigration and Naturalization Amendments of 1991 (P.L. 102-232);
- the Immigration and Nationality Technical Corrections Act of 1994 (P.L. 103- 416), which created a probationary status to allow countries whose nonimmigrant visa refusal rates were higher than 2% but less than 3.5% to enter the program on a probationary basis; and
- the Illegal Immigrant Reform and Immigrant Responsibility Act of 1996 (P.L. 104-208), which created a new type of probationary status for countries in the program that failed to meet certain criteria, and removed the probationary status that had allowed countries with nonimmigrant visa refusal rates higher than 2% but less than 3.5% to enter the program.

The pilot program was scheduled to expire on September 30, 1997, but temporary extensions were included in the Continuing Resolutions passed in the 105th Congress.[81] The Commerce, Justice, State, and Judiciary (CJS) FY1998 Appropriations Act (P.L. 105-119) also contained an extension through April 30, 1998. In 1998, Congress passed legislation (P.L. 105-173) that not only extended the program through April 30, 2000, but made other changes to the standard by which countries are selected (designated) to participate in the VWP.[82] By 1999, program participation had grown to include 29 countries.[83]

Visa Waiver Permanent Program Act

On October 30, 2000, the Visa Waiver Permanent Program Act was signed into law (P.L. 106- 396). The statutory authority for the Visa Waiver Pilot Program had expired on April 30, 2000, but in the interim, the Commissioner of the former Immigration and Naturalization Service (INS)[84] exercised the Attorney General's parole authority to extend the program temporarily.[85] Besides making this program's authorization permanent, the Visa Waiver Permanent Program Act included provisions designed to strengthen documentary and reporting requirements. P.L. 106- 396 included provisions that

- mandate that by October 1, 2007 all entrants under the VWP must have machine-readable passports;
- require that all visa waiver program applicants be checked against lookout systems;
- require ongoing evaluations of participating countries (not less than once every five years);
- require the collection of visa waiver program arrival/departure data at air and sea ports of entry; and

- require that the calculation of visa refusal rates for determining country eligibility shall not include any refusals based on race, sex, or disability.[86]

At the time, many maintained that P.L. 106-396 balanced the competing concerns of facilitating travel and tightening immigration controls.

USA Patriot Act of 2001

The USA Patriot Act (P.L. 107-56), signed into law on October 26, 2001, advanced the deadline for all entrants under the VWP to have machine-readable passports to October 1, 2003, but allowed the Secretary of State to waive this requirement until October 1, 2007 if the VWP country can show that it is making progress toward issuing machine-readable passports. In addition, the USA Patriot Act directed the Secretary of State each year until 2007 to ascertain that designated VWP countries have established programs to develop tamper-resistant passports.

On September 24, 2003, the Secretary of State extended the deadline for visitors from 21 VWP countries to present a machine-readable passport at the ports of entry until October 26, 2004.[87] At this time, an entrant under the VWP with a passport which is not machine-readable must obtain a visa to travel to the United States.

Enhanced Border Security and Visa Entry Reform Act of 2002

The Enhanced Border Security and Visa Entry Reform Act of 2002 (Border Security Act),[88] signed into law on May 14, 2002, required all VWP countries to certify that they report in a timely manner the theft of blank passports, and required, prior to admission in the United States, that all aliens who enter under the VWP are checked against a lookout system. The Border Security Act also mandated that by October 26, 2004, the government of each VWP country needed to certify that it has established a program to issue to its nationals machine-readable passports that are tamper-resistant and incorporate a biometric identifier.[89] The Border Security Act specified that any person applying for admission to the United States under the VWP must have a tamper-resistant, machine-readable passport with a biometric identifier unless the passport was issued prior to October 26, 2004. The USA Patriot Act established the deadline for all foreign nationals entering under the VWP to have machine-readable, tamper-resistant passports, and the new requirement of biometrics in the passports did not change the deadline in the USA Patriot Act for the presentation of machine-readable, tamper-resistant passports. The biometric passport requirement deadline was extended to October 27, 2005, by P.L. 108-299.[90] Thus, as of October 27, 2005 (the day after the new deadline), all entrants under the VWP were required to present machine-readable, tamper-resistant passports (as required by the USA Patriot Act, and P.L. 108- 299), but only passports issued after October 26, 2005, were required to have a biometric identifier.

Although Congress extended the deadline for VWP countries to certify that they had a program to issue machine-readable passports with biometric identifiers, most VWP countries would have been unable to meet the new, October 26, 2005, deadline, especially if the biometric requirement could only have been fulfilled by countries who had electronic data chips in their passports (e-passports). In addition, there was resistance in Congress to grant another extension of the biometric deadline.[91] As a result, the U.S. government clarified that a digitized photograph printed on a data page in the passport would count as a biometric for the October 26, 2005, requirement. Thus, only France and Italy were unable to meet the new deadline, but have since come into compliance. In addition, any passports used by VWP travelers issued after October 26, 2006, requires integrated chips with information from the data page (e-passports).

The Intelligence Reform and Terrorism Prevention Act of 2004

P.L. 108-458,[92] the Intelligence Reform and Terrorism Prevention Act of 2004, added the requirement that by October 26, 2006, as a condition of being in the VWP, each VWP country must certify that it is developing a program to issue tamper-resistant, machine-readable visa documents that incorporate biometric identifiers which are verifiable at the country's port of entry.

Implementing the 9/11 Commission Recommendations Act of 2007

Signed into law on August 3, 2007, §711 of P.L. 110-53 (H.R. 1) allowed the Secretary of DHS, in consultation with the Secretary of DOS, to waive the nonimmigrant refusal rate requirement for admission to the VWP on the date on which the Secretary of DHS certified to Congress that an air exit system is in place that can verify the departure of not less than 97% of foreign nationals that exit through U.S. airports. In addition, the Secretary of DHS also had to certify to Congress that the electronic travel authorization system (discussed below) is operational, prior to being able to waive the nonimmigrant refusal rate requirement. Until June 30, 2009, the air exit system did not need to incorporate biometric identifiers; however, after that date, if the air exit system is unable to match an alien's biometric information with relevant watch lists and manifest information, the Secretary of DHS's authority to waive the nonimmigrant refusal rate is suspended until the air exit system has the specified biometric capacity.

For admission to the VWP, a country who receives a refusal rate waiver also has to

- meet all the security requirements of the program;
- be determined by the Secretary of DHS to have a totality of security risk mitigation measures which provide assurances that the country's participation in the program would not compromise U.S. law enforcement and security interests, or the enforcement of U.S. immigration laws;
- have had a sustained reduction in visa refusal rates, and have existing conditions for the rates to continue to decline;
- have cooperated with the United States on counterterrorism initiatives and information sharing before the date of its designation, and be expected to continue such cooperation; and
- have, during the previous fiscal year, a nonimmigrant visas refusal rate of not more than 10%, or an overstay rate that did not exceed the maximum overstay rate

established by the Secretaries of DHS and DOS for countries receiving waivers of the nonimmigrant refusal rate to participate in the VWP the program.

P.L. 110-53 also specified that in determining whether to waive the nonimmigrant refusal rate requirement, the Secretary of DHS, in consultation with the Secretary of DOS, may take into consideration other factors affecting U.S. security, such as the country's airport security and passport standards, whether the country has an effective air marshal program, and the estimated overstay rate for nationals from the country.

In addition, P.L. 110-53 made several changes to the criteria to qualify as a VWP country, which were intended to enhance the security of the program. As previously mentioned, the act mandated that the Secretary of DHS, in consultation with the Secretary of State, develop and implement an electronic travel authorization system (the system),[93] through which each alien electronically provides, in advance of travel, the biographical information necessary to determine whether the alien is eligible to travel to the United States and enter under the VWP. Aliens using the system are charged a fee that is required to be set at a level so that the cost of creating and administering the system is covered by the fees.

P.L. 110-53 also required the Secretary of DHS, no later than one year after enactment, to establish an exit system that records the departure of every alien who entered under the VWP and left the United States by air. The exit system is required to match the alien's biometric information against relevant watch lists and immigration information, and compare such biographical information against manifest information collected by airlines to confirm that the alien left the United States.[94]

Furthermore, under P.L. 110-53, to participate in the VWP, countries are required to enter into an agreement with the United States to report or make available through INTERPOL information about the theft or loss of passports. The agreements have to specify strict time limits for the reporting of this information. In addition, to be part of the VWP, countries have to accept the repatriation of any citizen, former citizen, or national against whom a final order of removal is issued no later than three weeks after the order is issued. Also, the countries are required to enter into an agreement with the United States to share information regarding whether a national of that country traveling to the United States represents a threat to U.S. security or welfare. The act requires the Secretary of DHS to provide technical assistance to VWP countries to assist the countries in fulfilling the requirements of the program.

In addition, P.L. 110-53 requires the Director of National Intelligence to conduct intelligence assessments of countries. For new VWP countries, the reviews must occur prior to their admittance into the VWP. For existing VWP countries, the reviews should be done in conjunction with the biannual country reviews.

The act also requires the Director of National Intelligence to immediately inform the Secretary of DHS of any current and credible threat of imminent danger to the United States or its citizens that originates from a VWP country. Upon receiving such notification, the Secretary of DHS, in consultation with the Secretary of DHS, may suspend a country from the VWP without any prior notice. Once the country's participation in the VWP no longer poses a security threat, the Secretary of DHS shall reinstate the country in the VWP.

End Notes

[1] The Secretary of Homeland Security administers the VWP program. Section 402 of the Homeland Security Act of 2002 (HSA; P.L. 107-296), signed into law on November 25, 2002, states: "The Secretary [of Homeland Security], acting through the Under Secretary for Border and Transportation Security, shall be responsible for the following: ... (4) Establishing and administering rules, ... governing the granting of visas or other forms of permission, including parole, to enter the United States to individuals who are not a citizen or an alien lawfully admitted for permanent residence in the United States."

[2] "B" visa refers to the subparagraph in the Immigration and Nationalization Act (INA § 101(a)(15)(B)).

[3] ESTA became operational for all VWP countries on January 12, 2009.

[4] These countries are: Andorra, Australia, Austria, Belgium, Brunei, Czech Republic, Denmark, Estonia, Finland, France, Germany, Greece, Hungry, Iceland, Ireland, Italy, Japan, Latvia, Liechtenstein, Lithuania, Luxembourg, Monaco, Malta, the Netherlands, New Zealand, Norway, Portugal, San Marino, Singapore, Slovakia, Slovenia, South Korea, Spain, Sweden, Switzerland, and the United Kingdom.

[5] To obtain a nonimmigrant visa, individuals submit written applications and undergo interviews and background checks. For more information on temporary admissions, see CRS Report RL31381, *U.S. Immigration Policy on Temporary Admissions*, by Chad C. Haddal and Ruth Ellen Wasem.

[6] For more information on visa issuances, see CRS Report RL31512, *Visa Issuances: Policy, Issues, and Legislation*, by Ruth Ellen Wasem.

[7] This provision was amended by P.L. 106-406 to provide extended voluntary departure to nonimmigrants who enter under the VWP and require medical treatment.

[8] INTERPOL is the world's largest international police organization, with 188 member countries. For more information on INTERPOL see, http://www.interpol.int/public/icpo/default.asp, visited September 28, 2010.

[9] Prior to P.L. 110-53 (signed into law on August 3, 2007), VWP countries only had to certify that they were reporting thefts of blank passports.

[10] An emergency is defined as (1) the overthrow of a democratically elected government; (2) war; (3) a severe breakdown in law and order in the country; (4) a severe economic collapse; and (5) any other extraordinary event in the program country where that country's participation could threaten the law enforcement or security interests of the United States. INA § 217(c)(5)(B).

[11] Beginning in December 2001, Argentina experienced a serious economic crisis, including defaulting on loans by foreign creditors, devaluation of its currency, and increased levels of unemployment and poverty. For more information on the financial collapse in Argentina see CRS Report RS21072, *The Financial Crisis in Argentina*, by J. F. Hornbeck.

[12] In addition, many Argentine nationals were trying to use the VWP to obtain entry to the United States solely for the purpose of proceeding to the Canadian border and pursuing an asylum claim in Canada. According to Citizenship and Immigration Canada, between 1999 and 2001, more than 2,500 Argentines filed refugee claims in Canada after transiting the United States under the VWP. *Federal Register*, February 21, 2002, vol. 67, no. 35, p. 7944.

[13] While the number of Argentine nonimmigrant travelers to the United States declined between 1998 and 2000, the number of Argentines denied admission at the border and the number of interior apprehensions increased. The Department of Justice (DOJ) in consultation with DOS determined that Argentina's participation in the VWP was inconsistent with the United States' interest in enforcing it's immigration laws. (The Department of Homeland Security did not exist in February 2002, and authority for the VWP resided with the Attorney General in the DOJ.) *Federal Register,* February 21, 2002, vol. 67, no. 35, pp. 7943-7945.

[14] Between 2000 and 2003 Uruguay experienced a recession causing its citizens to enter under the VWP to live and work illegally in the United States. In 2002, Uruguayan nationals were two to three times more likely than all nonimmigrants on average to have been denied admission at the border. Uruguayan air arrivals had an apparent overstay rate more than twice the rate of the average apparent overstay rate for all air arrival nonimmigrants. *Federal Register*, March 7, 2003, vol. 68, no. 45, pp. 10954-10957.

[15] "Disqualification rate" is defined as the percentage of nationals from a country who applied for admission as a nonimmigrant who either violated the terms of the nonimmigrant visa, who were excluded from admission or who withdrew their application for admission as a nonimmigrant.

[16] The Illegal Immigration Reform and Immigrant Responsibility Act of 1996 (P.L. 104-208).

[17] *Federal Register*, March 7, 2003, vol. 68, no. 45, pp. 10954-10957.

[18] P.L. 110-53 (H.R. 1), signed into law on August 3, 2007. For more details on the changes to the VWP in this act, see the Appendix, "Legislative History."

[19] There was some disagreement between certain critics and DHS regarding exactly what needed to be verified. Some contend that Congressional intent was to have a functional entry-exit system that would be able to match arrival and departure records and know which aliens failed to depart from the United States rather than just matching the entry records with the records of those who were known to have departed from the United States. For example, see S. 203 introduced in the 111th Congress, which attempts to clarify the language in this provision. U.S. Congress, Senate Committee on Judiciary, Subcommittee on Terrorism, Technology and Homeland Security, *The Visa Waiver Program: Mitigating Risks to Ensure Safety to All Americans*, 110th Cong., 2nd sess., September 24, 2008.

[20] DHS determined that the law permitted it to utilize the waiver when ESTA was functional but before it was mandatory for all VWP travelers. Critics did not agree with this interpretation and thought that ESTA should have been mandatory for all VWP travelers before new countries were admitted to the program. When the new countries entered the program, their citizens were required to use ESTA before travelling to the United States. U.S. Government Accountability Office, *Visa Waiver Program: Actions Are Needed to Improve Management of the Expansion Process, and to Assess and Mitigate Program Risks,* GAO-08-967, September 2008. *(Hereafter GAO, Visa Waiver Program: Actions Are Needed to Improve Management of the Expansion Process, and to Assess and Mitigate Program Risks.)*

[21] U.S. Government Accountability Office, *Homeland Security: Key US-VISIT Components at Varying Stages of Completion, but Integrated and Reliable Schedule Needed*, GAO-10-13, November 19, 2009, p. 1, http://www.gao.gov/products/GAO-10-13.

[22] Under law, ESTA became operational 60 days after the Secretary of DHS published a notice in the *Federal Register*. The interim final rule was published on June 9, 2008, and a final rule was published on November 13, 2008. Department of Homeland Security, "Changes to the Visa Waiver Program To Implement the Electronic System for Travel Authorization (ESTA) Program," *Federal Register*, June 9, 2008, vol. 73, no. 11, pp. 32440-32453. .Department of Homeland Security, "Electronic System for Travel Authorization: Mandatory Compliance Required for Travel Under the Visa Waiver Program," 73 *Federal Register* 67354, Nov. 13, 2008.

[23] Entrants under the VWP from the newly admitted VWP countries (Czech Republic, Estonia, Hungry, Latvia, Lithuania, Malta, Slovakia, and South Korea) had to use to system starting on the date of their formal admission to the program. For all the countries except Malta, that date was November 17, 2008. Malta was formally admitted to the VWP on December 30, 2008. Department of Homeland Security, "Electronic System for Travel Authorization (ESTA) Advisory Statement," Nov. 6, 2008. Department of Homeland Security, "Electronic System for Travel Authorization: Mandatory Compliance Required for Travel Under the Visa Waiver Program," 73 *Federal Register* 67354, Nov. 13, 2008.

[24] The fee was instituted on September 8, 2010. The $14 fee includes $4 to cover the costs of administering ESTA and $10 for the travel promotion fee established by Congress in the Travel Promotion Act of 2009 (§9 of P.L. 111-145). Department of Homeland Security, Customs and Border Protection, "DHS, CBP Announce Interim Final Rule For ESTA Fee," press release, August 6, 2010, http://www.cbp.gov/xp/cgov/newsroom/news_releases/national/ 08062010_2.xml#contacts.

[25] Absent of ESTA, the first time an alien traveling to the United States under the VWP was screened was at the airport after the alien checked in for the flight.

[26] A person is not required to apply for their own travel authorization under ESTA. Friends, relatives, personnel in the travel industry, and other third parties may apply for the traveler.

[27] Personal Conversation with Department of Homeland Security, Office of Congressional Affairs, Nov. 7, 2008.

[28] In most cases, the approval process is almost instantaneous. Under statute, ESTA determinations are not reviewable by the courts.

[29] The following information is required for ESTA and on the I-94W form:

- biographical information including name, birth date, country of citizenship, country of residence, telephone number;
- passport information including number, issuing country, issuance date, and expiration date; and
- travel information including city where departing from, flight number, and address while in the United States.

According to DHS, when developing ESTA, the department had to balance the need for biographic information with the requirement that the participating countries did not view applying for an approval under ESTA as equivalent to applying for a visa. If countries had interpreted applying for an authorization under ESTA as having the same burden as applying for a visa, these countries might have required that U.S. citizens traveling to their countries obtain a visa.

[30] These eligibility questions pertain to whether the alien would be inadmissible on health, criminal, or terrorist grounds, or because the alien had previously violated immigration law (e.g., been deported). Other eligibility questions include whether the alien has: (1) violated a child custody agreement with a U.S. citizen; (2) previously been denied a visa to travel to the United States; and (3) asserted immunity from prosecution.

[31] Department of Homeland Security, "Changes to the Visa Waiver Program To Implement the Electronic System for Travel Authorization (ESTA) Program," *Federal Register*, June 9, 2008, vol. 73, no. 11, pp. 32440-32453.

[32] All VWP applicants are issued nonimmigrant visa waiver arrival/departure forms (Form I-94W).

[33] ADIS feeds information to the Interagency Border Inspection System (IBIS). IBIS is a database of suspect individuals, businesses, vehicles, aircraft, and vessels that is used during inspections at the border. IBIS interfaces with the FBI's National Crime Information Center (NCIC), the Treasury Enforcement and Communications System (TECS II), National Automated Immigration Lookout System (NAILS), Non-immigrant Information System (NIIS), CLASS and TIPOFF terrorist databases. Because of the numerous systems and databases that interface with IBIS, the system is able to obtain such information as whether an alien is admissible, an alien's criminal information, and whether an alien is wanted by law enforcement. Department of Homeland Security, Customs and Border Protection, *IBIS- General Information*, Washington, DC, https://help.cbp.gov/app/answers/detail/a_id/151/related/1/~/ibis.

[34] For more information on US-VISIT see, CRS Report RL32234, *U.S. Visitor and Immigrant Status Indicator Technology (US-VISIT) Program*, by Lisa M. Seghetti and Stephen R. Vina.

[35] Lookout databases such as TIPOFF, which is integrated with CLASS, contain information on aliens who are inadmissible for entry into the United States. The National Security Entry-Exit System (NSEERS) and the Student and Exchange Visitor Information System (SEVIS) are also used during secondary inspections. Immigration inspectors may access the National Automated Immigration Lookout System (NAILS II), which is a text-based system that interfaces with IBIS and CLASS. For more information, see CRS Report RL31381, *U.S. Immigration Policy on Temporary Admissions*, by Chad C. Haddal and Ruth Ellen Wasem.

[36] Department of Homeland Security, "Collection of Alien Biometric Data Upon Exit From the United States at Air and Sea Ports of Departure," 73 *Federal Register* 22065, April 24, 2008.

[37] Personal conversation with Department of Homeland Security Congressional Affairs, September 22, 2008.

[38] P.L. 110-329.

[39] One pilot will test DHS's recommended solution that carriers collect biometrics from passengers; the other pilot will test CBP officers collecting passenger biometrics at the boarding gate.

[40] U.S. Government Accountability Office, *Homeland Security: Key US-VISIT Components at Varying Stages of Completion, but Integrated and Reliable Schedule Needed*, GAO-10-13, November 19, 2009, p. 1, http://www.gao.gov/products/GAO-10-13.

[41] Temporary visitors include aliens who entered with B visas, those who entered under the Guam Visa Waiver Program, and those who entered under the VWP.

[42] The example of Argentina was frequently used to illustrate this relationship; during the first year Argentina was in the VWP, tourism from that country to the United States grew by 11.5%. Some argue that because of the trade and tourism growth additional VWP membership could generate for the United States, this factor should be added to the criteria used to select participating countries. Other proponents of the VWP, however, contend that the criteria should not be broadened to include tourism potential if the thresholds of refusal rates and visa overstay violations are weakened, arguing that these provisions are essential to safeguard and control our borders.

[43] In his testimony before the House Immigration and Claims Subcommittee on February 28, 2002, William S. Norman, President and Chief Executive Officer of the Travel Industry Association of America, stated that it would take hundreds of new consular staff and tens of millions of dollars to issue visas to visitors currently entering under the VWP.

[44] U.S. Department of Justice, Office of Inspector General Report I-2002-002, *Follow-Up Report on the Visa Waiver Program*, December 2001. (Hereafter cited as DOJ, *Follow-Up Report.*)

[45] U.S. Congress, House Committee on the Judiciary, Subcommittee on Immigration and Claims, *Implications of Transnational Terrorism for the Visa Waiver Program* , 107th Cong., 2nd sess., February 28, 2002.

[46] Testimony of Jess T. Ford, Director International Affairs and Trade, General Accounting Office, in U.S. Congress, Senate Committee on the Judiciary Committee, Subcommittee on Terrorism, Technology, and Homeland Security, *Keeping Terrorists Off The Plane: Strategies For Pre-Screening International Passengers Before Takeoff*, hearings, 109th Cong., 2nd sess., September 7, 2006.

[47] IAFIS is a national fingerprint and criminal history system. IDENT is a DHS-wide system for the storage and processing of biometric and limited biographic information. IDENT is the primary DHS-wide system for the

biometric identification and verification of individuals encountered in DHS mission-related processes. For more information on IAFIS, see Federal Bureau of Investigation, "The Integrated Automated Fingerprint Identification System (IAFIS)," press release, http://www.fbi.gov/hq/cjisd/iafis.htm. For more information on IDENT, see Department of Homeland Security, *Privacy Impact Assessment for the Automated Biometric Identification System (IDENT)*, Washington, DC, July 31, 2006, p. 2, http://www.dhs.gov/xlibrary/assets

[48] CRS Report RL32234, *U.S. Visitor and Immigrant Status Indicator Technology (US-VISIT) Program.*

[49] For an example of this argument, see Heritage Foundation, *The Visa Waiver Program: A Security Partnership*, Fact Sheet #66, Washington, DC, June 25, 2010.

[50] There is not a specific requirement to present an e-passport when entering under the VWP. As discussed above, any passports issued after October 26, 2006, and used by VWP travelers to enter the United States are required to have integrated chips with information from the data page (e-passports). Most passports are valid for 10 years, and thus, it is likely that by October 2016, all VWP entrants will have e-passports.

[51] The length of validity of a visa is mostly dependent on reciprocity with the United States (i.e., that visas from that country for U.S. citizens are valid for the same period of time). For a full list of reciprocity schedules, see Department of State, Reciprocity Schedules, at http://travel.state

[52] For an example of this argument, see James Jay Carafano, With a Little Help from Our Friends: Enhancing *Security by Expanding the Visa Waiver Program*, Heritage Foundation, Executive Memorandum no. 991, February 3, 2006; and Jena Baker McNeill, *Time to Decouple Visa Waiver Program from Biometric Exit*, Heritage Foundation, Web Memorandum no. 2867, April 15, 2010.

[53] There were 13 "road map" countries. They were Bulgaria, Cyprus, Czech Republic, Estonia, Greece, Hungary, South Korea, Latvia, Lithuania, Malta, Poland, Romania, and Slovakia. Eight of these countries have been admitted to the VWP.

[54] For example, on February 8, 2006, the Heritage Foundation held an event entitled *Fighting a More Effective War on Terrorism: Expanding the Visa Waiver Program.* The featured speakers were Ambassadors Petr Kolar of the Czech Republic, John Bruton of the EU, Janusz Reiter of Poland, and András Simonyi of Hungary. A recording of the event is available at http://www.heritage.org/Press/Events/ev020806a.cfm.

[55] Twelve of the 13 roadmap countries were EU countries, but seven of those countries have been admitted to the VWP.

[56] Non-VWP EU countries could contend that the fact that other countries in the EU are part of the VWP constitutes unequal treatment.

[57] The same visa rules do not apply to U.S. citizens traveling to the Non-VWP EU countries, and Non-VWP EU citizens traveling to the United States.

[58] Conversation with Telmo Baltazar, Justice and Home Affairs Counselor, European Union, April 18, 2005.

[59] The Schengen area comprises the EU countries which have signed the convention implementing the Schengen Agreements of 1985 and 1990 on the free movement of persons and the standardization of border controls.

[60] DHS began its review of Greece for participation in the VWP in late 2007.

[61] For example, see "Poland Excluded from Visa-Waiver List," *Washington Times*, October 18, 2008, http://www.washingtontimes.com/news/2008/oct/18/poland-excluded-from-visa-waiver-l and Ewa Kern-Jedrychowska , "Polish-American Voters' Top Issues: the Visa Waiver Program and Missile Defense," *Feet in Two Worlds*, July 1, 2008, http://news.feetintwoworlds.org/2008/07/01/polish-american-voters-

[62] All applicants pay the visa application fee, but depending on the person's nationality, there may also be a visa issuance fee because nonimmigrant visa fees are based on "reciprocity," (i.e., what another country charges a U.S. citizen for a similar type of visa). For a list of visa issuance fees by country, see Department of State, Reciprocity by Country, http://travel.state

[63] Craig Whitlock, "Poland's Leader Hopes To Gain from Support of U.S. Policies," *Washington Post*, February 7, 2006; Discussions with U.S. and European officials.

[64] Commission of the European Communities, *Report from the Commission to the Council on Visa Waiver Reciprocity with Certain Third Countries,* October 1, 2006, pp.11-12.

[65] Josh Rogin, "Obama: Poland will be admitted to the visa waiver program," *http://thecable.foreignpolicy.com*, December 8, 2010, http://thecable.foreignpolicy.com/posts/2010/12/08/ obama_poland_will_be_admitted_ to_the_visa_ waiver_program.

[66] Poland's FY2010 adjust B-visa refusal rate was 9.8%. Thus, Poland would meet the refusal rate requirement if the nonimmigrant refusal rate waiver was reinstated. Department of State, *Adjusted Refusal Rate- B-Visas Only by Nationality: Fiscal Year 2010*, http://www.travel.state

[67] In a meeting with CRS, DHS said that the countries who had previously been "road map" countries were given priority, since in some respects, they were "first in line." Also, DHS expected, and was correct, that the countries with FY2007 refusal rates above 10% with whom DHS signed MOUs would have FY2008 refusal rates below the 10% threshold.

[68] U.S. Government Accountability Office, *Visa Waiver Program: Actions Are Needed to Improve Management of the Expansion Process, and to Assess and Mitigate Program Risks,* GAO-08-967, September 2008. *(Hereafter GAO, Visa Waiver Program: Actions Are Needed to Improve Management of the Expansion Process, and to Assess and Mitigate Program Risks.)*

[69] The issue of LASP has been ongoing. VWP passports are supposedly highly valued since the bearer does not need a visa to enter the United States. For examples of past issues, see U.S. Government Accountability Office, *Border Security: Stronger Actions Needed to Assess and Mitigate Risks of the Visa Waiver Program,* GAO-06-854, July 2006; and U.S. Department of Homeland Security, Office of Inspections, Evaluations, and Special Reviews, *A Review of the Use of Stolen Passports from Visa Waiver Countries to Enter the United States*, OIG-05-07, December 2004.

[70] The United States has signed MOUs with the nine newest VWP entrants (those who received a waiver of the nonimmigrant refusal rate before it was suspended in July 2009, and Greece). All but four of the other VWP countries share LASP data via an exchange of Diplomatic Notes. Personal Conversations with Department of Homeland Security, Office of Congressional Affairs, July 20, 2010.

[71] The United States began providing information on LASP to the U.S. National Central Bureau of the International Criminal Police Organization (INTERPOL) in May 2004. The INTERPOL LASP database is available to law enforcement and immigration authorities worldwide. U.S. Department of Homeland Security, Office of Inspections, Evaluations, and Special Reviews, *A Review of the Use of Stolen Passports from Visa Waiver Countries to Enter the United States*, OIG-05-07, December 2004, pp. 7-8.

[72] In the past, before access to, and the content of, the INTERPOL database was reliable, DHS required countries to submit LASP data to the U.S. Embassies in those countries.

[73] U.S. Government Accountability Office, *Visa Waiver Program: Actions Are Needed to Improve Management of the Expansion Process, and to Assess and Mitigate Program Risks,* GAO-08-967, September 2008, p.5.

[74] If a person submits five visa applications in a year and all are denied, they are all counted toward the refusal rate. However, if such a person submits five applications that are denied and then a sixth application that is approved, none of the previous applications are counted as refusals in the calculation of the adjusted refusal rate that is used in the determination of VWP eligibility. Personal Communication with the Department of State, Office of Congressional Affairs, July 19, 2010.

[75] CRS Report RL32234, *U.S. Visitor and Immigrant Status Indicator Technology (US-VISIT) Program*, by Lisa M. Seghetti and Stephen R. Vina.

[76] §214(b) of the INA generally presumes that all aliens seeking admission to the United States are coming to live permanently; as a result, aliens seeking to qualify for a B visa (and most other nonimmigrant visas) must demonstrate that they are not coming to reside permanently in the United States. CRS Report R41104, *Immigration Visa Issuances and Grounds for Exclusion: Policy and Trends*, by Ruth Ellen Wasem.

[77] This determinations of inadmissibility are also made by CBP officers at ports of entry.

[78] The so-called grounds of inadmissibility under INA §212(a) include health-related grounds; criminal history; security and terrorist concerns; public charge (e.g., indigence); seeking to work without proper labor certification; illegal entrants and immigration law violations; ineligibility for citizenship; and aliens who are illegally present or have previously been removed.

[79] Under current statute, country evaluations must be completed every two years.

[80] Under current law, the refusal rate waiver became available on the day that an air exit system is in place that could verify the departure of at least 97% of foreign nationals departing from the United States.

[81] An extension of the pilot program was included in the first Continuing Resolution (P.L. 105-56 §117) for FY1998. The five subsequent Continuing Resolutions—P.L. 105-64, P.L. 105-68, P.L. 105-69, P.L. 105-71, and P.L. 105-84— simply extended the expiration date of the provisions in the first Continuing Resolution for FY1998 (P.L. 105-56).

[82] Originally, to qualify for the Visa Waiver Pilot Program countries needed to have had an average nonimmigrant refusal rate of no more than 2% over the past two fiscal years with neither year going above 2.5%. P.L. 105-173 added the criteria that a country could have a nonimmigrant refusal rate of less than 3% for the previous year and qualify for the program.

[83] The 29 countries were: Andorra, Argentina, Australia, Austria, Belgium, Brunei, Denmark, Finland, France, Germany, Iceland, Ireland, Italy, Japan, Liechtenstein, Luxembourg, Monaco, the Netherlands, New Zealand,

Norway, Portugal, San Marino, Singapore, Slovenia, Spain, Sweden, Switzerland, the United Kingdom, and Uruguay. Argentina was removed from the VWP in February 2002, and Uruguay was removed in April 2003. From April 2003 until November 2008, the VWP included 27 countries. As of October 2010, there are 36 countries participating in the VWP.

[84] The Homeland Security Act of 2002 (P.L. 107-296) abolished the Immigration and Naturalization Service (INS) and effective March 1, 2003, transferred most of its functions to three bureaus in the new Department of Homeland Security (DHS): Citizenship and Immigration Services (USCIS); Bureau of Immigration and Customs Enforcement (ICE); and, Bureau of Customs and Border Protection (CBP).

[85] Parole is a temporary authorization to enter the United States and is normally granted when the alien's entry is determined to be in the public interest (INA § 212(d)(5)(A)).

[86] Many of these requirements were included to address shortcomings in the program, as identified by the Inspectors General of both the Departments of Justice and State.

[87] The 21 countries granted a postponement were: Australia, Austria, Denmark, Finland, France, Germany, Iceland, Ireland, Italy, Japan, Monaco, the Netherlands, New Zealand, Norway, Portugal, San Marino, Singapore, Spain, Sweden, Switzerland, and the United Kingdom. On November 11, 2003, Luxembourg was granted an extension of the deadline.

[88] P.L. 107-173. The original bill, H.R. 3525, was sponsored by Representative F. James Sensenbrenner.

[89] The act tasked the International Civil Aviation Organization (ICAO) with developing the biometric standard.

[90] Signed into law on August 9, 2004.

[91] For example, see letter from Rep. F. James Sensenbrenner, Jr., to Luc Frieden, President of the European Counsel of Ministers, and Franco Frattini, Vice-President of the European Commission, April 7, 2005.

[92] The original bill, H.R. 2845, was sponsored by Senator Susan M. Collins and signed into law on December 17, 2004.

[93] The system as implemented is known as the Electronic System for Travel Authorization (ESTA).

[94] This exit system is not necessarily the same as the exit system required for the nonimmigrant refusal rate waiver authority. DHS appears to have incorporated this requirement as part of the exit portion of automated entry and exit data system known as US-VISIT.

In: U.S. Visa Policies, Programs and Considerations
Editor: Aaron R. Miller
ISBN: 978-1-61470-333-4

Chapter 5

FOREIGN INVESTOR VISAS: POLICIES AND ISSUES*

Alison Siskin and Chad C. Haddal

SUMMARY

With the current economic downturn, Members of the 111th Congress are likely to be faced with many policy options aimed at economic improvement, including the possible consideration of amending visa categories for foreign investors. Foreign investors are often viewed as providing employment opportunities for U.S. citizens rather than displacing native workers. Yet, extending foreign investor visas provides several potential risks as well, such as visa abuses and security concerns. Thus, a potential policy question for Congress—and particularly legal permanent resident (LPR) investors—is whether the benefits reaped from allocating visas to foreign investors outweigh the costs of denying visas to other employment-based groups.

There are currently two categories of nonimmigrant investor visas and one category of immigrant investor visa for legal permanent residents (LPR). The visa categories used for nonimmigrant investors are: E-1 for treaty traders; and the E-2 for treaty investors. The visa category used for immigrant investors is the fifth preference employment-based (EB-5) visa category. According to Department of Homeland Security (DHS) statistics, there were 230,647 nonimmigrant treaty trader and investor visa arrivals in the United States in FY2008. For the same time frame, DHS reported the granting of 1,360 investor visas.

When viewed from a comparative perspective, the investor visas of the United States are most closely mirrored by those of Canada. The LPR investor visa draws especially strong parallels to the Canadian immigrant investor visa, since the latter served as the model for the former. Comparing the admissions data between these two countries, however, reveals that the Canadian investor provision attracts many times the number of investors of its United States counterpart. Yet, both countries showed an upward trend in immigrant investor visas in the last two years.

The investor visas offered by the United States operate on the principle that foreign direct investment into the United States should spur economic growth in the United States. According to the classical theory, if these investments are properly targeted

---

* This is an edited, reformatted and augmented version of a Congressional Research Service publication, CRS Report for Congress RL33844, from www.crs.gov, dated January 27, 2010.

towards the U.S. labor force's skill sets, it should reduce the international migration pressures on U.S. workers. To attract foreign investors, research indicates that temporary migrants are motivated most significantly by employment and wage prospects, while permanent migrants are motivated by professional and social mobility. Theoretically, however, it is unclear to what extent potential migration provides additional incentive for investment activity. Investors from developed countries may sometimes lack incentive to settle in the United States since they can achieve foreign direct investment (FDI) and similar standards of living from their home country. Yet, in cases where foreign investors have been attracted, the economic benefits have been positive and significant.

Immigrant investors have been subject to notable administrative efforts in the past couple of years. In 2005, DHS developed the Investor and Regional Center Unit (IRCU) to govern matters concerning LPR investor visas and investments to better adjudicate petitions and coordinate investments. In the 111th Congress, authorizing language in the Department of Homeland Security Appropriations Act, 2010 (P.L. 111-83, §548), extends the authorization of the Regional Center Pilot Program through September 30, 2012.

INTRODUCTION

With the current economic downturn, Members of the 111th Congress are likely to be faced with many policy options aimed at economic improvement. A focus of past debates has been on the impact immigrants have on jobs and wages. Yet, these discussions frequently take on a different focus when it comes to foreign investors, in part because such visas are targeted at immigrants that are poised to inject capital into the economy and create employment. Foreign investors are often viewed as providing employment opportunities for U.S. citizens rather than displacing native workers. Thus, Congress has in previous years been willing to set aside both temporary and permanent visas for foreign investors with the goal that this visa distribution would net positive economic effects. Yet, extending foreign investor visas provides several potential risks as well, such as visa abuses and security concerns.

With the extension of the immigrant investor visa pilot program—a program aimed at granting permanent immigrant visas for investments into certain limited liability corporations—by a continuing resolution until March 6, 2009,[1] Members of Congress will have to decide if the current policy towards foreign investors should be maintained, or if a different set of policies should be implemented. The central policy question surrounding foreign investors—and particularly legal permanent resident (LPR) investors—is whether the benefits reaped from allocating visas to foreign investors outweigh the costs of denying visas to other employment-based groups. The subsequent analysis provides a background and contextual framework for the consideration of foreign investor visa policy. After a brief legislative background, this report will provide discussions of immigrant and nonimmigrant investors visas, a comparison of U.S. and Canadian immigrant investor programs, an analysis of the relationship between investment and migration, and finally a review of current issues.

BACKGROUND

Since the Immigration Act of 1924[2] the United States has expressly granted visas to foreign nationals for the purpose of conducting commerce within the United States. Although foreign investors had previously been allowed legal status under several Treaties of Friendship, Commerce and Navigation treaties, the creation in 1924 of the nonimmigrant treaty trader visa provided the first statutory recognition of foreign nationals as temporary traders. With the implementation of the Immigration and Nationality Act of 1952 (INA), the statute was expanded to include nonimmigrant treaty investors—a visa for which trade was no longer a requirement.[3] Nonimmigrant visa categories for traders and investors have always required that the principal visa holder stems from a country with which the United States has a treaty.[4] The nonimmigrant visa classes are defined in §101(a)(15) of the INA. These visa classes are commonly referred to by the letter and numeral that denotes their subsection in §101(a)(15) of the INA, and are referred to as E-1 for nonimmigrant treaty traders and E-2 for nonimmigrant treaty investors.

Unlike nonimmigrant investors, who come to the United States as temporary admissions, immigrant investors are admitted into the United States as LPRs.[5] With the Immigration Act of 1990,[6] Congress expanded the statutory immigrant visa categories to include an investor class for foreign investors. The statute developed an employment-based (EB-5) investor visa for LPRs,[7] which allows for up to 10,000 admissions annually and generally requires a minimum $1 million investment. Through the Regional Center Pilot Program, investors may invest in targeted regions and existing enterprises that are financially troubled. This pilot program was extended by the Basic Pilot Program Extension and Expansion Act of 2003[8] to continue through FY2008.

Foreign investors are generally considered to help boost the United States economy by providing an influx of foreign capital into the United States and through job creation. For investor immigrants, job creation is an explicit criterion, while with the nonimmigrant visa categories economic activity is assumed to spur job growth. Additionally, foreign investors are often associated with entrepreneurship and increased economic activity. Critics, however, believe that such investors may be detrimental since they potentially displace potential entrepreneurs that are United States citizens.

Immigrant Investors

There is currently one immigrant class set aside specifically for foreign investors coming to the United States.[9] Falling under the employment-based class of immigrant visas, the immigrant investor visa is the fifth preference category in this visa class.[10] Thus, the immigrant investor visa is commonly referred to as the EB-5 visa.

Goals

The basic purpose of the LPR investor visa is to benefit the United States economy, primarily through employment creation and an influx of foreign capital into the United States.[11] Although some members of Congress contended during discussions of the creation of the visa that potential immigrants would be "buying their way in," proponents maintained that the program's requirements would secure significant benefits to the U.S. economy.[12] Proponents of the investor provision offered predictions that the former-Immigration and

Naturalization Service (INS) would receive approximately 4,000 applications annually. These petitioners' investments, the drafters speculated, could reach an annual total of $4 billion and create 40,000 new jobs.[13] The Senate Judiciary Committee report on the legislation states that the provision "is intended to provide new employment for U.S. workers and to infuse new capital into the country, not to provide immigrant visas to wealthy individuals" (S.Rept. 101-55, p.21).

Requirements

As amended by the Immigration Act of 1990,[14] the Immigration and Nationality Act (INA) provides for an employment-based LPR investor visa[15] program designated for individuals wishing to develop a new commercial enterprise[16] in the United States (INA §203(b)(5)). The statute stipulates that

- The enterprise must employ at least 10 U.S. citizens, legal permanent residents (LPRs), or other work-authorized aliens in full time positions. These employees may not include the foreign investor's wife or children.
- The investor must further invest $1 million[17] into the enterprise, such that the investment goes directly towards job creation and the capital is "at risk."[18] However, if an investor is seeking to invest in a "targeted area"[19] then the required capital investment may be reduced to $500,000.[20] For each fiscal year, 7.1% of the worldwide employment-based visas (roughly 10,000 visas) are set aside for EB-5 investors, of which 3,000 are reserved for entrepreneurs investing in "targeted areas."[21]
- The business and jobs created must be maintained for a minimum of two years.[22]

According to regulations, enterprises being proposed need not be backed by a single applicant.[23] Multiple applicants may provide financial backing in the same enterprise, provided that each applicant invests the required minimum sum and each applicant's capital leads to the creation of 10 full-time jobs. The applicant may also combine the investment in a new enterprise with a non-applicant who is authorized to work in the United States. Furthermore, each individual applicant must demonstrate that he or she will be actively engaged in day-to-day managerial control or as a policymaker.[24] Petitions as a passive investor will not qualify.[25] However, since limited partnership is acceptable, regulations do not prevent the investor from living in another location or engaging in additional economic activities.

Regional Center Pilot Program

The Regional Center Pilot Program differs in certain ways from the standard LPR investor visa. Established by §610 of P.L. 102-395 (October 6, 1992), the pilot program was established to achieve the economic activity and job creation goals of the LPR investor statute by encouraging investors to invest in economic units known as "Regional Centers."[26] Regional Center designation must be approved by the Department of Homeland Security's (DHS) United States Citizenship and Immigration Service (USCIS), and is intended to provide a coordinated focus of foreign investment towards specific geographic regions. Areas with high unemployment are especially likely to receive approval as a Regional Center, since they are less likely to receive foreign capital through foreign direct investment (FDI)[27] (although the basic requirements apply to all regional petitions).[28] Up to 5,000 immigrant visas[29] may be set aside annually for the pilot program. These immigrants may invest in any of the Regional Centers that currently exist to qualify for their conditional LPR status.[30]

The Basic Pilot Program Extension and Expansion Act of 2003[31] scheduled the program to sunset in FY2008. However, the Department of Homeland Security Appropriations Act, 2010 (P.L. 111- 83, §548), extends the authorization of the Regional Center Pilot Program through September 30, 2012. Following the 2003 legislation, USCIS decided to develop a new unit to govern matters concerning LPR investor visas and investments.[32] On January 19, 2005, the Investor and Regional Center Unit (IRCU) was created by the USCIS, thereby establishing a nationwide and coordinated program. USCIS believes that the IRCU will serve the dual purpose of guarding against EB-5 abuse and encouraging investment.[33]

The USCIS approximates that between 75-80% of EB-5 immigrant investors have come through the pilot program since it began, and that limited partnerships constitute the most significant portion of this group.[34]

LPR Investor Visa Numbers

In contrast to the high number of applications for other employment-based LPR visas,[35] the full allotment of almost 10,000 LPR investor visas per fiscal year has never been used. As Table 1 below shows, the number of LPR investor admissions reached 1,361 admissions in FY1997, or 13.6% of the program's visa supply. In subsequent years, the program declined markedly, before increasing up to 1,360 in FY2008. Despite the low numbers of overall investor admissions, the program has seen a marked increase since the implementation of the Regional Center Pilot Program expansion in 2004.

From FY1992 to FY2004, the cumulative total amount invested into the United States by LPR investor visa holders was approximately $1 billion and the cumulative number of LPR investor visas issued was 6,024.[36] Since FY2004, an additional 1,901 immigrant investor visas have been issued. In the earlier years of the program, it attracted a relatively higher rate of derivatives than principals.[37] However, in the last three years the distribution of visas between principals and derivatives has more closely approximated parity. Derivatives have historically accounted for approximately 66% of immigrant investor visa recipients, while principals account for 34%.

According to data from DHS, in the time span of FY1992 through May 2006, authorities had received a cumulative total of 8,505 petitions for immigrant investor visas. Of these petitions, 4,484 petitions had been granted while 3,820 had been denied[38]—an approval rate of 52.7%.

Furthermore, in this same time span, officials received 3,235 petitions for the removal of conditional status[39] from the LPRs of immigrant investors. These petitions were granted in 2,155 cases (a 66.6% approval rate), while the remaining 910 petitions for the removal of conditional status were denied.

Although numerous possible explanations for the overall low admission levels of LPR investor visas exist, the notable drop in admissions in FY1998 and FY1999 is due in part to the altered interpretations by the former-INS of the qualifying requirements that took place in 1998.[40] The 21st Century Department of Justice Appropriations Act (2002)[41] provided remedies for those affected by the former-INS' 1998 decision, and provided some clarification to the requirements to promote an increase in petitions.[42]

Table 1. United States LPR Investor Visa Admissions, FY1996-FY2007

Fiscal Year	EB-5 Visa Admissions	Principals[a]	Derivatives[a]
1992	59	24	35
1993	583	196	387
1994	444	157	287
1995	540	174	366
1996	936	295	641
1997	1,361	444	917
1998	824	259	565
1999	285	99	187
2000	218	79	147
2001	191	67	126
2002	142	52	97
2003	64	39	25
2004	129	60	69
2005	346	158	188
2006	749	252	497
2007	806	279	515
2008	1,360	427	922

Source: CRS presentation of U.S. Department of Homeland Security Office of Immigration Statistics FY2008 data.

Notes: In FY2008, of the total admissions, 1,029 were new arrivals and 331 were adjustments of status. The new arrivals included at least 304 principals and 714 dependents, while the adjustments of status included at least 123 principals and 208 dependents.

[a] DHS withheld the information on some individuals to limit disclosure. Thus, the total admissions does not reflect the sum of principals and derivatives for FY2007 and FY2008.

A 2005 report from GAO[43] listed a number of contributing factors to the low participation rates, including the rigorous nature of the LPR investor application process and qualifying requirements; the lack of expertise among adjudicators; uncertainty regarding adjudication outcomes; negative media attention on the LPR investor program; lack of clear statutory guidance; and the lack of timely application processing and adjudication. It is unknown how many potential investors opted to obtain a nonimmigrant investor visa or pursued other investment pathways. A recent law journal article on investor visas suggested that the two year conditional status of the visa and the alternate (and less expensive) pathways for LPR status often dissuaded potential investors from pursuing LPR investor visas.[44] Yet, since FY2003, the number of immigrant investor visas issued has increased on an annual basis.

According to the GAO study, of the LPR visas issued to investors, 653[45] had qualified for removal of the conditional status of LPR visa (not including dependents).[46] GAO estimates that these LPR investors invested approximately $1 billion cumulatively into their collective enterprises and 99% kept their enterprise in the same state where it was established.[47] The types of enterprises these investors established were often hotels/motels, manufacturing, real estate, or domestic sales, with these four categories accounting for 61% of the businesses established by LPR-qualified investors. Furthermore, an estimated 41% of the businesses by LPR-qualified investors were set up in California. The subsequent states with the highest percentages of established enterprises were Maryland, Arizona, Florida and Virginia with 11%, 8%, 7%, and 7% respectively (for examples of current investment projects see Appendix B).

As Figure 1 shows, persons obtaining LPR investor visas to the United States between FY1998 and FY2007 has fluctuated in number. While 824 persons obtained such LPRs in FY1998, the total for FY2003 was 64. From FY2003 through FY2008, the total number grew by 2,125% to a total of 1,360. Thus, despite a notable recent upward trend in growth, the issuance of LPR investor visas has not yet recovered to the levels of the mid-to-late 1990s. Additionally, during the time period depicted in Figure 1, 38.9% of the 3,754 visas issued were for individuals adjusting status. The remaining 61.1% were issued to new arrivals. The majority of these new arrivals occurred in FY2006-FY2008.

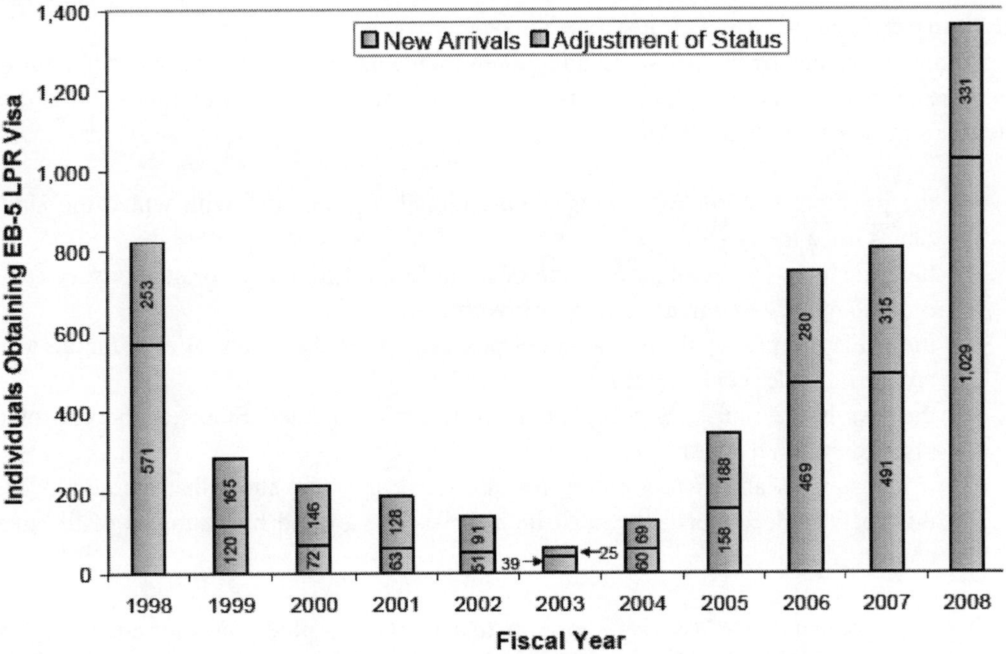

Source: CRS presentation of data from the *OHS Yearbook of Immigration Statistics 2008*.

Notes: Figure does not include information on some individuals where DHS chose to limit disclosure. Thus, the total admissions does not reflect the sum of new arrivals and adjustment of status individuals for FY2007 and FY2008.

Figure 1. LPR Investor Visas Issued by Type, FY1998-FY2008.

NONIMMIGRANT INVESTOR VISAS

When coming to the United States as a temporary investor, there are two classes of nonimmigrant visas which a foreign national can use to enter: the E-1 for treaty traders and the E-2 for treaty investors. An E-1 treaty trader visa allows a foreign national to enter the United States for the purpose of conducting "substantial trade" between the United States and the country of which the person is a citizen.[48] An E-2 treaty investor can be any person who comes to the United States to develop and direct the operations of an enterprise in which he or she has invested, or is in the process of investing, a "substantial amount of capital."[49] Both these E-class visas require that a treaty exist between the United States and the principal foreign national's country of citizenship.[50]

In the majority of cases, a commerce or navigation treaty serves as the basis for the E-class visa extension (though other bilateral treaties and diplomatic agreements can also serve as a foundation).[51] A number of countries offer both the E-1 and E-2 visas as a result of reciprocal agreements made with the United States, although many countries only offer one. Currently there are 75 countries who offer the treaty class visas. Of these countries, 28 offer only the E-2 treaty investor visa while 4 countries offer only the E-1 treaty trader visa (see Appendix A). In the cases where a country offers both types of visas, an applicant who qualifies for both types of visa may choose based upon his or her own preference. Such decisions, however, would depend upon the specific nature of the business as the E category visas carry different qualifying criteria for renewal.

Although each category has some unique requirements, other requirements cut across all categories of nonimmigrant investor visas. An applicant for any of the nonimmigrant investor categories must satisfy the following criteria:

- the principal visa recipient must be a national of a country with which the United States has a treaty.[52]
- the principal visa recipient must be in some form of executive or supervisory role in order to qualify as a treaty trader or investor[53]
- the skills the principal visa recipient possesses must be essential and unique to the enterprise under consideration[54]
- the visa holder must show an intent to depart the United States at the end of the visa's duration of status[55]
- if investing in an existing enterprise, the applicant must show that the employer of the treaty trader or investor must be at least 50% owned by nationals of the treaty country.[56]

A person granted an E-class visa is eligible to stay in the United States for a period of two years.[57] Although an applicant is obligated to show intent of departing the United States at the end of the visa duration, the E-class visas may be renewed for an indefinite number of two year periods provided that the individual still qualifies.[58] Spouses and child dependents are granted the same visa status and renewal as the principal visa holder so long as the child is under the age of 21, after which the child must apply and qualify for his or her own visa.[59]

Generally with the E-class visas, the individual may not engage in other employment than that which is stipulated,[60] although incidental activities are generally allowed.[61] If any E-class individual wishes to change employer, he or she is under obligation to contact the Department of State (DOS) and apply for adjustment of status.[62]

E-1 Treaty Trader[63]

The E-1 formally traces back to the 1924 Immigration Act, although merchants working under treaty terms were recognized visa holders prior to this act.[64] Under current law, the E-1 visa is to be issued to an individual who engages in substantial trade between the United States and his or her country of nationality. According to immigration regulations, trade is defined as "the exchange, purchase or sale of goods and/or services. Goods are tangible commodities or merchandise having intrinsic value. Services are economic activities whose outputs are other than tangible goods."[65] This expanded definition of trade into the service sector allows for a fairly broad understanding of what trade may entail.

The term "substantial trade" has never been explicitly defined in terms of monetary value. Rather, the term is meant to indicate that there is an amount of trade necessary to ensure a continuing flow of international trade items.[66] For smaller businesses, regulatory qualification for treaty trader status may be derived from demonstrating that the trading activities would generate an income sufficient to support the trader and his or her family.[67] The qualifications for sufficient volume or transaction have not been explicitly set in the regulations,[68] but a minimum qualification is that more than 50% of the business's trade must flow between the United States and the treaty country from which the E-1 visa holder stems.[69]

E-2 Treaty Investor

The E-2 investor visa is a visa category that stems from the 1952 Immigration and Nationality Act (INA). The qualifying applicant for such a visa is coming to the United States in order to "develop or direct the operations of an enterprise in which he has invested, or is in the process of investing a substantial amount of capital."[70] Unlike the E-1 visa, the business need not be engaged in trade of any kind. However, the same rules concerning ownership are still applicable.[71] In cases of ownership of an enterprise, the regulations require that the E-2 visa holder control at least a 50% interest in an enterprise.[72] The burden of proof for E-2 qualification lies with the applicant in the same manner as with the other E-class visas.[73]

There is no explicit monetary amount for what constitutes a "significant amount of capital." The DOS has operated under a regulatory proportionality principle that dictates that the amount an individual invests must be enough to ensure the successful establishment and growth of an enterprise, and there must be some level of investment risk assumed by the treaty investor.[74] Because of this proportionality regulation, an investment in a small to medium-sized enterprise is acceptable.[75] For smaller sized investments, the DOS generally requires that the investment amount be a higher percentage of the enterprise value.[76] For higher valued enterprises the investment percentage becomes less relevant, provided that the monetary amount is deemed substantial.[77]

As further grounds for regulatory qualification for an E-2 investor visa, investments in marginal enterprises are not eligible for acceptance.[78] Consequently, the DOS applies a two-pronged test for marginality.[79] On the one hand, the enterprise in which the applicant seeks to make an investment must be capable of providing more than a minimal living for the investor and his or her family. However, the rules are capable of recognizing that some businesses need time to establish themselves and become viable. Consequently, as a second prong of the test, the investor's enterprise must be deemed capable of making a significant economic impact within five years of starting normal business activity. If neither of these prongs is successfully passed, the enterprise is deemed marginal and the application is rejected.[80]

An additional category of E-class nonimmigrant visa—the E-3 visa for Australian nationals— does exist, but it is set aside for use by specialized workers, and not for investors or traders.[81]

Nonimmigrant Investor Visa Numbers

E-class visas are largely distributed to foreign nationals from the regions of Asia and Europe. This result is not surprising since the majority of treaty countries are in these two regions.

Furthermore, one could reasonably expect that the financial requirements embedded in nonimmigrant investor visa categories would result in a high correlation between the nationality of qualifying applicants and country membership in the Organization for Economic Cooperation and Development (OECD)—an organization of capital abundant countries.

As Figure 2 shows, the Asian region was issued the highest number of E-class visas in FY2009, with a total of 14,843 visas issued. These Asian issuances constitute more than any other region, and represent 45.5% of the worldwide total. Within the Asian region, the biggest user of the E-class visa is Japan, whose nationals accounted for 9,533 of the visa issuances in FY2009, a figure representing 29.2% of the 32,655 worldwide E-class visas issued that fiscal year. Europe's 10,943 E-Class visas accounted for 33.5% of the worldwide total, while the North American share of 3,897 visas represented 11.9%. Oceania's issuance accounted for 2,387 visas, or 7.3% of the total. South America and Africa each accounted for less than 1.7% of the worldwide total, and combined their nationals represented approximately 1.8% of the worldwide E-class visa issuances

The admissions data on nonimmigrant investors offers more detailed insights into the origins of the visa holders. Table 2 provides cumulative totals of E-class visa admissions into the United States in FY2008 by region of origin, with a detailed breakdown of the Asian region. The figures listed in Table 2 show that the Asian region accounted for approximately 47.7% of the nonimmigrant investor visa admissions into the United States. In FY2008, Japan accounted for the majority of nonimmigrant investor admissions with 85,175 admissions.[82] South Korea's 13,801 nonimmigrant investors admitted account for 6.0% of the United States total for FY2008. It is worth noting that the fast growing markets of China and India (the world's two largest population centers) combined for slightly less than 900 admissions. The second largest region of origin for nonimmigrant investor admissions was Europe, with slightly more investors admitted than Japan. And while Europe's 87,787 admissions accounted for 38.1% of the total U.S. nonimmigrant investor admissions in FY2008, the 276 admissions of nationals from African countries accounted for approximately one-tenth of 1% of this same total.

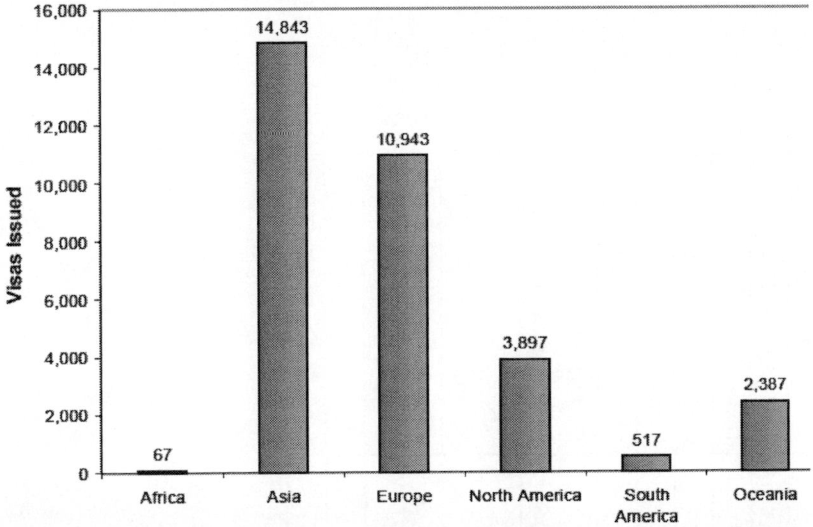

Source: Data are from the Department of State, Bureau of Consular Affairs, Report of the Visa Office, 2009.

Notes: The figure does not include the one visa issued to an individual with no registered nationality. E-3 visas issued are not included in the figure.

Figure 2. E Treaty Trader and Investor Visas Issued by Region, FY2009.

Table 2. Nonimmigrant Treaty Trader and Investor Admissions, FY2008

Country (or Region) of Origin	Number	Percentage of Total
Asia:		
Taiwan	3,569	1.5%
South Korea	13,801	6.0%
China[a]	573	0.2%
Japan	85,175	36.9%
India	302	0.1%
All other Asia	6,501	2.8%
Total for Asia	109,921	47.7%
All Other Regions:		
Europe	87,787	38.1%
South America	5,903	2.6%
Africa	276	0.1%
North America	23,513	10.2%
Oceania	2,795	1.2%
Unknown	452	0.2%
Total	230,647	100.0%

Source: CRS presentation of data from the *DHS Yearbook of Immigration Statistics 2008*.

Notes: The data not include the 12,739 admission of free trade workers with E-3 visas from Australia.

[a] Denotes People's Republic of China, Hong Kong, and Macau.

Table 3. E Treaty Traders and Investors Admitted by State of Destination, FY2008

State	Admissions	State	Admissions	State	Admissions	State	Admissions
Alabama	3,068	Indiana	3,393	Nevada	1,463	South Dakota	108
Alaska	371	Iowa	257	New Hampshire	179	Tennessee	2,855
Arizona	2,795	Kansas	436	New Jersey	11,748	Texas	22,126
Arkansas	648	Kentucky	3,626	New Mexico	300	Utah	352
California	46,835	Louisiana	858	New York	27,252	Vermont	138
Colorado	1,121	Maine	168	North Carolina	3,749	Virginia	2,552
Connecticut	2,834	Maryland	1,593	North Dakota	48	Washington	3,605
Delaware	209	Massachusetts	2,971	Ohio	7,357	West Virginia	159
District of Columbia	578	Michigan	12,331	Oklahoma	374	Wisconsin	753
Florida	24,668	Minnesota	671	Oregon	1,809	Wyoming	47
Georgia	7,008	Mississippi	251	Pennsylvania	3,528	Other	49
Hawaii	2,171	Missouri	579	Puerto Rico	415	Unknown	4,101
Idaho	2,265	Montana	80	Rhode Island	277		
Illinois	134	Nebraska	196	South Carolina	4,258	Total	230,647

Source: CRS presentation of data from the OHS Yearbook of Immigration Statistics 2008.

Notes: The data not include the 9,294 admission of free trade workers with E-3 visas from Australia.

The Department of Homeland Security (DHS) offers statistics on the admissions of nonimmigrants and their destination state. Table 3 indicates the destination states of nonimmigrant treaty trader and investor visa admissions into the United States for FY2008. The state with the highest number of nonimmigrant investors as their destination in FY2008 was California with 46,835 admissions, accounting for 20.3% of the admissions total. Following California, the next three biggest recipients of nonimmigrant investors were New York, Florida, and Texas with 27,252, 24,668, and 22,126 admissions each, respectively. In the respective order, these state admissions accounted for 11.8%, 10.7% and 9.6% of the admissions total in FY2008. The only other states with a combined total of more than 10,000 nonimmigrant treaty trader and investor visa admissions were Michigan and New Jersey. Michigan was the destination state of 12,331 nonimmigrant investors admitted, while New Jersey attracted 11,748 admissions. These totals accounted for 5.3% and 5.1% of the United States admissions total, respectively. The remaining states represented the destination states for approximately 37.2% of nonimmigrant traders and investors.

Historically, more investors have applied to enter the United States as nonimmigrants than immigrants, possibly because the less stringent requirements for the nonimmigrant investor visa make it easier to obtain. However, relative to other nonimmigrant categories, the admission levels of investor nonimmigrants are low. With the ease of movement, technological advances, and ease of trade restrictions, many investors may be choosing to invest in the United States from abroad and enter the United States on B-1 temporary business visas or visa waivers.[83]

U.S. AND CANADIAN COMPARISONS

Although there are many countries with investor visa programs—including the United Kingdom, Australia, and New Zealand—the Canadian investor program has the strongest parallels to those of the United States. These parallels are in part due to the fact that the U.S. immigrant investor program was modeled after its Canadian counterpart. The Canadian program allows investors who have a net worth of at least \$800,000 (Cdn) to make a \$400,000 (Cdn) investment through Citizenship and Immigration Canada (CIC).[84] The Canadian government additionally offers an entrepreneurial visa for foreign nationals with a net worth of \$300,000 (Cdn).[85] These nationals are required to invest and participate in the management of a certain sized business, and they must produce at least one new full-time job for a non-family member.[86] Between 1986 and 2002, the Canadian investor visa program attracted more than \$6.6 billion (Cdn) in investments.[87] From FY1992 through FY2004, United States LPR investor immigrants had invested an estimated \$1 billion in U.S. businesses.[88]

According to published accounts, the Canadian investor visa was developed initially to attract investors from the British colony of Hong Kong.[89] The visa was created in 1986 in response to the significant numbers of investors seeking to migrate from Hong Kong in anticipation of the transfer of the colony from British to Chinese control. For these investors, the visa offered an opportunity to establish legal permanent residence in a country that was perceived to be more embracing of individual property rights and open markets.[90] These immigrant investors from Hong Kong, along with other immigrant investors, have cumulatively invested over $3 billion in the Canadian economy.[91]

As Figure 3 demonstrates, the annual number of immigrant investor visas issued over the past decade has remained multiple times higher than that of its United States counterpart. The margin between these two programs was closest in 1997, when the Canadian issuance of 5,595 immigrant investor visas was approximately 400% higher than the U.S. total of 1,361 immigrant investor visas issued. Although these ratios have fluctuated, the sizable Canadian advantage in this measure has remained. In terms of the absolute levels, the Canadian immigrant visa level for 2008 represented a 13-year high, while the U.S. level for the same time period roughly equaled its 13-year high. Both countries have shown an upward trend in immigrant investor visas since 2003.

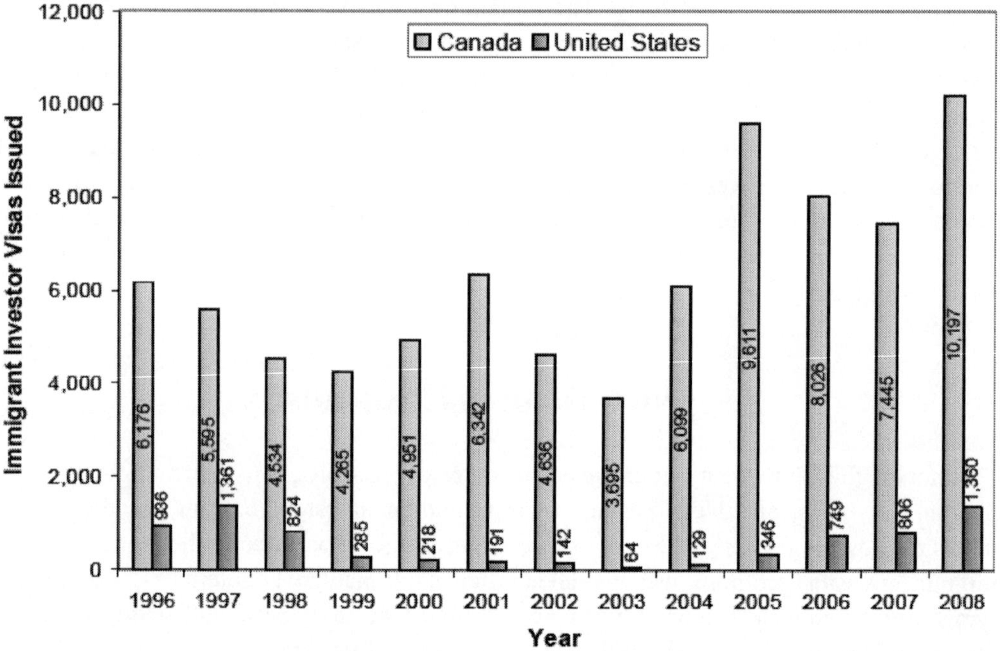

Source: Data are from the United States Government Accountability Office (2008) and Citizenship and Immigration Canada (2008).

Figure 3. Immigrant Investors to Canada and the United States, 1996-2008.

What is unclear from the data is whether the competition between the U.S. and Canadian program (as well as investor programs in other countries) constitutes a zero-sum game. There are no data available showing the motive for migration among investors, or if they perceive the United States and Canada as interchangeable investment locations. If the investors are motivated purely by the economic returns, then economic theory[92] suggests that equalizing the program financial requirements should result in more equal rates of petitions. Furthermore, a lowering of the financial requirements should increase the supply for both countries. However, if the immigrant investors are motivated to migrate by non-financial considerations, then equalizing the United States program requirements with its Canadian counterpart is likely to have little impact on the current trends.

ANALYSIS OF THE RELATIONSHIP BETWEEN INVESTMENTS AND MIGRATION

Classical economic theory has posited that trade liberalization (including the reduction of investment restrictions) establishes a conditional inverse theoretical relationship between foreign direct investment (FDI) and migration.[93] In other words, as trade increases, migration pressures decrease. The theory posits that an increased level of FDI should reduce migratory pressures through growth in the targeted economy. As economic growth produces a higher demand for labor, workers in that economy feel less pressure to seek employment in foreign economies, provided that the new jobs complement the workforce's skills. For example, if economic growth creates demand for skilled labor, then an unskilled labor force should not experience any reduced migration pressures. Thus, while FDI increases host-country growth, there is not necessarily a direct reduction in host-country migration pressures.

The investor visas offered by the United States operate on the principal that FDI into the United States should spur economic growth in the United States. According to the classical theory, if these investments are properly targeted towards the U.S. labor force's skill sets, it should reduce the migration pressures on U.S. workers. Such economic growth from FDI should further spur greater demand for trade. In FDI between capital abundant countries such as the OECD member states (between whom a marked majority of FDI flows), the empirical evidence has largely supported this notion.[94] Furthermore, it has provided an increased per capita income in these states, as well as boosted the general standard of living.

What is less clear from the empirical research is the degree to which potential migration provides any additional incentive for investment activity in the United States. The classical trade theory asserts that trade and migration are substitutes,[95] and that trade liberalization should reduce migratory pressures.[96] These basic propositions are generally agreed to hold in the long term. Consequently, in the long term classical trade theory suggests there should be little migration of investors from countries with liberalized trade arrangements with the United States.[97] Instead, these investors would achieve their investments through conventional FDI. Furthermore, the theory suggests that investors would be more likely to migrate from countries with restrictive trade policies (a policy more highly correlated with less economically developed countries).

Critics of the classical economic models contend that despite elegant predictions, the models produced by the theory frequently do not capture the costs of international finance. Such critics argue that foreign investments often occur at the expense of local businesses, and result in exploitive practices of local labor.[98] These criticisms are particularly common when critiquing the economic relationship between capital abundant countries and less economically developed countries (LEDC). According to the argument, more powerful countries can leverage their power to construct investment relationships that shift a disproportionate amount of profits to the capital abundant countries. Simultaneously, a greater share of the costs[99] are shouldered by the less powerful country. Classical economists generally respond by noting that these investments are still producing growth in the LEDCs, making the countries better off than without the investments. However, LEDCs remain a source of contention between the classical economic theorists and their critics.

Less Economically Developed Countries

Some scholars have expressed doubt about the posited trade/migration substitutability, suggesting that the relationship in the short or medium term could look different from the long term.[100] One of the arguments put forward is that trade and migration are complementary for countries with different levels of development.[101] Under such a scenario, economic growth in a sending country would provide potential migrants with the economic means to overcome relatively high migration costs. Other observers point to such factors as imperfect credit markets and currency fluctuations as significant "push" factors for potential migrants.[102] These latter factors, however, are generally more highly correlated with LEDCs. Therefore, both the complementary and substitutability theories of trade and migration suggest that higher demand for investor out-migration should currently lie in the populations of LEDCs. However, as noted earlier, investor visas issued to regions with LEDCs are relatively few.

What makes the visa program distinct from conventional FDI is that it involves trade through the import of human capital. Consequently, these visas have potential for creating a so-called "brain drain" migration out of less-developed sending-countries.[103] LEDCs are by definition limited in their capital levels, and economic theory would suggest that exporting capital from a capital scarce country would inhibit its growth and development.[104] Classical theorists would argue that the United States would be better served by sending FDI into LEDCs, thereby promoting economic growth in LEDCs and a subsequent higher demand for U.S. goods.[105] Such investment, the theory dictates, would promote job growth both in the United States and abroad.[106] Instead, targeting investors from capital abundant countries for sector specific investments would serve a more complementary role for the global market.[107] By attracting capital abundant country investors, the United States' economic growth and productivity could be stimulated without adversely affecting the consumption and trade potential of the investor's country of origin.

Temporary and Permanent Investors

Some recent scholarly work has drawn a distinction between the decision-making factors of potential temporary and permanent migrants.[108] Amongst temporary migrants, it is the employment prospects and wage differentials that are significant variables in deciding whether to migrate. Differences in both gains and price levels should affect the cost/benefit calculation of the potential migrants, as these variables will affect potential levels of consumption and savings. For permanent migrants, however, the prospects for professional and social mobility are the main motivating factors.

The distribution of visas among Asian countries shows marked country-specific tendencies among investor visa petitioners. Specifically, the polarization among petitioners towards either immigrant (permanent) or nonimmigrant (temporary) visas suggests that a significant proportion of applicants are substituting immigrant visas for nonimmigrant visas, or vice versa. For example, while Japan accounted for 36.9% of all the foreign nationals arriving on nonimmigrant treaty trader and investor visas in FY2008 (Table 2), its nationals represented only 1% of all the LPR investor visas issued since FY1992. Conversely, nationals of Taiwan accounted for roughly 40% of immigrant investors issued since FY1992, but only 1.5% of nonimmigrant arrivals in FY2008. In the context of the aforementioned theory, these opposite behaviors suggest that Japanese investors are seeking to capitalize on wage differentials, while Taiwanese, Chinese, and (to some extent) South Korean investors are pursuing professional and social mobility.

Although some considerations weigh more heavily on the decisions of immigrant and nonimmigrant investors, no single explanation accounts for the behavior of investor visa petitioners. Japan, for example, has some trade restrictions with the United States through voluntary export restraint agreements limiting auto and steel exports to the United States, suggesting from the theoretical standpoint that Japanese investors would choose to temporarily migrate.[109] The Japanese governments have also complained that the post-9/11 customs regulations and practices of the United States inhibit U.S./Japanese trade.[110] Despite the suggestion by these factors that Japanese investors are temporarily substituting trade with migration, it is also plausible that Japan's weak economic performance has reduced the professional mobility opportunities—a motivation associated with permanent migration. From 1991-2000, Japan's real (adjusted for inflation) average GDP growth rate was 1.4%, and it fell to 0.9% from 2001 to 2003.[111] Yet, regardless of motivation, Japanese investors are predominantly choosing to temporarily migrate to the United States.

The fact that China, Taiwan and South Korea have had strong economic performance in the last decade and relatively higher levels of immigrant investors to the United States, suggests that these investors are migrating for more than financial purposes. These investors may be more strongly motivated by the family and/or social network connections to previously migrated investors and other LPRs in the United States. These theoretically derived motives, however, must be further tested empirically before any conclusive behavioral statements can be made.

Multiplier Effects

Classical economic theory holds that investments provide for multiplier effects throughout the economy by increasing demand for other goods and services. For example, an increase in demand for corn may increase the demand for storage facilities, which results in an increase in construction contracts. The U.S. Department of Commerce has quantified these effects through the Regional Input-Output Modeling System (RIMS II).[112] The RIMS II multipliers have become a significant factor in assessing indirect economic activity and employment effects for Regional Center Pilot Program petitions.[113] Using the regional multipliers for various industries, foreign investment funds are frequently shown to yield increases in demand across an economy that are several times higher than the direct input by an investor. Thus, despite the relatively low number of investors entering the United States, the impact of each investment by a foreign investor is a multiplied factor greater than the direct investment, depending upon which industry and region is being invested in. Furthermore, studies showing the direct economic investments of foreign investors may not fully capture the economic impact of these investors upon a region.[114]

Administrative Efforts

In recent years, significant efforts have been made by administrative agencies to both promote investment by foreigners in the United States economy, and to close perceived loopholes for visa exploitation. At the center of these efforts has been the USCIS' changes to the Regional Center Pilot Program, which addressed fraud concerns and the development of a Regional Center unit for coordination and targeting of foreign investments.

Fraudulent Investments

During the late 1990's, the LPR investor visa was suffering from high levels of fraudulent applications.[115] There has been concern that potential immigrants could use schemes of pooling their funds and transferring the money to demonstrate the existence of sufficient capital.[116] Furthermore, applicants could potentially use promissory notes that would allow for their repayment after a six year time period. Since the LPR was only conditional for two years, some observers feared that these investors could pull out of their respective investments after being granted their LPR, have the promissory notes forgiven, and the enterprise would collapse. As a result, the USCIS has engaged in a policy of not accepting promissory notes, although the regulations state that petitions with promissory notes may be considered for approval.[117] Additionally, the creation of the Investor and Regional Center Unit (IRCU) within USCIS has allowed greater scrutiny of applications through increased resources and coordination of petitions processing. Petitioners now must provide extensive documentation that traces the source of their funds to show that the capital was legally obtained.[118]

IRCU Expansion

Prior to the creation of IRCU, the former-INS had been criticized for becoming more restrictive in application reviews for Regional Center designation, including allowing some applications to remain pending for more than three years.[119] In 2005, concerns were raised by both Members and advocates that the IRCU still did not process applications quickly enough,[120] and that staff members had competing obligations within IRCU.[121] Proponents of the Regional Center Pilot Program believe it has attracted a significant amount of capital and that addressing these criticisms would further increase the levels of foreign investments through the LPR investor visa.[122] USCIS has responded to these criticisms by expanding the number of Regional Centers available for LPR investor investments.

Working with foreign financing from the immigrant investor program has become highly attractive for many domestic investors. A number of current investment projects are using LPR investor financing because it is less costly for the domestic investors. For domestic investors, employing LPR investor funds becomes a significantly cheaper option than a bank loan, since there is no requirement to pay interest on the financing. Additionally, because the enterprises are less saddled with financing debt they are more quickly able to turn a profit. The LPR investor visa petitioners are still able to qualify for conditional LPR status under these investment structures through the multiplier rules for employment and capital that the USCIS employs. Thus, limited partnerships of domestic investors with LPR investor visas has become a popular option for financial stabilization and enterprise start-up in Regional Centers as diverse as Philadelphia and South Dakota.

New Orleans

In the efforts to rebuild the sections of New Orleans damaged by Hurricane Katrina, developers and officials alike have taken an interest in attracting foreign capital. USCIS officials are working closely with New Orleans officials to establish New Orleans as another Regional Center for LPR investor visa investments. Officials at USCIS are hopeful that the program success that the Philadelphia targeted center is experiencing can be replicated in New Orleans. Since being designated a Regional Center, Philadelphia has attracted over 100 LPR investors and most of their investments are being used to help finance the renovation and transformation of the 1,100 acre shipyard (for further discussion, see Appendix B).

CURRENT LEGISLATION AND POTENTIAL ISSUES FOR CONGRESS

In the 111th Congress, authorizing language in the Department of Homeland Security Appropriations Act, 2010 (P.L. 111-83, §548), extends the authorization of the Regional Center Pilot Program through September 30, 2012. The Senate-passed version of the act had included language to permanently reauthorize the EB-5 Regional Center Pilot Program, but this language was not included in the conference agreement. On July 22, 2009, the Senate Judiciary Committee held a hearing to assess the Regional Center Pilot Program, with some members expressing support for the program's permanent authorization.[123] Some legislation has also proposed modifying the qualifying criteria as a targeted area to lower the threshold for investment amounts in some geographic regions as a means of enticing more applications by potential immigrant investors.[124] There are currently no other programs for targeting investments by immigrant investors to the United States.

Additional investor visa issues that could surface may relate to temporary investors. In terms of nonimmigrant visas, the Danish government has been lobbying the United States to grant E-2 treaty investor visas to Danish nationals. Originally, this provision was granted to the Danes on May 2, 2001 as part of a protocol to the treaty granting nationals of Denmark E-1 nonimmigrant trader visa eligibility. The protocol was never ratified, however, due to congressional objections over the inclusion of immigration provisions in a trade agreement. Subsequently, Representative Sensenbrenner introduced H.R. 3647 in the 109th Congress, which was passed in the House on November 16, 2005, and would have allowed nationals of Denmark to enter and operate in the United States as investors under E-2 treaty investor nonimmigrant visas. Currently, Danish nationals are only allowed E-1 treaty trader visas. Denmark is one of four countries whose nationals are eligible for E-1 treaty trader visas, but not E-2 treaty investor visas (see Appendix A).

APPENDIX A. E-CLASS VISA PRIVILEGES BY YEAR OF ATTAINMENT

Table A-1. E-Class Visa Privileges by Year of Attainment

Country	Classification	Year of Visa
Albania[a]	E-2	1998
Argentina	E-1	1854
Argentina	E-2	1854
Armenia	E-2	1996
Australia	E-1	1991
Australia	E-2	1991
Australia	E-3	2005
Austria	E-1	1931
Austria	E-2	1931
Azerbaijan[a]	E-2	1901
Bahraina	E-2	1901
Bangladesh[a]	E-2	1989
Belgium	E-1	1963
Belgium	E-2	1963
Bolivia	E-1	1862
Bolivia	E-2	2001
Bosnia & Herzegovina	E-1	1982
Bosnia & Herzegovina	E-2	1982
Brunei[b]	E-1	1853
Bulgaria[a]	E-2	1954
Cameroon[a]	E-2	1989
Canada	E-1	1993
Canada	E-2	1993
Chile	E-1	2004
Chile	E-2	2004
Chile	H-1B-1	2004
China (Taiwan)	E-1	1948
China (Taiwan)	E-2	1948
Colombia	E-1	1948
Colombia	E-2	1948
Congo (Kinshasa)[a]	E-2	1989
Congo (Brazzaville)[a]	E-2	1994
Costa Rica	E-1	1852
Costa Rica	E-2	1852
Croatia	E-1	1982
Croatia	E-2	1982
Czech Republic[a]	E-2	1993
Denmark[b]	E-1	1961
Ecuador[a]	E-2	1997
Egypt[a]	E-2	1992
Estonia	E-1	1926
Estonia	E-2	1997
Ethiopia	E-1	1953
Ethiopia	E-2	1953
Finland	E-1	1934
Finland	E-2	1992
France	E-1	1960
France	E-2	1960
Georgia	E-2	1997
Germany	E-1	1956
Germany	E-2	1956

Country	Classification	Year of Visa
Greeceb	E-1	1954
Grenadaa	E-2	1989
Honduras	E-1	1928
Honduras	E-2	1928
Iran	E-1	1957
Iran	E-2	1957
Ireland	E-1	1950
Ireland	E-2	1992
Israel[b]	E-1	1954
Italy	E-1	1949
Italy	E-2	1949
Jamaica[a]	E-2	1997
Japan	E-1	1953
Japan	E-2	1953
Jordan	E-1	2001
Jordan	E-2	2001
Kazakhstan[a]	E-2	1994
Korea (South)	E-1	1957
Korea (South)	E-2	1957
Kyrgyzstana	E-2	1994
Latvia	E-1	1928
Latvia	E-2	1996
Liberia	E-1	1939
Liberia	E-2	1939
Lithuania[a]	E-2	2001
Luxembourg	E-1	1963
Luxembourg	E-2	1963
Macedonia	E-1	1982
Macedonia	E-2	1982
Mexico	E-1	1994
Mexico	E-2	1994
Moldova[a]	E-2	1994
Mongolia[a]	E-2	1997
Morocco[a]	E-2	1991
Netherlands	E-1	1957
Netherlands	E-2	1957
Norway	E-1	1928
Norway	E-2	1928
Oman	E-1	1960
Oman	E-2	1960
Pakistan	E-1	1961
Pakistan	E-2	1961
Panama[a]	E-2	1991
Paraguay	E-1	1860
Paraguay	E-2	1860
Philippines	E-1	1955
Philippines	E-2	1955
Poland[a]	E-2	1994
Romania[a]	E-2	1994
Senegal[a]	E-2	1990
Singapore	E-1	2004
Singapore	E-2	2004
Singapore	H-1B-1	2004
Slovak Republic[a]	E-2	1993
Slovenia	E-1	1982
Slovenia	E-2	1982

Table A-1. (Continued)

Country	Classification	Year of Visa
Spain	E-1	1903
Spain	E-2	1903
Sri Lanka[a]	E-2	1993
Suriname	E-1	1963
Suriname	E-2	1963
Sweden	E-1	1992
Sweden	E-2	1992
Switzerland	E-1	1855
Switzerland	E-2	1855
Thailand	E-1	1968
Thailand	E-2	1968
Togo	E-1	1967
Togo	E-2	1967
Trinidad & Tobago[a]	E-2	1996
Tunisiaa	E-2	1993
Turkey	E-1	1993
Turkey	E-2	1990
Ukraine[a]	E-2	1996
United Kingdom	E-1	1815
United Kingdom	E-2	1815

Source: CRS presentation of data from the U.S. Department of State Foreign Affairs Manual, 9 FAM §41.51.

[a] Countries with only E-2 visa privileges.

[b] Countries with only E-1 visa privileges.`

APPENDIX B. IMMIGRANT INVESTOR PILOT PROGRAM PROJECTS

There are currently numerous targeted economic regions set up for the Regional Center Pilot Program for the EB-5 visa category. These targeted areas have focused on different types of investments in order to achieve economic benefits for the given region. Below are descriptions of a couple of the projects that are currently in place under the Regional Center Pilot Program and the results these projects are producing.

South Dakota International Business Institute

The South Dakota International Business Institute (SDIBI), Dairy Economic Development Region (DEDR) is the only regional targeting center currently run by a state government. Approved in June 2005, this Regional Center was the result of a state-wide effort to find an improved method of attracting foreign capital to South Dakota. From the state's perspective, the EB-5 pilot investor program offered a more promising solution than the E-2 nonimmigrant visa, since officials could offer investors the benefit of LPR status.[125] Additionally, the job-creation criterion of the EB-5 visa aligned well with the state's focus on job creation from foreign investments (as opposed to isolated capital injections). In its application for Regional Center designation, the state said it would focus its efforts on attracting dairy farm investors. USCIS agreed to the designation on the condition that South

Dakota would allow for limited partnerships of foreign investors with domestic farmers.[126] As a result, South Dakota currently has enterprises fully owned and operated by foreign investors, as well as limited partnerships.

Since the regional designation took effect, South Dakota has attracted 60 foreign investors to its dairy industry (with an additional 10 applications still pending).[127] These foreign investors have injected approximately $30 million into the South Dakota economy, with an additional $6 million in matching funds coming from local farmers. Furthermore, this combined $36 million in invested funds has resulted in almost $90 million in bank financing for the various dairy investment projects. As a direct consequence of these foreign investments, 240 additional jobs have been created and 20,000 additional cows have been brought to South Dakota.[128] Using the RIMS II multipliers for investment and employment,[129] the foreign investments from EB-5 immigrants have resulted in a total of 638 additional jobs and over $360 million in additional funds to the regionally targeted economy.

According to SDIBI/DEDR Director Joop Bollen, the pilot program has afforded South Dakota “a tremendous opportunity,” not only because of the direct investments and multiplier effects, but because of the other investments made by the foreign investors.[130] According to Director Bollen, the attraction of foreign investors has had significant spillover effects into the restaurant and meat packing industries. As a result, SDIBI/DEDR hopes to focus on attracting additional investments for its meat packing plants. As such, Director Bollen stated that it was of paramount concern to the SDIBI/DEDR that USCIS have sufficient resources to quickly adjudicate EB-5 immigrant visa petitions. If the adjudication process is too long, Director Bollen stated, then the opportunity cost may make a South Dakota dairy investment unappealing to foreign investors.[131]

CanAm Enterprises

CanAm Enterprises is a private financial advising group which serves to structure, promote and administer the Philadelphia Industrial Development Center (PIDC) Regional Center.[132] The group works in conjunction with the City of Philadelphia through the PIDC to facilitate the city development (mainly in the city’s shipyard area) and provide investor credibility. This public/private partnership was developed to aid the transition of Philadelphia from a manufacture-based to a service based economy.[133] The main strategy has been to use collateralized loans to attract investments in industries that provide long-term full time employment. By doing so the city hopes that investors will wish to invest in other projects and sectors of the city’s economy.[134]

When the Philadelphia Naval Base was closed as part of the base closures of the 1970s, the base was handed over to the PIDC for transformation to civilian use. Despite the city’s efforts the shipyard was unable to remain competitive in the ship construction industry.[135] However, with the passage of requirements following the Exxon Valdez oil spill[136] (and the ongoing regulations from the Jones-Shafroth Act),[137] the civilian shipbuilding industry in the United States became economically viable again.[138] The federal government and the city of Philadelphia combined to invest over $400 million into the Philadelphia shipyard. Additionally Norwegian shipbuilding companies were brought in as investors in the shipyard and provided valuable training and human capital to the shipyard. Since production restarted, EB-5 investors have become increasingly important for providing funds to remove production bottlenecks. A recent example includes the use of EB-5 funds for the development of a more advanced painting technology for the ships.[139]

Philadelphia is one of the Regional Centers that has been most successful in attracting foreign investors through the EB-5 visa. There are approximately 60 EB-5 visa investors in Philadelphia who have invested a total of $75 million into the city.[140] Additionally, there are around 30 petitions that are under review for other investment projects. The lead official at CanAm Enterprises told CRS that while they believe the funds have been important to the city, the human capital the investors bring is equally important. This official stated that the investors being brought to the United States represented highly competent entrepreneurs, who not only made investments in the city beyond their initial investment, but also facilitated greater economic activity through exchanges with their existing foreign networks.[141]

End Notes

[1] P.L. 110-329, §144.

[2] 43 Stat 153.

[3] INA §101(a)(15)(e)(ii).

[4] INA §101(a)(15)(e).

[5] The two basic types of legal aliens are *immigrants* and *nonimmigrants*. As defined in the INA, immigrants are synonymous with legal permanent residents (LPRs) and refer to foreign nationals who come to live lawfully and permanently in the United States. The other major class of legal aliens are nonimmigrants—such as tourists, foreign students, diplomats, temporary agricultural workers, exchange visitors, or intracompany business personnel—who are admitted for a specific purpose and a temporary period of time. Nonimmigrants are required to leave the country when their visas expire, though certain classes of nonimmigrants may adjust to LPR status if they otherwise qualify.

[6] P.L. 101-649.

[7] INA §203(b)(5).

[8] P.L. 108-156, 8 USC §1324a note.

[9] The INA provides for a permanent annual worldwide level of 675,000 legal permanent residents (LPRs), but this level is flexible and certain categories of LPRs are permitted to exceed the limits, as described below. The permanent worldwide immigrant level consists of the following components: family-sponsored immigrants, including immediate relatives of U.S. citizens and family-sponsored preference immigrants (480,000 plus certain unused employment-based preference numbers from the prior year); employment-based preference immigrants (140,000 plus certain unused family preference numbers from the prior year); and diversity immigrants (55,000). Immediate relatives of U.S. citizens as well as refugees and asylees who are adjusting status are exempt from direct numerical limits. For further discussion, see CRS Report RL32235, *U.S. Immigration Policy on Permanent Admissions*, by Ruth Ellen Wasem.

[10] The INA provides that each category of immigrants has a set of preferences for the classes within that category. These preferences determine the priority of visa distribution for each category depending on certain formulas provided for in the INA. In the case of the LPR investor visa, being the fifth preference (and therefore the lowest) within the employment-based category, it has an annual maximum visa allocation of 10,000.

[11] 3 Charles Gordon, Stanley Mailman, and Stephen Yale-Loehr, *Immigration Law and Procedure*, § 39.07 (Matthew Bender, Rev. Ed.).

[12] For debate on this issue, see *Congressional Record,* vol. 136 (July 12, 1990), pp. S7768-S7775.

[13] The West Group. *New Pilot Program for Immigrant Investors*. 70 Interpreter Releases 1129. August 30, 1993.

[14] P.L. 101-649.

[15] This visa category is for permanent immigrants and should not be confused with the E-2 Treaty Investor nonimmigrant visa.

[16] Since 2002, applicants have also been allowed to invest funds in "troubled businesses." These businesses must have been in existence for at least two years, and must have incurred a net loss of at least 20% of the business' net worth (prior to the loss) during the twelve- or twenty-four-month period prior to filing the petition (8 CFR §204.6(e)).

[17] These funds must be demonstrated to have been obtained lawfully. Generally, any burden of proof to show qualifying status for an EB-5 lies with the applicant (8 CFR §204.6(j)).

[18] Depositing the funds into a corporate account does not qualify as making the investment "at risk." Clear guidelines for demonstrating that the capital is "at risk" do not exist in the regulations (8 CFR §204.6(j)).

[19] "Targeted areas" are either rural areas or areas with unemployment rates of at least 150% of the national average. A "rural area" is defined as one not within a metropolitan statistical area or the outer boundary of a city or town with a population of 20,000 or more.

[20] 8 CFR §204.6(f).

[21] INA §203(b)(5).

[22] 8 CFR §204.6(j).

[23] 8 CFR §204.6(g).

[24] This latter criterion may be demonstrated through board membership, status as a corporation officer, or qualifying as a limited partner under the Uniform Limited Partner Act (ULPA) (8 CFR §204.6(i)).

[25] 8 CFR § 206.6.

[26] A Regional Center is defined as any economic unit, public or private, engaged in the promotion of economic growth, improved regional productivity, job creation and increased domestic capital investment.

[27] FDI is defined as an investment made by a foreign individual or company in an enterprise residing in an economy other than where the foreign direct investor is based.

[28] The basic requirements for Regional Center designation state that applicants must show how their proposed program will:

- focus on a geographic region (8 CFR 204.6(m)(3)(i));
- promote economic growth through increased export sales, if applicable;
- promote improved regional productivity (8 CFR 204.6(m)(3)(i));
- create a minimum of 10 jobs directly or indirectly per investor (8 CFR 204.6(m)(3)(ii));
- increase domestic capital investment (8 CFR 204.6(m)(3)(i));
- be promoted and publicized to prospective investors (8 CFR 204.6(m)(3)(ii));
- have a positive impact on the regional or national economy through increased household earnings (8 CFR 204.6(m)(3)(iii)); and
- generate a greater demand for business services, utilities maintenance and repair, and construction jobs both in and around the center (8 CFR 204.6(m)(3)(iv)).

[29] These 5,000 visas represent a subset of the approximately 10,000 visas allocated for the LPR investor visa.

[30] USCIS does not publish an official list of the number of EB-5 Regional Centers that exist. However, in November 2007, USCIS released to the American Immigration Lawyers Association a list of regional centers that were "active" as of October 2007. This list included 20 active centers. The list is available at http://vkvisalaw.wordpress.com/2007/11/ 12/updated-list-of-eb-5-investor-visa-regional-centers-as-of-oct-2007/.

[31] P.L. 108-156.

[32] USCIS, *EB-5 Immigrant Investor Pilot Program, Background*, June, 2004.

[33] Ibid.

[34] Based on CRS discussions with Morrie Berez, Chief Adjudications Officer, USCIS Investor and Regional Center Program, November 20, 2006.

[35] According to the Department of State (DOS) *Visa Bulletin* (No. 111, Vol. VIII) there are backlogs only for all employment-based immigrants in the third preference categories, and for nationals of India and China in the second preference category. All other categories have numbers available for qualified applicants.

[36] U.S. Government Accountability Office, *Immigrant Investors: Small Number of Participants Attributed to Pending Regulations and Other Factors*, GAO-05-256, April 2005, pp. 8-11.

[37] Principals are the actual investors. Derivatives are comprised of spouses, children, and other dependents.

[38] The discrepancy between the petitions granted, denied, and received is due to some petitions remaining unadjudicated.

[39] "Conditional status" for an LPR immigrant means that the final approval of the LPR is contingent upon fulfilling certain requirements. For immigrant investors, the conditional status lasts for two years before the applicant is reviewed for final approval.

[40] The West Group, *Sections 203(b)(5) and 216A of the Immigration and Nationality Act*, 75 Interpreter Releases 332, March 9, 1998.

[41] P.L. 107-273.

[42] 3 Charles Gordon, Stanley Mailman, and Stephen Yale-Loehr, *Immigration Law and Procedure*, § 39.07 (Matthew Bender, Rev. Ed.)

[43] U.S. Government Accountability Office, *Immigrant Investors: Small Number of Participants Attributed to Pending Regulations and Other Factors*, GAO-05-256, April 2005, pp. 8-11.

[44] Mailman, Stanley, and Stephen Yale-Loehr. "Immigrant Investor Green Cards: Rise of the Phoenix?" *New York Law Journal*, April 25, 2005. At http://www.millermayer.com/EB5NYLJ0405.html, visited January 23, 2007.

[45] Of these investors, 247 (or 38%) applied for U.S. citizenship.

[46] The fact that they qualified for LPR status means that they had successfully maintained their business and 10 full-time qualifying employees for more than two years.

[47] GAO's report stated it could not provide reliable figures on the number of jobs created by these enterprises.

[48] §101(a)(15)(E)(i) of the Immigration and Nationality Act (INA).

[49] INA §101(a)(15)(E)(ii).

[50] 8 CFR §214.2(e)(6).

[51] 2 Charles Gordon, Stanley Mailman, and Stephen Yale-Loehr, *Immigration Law and Procedure*, § 17.06[2][a] (Matthew Bender, Rev. Ed.).

[52] Spouses and child dependents are not subject to the same nationality requirements as they can be nationals of any country, regardless of whether that country has treaties with the United States or not.

[53] There is no set formula for determining whether a person's role is sufficient to qualify, but is determined on a case by case basis using a number of different factors. These factors normally include such considerations as salary, position, duties, degree of control, and the number of employees under the applicant's supervision.

[54] A nominal position (e.g. having the title of manager) or title is not sufficient grounds to qualify for an E-class visa. Individuals with highly specialized skills or knowledge pertinent to the employer's business may also qualify, although if the individual's skills are determined to be of only a specialized nature that person must qualify for an H-1B visa (for highly skilled professionals). An example of a skill that has been rejected by DOS as an essential skill is knowledge of a foreign language.

[55] 8 CFR §214.2(e)(2)(iii).

[56] This criterion is more salient in the cases of smaller companies since ownership is more constant and concentrated. Large publically traded companies are largely not saddled with having to demonstrate ownership by nationals.

[57] 8 CFR §214.2(e)(19).

[58] 8 CFR §214.2(e)(20).

[59] 8 CFR §214.2(e)(4).

[60] 8 CFR §214.2(e)(8).

[61] The rules on such incidental activities are quite flexible. The governing principle of such incidental activities is that the primary trade or investment activity remains paramount (see 9 FAM §41.40 n7 (Visa TL-872 February 20, 1975, i.e. prior to 1987 revision) and 9 FAM §41.11 n.3.1).

[62] 8 CFR §214.2(e)(8).

[63] Although technically being a "trader" category as opposed to an "investor" category, there is sufficient grounds for believing that the E-1 traders should be included with the other investor categories. Although their activities must be related to trade, they are still allowed to make investments in United States enterprises. Also, investor categories such as the LPR investor visa have previously held requirements that investments must positively effect export levels in the industry where an investment is occurring (USCIS, *EB-5 Immigrant Investor Pilot Program*, Background, June, 2004).

[64] The term "treaty merchant," for example, traces its roots at least back to the 1880 treaty with China to conduct trade (Treaty Between the United States and China, Concerning Immigration, November 17, 1880, art. I, 22 Stat. 826).

[65] 8 CFR §214.2(e)(2), as amended by 56 Fed. Reg. 10978, 10979 (1989).

[66] 8 CFR §214.2(e)(10).

[67] Ibid.

[68] Ibid.

[69] 8 CFR §214.2(e)(11).

[70] INA §101(a)(15)(E)(ii).

[71] 8 CFR §214.2(e)(3)(ii).

[72] Certain joint ventures have been deemed permissible by the United States, provided that each joint venture partner have veto power over decisions by the other partner.

[73] 8 CFR §214.2(e)(12).

[74] 8 CFR §214.2(e)(14).

[75] 9 FAM §41.51 n.10.4, as amended, TL:VISA-322 (October 10, 2001).

[76] Visa Bulletin, Vol. V, No. 20—Nonimmigrant Treaty Investors U.S. Department of State, Visa Office (1982).

[77] Ibid.

[78] 8 CFR §214.2(e)(15).

[79] 2 Charles Gordon, Stanley Mailman, and Stephen Yale-Loehr, *Immigration Law and Procedure*, § 17.06[3][c] (Matthew Bender, Rev. Ed.).

[80] Ibid.

[81] A special category of nonimmigrants classified as the E-3 visa has been established and is only available to nationals of Australia. Although agreed upon under the Australian Free Trade Agreement, the agreement itself contained no explicit immigration provision. Rather, the FY2005 supplemental appropriations for military operations in Iraq and Afghanistan (P.L. 109-16) included §501 creating the E-3 visa category. This visa permits the employment by any United States employer of a qualifying Australian national for a specialty occupation. Unlike the other E-class visas, the E-3 carries an annual cap which is currently set at 10,500. However, the other rules generally remain the same as E1 and E-2 visas, with admissions for two years and unlimited extensions for qualifying individuals. The E-3 resembles the H-1B-1 visa which allows for similar admissions of specialized workers from Chile and Singapore. After legislation was passed implementing the Chile and Singapore Free Trade Agreements (P.L. 108-77 and P.L. 108-78, respectively), these new laws carved out a portion of §101(a)(15)(H) of the INA for professional workers entering through the free trade agreements. Unlike the other H-1B requirements, H-1B-1 recipients are only required to be *specialized* workers as opposed to *highly specialized*. This visa category also differs from the E-3 visa in that it allows for an 18 month admission and carries an annual cap of 1,400 for Chilean nationals and 5,400 for nationals of Singapore. For further discussion on the E-3 and H-1B-1 visas, see CRS Report RL30498, *Immigration: Legislative Issues on Nonimmigrant Professional Specialty (H-1B) Workers*, by Ruth Ellen Wasem, and CRS Report RL32982, *Immigration Issues in Trade Agreements*, by Ruth Ellen Wasem.

[82] Admissions figures differ significantly from visa issuance figures because individuals may leave the United States and return on the same visa, as long as the visa is still valid. Thus, some individuals may be counted multiple times in the admissions data.

[83] According to the DHS Office of Immigration Statistics' *2005 Yearbook of Immigration Statistics*, in FY2005 there were 2,432,587 admissions of B-1 visa holders and 2,261,354 admissions for business purposes on visa waivers.

[84] Citizenship and Immigration Canada, "Business Immigrant Links: FAQs," March 31, 2007, at http://www.cic.gc.ca/ english/information/faq/immigrate/business/index.asp.

[85] Ibid.

[86] Ibid.

[87] Mailman, Stanley, and Stephen Yale-Loehr. "Immigrant Investor Green Cards: Rise of the Phoenix?" *New York Law Journal*, April 25, 2005. At http://www.millermayer.com/EB5NYLJ0405.html.

[88] U.S. Government Accountability Office, *Immigrant Investors: Small Number of Participants Attributed to Pending Regulations and Other Factors*, GAO-05-256, April 2005, pp. 8-11.

[89] Denton, Herbert H. "Canada Lures Hong Kong Immigrants: Well-Off Businessmen Willing to Invest Are Granted Special Status." *Washington Post*, March 8, 1986, pp. A11, A18.

[90] Ibid.

[91] Citizenship and Immigration Canada, "Business Immigrant Links: FAQs," March 31, 2007, at http://www.cic.gc.ca/ english/information/faq/immigrate/business/index.asp.

[92] Xenogiani, Theodora. "Migration Policy and Its Interactions with Aid, Trade and Foreign Direct Investment Policies: A Background Paper." *OECD Development Centre*, Working Paper No. 249, June, 2006.

[93] For a brief discussion, see Xenogiani, Theodora. "Migration Policy and Its Interactions with Aid, Trade and Foreign Direct Investment Policies: A Background Paper." *OECD Development Centre*, Working Paper No. 249, June, 2006, p.36.

[94] Ibid.

[95] For further discussion on immigration and trade, see CRS Report RL32982, *Immigration Issues in Trade Agreements*, by Ruth Ellen Wasem.

[96] This migratory pressure reduction should occur through the increased exports of unskilled labor-intensive goods, as well as the resulting fact-price equalization and subsequent convergence of wages.

[97] There exists the possibility that foreign investment and capital trade objectives of many investors are accomplished through multinational corporations. Under the construct of a multinational corporation, returns

to the investor are achieved through the foreign direct investment by the corporation and through the migration of managers and technical experts to facilitate production efficiency.

[98] For example, see Banerjee, Subhabrata Bobby, and Stephen Linstead, "Globalization, Multiculturalism and Other Fictions: Colonialism for the New Millennium?" *Organization*, vol. 8, no. 4 (2001), pp. 683-722.

[99] These costs may include tax shelters, government sponsored benefits, subsidies, and the like.

[100] Schiff, M. "How Trade, Aid, and Remittances Affect International Migration." World Bank Policy Research Working Paper No. 1376, Washington, DC, 1994.

[101] Xenogiani, Theodora. "Migration Policy and Its Interactions with Aid, Trade and Foreign Direct Investment Policies: A Background Paper." *OECD Development Centre*, Working Paper No. 249, June, 2006, p. 31-33.

[102] Ibid.

[103] A large majority of the issued visas have been to foreign nationals from relatively capital abundant countries.

[104] For further discussion of FDI into the United States, see CRS Report RS21857, *Foreign Direct Investment in the United States: An Economic Analysis*, by James K. Jackson.

[105] FDI does entail some degrees of risk and reward for both the home and host economies. For the home economy, FDI can improve competitiveness and performance of firms by providing value-added activities, better employment opportunities, better export performance, and higher national income. At the same time, engaging in FDI also runs the risks of lower additions to both domestic investment and capital stock, as well as loss of competitiveness and jobs in certain parts of the economy. For the host economies, the benefits include increases in employment and potential multiplier effects on other parts of the economy through productivity growth. Accepting FDI, however, does run the risk that domestic firms are crowded out of the market (United Nations *World Investment Report*, 2006).

[106] From the classical economic perspective, the immigrant investor pilot program is counter-intuitive. In the case of investors from developed countries there is little incentive for them to settle in the United States since they can achieve similar standards of living and all of their FDI objectives from their home country. As for LEDCs, a drain of their capital may provide short-term benefits to the United States, but would inhibit growth and trade in the long run. The flight of investors from Hong Kong in the late-1980s and the 1990's was a unique economic situation that has since subsided. Other than the Hong Kong scenario, there is seemingly little incentive for investors to relocate.

[107] The complementary roles would be achieved through what economists refer to as "comparative advantage." Theoretically, each country should be able to produce a good or service more efficiently than the world average, thereby making the good or service exportable. By attracting investments in these comparatively advantaged sectors, costs should decrease while production increases. Thus, consumers at both ends of a trading relationship are able to consume more goods.

[108] Xenogiani, Theodora. "Migration Policy and Its Interactions with Aid, Trade and Foreign Direct Investment Policies: A Background Paper." *OECD Development Centre*, Working Paper No. 249, June, 2006, p. 31-33.

[109] CRS Report RL32649, *U.S.-Japan Economic Relations: Significance, Prospects, and Policy Options*, by William H. Cooper.

[110] Ibid.

[111] Ibid.

[112] For an explanation of the RIMS II multiplier, see U.S. Department of Commerce, *Regional Multipliers: A User Handbook for the Regional Input-Output Modeling System (RIMS II)*, Third Edition, March, 1997.

[113] According to the USCIS Chief Adjudications Officer for EB-5 visas, well established input-output models such as RIMS II are useful in assessing investments for limited partnerships, where the direct effects of an investment are difficult to demonstrate (based on CRS discussions with Morrie Berez, Chief Adjudications Officer, USCIS Investor and Regional Center Program, November 20, 2006). Such established economic models are permitted under regulations (8 CFR 204.6(m)(3)).

[114] A recent study commissioned by the National Venture Capital Association found that over the past 15 years, immigrants have started 15% of venture-backed U.S. public companies. The value of these companies currently exceeds $500 billion, and most of the companies were in technology-related industries. The study found that these companies employ 220,000 people in the United States, and 400,000 globally. Some of the more prominent companies included by the study's criteria include Google, Yahoo!, eBay, and Intel (Stuart Anderson and Michael Platzer, *American Made: The Impact of Immigrant Entrepreneurs and Professionals on U.S. Competitiveness*, National Venture Capital Association, November 15, 2006, pp. 5-8). Although the study shows the potential benefits of immigrant entrepreneurs, it does not directly reflect on the investor visa categories. Most of the immigrants that founded these enterprises came to the United States as children, teenagers, graduate students, or were hired on H-1B visas in their mid-twenties. Thus, it is unclear to what

extent these individuals would have qualified as either immigrant or nonimmigrant investors under the current regulations. Furthermore, the study's findings includes numbers from both companies wholly founded by immigrants and companies founded through partnerships with United States citizens (Ibid).

[115] Some have expressed concern regarding the investor visas being a means for some foreign nationals to channel illegal funds into the United States. Opponents of the LPR investor visa raised objections during congressional debates by asserting that the LPR investor category would allow individuals to become United States citizens who had profited from drug cartels. According to DHS, there does exist documented past abuses in the alien investor program (U.S. Government Accountability Office, *Immigrant Investors: Small Number of Participants Attributed to Pending Regulations and Other Factors*, GAO-05-256, April 2005, pp. 39.). However, since the implementation of the "no promissory notes" policy, the fraudulent cases have largely disappeared.

[116] Based on CRS discussions with Morrie Berez, Chief Adjudications Officer, USCIS Investor and Regional Center Program, November 20, 2006.

[117] Ibid.

[118] This practice has made it especially difficult for investors from countries with business practices based on convention (as opposed to legal documentation) to qualify for investor visas. Documentation requirements may force a potential investor to trace funds back several decades, effectively disqualifying investors from countries where credible historical records of income tax documents do not exist (Wolfsdorf, Bernard P., Naveen Rahman-Bhora, Tien-Li Loke Walsh, and Kim Tran. "A Review of the Immigrant Investor Program." Immigration Law Today, July/August, 2006, pp. 27-33).

[119] Lincoln Stone, *INS Decisions Cloud Future of Investor Pilot Program*, 6 Bender's Immigration Bulletin 233 (March 1, 2001).

[120] Rep. Sensenbrenner wrote a letter to USCIS Director Eduardo Aguirre on April 6, 2005 asking the USCIS to institute premium processing and concurrent filing for immigrant investor petitions (Mailman, Stanley, and Stephen Yale-Loehr. "Immigrant Investor Green Cards: Rise of the Phoenix?" *New York Law Journal*, April 25, 2005. At http://www.millermayer.com/EB5NYLJ0405.html, visited January 23, 2007.).

[121] Letter from Lincoln Stone, Chair of the Investor Committee of the American Immigration Lawyers Association, to Michael Aytes, USCIS Acting Associate Director of Operations, November 16, 2005.

[122] Lincoln Stone, the Chair of the Investor Committee of the American Immigration Lawyers Association, noted the generated level of capital in four targeted areas. According to an informal survey Stone had conducted of four targeted centers (California Consortium for Agricultural Export, Philadelphia Investment Development Corporation, Golden Rainbow Freedom Fund, and South Dakota international Business Institute), these centers had attracted $121.3 million in capital in their two-year existence (Letter from Lincoln Stone, Chair of the Investor Committee of the American Immigration Lawyers Association, to Michael Aytes, USCIS Acting Associate Director of Operations, November 16, 2005.).

[123] U.S. Congress, Senate Committee on the Judiciary, Promoting Job Creation and Foreign Investment in the United States: An Assessment of the EB-5 Regional Center Program, hearing on S.Amdt. 1407 to H.R. 2892, 111th Cong., 1st sess., July 22, 2009.

[124] For example, see H.R. 4321.

[125] Based on CRS discussion with Joop Bollen, Director of the South Dakota International Business Institute, November 28, 2006.

[126] Letter from William R, Yates, Associate Director of USCIS Office of Operations, to Joop Bollen, Director of the South Dakota International Business Institute, June 11, 2005.

[127] Based on CRS discussion with Joop Bollen, Director of the South Dakota International Business Institute, November 28, 2006.

[128] Ibid.

[129] For the South Dakota targeted region, the RIMS II multipliers are 2.9 for investment and 2.66 for employment.

[130] Based on CRS discussion with Joop Bollen, Director of the South Dakota International Business Institute, November 28, 2006.

[131] Ibid.

[132] On April 26, 2008, CanAm published a press release stating: "CanAm Enterprises, LLC is pleased to introduce the Los Angeles Film Regional Center, which was designated by USCIS on March 24, 2008, and will specifically target investments in the motion picture and television industry in Los Angeles County, California." (CanAm Enterprises, "CanAm Introduces the LA Film Regional Center," Press release, April 26, 2008, available at http://eb5dvd.com/ news.php?inc=3&nid=59.

[133] Based on CRS discussions with Tom Rosenfeld, President & CEO, CanAm Enterprises, November 28, 2006.

[134] Ibid.

[135] Based on CRS discussions with Tom Rosenfeld, President & CEO, CanAm Enterprises, November 28, 2006.

[136] P.L. 101-380.

[137] The Jones-Shafroth Act is a section of the Merchant Marine Act of 1920 (46 U.S.C. 883; 19 CFR 4.80 and 4.80b). Designed to protect the United States shipping fleet, the law requires that cargo moving between U.S. ports be carried by ships that are built in the United States and at least 75% owned by American citizens or corporations.

[138] Based on CRS discussions with Tom Rosenfeld, President & CEO, CanAm Enterprises, November 28, 2006.

[139] Ibid.

[140] Ibid.

[141] Ibid.

In: U.S. Visa Policies, Programs and Considerations
Editor: Aaron R. Miller
ISBN: 978-1-61470-333-4

Chapter 6

DHS's Visa Security Program Needs to Improve Performance Evaluation and Better Address Visa Risk Worldwide*

United States Government Accountability Office

Why GAO Did this Study

Since 2003, the Department of Homeland Security's (DHS) Visa Security Program (VSP) has participated in the visa process by reviewing applications at some embassies and consulates, with the intention of preventing individuals who pose a threat from entering the United States. The attempted bombing of an airline on December 25, 2009, renewed concerns about the security of the visa process and the effectiveness of the VSP. For this report GAO assessed (1) the ability of DHS's Immigration and Customs Enforcement (ICE) to measure the program's objectives and performance, (2) challenges to VSP operations, and (3) ICE efforts to expand the VSP program. To evaluate the VSP, we reviewed VSP data, guidance, and the ICE's 5-year expansion plan. We also interviewed ICE officials, and observed VSP operations at 6 posts overseas.

What GAO Recommends

GAO made several recommendations designed to address weaknesses we identified in the VSP. DHS concurred with the recommendations that the VSP provide consular officer training and develop a plan to provide more VSP coverage at high-risk posts. DHS did not concur with the recommendations that the VSP collect comprehensive data on all performance measures and track the time spent on visa security activities. GAO continues to maintain that these recommendations are necessary to accurately assess VSP performance.

---

* This is an edited, reformatted and augmented version of the United States Government Accountability Office publication, Report to the Committee on Homeland Security and Government Affairs, United States Senate, GAO-11-315, dated March 2011.

What GAO Found

ICE cannot accurately assess progress toward its VSP objectives. ICE outlined three primary objectives of the VSP—identifying and counteracting potential terrorist threats from entering the United States, identifying not-yet-known threats, and maximizing law enforcement and counterterrorism value of the visa process—and established performance measures intended to assess VSP performance, including situations where VSP agents provide information that results in a consular officer's decision to deny a visa. ICE's VSP tracking system, used to collect data on VSP activities, does not gather comprehensive data on all the performance measures needed to evaluate VSP mission objectives. In addition, data collected by ICE on VSP activities were limited by inconsistencies. ICE upgraded its VSP tracking system in April 2010 to collect additional performance data, but the system still does not collect data on all the performance measures. Therefore, ICE's ability to comprehensively evaluate the performance of the VSP remains limited. While ICE can provide some examples demonstrating the success of VSP operations, ICE has not reported on the progress made toward achieving all VSP objectives.

Several challenges to the implementation of the VSP affected operations overseas. DHS and the Department of State (State) have issued some guidance, including several memorandums of understanding, to govern VSP operations. However, some posts experienced difficulties because of the limited guidance regarding interactions between State officials and VSP agents, which has led to tensions between the VSP agents and State officials at some posts. In addition, most VSP posts have not developed standard operating procedures for VSP operations, leading to inconsistency among posts. Additionally, the mandated advising and training of consular officers by VSP agents varies from post to post, and at some posts consular officers received no training. Finally, VSP agents perform a variety of investigative and administrative functions beyond their visa security responsibilities that sometimes slow or limit visa security activities, and ICE does not track this information in the VSP tracking system, making it unable to identify the time spent on these activities.

In 2007, ICE developed a 5-year expansion plan for the VSP, but ICE has not fully followed or updated the plan. For instance, ICE did not establish 9 posts identified for expansion in 2009 and 2010. Furthermore, the expansion plan states that risk analysis is the primary input to VSP site selection, and ICE, with input from State, ranked visa-issuing posts by visa risk, which includes factors such as the terrorist threat and vulnerabilities present at each post. However, 11 of the top 20 high-risk posts identified in the expansion plan are not covered by the VSP. Furthermore, ICE has not taken steps to address visa risk in high-risk posts that do not have a VSP presence. Although the expansion of the VSP is limited by a number of factors, such as budgetary limitations or limited embassy space, ICE has not identified possible alternatives that would provide the additional security of VSP review at those posts that do not have a VSP presence.

Abbreviations

DHS	Department of Homeland Security
DS	Bureau of Diplomatic Security

ICE	Immigration and Customs Enforcement
MOU	memorandum of understanding
SAO	security advisory opinion
TECS	Treasury Enforcement and Communications System
VSP	Visa Security Program

March 31, 2011

The Honorable Joseph I. Lieberman
Chairman
The Honorable Susan M. Collins
Ranking Member
Committee on Homeland Security and Governmental Affairs
United States Senate

Since its establishment in 2002, following the September 2001 terrorist attacks on the United States, the Department of Homeland Security (DHS) has been responsible for the issuance of visa policy.1 In 2003, DHS implemented the Visa Security Program (VSP), and has since deployed DHS officials to certain U.S. embassies and consulates to strengthen the visa process by working with Department of State (State) officials in reviewing visa applications.2 However, the attempted bombing of Northwest Airlines flight 253 on December 25, 2009, by a Nigerian citizen in possession of a valid U.S. visa renewed concerns about the security of the visa process.

In 2005, we reported on VSP activities in Saudi Arabia—at that time, the only country where DHS had implemented the program—and on the department's plans to expand the program to other countries.3 To help ensure effective management of the VSP and its expansion, we recommended that the Secretary of Homeland Security develop a strategic plan that includes, among other things, information on criteria for selecting locations for expansion. We also recommended that the Secretary maintain performance data that could be used to assess the program's impact at each post.4 In response to our recommendations, DHS's Immigration and Customs Enforcement (ICE), which oversees the program, developed a 5-year expansion plan and deployed a tracking system to capture performance data. As of December 2010, ICE had established VSP units at 19 posts in 15 countries.

In response to your request, this report (1) assesses the ability of DHS to measure the program's objectives and performance, (2) identifies potential challenges to VSP operations overseas, and (3) examines DHS efforts to expand the VSP program.

To conduct our evaluation, we reviewed relevant legislation, such as the Homeland Security Act of 2002, and documentation including internal guidance and interagency memorandums. To assess ICE's ability to measure the objectives and performance of the VSP, we reviewed the VSP mission objectives and performance measures identified by ICE. We also reviewed data from VSP's tracking system, and compared the data collected with the performance measures to identify the ability of ICE to assess its performance and progress toward the identified objectives. To evaluate the challenges to VSP operations, we reviewed the issued guidance governing the implementation of the VSP. We met with ICE and State officials in Washington, D.C., and interviewed VSP agents and consular officials, via telephone and e-mail, at 13 VSP posts that were operational as of April 2010 to identify some VSP operational challenges. We also visited six U.S. embassies and consulates with VSP operations to observe VSP operations. To assess ICE's efforts to expand the VSP, we reviewed the VSP 5-year expansion plan and compared the expansion with the plan. We also reviewed the criteria for the selection of posts identified for expansion. We also interviewed ICE and State officials regarding the expansion plan and the challenges of expanding the VSP.

We conducted this performance audit from March 2010 through March 2011 in accordance with generally accepted government auditing standards. Those standards require that we plan and perform the audit to obtain sufficient, appropriate evidence to provide a reasonable basis for our findings and conclusions based on our audit objectives. We believe that the evidence obtained provides a reasonable basis for our findings and conclusions based on our audit objectives.

BACKGROUND

Legislative Authority for the Visa Security Program

The Homeland Security Act of 2002 established DHS and gave the agency responsibility for visa policy. Specifically, the act granted DHS the authority to issue regulations on, administer, and enforce the Immigration and Nationality Act and other immigration and nationality laws relating to the functions of U.S. consular officers in connection with the granting and denial of visas. Section 428 of the act also authorized DHS to immediately assign personnel to Saudi Arabia to review all visa applications prior to final adjudication, and authorized DHS to assign officers to other locations overseas to review visa applications. Section 428 designated the following functions for DHS officers assigned overseas:

1. provide expert advice and training to consular officers regarding specific security threats relating to the adjudication of individual visa applications or classes of applications,
2. review visa applications either on the initiative of the employee of the department or at the request of a consular officer, or other persons charged with adjudicating such applications, and
3. conduct investigations with respect to consular matters under the jurisdiction of the Secretary of Homeland Security.

Establishment of the Visa Security Program

DHS designated ICE to handle the operational and policy-making responsibilities outlined in section 428 in January 2004. Subsequently, ICE established the Office of International Affairs and gave it responsibility for overseeing the Visa Security Program. Figure 1 shows the organization of the Visa Security Program within DHS.

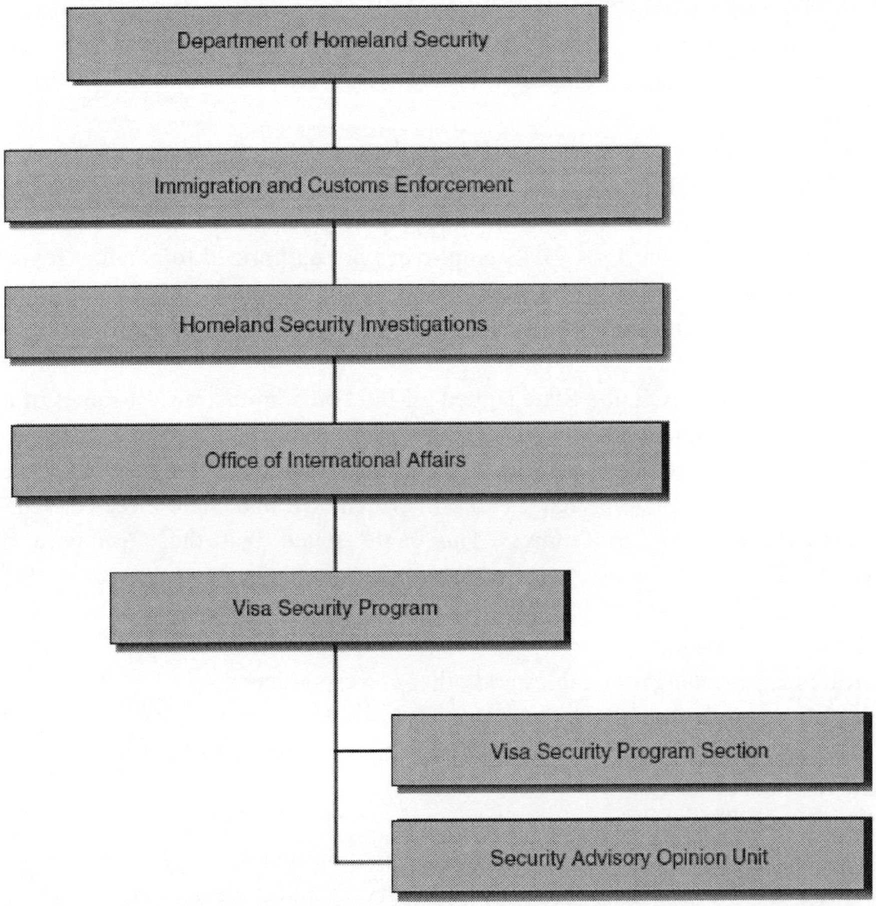

Source: GAO analysis of DHS documents.

Figure 1. Organizational Chart of DHS and the VSP.

Primary Guidance Governing Visa Security Program Operations

Since the establishment of the Visa Security Program, ICE and State have issued four primary forms of guidance governing VSP operations overseas: (1) a 2003 memorandum of understanding (MOU) concerning implementation of the Homeland Security Act; (2) a 2004 MOU on administrative aspects of assigning personnel overseas; (3) a 2008 cable directing State Bureau of Diplomatic Security (DS) officers,[5] VSP agents, and the senior consular officer at each post to develop standard operating procedures; and (4) a 2011 MOU delineating the roles and responsibilities of VSP agents, consular officers, and diplomatic security officers in daily operations of VSP at posts overseas.

2003 MOU. In 2003, DHS and State issued a memorandum of understanding to govern the implementation of section 428. In accordance with the legislation, the memorandum outlined the following responsibilities of DHS officers assigned to posts overseas to perform visa duties:

- *Advising and training consular officers.* DHS employees are to provide expert advice to consular officers regarding specific security threats relating to visa adjudication and provide training to consular officers on terrorist threats and detecting applicant fraud.
- *Reviewing visa applications.* DHS employees have the authority to review visa applications on their own initiative or at the request of consular officers, and provide input on or recommend security advisory opinion requests.
- *Conducting investigations.* DHS employees are authorized to conduct investigations on consular matters under the jurisdiction of the Secretary of Homeland Security, as well as conduct and support investigations under other DHS authorities.

2004 MOU. In 2004, ICE and State signed a MOU on administrative aspects of assigning personnel overseas. Among other things, this MOU described administrative support, security, facilities, security awareness training, and information systems for VSP personnel.

2008 cable. In 2008, State issued a cable in which ICE and State directed VSP posts to develop standard operating procedures. The cable stated that these standard operating procedures should include, but not be limited to,

- chain of command;
- clearance procedures for cables and other correspondence;
- dispute resolution practices;
- specific coordination procedures among the fraud prevention unit, VSP agents, and the regional security officer;
- procedures for determining case selection;
- specific hours of operation and other coordination issues;
- stating how electronic reviews will be conducted and documented;
- stating how physical reviews will be conducted and documented;
- coordination of procedures for handling expedited or exceptional visa cases;
- procedures for sharing and documenting applicant information constituting grounds for ineligibility; and
- procedures for VSP applicant interviews and re-interviews.

2011 MOU. On January 11, 2011, ICE and State issued a MOU that explains the roles, responsibilities, and collaboration of VSP agents, consular officers, and diplomatic security officers in daily operations of VSP at posts overseas. The MOU outlines the following, among other things:

- general collaboration between ICE and State for VSP operations;
- roles and responsibilities of VSP agents and consular officers and routine interaction between the officers and agents;
- development of formal, targeted training and briefings by VSP agents for consular officers and other U.S. government officials at post;
- clarification of the dispute resolution process; and
- collaboration between diplomatic security officers and VSP agents on visa and passport fraud investigations.

Visa Adjudication Process

The review of visa applications by VSP agents is incorporated into the visa process at overseas posts where the VSP is located. After consular officers interview an applicant and review the relevant supporting documentation, they make a preliminary determination about whether to issue or refuse the visa or refer the case to Washington for additional security clearances.[6] The VSP agents screen the applicant information against DHS's Treasury Enforcement and Communications System (TECS) database to identify applicants that potentially match records of individuals who are known threats to the United States.[7] The VSP agents then perform a vetting process on a smaller number of applications, based upon a threat-based targeting plan. During vetting, the VSP agents perform checks against additional law enforcement and other databases, and review the applications and supporting documentation for evidence of fraud or misrepresentation, indicators of potential national security risks, criminal activity, and potential illegal immigration risks. During the review, the VSP agents may also consult consular officers and other law enforcement officials as needed. On the basis of these reviews, the VSP agents will either agree with the consular officer's original decision or recommend refusal of the visa. The consular officer decides to issue or deny the visa.[8] If the consular section chief and the VSP agents disagre e on a case, a dispute resolution process is started to render a final determination of the application.

Several other agencies stationed overseas have roles in the visa process. For example, State regional security officers assist the consular section by investigating passport and visa fraud detected through the consular officers' reviews of visa applications and supporting documents. In addition, officials from the Federal Bureau of Investigation overseas can assist consular officers when questions about an applicant's potential criminal history arise during adjudication. DHS's Bureaus of Citizenship and Immigration Services and Customs and Border Protection have responsibility for some immigration and border security programs overseas. For example, consular officers may seek advice from these officials on issues such as DHS procedures at U.S. ports of entry.

Expansion Plan for the Visa Security Program

ICE's 5-year plan for expanding the VSP, which ICE released in consultation with State in 2007, states that global visa risk is substantial and that the VSP must be expanded in order to mitigate threats identified through the visa process and to address visa risk. The plan also includes the following principles to guide the program's expansion:

- concentrate expansion on risk by deploying personnel sooner to the highest-risk visa-issuing locations;
- develop a global capacity by expanding to select high-risk posts in diverse regions; and
- cover the highest-risk visa activity while incorporating dynamic conditions such as funding, personnel, and logistical issues such as the availability of space.

The 5-year plan also includes the following site selection methodology to inform the expansion process:

- *Initial quantitative risk analysis*. ICE and State developed a list of 216 visa-issuing locations that are ranked according to risk. The underlying analysis incorporates information on terrorist activity, DHS enforcement and removals, host government circumstances, corruption, visa activity, and several other factors.
- *Interagency and interdepartmental consultation*. Throughout the site selection process, ICE coordinates with State, law enforcement and intelligence communities, and other components of DHS. This coordination helps to establish mutual understanding among interested parties and to inform and refine the decision-making process.
- *Site assessments*. ICE selects a smaller number of locations for on-site assessments to further improve communication and gather information about local conditions at post.
- *Final evaluation and selection*. Using all of the information gathered, ICE makes a final evaluation and selection for new VSP unit locations.

Figure 2 shows a timeline for the establishment of the VSP and the expansion of the program. As of December 2010, ICE had established VSP units at 19 posts in 15 countries.

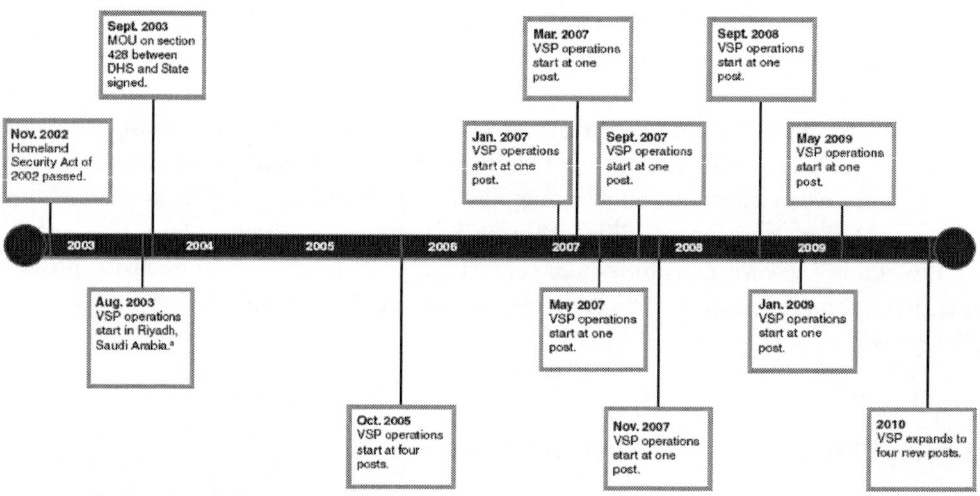

Note: Locations are not specified for security reasons.
[a] VSP operations start at other posts in Saudi Arabia in October 2003.
Source: GAO analysis of DHS documents.

Figure 2. Timeline for the Establishment and Expansion of the VSP.

Visa Security Program Funding

For fiscal years 2007 through 2010, ICE reported that approximately $94 million in appropriated funds was allotted for the Visa Security Program. Of these amounts, in fiscal years 2009 and 2010, Congress specified that $6.8 million and $7.3 million, respectively, would remain available for 1 additional year. In fiscal year 2010, the Visa Security Program received $30.7 million in appropriated funds, and the agency requested $30.7 million in the fiscal year 2011 budget request.

ICE REMAINS UNABLE TO ACCURATELY MEASURE THE PERFORMANCE OF THE VISA SECURITY PROGRAM

ICE does not maintain comprehensive performance data to accurately evaluate progress toward all VSP mission objectives. In 2007, ICE outlined three primary objectives of the Visa Security Program in its 5-year expansion plan and identified and established performance measures intended to assess performance toward the stated objectives. However, the initial VSP tracking system did not gather data on all the performance measures and mission objectives identified in the VSP expansion plan. Although ICE upgraded the VSP tracking system in April 2010 to collect additional performance data, the system still does not collect data on all the performance measures, hampering ICE's efforts to comprehensively evaluate the performance of the VSP. While ICE can provide some examples demonstrating the success of VSP operations, ICE has not produced reports identifying the progress made toward achieving VSP objectives. In addition, data collected by ICE on VSP activities prior to 2010 were limited by inconsistencies.

ICE Unable to Accurately Assess the Value of the VSP

From 2003 to 2010, ICE did not maintain comprehensive data on its identified performance measures to fully assess progress toward VSP objectives. As we reported in 2005, ICE did not maintain data on VSP activities in order to assess the program's performance since its establishment in 2003.[9] In the fall of 2005, in response to GAO recommendations, ICE developed a database to track VSP workload and to serve as a performance management tool. The initial VSP tracking system, which was operational until 2010, collected information on the results of the review of visa applications by VSP agents, including tracking the number of visas screened, the number of visas vetted, and the number of visas recommended for denial by VSP agents.

While the initial tracking system allowed ICE to track VSP workload and assist with performance assessment, the VSP did not establish program objectives until 2007. The Government Performance and Results Act of 1993 requires agencies to develop objective performance goals and report on their progress.[10] In addition, GAO's *Standards for Internal Control in the Federal Government* state that U.S. agencies should monitor and evaluate the quality of performance over time.[11] ICE's 5-year expansion plan for the VSP, issued in 2007, identified three primary mission objectives to enhance national security and public safety:

1. identify and counteract threats before they reach the United States,
2. identify not-yet-known threats to homeland security, and
3. maximize the law enforcement and counterterrorism value of the visa process.

Furthermore, the expansion plan indicates that the program must measure its performance and demonstrate the value it contributes to homeland security, with mechanisms in place to adequately and accurately measure its performance. ICE identified six categories of performance measures to assess the progress toward the objectives of the program (see table 1):

Table 1. Objectives and Performance Measures of the Visa Security Program

VSP objective	VSP activities	Performance measures	Description
Identify and counteract threats before they reach the United States	Review of visa applications	1. Recommendations for refusal	Any instance in which a VSP agent provides input, advice, or information that results in a consular officer's decision to deny a visa to an ineligible applicant.
		2. Additional enforcement outputs	Represents the generation of additional law enforcement value, including terrorist watchlist entries, intelligence reports, investigative leads, andidentification of terrorist trends and tactics.
		3. Derogatory information removal	This measure reflects the removal of derogatory information by VSP agents that assists the travel of legitimate, eligible applicants.
Identify not-yet-known threats	Initiate investigations	4. Open/closed investigations	Captures the number of investigations opened and closed and the hours spent supporting domestic and foreign investigations.
Maximizing law enforcement and counterterrorism value	Advice and training	5. Consular and other training	Tracks the expert advice and training provided to consular officers.
	Information sharing and liaison	6. Assistance and liaison provided	Measure the ways in which VSP agents liaise with other law enforcement, intelligence, and host country officials.

Source: DHS 5-year expansion plan.

The VSP tracks and reports on activities through reports submitted regularly by VSP agents at overseas posts, through the activities recorded in the TECS database, and through the VSP tracking system. The VSP tracking system is used by ICE to monitor and report on performance of its VSP agents overseas.

While ICE developed a VSP tracking system before the expansion plan identified the VSP objectives in 2007, ICE did not modify the system to collect data related to the performance measures and objectives in the expansion plan. The initial VSP tracking system tracked the results of one of the six identified performance measures—the number of recommendations for refusal—and the system did not track the other five performance measures (see table 1). Furthermore, the initial VSP tracking system did not collect performance data to evaluate progress toward two of its overall objectives, identifying not-yet-known threats and maximizing law enforcement and counterterrorism value.

According to VSP officials, in April 2010, ICE implemented a new data tracking system intended, among other things, to better track performance, to better reflect the work performed by the VSP agents overseas, and to provide management with improved reports to better evaluate the VSP activities performed overseas. However, the new system does not collect performance data on three of the measures identified in the plan: (1) investigations opened or closed and hours spent supporting investigative activity, (2) consular and other training provided, and (3) assistance and liaison provided by VSP agents. Furthermore, while ICE has some information regarding the hours charged to VSP activities at posts, it cannot accurately determine the time VSP agents spend on nonVSP activities. An ICE official indicated that some activities are recorded outside of the VSP tracking system. For example, training for consular officers performed by VSP agents are often included in the weekly reports submitted to ICE. In addition, some of the liaison activities and assistance VSP agents provide to local law enforcement is captured in TECS and other DHS reports, such as search, arrest, and seizure reports. However, ICE does not track these activities systematically and cannot evaluate the comprehensive effort of these activities. ICE has requested upgrades to the VSP tracking system to capture additional data on training and liaison activities, but according to an ICE official, because of development delays, the system upgrades are not complete.

ICE Does Not Produce Reports Evaluating VSP Performance

ICE has reported on the results of some VSP activities, but these reports do not address all of the VSP performance measures and therefore do not show progress toward each of the VSP mission objectives. For example, ICE annual reports and DHS's performance report for fiscal years 2008 to 2010 address only one of the six VSP performance measures—the number of visa applications denied because of recommendations from VSP agents. For example, ICE reported that the VSP recommended refusal of more than 900 visa applications in fiscal year 2008. ICE has presented some anecdotal examples of VSP participation in the visa process. For example, in testimony in 2009, the Assistant Secretary of ICE stated that the review of a specific visa applicant revealed information that resulted in the denial of the applicant's visa on the basis of national security. However, because these reports do not address all VSP performance measures, they do not comprehensively show progress toward all of the VSP objectives identified in the expansion plan. According to ICE officials, the VSP reviews monthly statistical reports on the activities performed by the VSP agents at each post, which allows management to identify discrepancies in the VSP activities and eliminate potential errors in the system. According to ICE, reports and information from the VSP tracking system are routinely used to inform budget decisions as well as other resource decisions including permanent and temporary duty staffing of VSP posts.

VSP Data Collected at Posts Have Not Been Reliable

VSP data collected through the initial tracking system are significantly limited by inconsistencies. As we reported in 2005, ICE had not maintained measurable data to fully demonstrate the impact of VSP agents on the visa process.

We have reported that for agencies to be able to assess progress toward performance goals, the performance measures, and the quality of the data supporting those measures, must be reliable and valid.[12] Our analysis of VSP data collected at posts in fiscal years 2007 to 2010 identified significant limitations to the data's reliability. For example, at one post the data recorded for the category "sum of post-adjudication: vetted" rose from 1,630 applications in fiscal year 2007 to 28,856 in fiscal year 2008, and then decreased to 2,754 in fiscal year 2009. In addition, another post recorded in fiscal year 2007 that VSP agents screened and vetted over 13,000 applicants that received security advisory opinions, but recorded zero applicants in the security advisory opinion categories in any subsequent year. ICE officials indicated that ICE did not provide guidance to the VSP agents on the proper use of the tracking system, which likely resulted in inconsistent use of the system. Furthermore, according to an ICE official, the accuracy of the data in the tracking system is contingent upon VSP agents at post entering the data and using the system consistently across all posts. ICE officials acknowledged that turnover of VSP agents at many posts likely resulted in inconsistent use of the tracking system.

SEVERAL CHALLENGES AFFECT VISA SECURITY OPERATIONS OVERSEAS

The Visa Security Program faces several key challenges in implementing operations at overseas posts. First, limited guidance from headquarters regarding VSP operations has led to confusion and inconsistency among posts. Both VSP and consular officials indicated that ICE and State have issued limited official guidance about how VSP agents, consular officers, and DS officials should interact with one another at post or resolve disputes concerning specific visa applications. Second, VSP agents' advising and training of consular officers, as mandated by section 428 of the Homeland Security Act, varies from post to post, and some posts provided no training to consular officers. Third, VSP agents perform a variety of investigative and administrative functions beyond their visa security responsibilities, including criminal investigations, attaché functions, and regional responsibilities. Fourth, ICE's use of 30-day temporary duty assignments has created challenges and affected continuity of operations at some posts. Last, ICE does not provide language or country-specific training for its agents serving overseas, thereby limiting agents' ability to conduct interviews and coordinate with host country officials.

VSP and Consular Interaction Has Been Difficult at Some Posts, and ICE Has Provided Limited Guidance for Such Interaction

Some VSP posts reported difficulties in the interactions between VSP agents and consular officers at post, and ICE and State had provided limited guidance in this regard. During our visits to several posts in 2010, both VSP agents and consular officers at several posts we visited indicated that difficulties arose from confusion surrounding the VSP-consular relationship. For example, a consular official at one post stated that he does not know how to interact with the VSP agents or what to do with the information VSP agents provide on visa applicants, particularly when that information is insufficient to render an applicant ineligible for a visa. This official suggested State's Visa Office provide yearly guidance on the VSPconsular relationship and instructions on how to use information from the VSP tracking system reports. At another post, disagreement over how the consular section should share information with law enforcement agencies at post led to significant tension between VSP agents and DS officials. One consular official at this post stated that tension between VSP agents and DS officials at post sometimes prevents the consular section from receiving information in a timely manner. At a third post, the Consular Chief stated that VSP agents and consular officials rarely interacted with one another and that visa applications sometimes "disappeared" in the VSP unit. Consular officers at this post stated they did not understand the VSP's mission.

ICE had issued limited guidance for VSP-consular interaction. ICE guidance, including the 2003 joint DHS-State MOU and the 2008 cable, does not explicitly address VSP-consular interaction at posts. The 2003 MOU states that DHS, in consultation with State, will develop policies and procedures for DHS employees' overseas functions, but does not detail such policies. The 2008 cable directs VSP posts to develop standard operating procedures for a number of operational areas requiring interaction among VSP, consular officers, and DS officials, such as chain of command, dispute resolution practices, specific coordination procedures between VSP agents and State officials at post, and case selection procedures. However, the cable does not include guidelines for such procedures. The most recent ICE-State MOU, issued in January 2011, addresses roles, responsibilities, and collaboration at VSP posts abroad. Specifically, the new MOU provides additional information on routine interaction between VSP agents and consular officers at post. For example, it indicates that interviewing officers can request VSP screening prior to an interview, VSP can request cases to be put on hold for additional investigation, and the consular chief may ask VSP to expedite cases.

Most VSP Posts Have Not Developed Standard Operating Procedures

Most of the VSP posts had not developed written standard operating procedures as recommended by the 2008 ICE-State cable. Two of the 13 posts had developed written standard operating procedures, but those procedures did not include all of the components identified in the 2008 cable. Nine of the 13 consular sections and 13 of 13 VSP units reported having developed informal standard operating procedures, but the scope and content of these procedures varied widely. VSP agents at 1 post told us that they were waiting for the issuance of the 2011 MOU before developing standard operating procedures and hoped that the MOU would provide additional operational guidance. At 1 post, VSP agents said that they had declined to develop standard operating procedures with the consular section and told consular officials that headquarters did not want them to develop "post-specific" standard operating procedures.

The 2008 cable issued by ICE and State—intended to address consular concerns about the VSP, according to VSP officials—recommends that VSP posts develop standard operating procedures. The 2008 cable also directs regional security officers and VSP agents to work with consular officers to establish post-specific procedures to manage fraud investigations that comply with the 2003 MOU. However, VSP officials told us that they later instructed VSP agents to postpone development of post-specific standard operating procedures pending completion of the new MOU with State. The 2011 MOU states that ICE and State may develop post-specific standard operating procedures or other agreements regarding VSP operations, adding that these procedures may further refine, but must remain consistent with, the roles, responsibilities, and collaboration described in previous guidance.

At posts that had developed standard operating procedures, consular officers stated that these procedures had improved the VSP-consular relationship. For example, a VSP agent at 1 post developed standard operating procedures with both the consular section and DS officials. The standard operating procedures at this post address the timing of VSP screening and vetting activities, how much time those activities will take, and points of contact in each agency. One VSP agent at this post described the process of developing these standard operating procedures as "painless," and the Consular Chief at post indicated that the VSP agents' reviews of visa applications were helpful because they provided a second review of visa applicants. In addition, a State official at another post that had developed standard operating procedures stated that having written guidance is crucial to a good relationship and valuable for new consular officers.

Advising and Training Performed by VSP Agents Varies among Posts

Although the Homeland Security Act requires DHS to advise and train consular officers, VSP agents' training and advising of consular officers varies among posts. Section 428 of the Homeland Security Act directs VSP agents to provide "expert advice and training to consular officers regarding specific security threats relating to the adjudication of individual visa applications or classes of applications." In addition, the 2003 and 2011 MOUs also state that VSP agents will provide training to consular officers.

Five of the 13 consular sections we interviewed stated that they had received no training from the VSP agents in the last year, and none of the VSP agents we interviewed reported providing training on specific security threats. At posts where VSP agents provided formal training for consular officers, topics covered included fraudulent documents, immigration law, human smuggling, and interviewing techniques.[13] In addition, 6 of the 13 VSP agents interviewed provided introductory briefings to new consular officers during the past year, but the VSP agents at the other 7 posts did not provide these briefings. VSP agents at 3 posts stated that they do not have time to deliver advice and training to consular officers. At 1 post, VSP agents refused to allow consular officers to observe VSP screening and vetting activities on the ground that they did not have a law enforcement "need to know." At the embassy in Riyadh, consular officers generally agreed that the VSP agents do not provide advice and training and are not proactive in developing such programs. Additionally, Riyadh consular officers stated that the VSP agents do not advise them on the security situation, current trends, or types of information to collect to assist the agents.

During our site visits and interviews, consular officers at several posts stated that they do not understand either the VSP's mission, or what the VSP agents do, or what types of information they collect. Officers at 6 of 13 consular sections interviewed requested additional training on the VSP's procedures and activities. For example, in Riyadh, consular officers generally agreed that greater knowledge of VSP activities would inform their interviews of visa applicants. At 1 post the VSP agents provided lunchtime briefings on patterns or trends with implications for visa issuance, as well as an orientation for all new consular officers and allow consular officers to observe screening and vetting activities. The

Consular Chief at this post stated that the training was very useful to consular officers and provided a better appreciation for how the VSP operates.

Guidance for Visa Dispute Resolution Mechanism Has Not Helped Resolve Some VSP-Consular Disagreements

Although ICE and State have developed formal and informal procedures for resolving disputes about specific visas, both VSP and consular officials stated that these procedures are sometimes insufficient for resolving such disputes. Disagreement between VSP and consular officials about specific visa applications is generally infrequent, and posts usually resolve these disputes through informal discussions between VSP and consular officials. However, 4 of 6 posts we visited reported disagreements about specific visa cases that could not be resolved informally at the post, and that in some cases, unresolved disputes have led to tension at post.

ICE and State officials told us that the two agencies sometimes have different interpretations of visa law, such as criteria for ineligibility based on "fraud or misrepresentation" or "crimes of moral turpitude." VSP officials also told us that they sometimes disagree with consular officials as to what degree of "association" with a terrorist is sufficient to render an applicant ineligible for a visa. Further, according to State officials, ICE and State have differing understandings of the VSP's jurisdiction under the Homeland Security Act.

Although the 2003 MOU outlines a dispute resolution mechanism, both ICE and State officials told us in May 2010 that this mechanism is not sufficient. The 2003 MOU states, "If the chief of section or supervisory consular officer does not agree that the visa should be refused or revoked, the post will initiate a request for a security or other advisory opinion and the DHS employee will be consulted in its preparation." The MOU goes on to state that no advisory opinion will be issued thereafter without the full consultation of State and DHS. However, both VSP and consular officials told us that this process has not always worked well in practice and that security advisory opinions sometimes do not result in the resolution of the dispute. According to ICE and State officials, because the Secretary of Homeland Security has not delegated authority to refuse visas under section 428 of the Homeland Security Act, any irreconcilable dispute about a visa application ultimately must be elevated to the Secretary level for final resolution. ICE and State officials stated that to supplement this process, ICE and Consular Affairs officials at headquarters have sometimes used other informal methods to reach agreement on the adjudication of a visa. For example, ICE and State tried to resolve disagreements at the unit chief level when possible.

The 2011 MOU addresses some of these issues by specifying that posts can raise disputes to the Managing Director of the Visa Office and the Assistant Director of ICE Homeland Security Investigations–International Affairs and, subsequently, to the State Assistant Secretary for Consular Affairs and the Director of ICE.

VSP Agents' Performance of Nonconsular Activities Sometimes Constrains Visa Security Operations

In some cases, VSP agents' performance of activities unrelated to visa security has limited their ability to carry out visa security activities. VSP agents perform a variety of investigative and administrative functions in addition to their visa security workload, such as conducting nonconsular investigations, serving as ICE's official presence in the region, and performing the duties of DHS attachés. According to ICE officials, VSP agents perform non-VSP functions only after completing their visa security screening and vetting workload. However, both VSP agents and State officials at some posts told us that these other investigative and administrative functions sometimes slow or limit VSP agents' visa security-related activities.

Existing guidance for VSP agents' performance of other non-VSP functions is limited. Section 428 of the Homeland Security Act states that one of the functions of VSP employees assigned to overseas posts is to conduct investigations with respect to consular matters under the jurisdiction of the Secretary of Homeland Security. For example, VSP agents may uncover and follow up on leads as a result of their screening and vetting activities. While the 2003 MOU between DHS and State states that DHS employees may conduct investigations with regard to consular matters under the jurisdiction of the Secretary of Homeland Security, those officials shall not conduct investigations that are within the jurisdiction of the Bureau of Diplomatic Security or the State Inspector General. Furthermore, VSP agents have the same position description as other ICE agents and have the authority to perform a wide range of tasks unrelated to visa security, including the ability to investigate a wide range of cases within ICE's jurisdiction. For example, VSP agents pursue cases related to bulk cash smuggling or human rights violations. According to ICE officials, ICE has not issued formal guidance that dictates how VSP agents should spend their time. ICE officials told us that, in some cases, requests to VSP agents come directly from other agencies, not from ICE itself. The 2011 MOU states that the primary responsibility of VSP agents is visa security. However, the 2011 MOU acknowledges that ICE personnel perform functions of regional or worldwide scope related to the post where they are assigned and that VSP agents may be called upon to perform other functions in support of the consulate.

ICE officials told us that, at most Visa Security Program posts, the VSP units represent the only ICE presence at post, and that some VSP agents have ICE responsibilities for other countries in the region. ICE officials told us that VSP agents are frequently tasked with collateral requests to assist other ICE offices with investigations. For example, as part of an ongoing investigation into a U.S.-hosted Web site, one VSP agent assisted in the arrest of two individuals who were producing and distributing child pornography. VSP agents are also tasked with a variety of attaché functions, including serving as the liaison between ICE and other U.S. government agencies. For example, as the only DHS representative in Saudi Arabia, the VSP in Riyadh is also responsible for supporting the Coast Guard, Transportation Security Administration, official visitors, and detention and removal operations. In addition, the regional responsibilities of the VSP agent may require the agent to work on other investigations or respond to collateral requests in other countries in the region. At one post, VSP agents told us that these responsibilities were essentially nominal and involved very little additional work. In Riyadh, these regional responsibilities involved frequent travel throughout the region to perform other investigations.

ICE officials told us that agents pursue these other investigations only after completing Visa Security Program responsibilities. However, consular officers at some posts told us that these additional investigations interfered with completion of visa security work and made ICE agents less available to consular officers. For example, at one post, the VSP agent told us he was sometimes unable to complete his screening and vetting activities because of other ICE responsibilities. At another post, VSP agents worked alongside other ICE agents, and the VSP agent at this post told us he focused primarily on visa security work. In our interviews, VSP agents' estimates of the amount of time spent on nonvisa requests and investigations ranged from 5 percent to 40 percent. ICE does not track the time VSP agents spend on both its visa security activities and its nonvisa requests and investigations. While the VSP expansion plan identifies the hours spent performing investigations as a performance measure, ICE can not accurately determine the amount of time that VSP agents spend on investigative and visa security activities, as its systems do not distinguish between the time VSP agents and other ICE officials spend on investigations at post. Furthermore, the VSP tracking system does not collect data on the time VSP agents spend on visa security activities. ICE cannot identify the time VSP agents spend on visa security operations or on the other investigation and attaché functions performed by VSP agents stationed overseas.

VSP agents' additional investigations also overlap with consular and DS investigations at some posts, leading to confusion in the consular section. According to the 2008 joint ICE-State cable to VSP posts, VSP agents' responsibility to identify the potential exploitation of the visa process by terrorists frequently overlaps the responsibilities of consular units investigating fraud and criminal investigations. According to one State official, all three units have a general understanding of their respective jurisdictions but sometimes interpret these jurisdictions differently. Generally, consular fraud investigations begin with consular officers, who check for fraudulent documentation and application information. When consular officers notice organized fraud activity, they refer the case to the post's Fraud Prevention Unit. When this organized activity is criminal, the post's DS office launches an investigation. When the activity is terrorism-related, the post's VSP agents investigate. However, some posts we visited had experienced tension between VSP agents and other law enforcement agency officials at post. For example, at one post, the VSP agents and DS officials disagreed about whether the VSP agent had authority and responsibility to conduct investigations locally. Consular officials at another post wanted a DS officer to serve as a liaison between VSP and the consular section. The 2011 MOU describes the types of cases that fall under the jurisdiction of diplomatic security investigators and VSP agents, and states that cases that fall under the responsibility of both parties will require the officials to notify each other.

Staffing Shortages and Use of Temporary Duty Agents Have Caused Difficulties at Some Posts

Staffing shortages, and a reliance on temporary duty VSP agents to fill such shortages, have led to difficulties at some posts. Consular officers at 3 of 13 posts we interviewed discussed challenges caused by this use of temporary duty agents. For example, the VSP unit in Riyadh used two temporary duty agents per month in fiscal year 2009 and one temporary duty agent per month in fiscal year 2010. Although ICE officials indicated that the VSP filled its positions in Riyadh as of December 2010, both VSP and consular officials stated that this reliance on temporary duty agents affected continuity of operations. One consular official pointed to a "severe lack of coverage" for consular operations in Riyadh, because the unit was not fully staffed and relied on temporary duty agents. Consular officers stated that agents in Riyadh are rarely available to answer questions and that the value of these temporary duty agents was limited, because it took them several weeks of their 30-day tour to learn VSP policies and procedures. Additionally, consular officers stated that temporary duty agents' grounds for recommending refusal of visa applications were sometimes inconsistent or insufficient. Lack of staff at VSPs in Jeddah and Dhahran also created delays and forced consular officers to re-adjudicate cases because VSP agents delayed an application beyond the point where consular "name checks" of applicants expire. According to one VSP official, reliance on temporary duty agents limits continuity of operations at post.

The Visa Security Program's 5-year plan identified recruitment of qualified personnel as a challenge and recommended incentives for VSP agents as critical to the program's mission, stating, "These assignments present significant attendant lifestyle difficulties. If the mission is to be accomplished, ICE, like State, needs a way to provide incentives for qualified personnel to accept these hardship assignments." However, according to ICE officials, ICE has not has not provided incentives to facilitate recruitment for hardship posts.[14] ICE officials stated that they have had difficulty attracting agents to Saudi Arabia, and ICE agents at post told us they have little incentive to volunteer for Visa Security Program assignments. ICE officials in headquarters stated that opportunities to gain international experience and earn danger pay are the primary recruitment incentives for VSP service. Additionally, according to ICE officials, some hardship posts, such as Riyadh, now allow spouses to accompany agents during their tour. However, according to an ICE official, ICE does not offer career and financial incentives for personnel at hardship posts, such as Washington, D.C.-based locality pay or priority consideration for onward assignments, which State Foreign Service Officers receive when posted at the same locations.[15]

VSP Agents Do Not Receive Language Training, and Additional Training May Be Helpful

VSP agents generally do not receive foreign language training before deployment overseas. Section 428 of the Homeland Security Act allows that, to the extent possible, VSP agents shall be provided the necessary training to enable them to perform their designated functions—reviewing visa applications, and conducting investigations on consular matters—including training in foreign languages, interview techniques, and fraud detection techniques, in conditions in the particular country where each employee is assigned, and in other appropriate areas of study. The 2003 MOU states that DHS training and assignment policies will emphasize identification or development of personnel with the ability to speak the host country language and "experience in or knowledge of the host country and extensive understanding of terrorism or other homeland security concerns in the host country." The 2011 MOU states that whenever practical, VSP staff should receive interagency training and, prior to deployment, should undergo orientation including, if possible, appropriate specialized consultations and briefings with Consular Affairs and Diplomatic Security officers.

ICE provides some training for VSP agents. ICE trains agents for Visa Security Program duties in a 3-week training course, sponsored by ICE and two other DHS divisions and conducted three times per year at the Federal Law Enforcement Training Center in Glynco, Georgia. This training includes, among other things, interview techniques, VSP systems, document examination, and terrorist trends.

However, ICE does not have a program for language training and has not established language training as a requirement for VSP agents. To date, VSP agents at one post have received language training. This was because, at one post, the Chief of Mission required language training as a condition for approving the VSP's request to send personnel to post. According to a VSP agent who received this training at the start of his deployment, language skills were "critical" because he was able to interact with host country law enforcement and conduct interviews. Both the VSP agent and Consul General at this post recommended that all VSP agents receive language training. According to ICE officials, ICE's ability to provide language training for VSP agents is limited by budgetary constraints. Because some VSP agents serve 1- or 2-year tours, language training can be an expensive investment given the amount of time an agent would actually use this training. ICE officials told us that, when possible, they deploy ICE agents with existing language skills. ICE also indicated that self-study language training is available for VSP agents.

According to some consular officers and VSP agents, VSP agents who have prior experience with immigration law may be better able to advise consular officers than officers whose training on the subject is limited to the VSP training course. For example, a consular official at one post stated that she found VSP agents with backgrounds in the former Immigration and Naturalization Service to be particularly helpful because they have extensive expertise on immigration law. All ICE agents receive basic instruction on immigration law, and ICE provides additional instruction to its agents during VSP training. One VSP agent stated he was unsure whether this training would provide sufficient expertise in immigration law for less experienced agents. VSP agents do not attend State's Consular General training at the Foreign Service Institute, although VSP agents and consular officials at some posts stated that attending such training would be beneficial. VSP agents at several posts also expressed a desire for more frequent opportunities to share problems, techniques, and best practices with headquarters and other VSP units.

ICE Has Not Fully Adhered to the VSP Expansion Plan

Although ICE developed a plan to expand the VSP to additional high-risk visa-issuing posts, ICE has not fully adhered to the plan or kept it up to date. The VSP 5-year expansion plan, developed in 2007, identifies 14 posts for expansion between 2009 and 2010, but 9 of these locations have not been established, and ICE has not updated the plan to reflect the current situation. Furthermore, ICE has not fully addressed remaining visa risk in high-risk posts that do not have a VSP presence. ICE, with input from State, developed a list of worldwide visa-issuing posts that are ranked according to visa risk. Although the expansion plan states that risk analysis is the primary input to VSP site selection and that the expansion plan represents an effort to address visa risk, ICE has not expanded the VSP to some high-risk posts. For example, 11 of the top 20 high-risk posts identified by ICE and State are not covered by VSP. The expansion of the VSP may be limited by a number of factors—including budget limitations and objections from State officials at some posts—and ICE has not identified possible alternatives that would provide the additional security of VSP review at those posts that do not have a VSP presence.

VSP Expansion Plan Has Not Been Fully Followed or Updated

Although ICE has expanded the VSP to a total of 19 posts in 15 countries, the agency has not fully followed the 5-year expansion plan. ICE's plan identified 14 posts for expansion in 2009 and 2010, but ICE did not establish VSP units at 9 of these 14 posts. Further, ICE officials stated that 3 locations planned for 2011 may not be opened because of budget constraints. Moreover, the expansion plan has not been updated since its release in 2007, although ICE officials said that the expansion plan will be revised in 2011. In the expansion plan, ICE notes that the locations it identifies for expansion reflect its best current assessment of the factors relevant to decision makers and that evolving variables, including changes in risk and the results of site assessments to determine the feasibility and timing of deployment, may affect, among other things, the ultimate selection of locations for VSP expansion. The plan states that ICE will continue to update its assessment of conditions based on the most current information and intelligence.

A number of factors have limited the VSP's expansion and consequently its coverage of global visa risk. According to ICE officials, expansion of the VSP has been constrained by budget limitations, difficulties in obtaining visas to certain countries, State's mandate to reduce personnel overseas, and objections from State officials at some posts for reasons such as limited embassy space and security concerns. For example, space limitations and security concerns are currently hindering VSP's expansion to a high-risk post of interest to ICE officials. The inability to obtain visas to another country is preventing ICE officials from conducting a preliminary site assessment at a possible expansion post in that country.

ICE Has Not Taken Steps to Address Remaining Visa Risk

ICE has not consistently located VSP units at the posts identified as highest risk and has not ensured VSP coverage for the posts without a VSP unit, leaving significant gaps in the program's capacity to address global visa risk. The VSP expansion plan states that global visa risk is substantial and that the VSP addresses threats that could exploit the visa process. ICE, in consultation with State, ranked 216 overseas posts based upon the visa security risk posed at each location. However, 5 of the 19 established VSP units are located at posts other than the 50 posts in the top tier, or critical quartile, of the agencies' rankings of high-risk posts. One established location ranks 70th on the list, while another ranks 86th. ICE officials explained that certain posts were opened to achieve regional coverage for other ICE activities. Moreover, of the 20 posts identified by ICE and State as highest risk, 11 do not have a VSP unit.

ICE officials stated that visa risk at posts without a VSP presence is addressed through the security advisory opinion (SAO) process, which provides in-depth screening and vetting of certain visa applicants at posts worldwide, regardless of whether the post has a VSP unit.[16] SAOs are initiated when an applicant meets certain predefined criteria or when a consular officer requests an SAO for a specific visa application. Officials from several agencies, including ICE and State, participate in certain categories of SAO reviews in Washington, D.C. However, while the SAO process can mitigate some visa risk at those locations without a VSP unit, it does not ensure the breadth of coverage provided by VSP agents through the routine screening and vetting of applicants who are not subjected to the SAO process.

ICE's expansion plan does not identify ways in which to address this lack of VSP coverage at the remaining high-risk posts it identified. However, ICE officials in headquarters indicated that they have used TECS, the primary database used by VSP agents to screen and vet visa applicants, to conduct screening and vetting domestically when a VSP unit at a post experienced computer problems or temporary personnel shortages. TECS interfaces with other law enforcement databases can be accessed by ICE officials. Similarly, one VSP agent stated that agents can perform screening and vetting for other posts in the event of a computer systems outage. In addition, ICE officials stated that they are currently developing a system that will make the screening and vetting process more automated and will provide information to consular officers in advance of the visa applicant's interview and adjudication decision. Further, several ICE and State officials at post indicated that the screening and vetting of visa applicants could be performed domestically on a permanent basis.

CONCLUSION

The Visa Security Program is intended to build additional security into the visa process by incorporating a law enforcement function at posts with the highest risk. However, the program is hampered in its efforts to strengthen visa security globally. A lack of comprehensive performance data collected since the establishment of the VSP in 2003 hinders ICE's ability to evaluate and report on the extent to which the VSP enhances the security of the visa process. Although ICE officials state that they have made improvements to their data tracking systems, the agency cannot demonstrate the progress of the VSP prior to 2010 toward its stated objectives of enhancing public safety and national security. Furthermore, the responsibility of VSP agents to perform investigations unrelated to visa security may limit their ability to carry out visa security activities, their primary responsibility, further affecting the relationship with consular officials, and may limit the VSP's performance and its ability to enhance national security and public safety. In addition, the VSP is not contributing to the visa process at many high-risk posts. As a result, there is a significant gap in the additional scrutiny that VSP provides in the visa process among many posts considered to be of high risk. ICE has not considered other options to strengthen security at those posts where VSP does not have a physical presence. The VSP will be limited in its goal to minimize global visa risk until DHS addresses the challenges of guidance, staffing, and data collection, and provides coverage and support to those high-risk posts without VSP agents at post.

Recommendations for Executive Action

To ensure that the Visa Security Program enhances the security of the visa process at posts overseas, we recommend that the Secretary of Homeland Security take the following four actions:

1. ensure that the VSP tracking system collects reliable data on all performance measures, to allow ICE to accurately evaluate VSP performance and report to Congress on progress toward the VSP mission objectives;
2. issue guidance requiring VSP agents to provide training for consular officers as mandated by section 428 of the Homeland Security Act;
3. develop a mechanism to track the amount of time spent by VSP agents on visa security activities and other investigations, in order to determine appropriate staffing levels and resource needs for VSP operations at posts overseas to ensure visa security operations are not limited; and
4. develop a plan to provide VSP coverage at high-risk posts where the possibility of deploying agents may be limited.

Agency Comments and our Evaluation

We provided a draft of our report to DHS and State. DHS provided written comments about the draft, which are reproduced in appendix II. State did not provide official comments on the draft. In addition, DHS and State provided technical comments, which we incorporated as appropriate.

DHS agreed with our recommendation that the department issue guidance instructing VSP agents to provide training to consular officers as mandated by section 428 of the Homeland Security Act. In addition, DHS concurred with our recommendation that it develop a plan to provide coverage for posts that lack a VSP presence and indicated that it is taking steps to address this recommendation.

DHS did not agree with our recommendation that it ensure that the VSP tracking system collected reliable data on all performance measures. In its written comments, DHS stated that the VSP currently captures all the required performance metrics identified in its 5-year expansion plan through the VSP tracking system and TECS. Although we acknowledge that ICE is collecting some data on the performance measures identified in the VSP expansion plan, our analysis showed that the data were not sufficient to accurately demonstrate the progress made toward the stated objectives. As we report, the 5-year expansion plan identifies six performance measures to assess VSP performance. The documents that ICE provided us indicate that ICE has collected comprehensive data on three of the performance measures, but not on the three remaining performance measures. Specifically, ICE did not provide us evidence that it collected data on the assistance and liaison activities performed by VSP. Furthermore, although ICE collects some information on the hours that VSP agents spend on investigations and the training they provided to consular officials, the VSP tracking system and TECS do not collect comprehensive data on the activities performed by all of its VSP agents abroad. Without collecting comprehensive data on the performance measures identified by ICE, DHS cannot accurately demonstrate progress toward its stated objectives of enhancing national security. Therefore we have retained our recommendation.

DHS did not agree with our draft recommendation to issue operational guidance for VSP posts. DHS stated that the 2011 MOU provides general guidance for the visa process and the development of standard operating procedures. We acknowledge that the MOU between ICE and State, signed on January 11, 2011, clarifies the respective roles and responsibilities of VSP agents and consular officers at post and states that posts may develop standard operating procedures that were identified in the 2008 cable. Therefore, we are removing our draft recommendation from the report. However, although the 2011 MOU and the 2008 cable provide a basis for developing effective standard operating procedures, we remain concerned that, during our review, most posts had not developed these procedures. Only 2 of 13 posts we contacted had developed standard operating procedures as recommended in the 2008 cable. At the 2 posts that developed standard operating procedures, consular officers stated that procedures had improved the consular-VSP relationship. It is critical for DHS to encourage posts to develop standard operating procedures to improve the VSP-consular relationship and strengthen VSP operations at posts.

DHS also did not agree with our recommendation to develop a mechanism to track the amount of time that VSP agents spend on visa security activities and other investigations. DHS states that ICE currently tracks case investigation hours through TECS, and that adding the metric to the VSP tracking system would be redundant. DHS's response does not address our finding that ICE does not have a mechanism that allows the agency to track the amount of time VSP agents spend on both investigation hours and hours spent on visa security activities. Although ICE states that its system tracks case hours of its agents, we found, based on ICE documentation, that ICE cannot accurately determine the amount of time that VSP agents spend on investigative and visa security activities. First, the reports that ICE provided us show the hours ICE officials spent on investigative and noninvestigative activities, but do not distinguish between the hours logged by VSP agents and hours logged by other ICE officials at posts abroad. During our structured interviews, VSP agents indicated that the time they spent on activities other than visa security reviews ranged from 5 to 40 percent. Second, our analysis of the VSP tracking system, which is intended to track visa-related activities of VSP agents, identified significant limitations to the reliability of the data. Thus, ICE does not maintain accurate data on the time VSP agents spend on visa security activities at posts. The VSP is intended to add additional security to the visa process through the screening and vetting of visa applications by experienced law enforcement officers. Without accurate data to determine the amount of time VSP agents spend on the visa security activities, ICE will not be able to determine whether the current allocations of staffing and resources at posts are adequate to carry out the visa security reviews and thereby fulfill the VSP objective of enhancing national security and public safety. Therefore, we have not changed our recommendation.

As agreed with your offices, unless you publicly announce the contents of this report earlier, we plan no further distribution until 30 days from the report date. At that time, we will send copies to the Secretaries of Homeland Security and State, as well as other interested Members of Congress. In addition, this report will be available at no charge on the GAO Web site at http://www.gao.gov.

If you or your staff have any questions, please contact me at (202) 512-4128 or fordj@gao.gov. Contact points for our Offices of Congressional Relations and Public Affairs may be found on the last page of this report. GAO staff who made major contribution to this report are listed in appendix III.

Jess T. Ford
Director,
International Affairs and Trade

APPENDIX I: SCOPE AND METHODOLOGY

To assess the ability of the Department of Homeland Security (DHS) to measure the objectives and performance of the Visa Security Program (VSP), we reviewed VSP mission objectives and performance measures identified in Bureau of Immigration and Custom Enforcement's (ICE) 5- year expansion plan. We reviewed data from the VSP tracking system, used to collect information on daily VSP activities, and compared the data collected from the system with the measures and mission objectives identified in the expansion plan. On the basis of inconsistencies of the data from the reporting systems prior to 2010 that we identified through our analysis of the reports and confirmed with ICE officials, we determined that the data that we received were not sufficiently reliable for the purposes of this report. We also reviewed performance reports from DHS and ICE that included references to the VSP. In addition, we met with ICE officials in Washington, D.C., who manage the VSP. We also observed VSP agents at six U.S. embassies and consulates conducting their daily screening and vetting activities and using the VSP Tracking System.

To identify challenges to the VSP's capacity to accomplish its goals, we reviewed the Homeland Security Act of 2002, which authorized DHS to assign DHS employees to posts overseas to support the visa process through various functions. We also reviewed documentation including the 2003 memorandum of understanding (MOU) between DHS and the Department of State (State) governing the implementation of section 428 of the Homeland Security Act; the 2004 administrative MOU; the 2008 cable directing VSP units to develop standard operating procedures; the 2011 MOU explaining the roles, responsibilities, and collaboration of VSP agents and other officials at posts overseas; VSP's training curriculum; and the VSP expansion plan. We met with ICE officials in Washington, D.C., who manage the VSP and State officials from the Bureaus of Consular Affairs and Diplomatic Security. We also visited six U.S. embassies and consulates with established VSP units where we interviewed and observed VSP agents, State officials from the Bureaus of Consular Affairs and Diplomatic Security, and chiefs of mission or deputy chiefs of mission. In order to allow for post-by-post comparison, we administered a set of structured interview questions to both the VSP units and consular sections in person at the six previously mentioned posts and by phone at an additional seven VSP locations. The five most recently established VSP posts, as well as one unit that underwent recent personnel turnover, were not included in our review.

To examine DHS's efforts to expand the Visa Security Program, we reviewed relevant documents such as the VSP 5-year expansion plan, which includes the mission and contributions of the program, criteria for selecting new expansion posts, cost estimates for establishing and maintaining VSP posts, and projected budget information. In addition, we reviewed the ranked list of visa-issuing posts identified by ICE, in consultation with State.

We then compared the expansion plan and the ranked list of posts with the VSP's actual expansion between 2005 and 2010. In addition, we reviewed the requests submitted by ICE to overseas posts for expansion of the program. Our interviews with ICE and State officials at 13 VSP locations worldwide and in Washington, D.C., also informed this analysis.

APPENDIX II: COMMENTS FROM THE DEPARTMENT OF HOMELAND SECURITY

U.S. Department of Homeland Security
Washington, DC 20528

Homeland Security

March 21, 2011

Jess Ford
Director, International Affairs and Trade
U.S. Government Accountability Office
441 G Street, NW
Washington, DC 20548

Re: Draft Report GAO-11-315: "BORDER SECURITY: The Department of Homeland Security's Visa Security Program Needs to Improve Performance Evaluation and Better Address Visa Risk Worldwide

Dear Mr. Ford:

The Department of Homeland Security (DHS) and U.S. Immigration and Customs Enforcement (ICE) appreciate the opportunity to comment on the draft report. We have addressed each recommendation separately below:

Recommendation 1: Ensure that the VSP tracking system collects reliable data on all performance measures, to allow ICE to accurately evaluate VSP performance and report to Congress on progress toward the VSP mission objectives.

Response: DHS does not concur. The Visa Security Program (VSP) captures all required metrics associated with its five-year plan through the VSPTS and Treasury Enforcement Communications System (TECS). The VSPTS and TECS are the two systems of record for VSP. Currently, the VSPTS records: recommendations for refusal, additional enforcement outcomes, derogatory information removal, opened investigations (with supplementary information such as case hours regarding investigations recorded into TECS), and assistance and liaison activities. Consular and other training is reported to the ICE Homeland Security Investigations, Office of International Affairs (HSI OIA) directly from ICE Attaché offices in a weekly metrics report. This formalized procedure for reporting training would make reporting in the VSPTS redundant.

Recommendation 2: Issue additional operational guidance for VSP posts, including standard operating procedures for the visa process and the dispute resolution process.

Response: DHS does not concur. The 2011 "Memorandum of Understanding among U.S. Immigration and Customs Enforcement of the Department of Homeland Security and the Bureaus of Consular Affairs and Diplomatic Security of the Department of State on Roles, Responsibilities and Collaboration at Visa Security Units Abroad" (MOU) recognizes that the circumstances at each post are unique. The MOU provides general guidance and recommends that management at each post negotiate a local standard operating procedure (SOP) to fit their needs. ICE headquarters' program managers assist posts in developing these SOPs according to post specific needs. Standard procedures across all posts would prove overly restrictive, given the dynamic environment of overseas operations. Each VSP post currently has an individualized plan that is specific to their location.

Recommendation 3: Issue guidance requiring VSP agents to provide training for consular officers as mandated by section 428 of the Homeland Security Act.

Response: DHS concurs. While VSP headquarters can provide general training guidance for all posts, it is incumbent upon each ICE Attaché and corresponding Department of State (DOS) manager to identify post-specific training needs relative to their respective environments.

Recommendation 4: Develop a mechanism to track the amount of time spend by VSP agents on visa security activities and other investigations, in order to determine appropriate staffing levels and resource needs for VSP operations at posts overseas to ensure visa security operations are not limited.

Response: DHS does not concur. ICE currently tracks case hours through existing ICE systems which are standardized throughout the agency. TECS is the system of record that tracks case investigation hours of all ICE agents worldwide. Adding this function to the VSPTS would be redundant.

Recommendation 5: Develop a plan to provide VSP coverage at high-risk posts where the possibility of deploying agents may be limited.

Response: DHS concurs. ICE is actively addressing this recommendation.

ICE identified alternatives for VSP review at high risk posts that currently do not have a physical VSP presence. ICE currently participates in the interagency Security Advisory Opinion (SAO) process, which reviews the highest risk visa applicants, covering all worldwide posts.

ICE is currently enhancing its IT systems, in coordination with U.S. Customs & Border Protection (CBP) and DOS. These changes will allow the screening and reviewing of all applicants at all posts worldwide. Use of TECS and CBP's Automated Targeting System (ATS), in addition to improved transfer of information with DOS's Consular Consolidated Database (CCD) and Visa Opinion Information System (VOIS) will enhance communication within DHS (ICE / CBP) and DOS, thereby strengthening the layered defense strategy.

Both the physical presence of ICE special agents abroad and worldwide coverage via IT enhancements are integral parts of VSP. IT enhancements will enable ICE to conduct visa security investigations at all existing ICE Attaché offices thereby providing coverage to an additional 34 high risk posts in furtherance of the VSP expansion plan.

DHS generally concurs with Government Accountability Office (GAO) recommendations three and five; however, DHS does not concur with recommendations one, two and four. DHS is taking corrective actions to address the overall recommendations. Thank you for the opportunity

to comment on this Draft Report. We look forward to working with you on future Department of Homeland Security issues.

Sincerely,

Jim H. Crumpacker
Director
Departmental GAO/OIG Liaison Office

End Notes

[1] The Homeland Security Act of 2002 (P.L. 107-296) established DHS and gave the Secretary of Homeland Security authority to issue regulations with respect to the issuance and refusal of visas.

[2] Section 428 of the Homeland Security Act authorizes the Secretary of Homeland Security to assign DHS employees to consular posts overseas to support the visa process through various functions.

[3] GAO, *Border Security: Actions Needed to Strengthen Management of Department of Homeland Security's Visa Security Program*, GAO-05-801 (Washington, D.C.: July 2005).

[4] In this report, we use the word "post" to identify U.S. embassies and consulates.

[5] The State Department Bureau of Diplomatic Security is responsible for personal protection, protection of facilities, investigations, threat analysis, and training. Overseas, Diplomatic Security personnel include regional security officers, who are responsible for the security of facilities, personnel, and information at U.S. overseas facilities, and assistant regional security officer-investigators, who focus on investigations into passport and visa fraud at posts with high levels of fraud.

[6] The security advisory opinion process is a multi-agency review process that collects additional information on applicants to provide a recommendation to posts to issue or refuse a visa.

[7] TECS is an updated and modified version of the former Treasury Enforcement Communications System, which is principally owned and managed by U.S. Customs and Border Protection. TECS is an automated enforcement and antiterrorism database that provides information for law enforcement and border security purposes, and can exchange information automatically with other U.S. government systems.

[8] Prior to adjudication, every visa application undergoes biometric and biographic clearances against several databases, including Facial Recognition, Consular Lookout and Support System, and Terrorist Screening databases.

[9] GAO-05-801.

[10] P.L. 103-62.

[11] GAO, *Standards for Internal Control in the Federal Government*, GAO/AIMD-00-21.3.1 (Washington, D.C.: November 1999).

[12] GAO/GGD-10.1.20, *The Results Act: An Evaluator's Guide to Assessing Agency Annual Performance Plans* (Washington, D.C.: April 1998).

[13] In our structured interview, we provided several examples of training, including "briefings, brown bags, hands-on exercises, reports or other written products" We asked both the VSP agents and the consular section to determine whether these sessions were "formal" or "informal."

[14] State has designated roughly two-thirds of its 268 overseas posts as hardship posts. Staff working in such locations often encounter harsh environmental and living conditions that can include inadequate medical facilities, limited opportunities for spousal employment, poor schools, high levels of crime, and severe climate.

[15] Locality pay is a salary comparability benefit, typically available to domestic federal employees only to attract workers in the continental United States to the federal government versus the private sector.

[16] SAOs provide an opinion or clearance from Washington on whether to issue a visa to an applicant. These clearances are required for a number of reasons, including whether an applicant's name appears as a "hit" in the name-check system, or if the applicant's country of origin is a state sponsor of terrorism.

In: U.S. Visa Policies, Programs and Considerations
Editor: Aaron R. Miller
ISBN: 978-1-61470-333-4

Chapter 7

H-1B VISA PROGRAM: REFORMS ARE NEEDED TO MINIMIZE THE RISKS AND COSTS OF CURRENT PROGRAM*

United States Government Accountability Office

WHY GAO DID THIS STUDY

Congress created the H-1B program in 1990 to enable U.S. employers to hire temporary, foreign workers in specialty occupations. The law capped the number of H-1B visas issued per fiscal year at 65,000. Since then, the cap has fluctuated with legislative changes. Congress asked GAO to assess the impact of the cap on the ability of domestic companies to innovate, while ensuring that U.S. workers are not disadvantaged. In response, GAO examined what is known about (1) employer demand for H-1B workers; (2) how the cap affects employer costs and decisions to move operations overseas; (3) H-1B worker characteristics and the potential impact of raising the cap; and (4) how well requirements of the H-1B program protect U.S. workers. GAO analyzed data from 4 federal agencies; interviewed agency officials, experts, and H-1B employers; and reviewed agency documents and literature.

WHAT GAO RECOMMENDS

This report offers several matters for congressional consideration, including that Congress re-examine key H-1B program provisions and make appropriate changes as needed. GAO also recommends that the Departments of Homeland Security and Labor take steps to improve efficiency, flexibility, and monitoring of the H-1B program. Homeland Security disagreed with two recommendations and one matter, citing logistical and other challenges;

* This is an edited, reformatted and augmented version of the United States Government Accountability Office publication, Report to Congressional Committees, GAO-11-26, dated January 2011.

however, we believe such challenges can be overcome. Labor did not respond to our recommendations.

WHAT GAO FOUND

In most years, demand for new H-1B workers exceeded the cap: From 2000 to 2009, demand for new H-1B workers tended to exceed the cap, as measured by the numbers of initial petitions submitted by employers who are subject to the cap (see fig. 1). There is no way to precisely determine the level of any unmet demand among employers, since they tend to stop submitting (and the Department of Homeland Security stops tracking) petitions once the cap is reached each year. When we consider all initial petitions, including those from universities and research institutions that are not subject to the cap, we find that demand for new H-1B workers is largely driven by a small number of employers. Over the decade, over 14 percent of all initial petitions were submitted by cap-exempt employers, and only a few employers (fewer than 1 percent) garnered over one-quarter of all H-1B approvals.

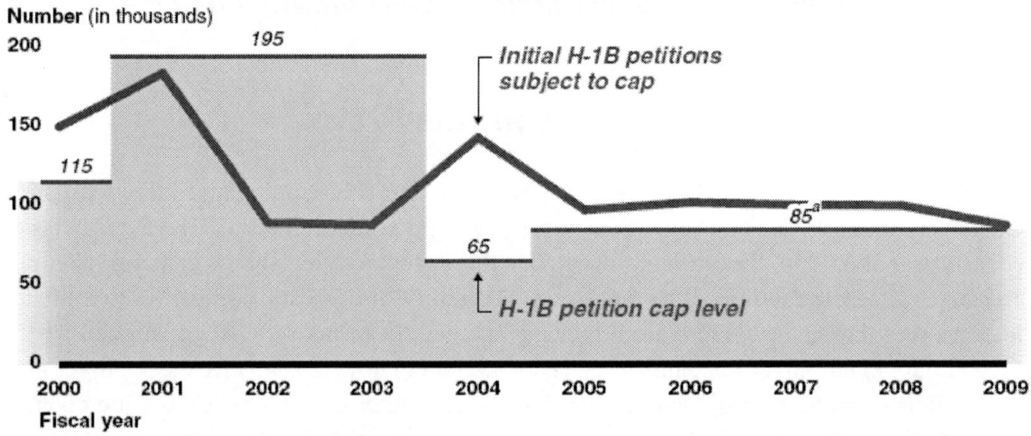

Source: GAO analysis of Department of Homeland Security CLAIMS 3 data on initial petitions.
[a] Includes 20,000 visas allocated to workers graduating from U.S. master's programs or higher.

Figure 1. Number of Initial Petitions for New H-1B Workers Submitted by Employers Subject to the Cap.

Most interviewed companies said the H-1B cap and program created costs, but were not factors in their decisions to move R&D overseas: The 34 H-1B employers GAO interviewed reported that the cap has created some additional costs, though the cap's impact depended on the size and maturity of the company. For example, in years when visas were denied by the cap, most large firms reported finding other (sometimes more costly) ways to hire their preferred job candidates. On the other hand, small firms were more likely to fill their positions with different candidates, which they said resulted in delays and sometimes economic losses, particularly for firms in rapidly changing technology fields. Interviewed employers also cited costs due to the H-1B lottery process employed when the cap is reached—noting that it does not allow them to prioritize their candidates if they have submitted more than one petition or to make timely hires in response to business needs. On the other hand, most employers told us that the global marketplace and access to skilled labor drive their decisions on whether to move R&D and other activities overseas, not the H-1B cap.

Limitations in agency data and systems hinder tracking the cap and H-1B workers over time: The total number of H-1B workers in the U.S. at any one time—and information about the length of their stay—is unknown, because (1) data systems among the various agencies that process such individuals are not linked so individuals cannot be readily tracked, and (2) H-1B workers are not assigned a unique identifier that would allow for tracking them over time—particularly if and when their visa status changes. Although information on the total H-1B workforce is lacking, data on approved petitions show that, since 2000, most people that were approved to be H-1B workers were born in China or India, were hired for technology positions, and increasingly held advanced degrees. System limitations also hinder the Department of Homeland Security from knowing precisely when and whether the annual cap has been reached each year, although this problem might be remedied through the agency's data-modernization plan. Finally, data limitations, along with complex economic relationships, hinder our ability to estimate the potential impact raising the cap would have on U.S. worker wages and employment.

Restricted agency oversight and statutory changes weaken protections for U.S. workers: Elements of the H-1B program that could serve as worker protections—such as the requirement to pay prevailing wages, the visa's temporary status, and the cap itself— are weakened by several factors. First, program oversight is fragmented and restricted. For example, the Department of Labor's review of H-1B applications from employers is cursory and limited by law to only looking for missing information and obvious inaccuracies. Yet a recent Department of Homeland Security study reported that 21 percent of the H-1B petitions they examined involved fraud or technical violations.

Second, the H-1B program lacks a legal provision for holding employers accountable to program requirements when they obtain H-1B workers through a staffing company (see fig. 2). Officials from the Department of Labor's investigative office reported receiving the bulk of their complaints from H-1B workers contracted by staffing companies.

Third, statutory changes made to the H-1B program have, in combination and in effect, increased the pool of H-1B workers beyond the cap and lowered the bar for eligibility. Specifically, these changes have increased the available exemptions to the cap; offered unlimited extensions on the visa while holders apply for permanent residency; and broadened the job and skill categories for eligibility. Regarding the latter, over 50 percent of employers requesting H-1B workers between June 2009 and July 2010 categorized their prospective H-1B workers as receiving entry-level wages, although we cannot tell whether this trend reflects lower skill levels or other factors.

Taken together, the multifaceted challenges identified in this report show that the H-1B program, as currently structured, may not be used to its full potential and may be detrimental in some cases. Although executive agencies overseeing the program can take steps to improve tracking, administration, and enforcement, the data we present raise difficult policy questions about key program provisions that are beyond the jurisdiction of these agencies. Such questions include the adequacy of the qualifications of foreign workers the U.S. admits through the program, the appropriateness of H-1B hiring by staffing companies, and the role of the program with respect to permanent residency. The H-1B program presents a difficult challenge in balancing the need for high-skilled foreign labor with sufficient protections for

U.S. workers. As Congress considers immigration reform in consultation with diverse stakeholders and experts, and the Department of Homeland Security moves forward with its modernization efforts, this is an opportune time for Congress to re-examine key provisions of the H-1B program.

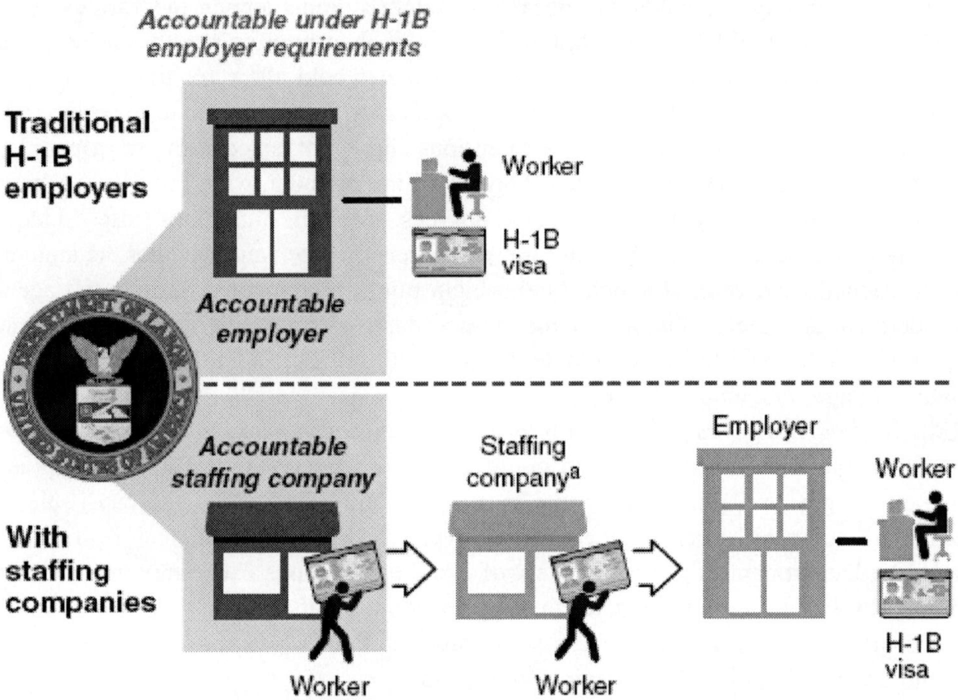

Source: GAO review of Department of Labor information.
[a] In some cases there may be more than one staffing company involved in placing the H-1B worker.

Figure 2. Limited Accountability for Employers Hiring H-1B Workers through Staffing Companies.

ABBREVIATIONS

AC21	American Competitiveness in the Twenty-First Century Act of 2000
ADIS	Arrival Departure Information System
BFCA	Benefit Fraud and Compliance Assessment Program
BLS	Bureau of Labor Statistics
CLAIMS 3	Computer Linked Application and Management System, Version 3
CPS	Current Population Survey
Employment and Training	Labor's Employment and Training Administration
FDNS	Homeland Security's Directorate of Fraud Detection and National Security
Homeland Security	Department of Homeland Security
IT	information technology
Justice	Department of Justice

Labor	Department of Labor
LAN	local area network
LCA	Labor Condition Application
NAICS	North American Industry Classification System
R&D	research and development
State	Department of State
USCIS	Homeland Security's U.S. Citizenship and Immigration Services
US-VISIT	United States Visitor and Immigrant Status Indicator Technology
Wage and Hour	Labor's Wage and Hour Division

January 14, 2011
The Honorable Thad Cochran

The Honorable Daniel K. Inouye
United States Senate
The Honorable Harold Rogers
Chairman
The Honorable Norman D. Dicks
Ranking Member
Committee on Appropriations
House of Representatives

The current H-1B program, which permits U.S. employers to hire foreign workers in specialty occupations, was authorized in 1990.[1] The same law also placed a cap of 65,000 on H-1B visas issued per fiscal year beginning in fiscal year 1992. However, since then, the cap has fluctuated with legislative changes, reaching a peak of 195,000 in fiscal years 2001 to 2003. Today, the cap is set at 65,000 and continues to be a topic of debate. Proponents of raising the H-1B cap argue that doing so would allow companies to better fill an important and growing gap in the supply of U.S. workers, especially in the science and technology fields. Opponents of raising the cap argue that there is no skill shortage, that the H-1B program displaces U.S. workers and undercuts their pay, and that the cap is an essential tool to protect U.S. workers. Others argue that the skill criteria for the H-1B visa should be revised to better target foreign nationals whose talents are undersupplied in the domestic workforce.

This report responds to a congressional request that GAO assess the impact of the current H-1B visa cap on the ability of domestic companies to develop modern technology and perform innovative research and development (R&D) while ensuring that U.S. workers are not unfairly disadvantaged or displaced by H-1B visa holders.[2] With respect to H-1B employers, we examined what is known about (1) their demand for H-1B workers and (2) how the H-1B cap affects costs, offshoring,[3] and R&D decisions for companies doing business in the United States. With respect to H-1B and U.S. workers, we examined what is known about (3) H-1B worker characteristics, (4) how raising the H-1B cap might affect the employment and wages of U.S. workers, and (5) how well H-1B program requirements ensure that U.S. workers are not displaced or otherwise disadvantaged by the program.

To address these questions, we drew upon a range of information sources. Specifically, to determine what is known about the demand for H-1B workers and their characteristics, we obtained and analyzed administrative data on employer applications for H-1B visas from the Department of Labor (Labor) for fiscal year 2002 through fiscal year 2009[4] and from the Department of Homeland Security (Homeland Security) from fiscal year 2000 through fiscal year 2009; collected and analyzed data on the 150 H-1B employers with the greatest number of approvals in 2009; and analyzed data on visa issuances published by the Department of State (State).

To understand the impact of the cap on companies' costs and their decisions to offshore work and invest in R&D, we interviewed a nongeneralizable sample of 34 H-1B hiring companies spanning the country in six industrial sectors, with a range of sizes from a few workers based in one location to thousands of workers positioned around the globe.[5] We also conducted interviews with representatives from immigration law firms, venture capital companies, industry advocacy organizations, and academic institutions, and conducted an extensive literature review.

To examine the impact of the H-1B program on domestic employment, we obtained data from Homeland Security on the long-run immigration outcomes of prospective H-1B workers that were approved to start work in H-1B status between January 1, 2004, and September 30, 2007, for whom data were available; analyzed Homeland Security data and Bureau of Labor Statistics' (BLS) Current Population Survey (CPS) data from 2009 to compare the wages of H-1B workers with those of U.S. citizens in three occupation groups; and analyzed CPS employment, unemployment, and earnings data for the top H-1B occupations.

To assess the effectiveness of the H-1B program's current protections for U.S. workers, we conducted site visits to Labor and Homeland Security processing centers for H-1B applications and to Labor's regional office that receives the highest number of H-1B-related complaints in the country; conducted interviews with agency officials from Labor, Homeland Security, the Department of Justice (Justice), and State involved with various facets of the program including complaint and fraud investigations, as well as with labor advocates and experts knowledgeable in this area; and obtained and analyzed agency data collected on complaints about the H-1B program.

To address all objectives, we reviewed relevant federal laws and regulations, articles, and the temporary immigration programs of several other countries that we selected based on our literature review and discussions with experts.

We conducted this performance audit from May 2009 through January 2011 in accordance with generally accepted government auditing standards. Those standards require that we plan and perform the audit to obtain sufficient, appropriate evidence to provide a reasonable basis for our findings and conclusions based on our audit objectives. We believe that the evidence obtained provides a reasonable basis for our findings and conclusions based on our audit objectives.

See appendix I for a detailed account of the objectives, scope, and methods for this report.

BACKGROUND

The H-1B program enables companies in the United States to hire foreign workers for work in specialty occupations on a temporary basis. A specialty occupation is defined as one requiring theoretical and practical application of a body of highly specialized knowledge and the attainment of a bachelor's degree or higher (or its equivalent) in the field of specialty.[6]

The law originally capped the number of H-1B visas at 65,000 per year, but the cap has changed several times pursuant to legislation. The American Competitiveness and Workforce Improvement Act of 1998 increased the cap to 115,000 for fiscal year 1999 and fiscal year 2000.[7] The American Competitiveness in the Twenty-First Century Act of 2000 (AC21) further increased the limit to 195,000 for fiscal year 2001 through fiscal year 2003.[8] In fiscal year 2004, the cap reverted to its original level of 65,000.

Over this period, statutory changes also allowed for certain categories of individuals and companies to be exempt from or to receive special treatment under the cap. In 2000, AC21 exempted all individuals being hired by institutions of higher education, as well as nonprofit and government-research organizations, from the cap.[9] More recently, the H-1B Visa Reform Act of 2004 allowed for an additional 20,000 visas each year for foreign workers holding a master's degree or higher from an American institution of higher education to be exempted from the numerical cap limitation.[10] In addition, in 2004, consistent with free trade agreements, amendments allowed for up to 6,800 of the 65,000 H-1B visas to be set aside for workers from Chile and Singapore.[11] Figure 1 depicts the cap levels over the last 20 years and important changes to provisions related to their application.[12] See appendix V for a list of selected H-1B program laws, with descriptions of key provisions.

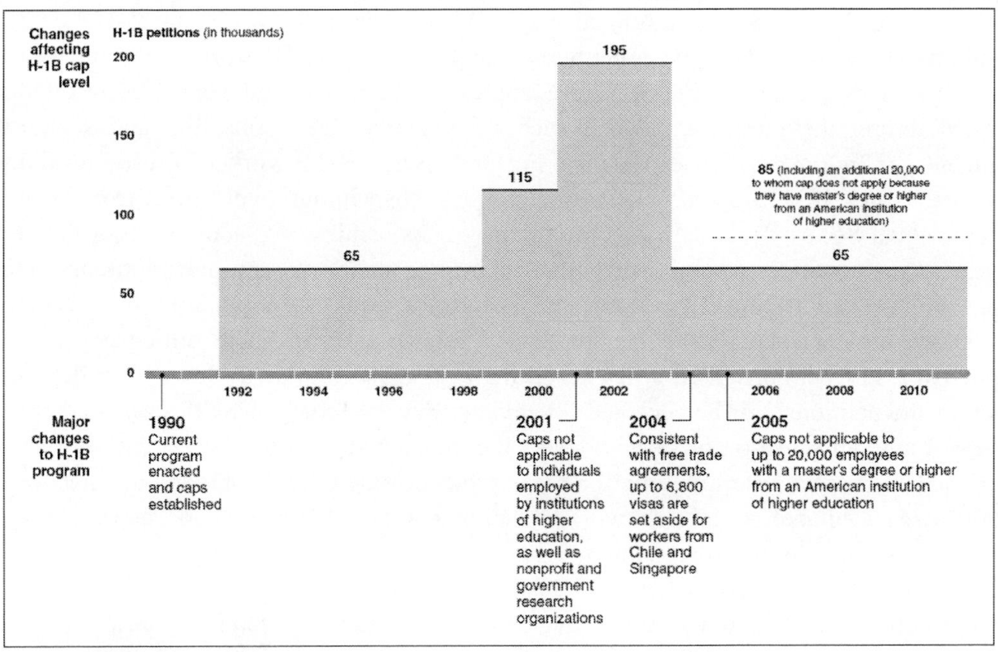

Note: Unless otherwise indicated, changes are shown in the fiscal year when they became effective.
Source: GAO analysis of federal law.

Figure 1. Legislative Changes Affecting H-1B Cap Level, by Fiscal Year.

While the H-1B visa is not considered a permanent visa, H-1B workers can apply for extensions and pursue permanent residence in the United States. Initial petitions are those filed for a foreign national's first-time employment as an H-1B worker and are valid for a period of up to 3 years. Generally, initial petitions are counted against the annual cap. Extensions—technically referred to as continuing employment petitions— may be filed to extend the initial petitions for up to an additional 3 years. These extensions may be filed for extended employment; sequential employment (when an H-1B worker changes employers within his or her 6- year time period); or for concurrent employment (when an H-1B worker intends to work simultaneously for a second employer). Extensions do not count against the cap. While working under an H-1B visa, an H-1B worker may apply for legal permanent residence in the United States. After filing an application for permanent residence, H-1B workers are eligible to obtain additional 1-year visa extensions until their green card is issued.[13] To obtain such extensions, the green card application must be employment-based (i.e. not a green card sponsored by a family member). Employment-based green cards can take a number of years to obtain due to limits on the number of green cards issued to individuals from different countries and in particular employment categories.[14]

Program Administration

Labor, Homeland Security, and State each play a role in administering the application process for an H-1B visa. Labor's Employment and Training Administration (Employment and Training) receives and approves an initial application, known as the Labor Condition Application (LCA), from employers. Homeland Security's U.S. Citizenship and Immigration Services (USCIS) reviews an additional employer application, known as the I-129 petition, and ultimately approves H-1B visa petitions. For prospective H-1B workers residing outside the United States, State interviews these approved applicants and compares information obtained during the interview against each individual's visa application and supporting documents, and ultimately issues the visa. For prospective H-1B workers already residing in the United States, USCIS updates the workers' visa status without involvement from State.

Homeland Security's USCIS has the primary responsibility for administering the H-1B program, which includes responsibility for tracking the number of approved petitions against the established cap.[15] Generally, Homeland Security accepts H-1B petitions in the order in which they are received. However, for those years in which USCIS anticipates that the number of I-129 petitions filed will exceed the cap, USCIS holds a "lottery" to determine which of the petitions will be accepted for review. For the lottery, USCIS uses a computer-generated random selection process to select the number of petitions necessary to reach the cap. USCIS runs two lotteries—one for cases subject to the 65,000 cap, and another for the 20,000 visas available to foreign workers holding a master's degree or higher from an American institution of higher education.

With regard to enforcement, Labor, Justice, and Homeland Security each have specific responsibilities. Labor's Wage and Hour Division (Wage and Hour) is responsible for enforcing program rules by investigating complaints made against employers by H-1B workers or their representatives and assessing penalties when employers are not in compliance with the requirements of the program.[16] Justice is responsible for investigating complaints made by U.S. workers who allege that they have been displaced or otherwise harmed by the H-1B visa program.[17] Finally, Homeland Security's Directorate of Fraud Detection and National Security (FDNS) collaborates with its Immigration and Customs Enforcement Office to investigate fraud and abuse in the program.

Employer Application Requirements

The application and approval process for an employer to hire an H-1B worker requires submission of an LCA and the I-129 petition. The employers must first submit the LCA to Employment and Training for certification.[18] The LCA may reflect requests for one or more workers. On this form, employers must provide their company name, address, Employer Identification Number, and the rate of pay and work location for the anticipated H-1B workers among other information. Submission of the LCA to Employment and Training also involves employers making four attestations: (1) that they will pay H-1B workers the amount they pay other employees with similar experience and qualifications or the prevailing wage; (2) that the employment of H-1B workers will not adversely affect the working conditions of U.S. workers similarly employed; (3) that no strike or lockout exists in the occupational classification at the place of employment; and (4) that the employer has notified employees at the place of employment of the intent to employ H-1B workers.[19] These attestations are designed to protect both the jobs of domestic workers and the rights and working conditions of foreign temporary workers.

H-1B-dependent employers or employers found to have committed a willful failure or misrepresentation during the 5-year period preceding the filing of the LCA must make additional attestations on their LCA.[20] They must attest (1) that they did not displace a U.S. worker within the period of 90 days before and 90 days after filing a petition for an H-1B worker; (2) that they took good-faith steps prior to filing the H-1B application to recruit U.S. workers and that they offered the job to a U.S. applicant who was equally or better qualified than an H-1B worker;[21] and (3) that they not place the H-1B worker with any other employer, unless they inquired and have no knowledge that, within the 90 days before and 90 days after the placement, the other employer has displaced or intends to displace a U.S. worker with the H-1B worker.

Unlike some other temporary visa programs, the H-1B program does not require employers to provide evidence that they have first "tested" the U.S. labor market by trying to hire a U.S. worker. Under other temporary visa programs, such as the H-2A program for temporary agricultural workers[22] and the H-2B program for temporary nonagricultural seasonal or intermittent workers,[23] an employer must, for example document that it has conducted detailed recruitment efforts, advertised the job as specified, listed the job with its State Workforce Agency, and under certain circumstances, document why it did not hire applicants it rejected.[24] In the H-1B program, only those employers that are designated as H-1B-dependent or willful violators are subject to any type of labor market test. However, these employers need only attest, rather than demonstrate, that they took good faith steps to hire a U.S. worker.

Once Labor has approved the LCA, employers must submit the certified LCA to Homeland Security, along with the I-129, for additional review. The I-129, submitted by employers to Homeland Security for each prospective H-1B worker, must show the wage that will be paid, the location of the position, and the worker's qualifications, among other information. Figure 2 summarizes the steps required to obtain an H-1B visa.

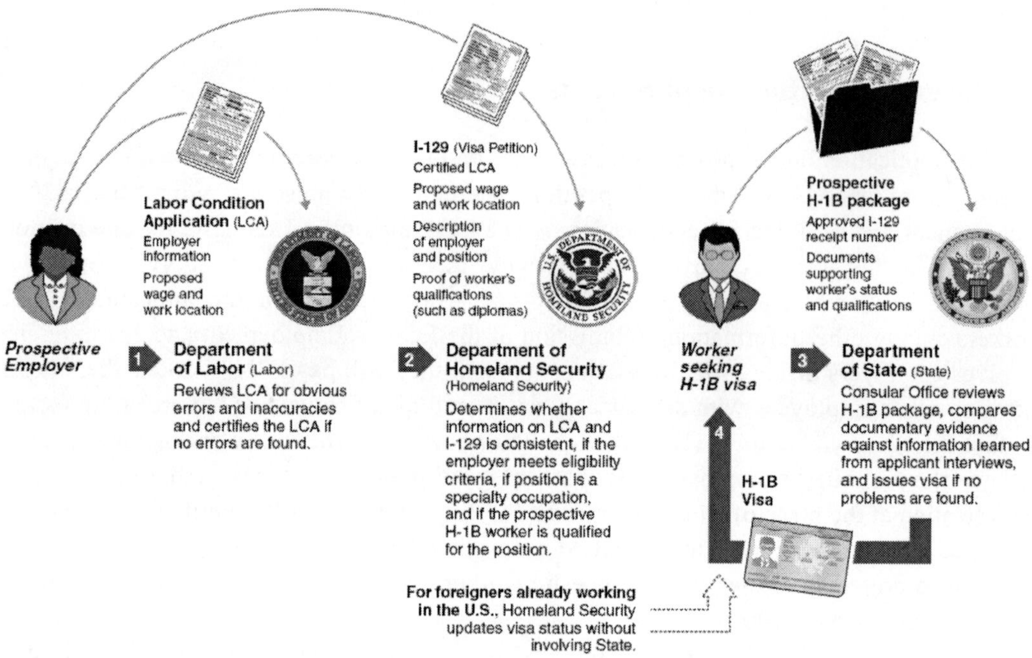

Source: GAO analysis of agency procedures.

Figure 2. Process of Obtaining an H-1B Visa.

DEMAND FOR H-1B WORKERS EXCEEDED THE CAP IN MOST YEARS AND WAS LARGELY DRIVEN BY A SMALL NUMBER OF COMPANIES

Available data show that, while demand for H-1B workers by employers has fluctuated with the economy over the past decade, the demand for H-1B workers tended to exceed the cap, as measured by the numbers of initial petitions submitted by employers. In addition, although the vast majority of employers for which Homeland Security processed petitions were approved to hire just one worker, a small number of employers consistently garnered about 30 percent of all approved petitions.

In Most Years, Demand for H-1B Workers Exceeded the Cap, but Precise Measures of Demand Do Not Exist

Although a precise measure of demand for H-1B workers does not exist, a key proxy—the number of initial petitions for new H-1B workers submitted to Homeland Security annually—indicates that demand for H-1B workers tended to exceed the cap over the last decade.[25] As shown in figure 3, from 2000 to 2009, initial petitions for new H-1B workers submitted to Homeland Security by employers who are subject to the cap exceeded the cap in all but 3 fiscal years. If initial petitions submitted by employers exempt from the cap are also included in this measure, the demand for new H-1B workers is higher, since over 14 percent of all initial petitions across the decade were submitted by employers who are not subject to the cap.[26] However, the number of initial petitions submitted annually is likely to be an underestimate of demand for two reasons. First, employers subject to the cap may stop submitting initial petitions once they know the cap has been reached.[27] Second, according to Homeland Security officials, Homeland Security stops accepting petitions that are subject to the cap once the cap is reached.[28] Consequently, we cannot precisely determine the level of any unmet demand among those employers who are subject to the cap.

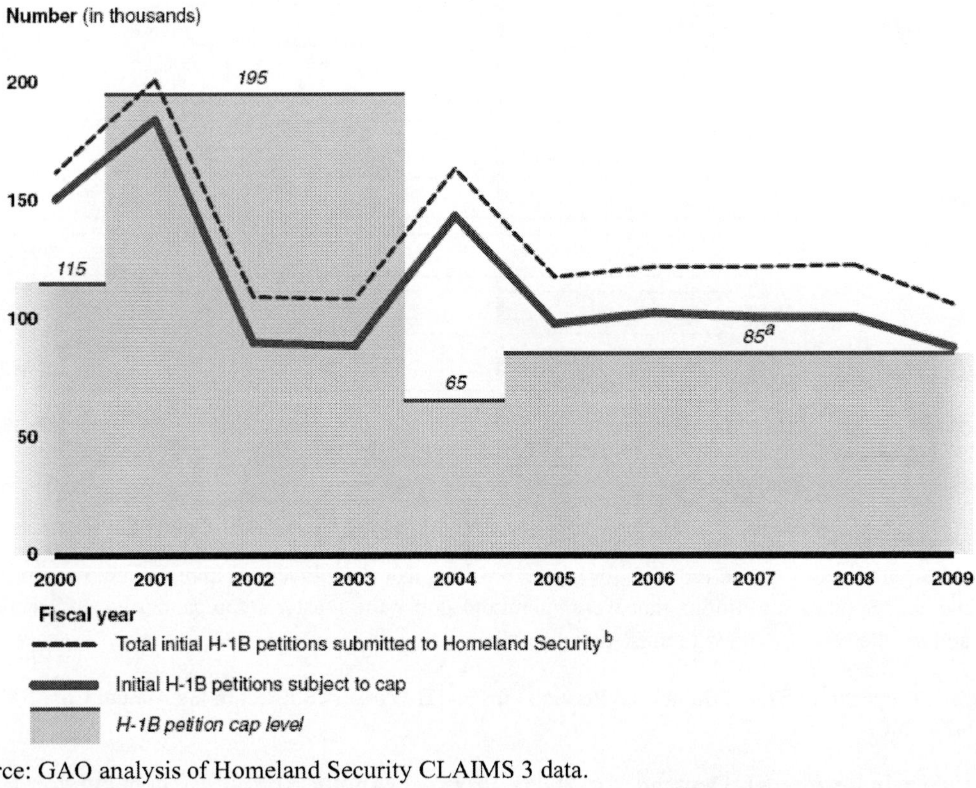

Source: GAO analysis of Homeland Security CLAIMS 3 data.

[a] Includes 20,000 visas allocated to workers graduating from U.S. master's programs or higher.

[b] Total initial petitions submitted to Homeland Security includes all initial petitions that were entered into Homeland Security's data system, including those from cap-exempt employers. Reported numbers only reflect petitions entered into Homeland Security's CLAIMS 3 data system and processed by Homeland Security, not the total number submitted which is likely higher in years when the cap is reached. Petitions submitted under the master's cap cannot be differentiated and are therefore included in these data.

Figure 3. Number of Initial Petitions for New H-1B Workers Submitted by Employers Relative to the Cap, FY 2000–FY 2009.

When requests to extend H-1B workers' visas (i.e., extensions)[29] are included in the total count of submitted petitions, we found that submitted petitions not subject to the cap generally increased as a proportion of overall petitions submitted from fiscal years 2000 to 2009, and greatly exceeded those that were subject to the cap in the last half of the decade. As shown in figure 4, during this time period, the proportion of all submitted petitions that were not subject to the cap increased from 48.9 percent in 2000 to 64.6 percent in 2009. However, as noted previously, submitted petitions for H-1B workers subject to the cap are likely to be underestimated. Additionally, Homeland Security's data system does not enable us to determine which petitions for H-1B workers were subject to the 20,000 master's cap.[30]

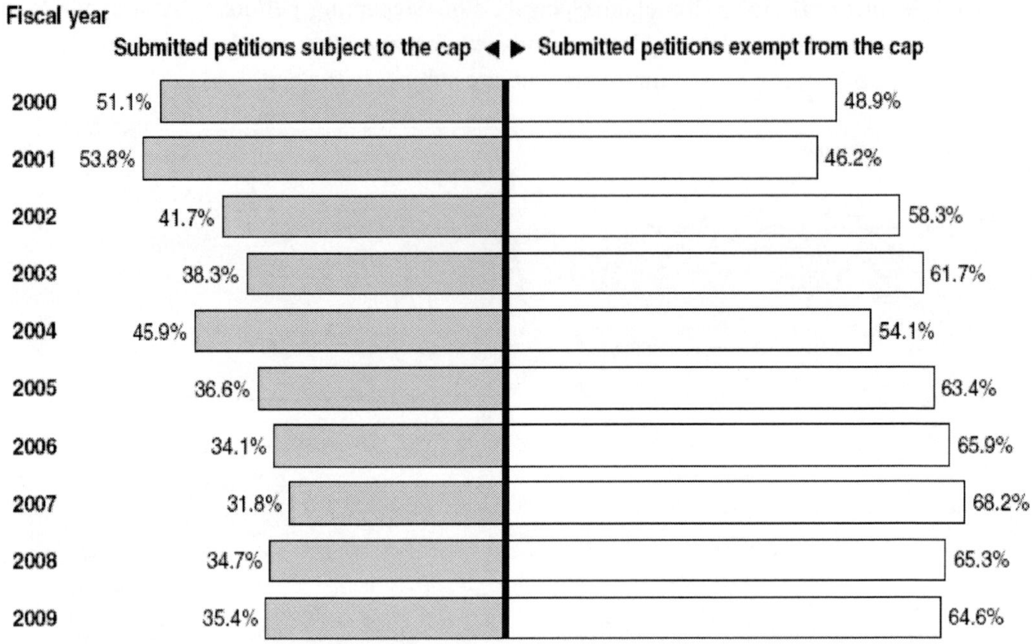

Source: GAO analysis of Homeland Security CLAIMS 3 data.

[a] Includes initial petitions and requests for visa extensions from employers exempt and not exempt from the cap. Submitted petitions that were submitted under the master's cap cannot be differentiated and are therefore included in these data.

Figure 4. Proportion of Total Submitted Petitions for H-1B Workers Subject to the Annual Cap, FY 2000–FY 2009[a].

Other Indicators of Demand for H-1B Workers Another proxy of demand for H-1B workers is the number of employers that submitted petitions for H-1B workers to Homeland Security each year. As shown in figure 5, the overall number of employers submitting petitions for H-1B workers—both initial petitions and requests for visa extensions—fluctuated from 44,675 in fiscal year 2000 to 58,956 in fiscal year 2009 with a high of 80,945 in fiscal year 2004, showing much less annual fluctuation than the overall number of H-1B workers they requested.[31] This proxy is also likely to underestimate demand because any additional employers submitting petitions for H-1B workers subject to the cap were not counted after the cap was reached.

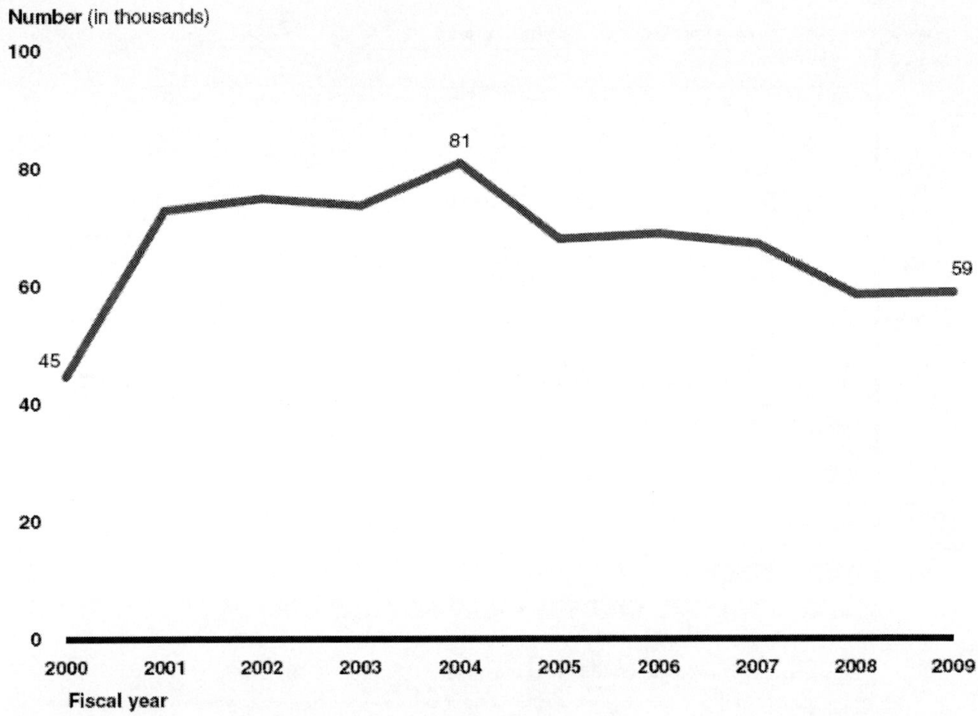

Source: GAO analysis of Homeland Security CLAIMS 3 data.

[a] Includes employers who submitted initial petitions and visa extensions and who were both exempt and not exempt from the cap. Employers who submitted petitions under the master's cap cannot be differentiated and are therefore included in these data. All employer-based analyses were restricted to petitions with valid Employer Identification Numbers. About 220,000 of 2.8 million petitions were excluded from our analysis due to missing or invalid Employer Identification Numbers.

Figure 5. Overall Number of Employers Submitting Petitions for H-1B Workers (Initial and Extensions) Processed by Homeland Security, FY 2000–FY 2009[a].

The time it takes to reach the cap—the date on which Homeland Security stops processing initial petitions for new H-1B workers from employers subject to the cap—is another proxy for demand. Employers may submit petitions for new H-1B workers starting on April 1 of each year for the following fiscal year. In some years, the cap was reached within a few days of April 1, while in other years the cap was never reached. The time it takes to reach the cap is also affected by the cap level, which fluctuated over the last decade. However, from fiscal year 2005 to fiscal year 2009, the cap level remained constant at 65,000 for regular requests and 20,000 for master's requests. For fiscal year 2005 through fiscal year 2007, the cap was reached in October, August, and May, respectively, likely indicating lower demand for new H-1B workers than in fiscal years 2008 and 2009, when the cap was reached within a few days (see fig. 6). Although Homeland Security's CLAIMS 3 Mainframe data do not allow us to distinguish which submitted initial petitions were eligible for but not counted against the master's cap, an indication of demand for that category of H-1B workers is how quickly the master's cap is reached. In fiscal years 2008 and 2009, the master's cap was reached in April, likely indicating a high level of demand for those H-1B workers in *recent years. In fisc al year 2010, the master's cap was reached before the general 65,000 cap.*

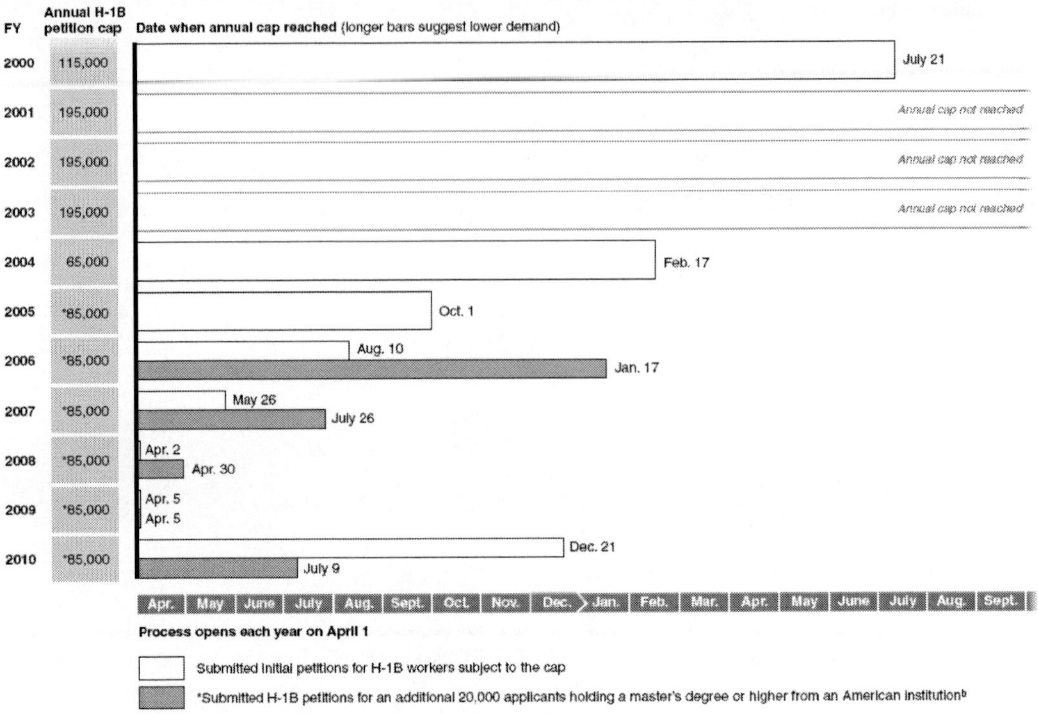

Source: GAO analysis of Homeland Security data.

[a] The cap filing period typically remains open for a total of a year-and-a-half—from April 1 preceding a given fiscal year until the end (September 30) of the following fiscal year (e.g. April 1, 2001, through September 30, 2002, for fiscal year 2002).

[b] According to Homeland Security officials, the agency first began tracking the master's cap in fiscal year 2006. Therefore, there is not a separate bar for the master's cap for fiscal year 2005.

Figure 6. Time to Reach Annual Cap and Cap Level, Regular and Master's Cap, FY 2000–FY 2010[a].

Finally, another potential indicator of demand, especially in years that the cap has been reached, might be requests for high-skilled workers via other visa programs, such as the L-1 visa for intracompany transfer of managers.[32] From fiscal year 2000 to fiscal year 2008, the number of L-1 visas issued— which is not subject to a cap—increased by almost 53 percent, *while the number of H-1B visas issued decreased slightly (see fig. 7).*

Influence of Economy on Demand

The economy was likely a key contributor to fluctuations in the demand for H-1B workers. As shown in figure 8, overall submitted petitions for H-1B workers (initial and extensions) went up and down, and ranged from a low of 214,654 in fiscal year 2002 to a high of 342,035 in fiscal year 2001 over the 10-year period. For example, in fiscal years 2002 and 2003 there was a downturn in hiring within the technology industry; concurrently, the number of submitted petitions for H-1B workers—both initial and requests for visa extensions—dropped dramatically to 214,654 and 230,423, respectively, even though the cap was increased to 195,000 for these years. In subsequent years, the number of submitted petitions increased as the economy rebounded, such that submitted petitions reached 316,065 in fiscal year 2007.

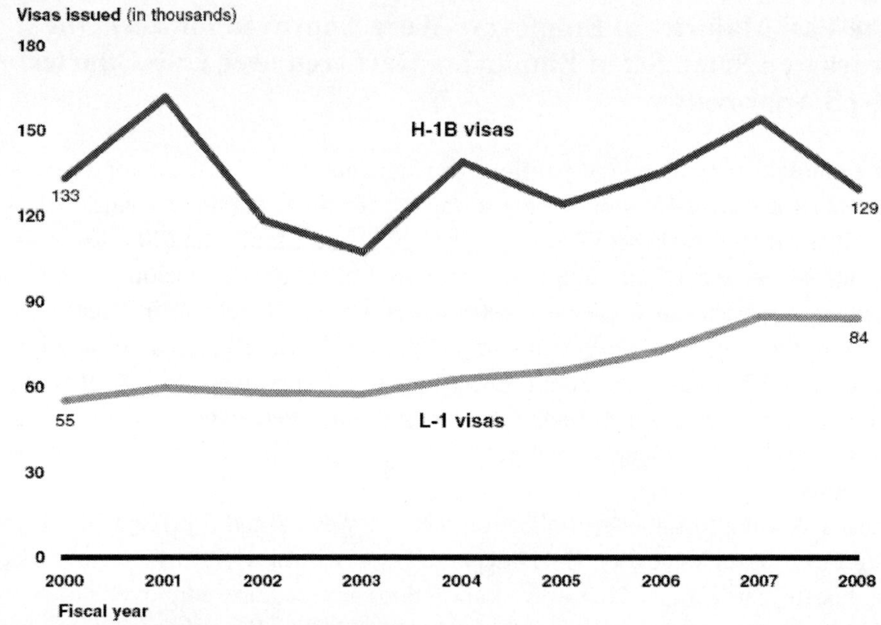

Source: GAO analysis of State visa issuance data.

Figure 7. L-1 and H-1B Visas Issued, FY 2000–FY 2008.

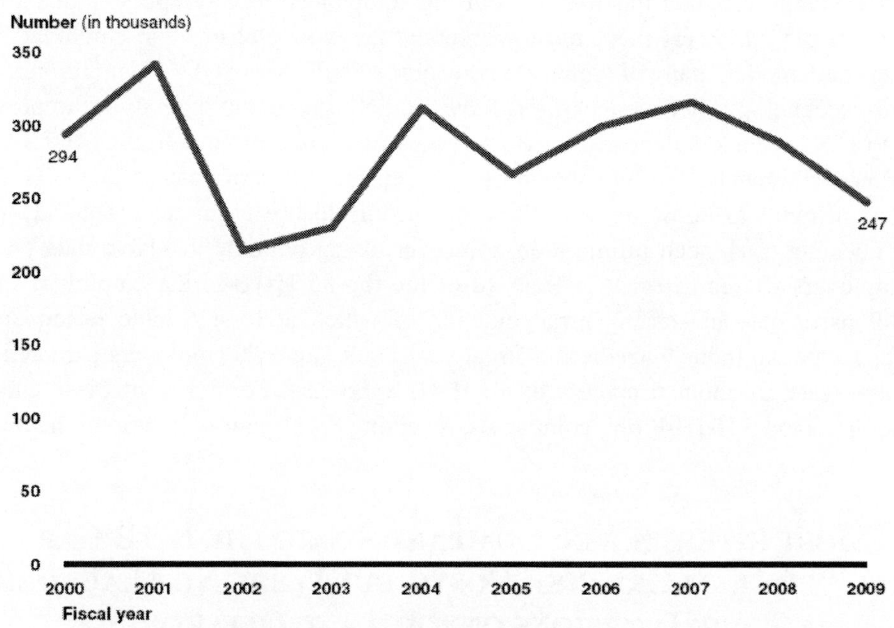

Source: GAO analysis of Homeland Security CLAIMS 3 data.

[a] Includes initial petitions and requests for visa extensions from employers exempt and not exempt from the cap. Reported numbers only reflect petitions entered into Homeland Security's CLAIMS 3 data system and processed by Homeland Security, not the total number submitted which is likely higher in years when the cap is reached.

Figure 8. All Submitted Petitions for H-1B Workers (Initial and Extensions), FY 2000–FY 2009[a].

While the Vast Majority of Employers Were Approved for Just One H-1B Worker, a Small Set of Employers Garnered over One-Quarter of All H-1B Approvals

Most employers that submitted petitions to Homeland Security were approved, and most were approved for one H-1B worker, but a small percent of employers garnered over one-quarter of all H-1B approvals between fiscal year 2000 and fiscal year 2009. Over the 10-year period, about 94 percent of all submitted petitions (initial and extensions) were approved, with a high of 97 percent in fiscal year 2006 and a low of 84 percent in fiscal year 2009.[33] With respect to the number of approved workers per employer, 68 percent of employers were approved for 1 H-1B worker and about 99 percent of all employers with approved petitions (627,922) were approved for 100 or fewer workers. However, over the decade, less than 1 percent of all employers with approved petitions were approved to hire almost 30 percent of all H-1B workers.

Further, according to Labor's application data, between 3 and 5 percent of all employers were categorized as being either H-1B-dependent or willful violators between fiscal year 2002 and fiscal year 2008.[34] However, Labor does not require employers to report (and therefore Labor's data do not indicate) the proportion of H-1B workers that comprise each employer's workforce.

Among the top H-1B-hiring employers—those approved for large numbers of H-1B workers—are employers that function as "staffing companies," (i.e., employers that apply for H-1B workers but ultimately place these workers at the worksites of other employers as part of their business model, many of which also outsource work overseas).[35] Some foreign-owned information technology (IT) services firms have publicly stated that their ability to provide IT services to U.S. customers depends in part on access to significant numbers of H-1B and L-1 visa workers. Ultimately, the prevalence of these employers participating in the H-1B visa program is difficult to know because there are no disclosure requirements and Homeland Security does not track such information. However, using publicly available data on H-1B-hiring employers we learned that at least 10 of the top 85 H-1B-hiring employers in fiscal year 2009 participate in staffing arrangements, of which at least 6 have headquarters or operations located in India. Together, in fiscal year 2009, these 10 employers garnered nearly 11,456 approvals, or about 6 percent of all H-1B approvals. Further, 3 of these employers were among the top 5 H-1B-hiring companies, receiving 8,431 approvals among them.[36]

Most Interviewed Companies Said the H-1B Cap and Program Created Costs, but Were Not Factors in Their Decisions on R&D and Offshoring

To better understand the impact of the H-1B cap and program on H-1B employers, GAO interviewed 34 companies—including individual structured interviews with 31 companies and group discussions with 3 companies—about how the H-1B program affects their costs of doing business, their R&D activities, and their decisions about whether to locate work overseas.[37] These companies reported that the H-1B cap created various costs, but those costs varied depending on the size[38] and maturity of the company. While many companies said that access to skilled labor is a significant factor in locating their R&D labs, few said that the H-1B cap was an important factor in their decisions about locating activities (either R&D or other skilled work) abroad, with the exception of IT services firms.

Depending on Their Size and Maturity, Some of the Interviewed Companies Said the Cap Resulted in Hiring Delays and Costs Associated with Uncertainty

Many of the 34 companies we spoke with cited a range of direct and indirect costs associated with the H-1B cap and program features, including staffing uncertainties, legal and administrative fees, and other costs. However, the nature and extent of some costs varied with the type of firm.

Costs of the H-1B Program

According to firms we interviewed, uncertainty in staffing due to the cap has imposed varied, and for some significant, costs to doing business, although they are difficult to quantify. Twenty-one of the 31 firms we interviewed individually reported that they had H-1B petitions denied due to the cap in years when the cap was reached early in the filing season. In these years, the firms did not know which, if any, of their H-1B candidates would obtain a visa, and several (7) firms said that this situation created uncertainty that interfered with both project planning and candidate recruitment. Two firms also said that delays in processing their petitions, such as requests for additional evidence, sometimes resulted in their candidates accepting other positions in the United States or abroad instead of waiting for a resolution. In addition, two firms mentioned that in order to get the petition application in before the deadline, they sometimes made job offers to candidates who required H-1B visas before they were certain of the need to hire them.

Firms cited other costs associated with acquiring H-1B hires, such as legal and administrative costs, and Homeland Security filing fees. For H-1B applications, the combined legal and filing fee costs among the 26 firms that reported this information to us ranged from an estimated $2,320 to $7,500 or more per petition.[39] However, several firms mentioned that petitions that generated additional requests for evidence from Homeland Security could result in higher legal costs, as well as additional administrative costs resulting from the staff hours required to collect extensive evidence. Several firms we spoke to also noted that Homeland Security filing fees have increased significantly in recent years—for example, Homeland Security fees for firms that are not exempt from the cap have risen from $110 in fiscal year 2000 to $2,320 in fiscal year 2009.[40]

With regard to firms that eventually file applications for permanent residency for their H-1B workers, some employers we spoke with noted that their total legal and administrative costs for the duration of the process are large. For example, one company official estimated the combined costs of the H-1B and green card process to be about $16,000 over the duration of the process. Two respondents noted that they have such long-term costs in mind when considering H-1B candidates. While only a few respondents brought up the cost of sponsoring an H-1B worker for permanent residency, nearly all (30 out of 31) of the firms we spoke with indicated that they had sponsored at least some of their H-1B visa holders for permanent residency, and 8 said that they typically sponsor all H-1B visa holders whose job performance was satisfactory.

Experience of Large Firms with H-1B Program

In years when firms did not receive approvals for all of their H-1B petitions, most of the large, multinational firms we spoke with reported that they were generally able to hire their preferred candidates because the firms were skilled at navigating the immigration system. Specifically, 12 of the 14 large, multinational firms we spoke with reported having found a way to hire a job candidate denied an H-1B visa due to the cap. They did so, for example, by sending the candidate to work in an overseas office and subsequently bringing him or her in on an L-1 visa, or by extending the practical training period allowed under their student visa for an additional year. Some firms noted, however, that these alternatives can be very costly. For example, after H-1B visas for preferred job candidates fell through, nine companies said they had sometimes placed their job candidates temporarily overseas, and three mentioned that this process required the company to pay an "expatriate package," with allowances for housing and living expenses. One company executive said hiring an employee on an expatriate package is often three times more costly than hiring the same employee in the U.S.—a point with which others we spoke with concurred.

Experience of Smaller Firms with H-1B Program

Of the 13 smaller H-1B employers we spoke with, 8 indicated that they had incurred significant business costs resulting from petitions denied due to the cap, delays in processing H-1B petitions, and other costs associated with the H-1B program. Six of the smaller companies we spoke with had petitions denied due to the cap, and of these, four indicated they did not have the resources or the infrastructure in place to pursue alternatives such as placing a desired employee abroad for a year. In addition, executives from four of the six small firms we spoke with who had petitions denied due to the cap told us that they had to delay or cancel projects, or hire second-choice employees, because they were unable to hire all of the employees for whom they sought H-1B petitions. Several firms in technology-intensive fields such as IT product development—both large and small—stressed that the product development cycles in their industries are extremely compressed, and in order to be competitive, they frequently need to develop new products in a matter of months, not years. Some of these firms told us that any delay in hiring an essential employee can, therefore, result in significant losses. One founder of a technology company, who valued his 3-year-old firm at about $100 million dollars, said a 3-month delay in product development could mean lost opportunities worth several million dollars.

Experience of Emerging Firms with Immigration System

To gain the perspective of entities that support and work with emerging technology companies (high-tech "start-up" firms), we spoke with venture capital and law firm representatives who reported that start-ups, in particular, often have less time and fewer resources for navigating the immigration system, and the impact of employee immigration problems on them can be substantial. Some founders of start-ups and venture capital firms with whom we spoke reported that the skills required by small firms and emerging companies in high-tech sectors are often extremely specialized, and sometimes these firms cannot readily find a "second-choice" employee in the U.S. labor market. For example, one start-up founder stressed that competition for "the best people" is fierce in "a high-growth, venture-backed business" where building "complex software faster and better than companies that are orders of magnitude larger" is critical to survival. In addition, foreign nationals seeking to found new companies in the United States can face a unique set of difficulties. Two lawyers we spoke with whose firms work with many emerging technology companies in Silicon Valley described cases in which entrepreneurs attempting to establish very early-stage technology start-ups were unable to obtain H-1B or other work visas for themselves and either relocated the project abroad or had to abandon the start-up.

Most Interviewed Companies Said the Cap Had Little Effect on R&D or Offshoring Decisions; However, Certain IT Services Firms Differed

When asked about how the H-1B cap affected their decisions on where to locate their R&D activities and other operations, 15 of the 28 companies who responded to these questions said the H-1B cap was not an important factor in their decisions on the location of these activities. The 20 firms we spoke with that conducted R&D were in a variety of industries—including semiconductor and electronics manufacturing, pharmaceutical companies, software publishing and financial services—and 7 of these 20 were in the manufacturing sector. Several firms that conducted R&D reported that their H-1B workers were essential to this work in the United States. Furthermore, access to skilled labor from around the world was very important to a number of the firms we interviewed; 15 of the companies we spoke with had R&D centers or labs overseas, and 8 of these firms told us that these centers or labs had been set up largely to access the skilled workforce in that country. However, only four said the H-1B cap was an important determinant in the creation of these overseas centers. Respondents from several of the multinational companies we spoke with—whether headquartered in the United States or not—regarded their firms as global entities, and five said that their decisions to expand overseas are primarily driven by the pursuit of new markets. In addition, firms said many other factors are involved in such decisions, including the cost of labor; access to a workforce in a variety of time zones; language and culture; proximity to universities; and tax law.[41]

While the majority of company officials we spoke to said they had not moved work offshore due to the H-1B program or cap, several respondents from one group of companies—IT services firms[42]—told us they have moved or would move work offshore as a result of the cap or changes in the administration of the H-1B program. One large IT services firm that had both an onshore staffing component and offshore outsourcing component[43] noted that in years when the H-1B cap prevented hiring all the foreign workers sought, the company could locate a larger portion of the work project overseas. Two IT staffing firms we spoke with—firms that place H-1B workers at the worksites of client companies—said their U.S. business relies heavily on the H-1B program because H-1B visa holders are more willing to relocate around the country, and one noted that H-1Bs accept lower wages than U.S. workers.

Several executives at IT staffing firms we interviewed noted that, since issuance of a January 2010 Homeland Security memo,[44] Homeland Security is more aggressively enforcing a requirement that staffing firms be able to provide evidence of an employer-employee relationship with the H-1B worker they sponsor by, for example, having a contract with their clients in place.[45] Executives from staffing firms told us they often cannot have a contract in place because they provide labor on short notice to their client firms. As a result of the increased enforcement of this provision, executives at one staffing firm told us that they no longer hired H-1Bs for their staffing business, and executives at several other staffing firms reported that they had ceased hiring new H-1B workers, hiring instead only foreign nationals already in the country with a current H-1B visa.[46,47] Executives at some companies who already had an offshore location reported expanding the portion of their work conducted overseas, and others reported that they had either opened an offshore location to access labor from overseas or were considering doing so.

Some researchers have noted that some IT services firms that conduct offshore outsourcing and employ large numbers of H-1B workers[48] offer engineering and R&D services.[49] Although 3 of the 10 IT services firms we spoke with described themselves as conducting R&D, 2 of the 3 noted that this R&D involved innovation while on-the-job. Some experts we spoke with also noted that learning and technological innovation is often attained on the job or through informal collaboration, as opposed to through formal R&D efforts. Thus, while the movement of IT services work offshore in response to the H-1B cap may not result in the direct transfer of formal R&D, it may nonetheless result in movement of innovation offshore.

Companies Also Cited Various Concerns about the Petition Review Process and Suggested Some Program Modifications

Companies we spoke with reported several concerns with the H-1B petition adjudication process, including the amount of paperwork required and the level of evidence requested during this process. Companies and experts we spoke with suggested several program modifications that could remedy some of these reported problems.

Increasingly Burdensome Adjudication Process

Eighteen of the firms we spoke with maintained that the review and adjudication process had become increasingly burdensome in recent years, with many of these firms complaining about the amount of paperwork they needed to provide as part of the adjudication process. Further, eight firms—of all sizes and across a range of industries—complained that the number of requests for additional evidence from Homeland Security increased significantly in recent years. Relatedly, in prior work, we suggested that Congress consider streamlining the H-1B approval process by eliminating the separate requirement that employers first submit an LCA to Labor for review and certification, since another agency (USCIS) subsequently conducted a similar review of the LCA.[50] Three years after our recommendation, in 2003, USCIS was moved under the newly formed Homeland Security; however, Congress has not taken action to streamline the process.

Inconsistencies in the Adjudication Process

Executives at several companies we spoke with provided examples of what they viewed as inconsistencies in the adjudication process. For example, one company executive noted that the petitions it sends to one of Homeland Security's two processing centers are often processed more efficiently than the petitions it sends to the other processing center. Another executive noted that at times, "decisions on approving or denying the H-1B visa applications seem arbitrary." This executive provided an example of a USCIS adjudicator who decided that the project for which the company sought an H-1B worker did not require "specialty education," but the executive felt that if the adjudicator had contacted the client firm, they could have easily seen that a specialist was required. Other firms noted that some adjudicators ask for evidence that seems unnecessary. For example, an immigration lawyer at a multinational pharmaceutical company said that agency requests for evidence do not always appear to be "thoughtful," and cited a Request for Evidence that demanded a review of the qualifications of an applicant who had received a science degree from Oxford University.

Adjudication Process Not Customized for Different Employers

Several companies we spoke with complained that the adjudication process is the same for all H-1B employers, irrespective of the employer's track record with the H-1B program. For example, the Immigration Policy Manager for a large, household-name Fortune 100 company recounted being asked to provide photographic evidence of its headquarters as part of the Request for Evidence in the petition review process. As another example, the Chief Executive Officer of a small software application developer who had been using the H-1B program for over 10 years recounted the frustration of interviewing 60 U.S. candidates before finding 3 candidates through international hiring, and then facing a vetting process that questioned his effort to hire a U.S. citizen. At the same time, Homeland Security staff we spoke with reported having to review large stacks of paperwork to adjudicate a single petition.

Experts we spoke with suggested that Homeland Security consider creating a risk-based adjudication process whereby businesses are ranked on their experience with the program and past compliance issues. Such a process could permit well-vetted businesses with a strong track-record of H-1B regulatory compliance access to a streamlined process for petition approval and reduced requests for evidence, thus reducing the burden to firms of providing evidence, and would permit Homeland Security investigators to focus their investigative efforts efficiently.

Rigidities in the Lottery System

Several company executives, industry representatives, and academic researchers we spoke with cited examples of what they viewed as rigidities in the lottery system, especially in years when the H-1B cap is hit early. Several industry representatives told us that the lottery process does not allow their clients to rank their top choices; as a result, firms do not necessarily receive approval for the most desired H-1B candidates. Several companies we spoke with also raised the issue that the annual allotment period does not allow firms to make their hiring decisions in response to business needs throughout the year, especially during years when the cap is hit early in the year. Some company executives and researchers we spoke with suggested the following:

- a more efficient system would permit employers to rank their applications so that they are able to hire the best qualified worker for the job in highest need; and
- to allow more flexible hiring of H-1B workers, Homeland Security consider distributing the allocation of H-1B permits throughout the year (such as quarterly) rather than annually.

Visas for Emerging Technology Companies

Entrepreneurs and venture capital firms we interviewed said that program rules can inhibit many emerging technology companies and other small firms from using the H-1B program to bring in the talent they need, constraining the ability of these companies to grow and innovate in the United States. For example, for the earliest stage ventures, when the person who needs the H-1B visa is the entrepreneur, there is sometimes no "firm" in existence yet that can meet legal criteria for employing H-1Bs. While it is not necessarily the role of the H-1B program to provide work visas for foreign entrepreneurs, several parties we spoke with discussed the risk of the United States losing its advantage in high-tech entrepreneurship if U.S. immigration policy undermines the ability and interest of new entrepreneurs to move to high-tech communities like Silicon Valley. Some venture capital firms and businesses we spoke with suggested that, in order to promote the ability of entrepreneurs to start businesses in the United States, Congress should consider creating a visa category for entrepreneurs, available to persons with U.S. venture backing.[51]

Agency officials expressed reservations about the feasibility of GAO's past recommendation and the suggestions from experts and company executives on improving the application process. Homeland Security officials believed that Labor would be better suited to review the LCA because Labor has specialized knowledge about the computation of prevailing wages. Labor officials, however, conceded that their review of the LCA is limited by statute, as discussed above. In regard to the potential adoption of a customized adjudication process, Labor officials noted that a strong track record of compliance with program rules does not guarantee future compliance. Homeland Security officials also noted that establishing a system for employers to rank their submitted petitions in order of priority might increase the likelihood of fraud if it also increased incentives for employers to submit applications for hypothetical workers in order to capture a larger proportion of those selected for the lottery. State officials raised questions about the logistics required for allocating H-1B petitions throughout the year—for example, whether or how employers would be permitted to resubmit petitions after receiving a denial in one quarter, and whether such a system might result in more employers being denied access to H-1B workers during peak seasons.

Homeland Security officials also noted two efforts currently under way to streamline the application process for prospective H-1B employers. Homeland Security is in the process of developing a product that would allow it to use data from a private data vendor to automatically download certain data on employers and update those data over time so that in the future, employers may not have as heavy a burden in filing their petitions. This product is currently being tested. Second, Homeland Security is currently preparing a proposed rule, which is being reviewed and considered within the agency, to allow employers to submit requests for H-1B slots before submitting an LCA. This rule would spare employers that were not chosen in the lottery from having to file an LCA and could also reduce workloads for Labor. The officials did not know whether and when a proposed rule would be published for comment and finalized.

Although Data Limitations Preclude Knowledge of the Total H-1B Workforce and Precise Tracking of the Cap, Characteristics of Those Approved to Be H-1B Workers Are Known

Data on the total number of H-1B workers in the United States are not available because of limitations in agency data. In addition, although Homeland Security is responsible for tracking the number of H-1B petitions approved under the cap or the number of H-1B visas issued,[52] it cannot precisely do so. However, Homeland Security is currently taking steps to address these limitations. Data on the annual cohort of people approved to be H-1B workers (referred to as "approved H-1B workers" in this report) offer some information on the characteristics of likely H-1B workers, including their countries of birth, occupations, and education levels.

Limitations in Agency Data Systems Hinder Tracking the Cap and H-1B Workers over Time, though Homeland SecurityIs Working to Improve its Systems

Although Homeland Security generally tracks the flow of likely H-1B workers into the United States on an annual basis, it cannot determine the size of the cumulative H-1B workforce because several agencies or departments manage data on this population over time, and the systems that capture the data are not easily linked. H-1B petition approvals are captured in Homeland Security's CLAIMS 3 data system, as are changes in visa status for approved H-1B workers who are already residing in the country at the time of approval. However, visas for H-1B workers living abroad at the time of approval are captured by a data system that is administered by State and not linked to CLAIMS 3. Further, information on visa holders who actually enter or exit the United States is tracked viaHomeland Security's United States Visitor and Immigrant Status Indicator Technology (US-VISIT) program, which is not systematically linked to CLAIMS 3. Because these data systems do not use a unique, person-centric identifier for H-1B workers, Homeland Security cannot determine, for example, how many approved H-1B workers living abroad actually received an H-1B visa and/or ultimately entered the country.[53] Similarly, Homeland Security does not track H-1B workers after their visas expire, and cannot readily determine if and when H-1B workers apply for or are granted legal permanent residency, leave the country, or remain in the country on an expired visa. The fact that electronic records from different systems are not linked also results in unnecessary duplication of efforts. For example, according to State officials, while State has some capacity to query Homeland Security's CLAIMS 3 database, its consular posts cannot import data from CLAIMS 3 to their own data system, so State contractors re-enter information from CLAIMS 3 manually into State's data system.

Further, although Homeland Security is responsible for tracking the number of H-1B petitions approved under the cap and the number of H-1B visas issued, it does not maintain precise information on this. To implement the statutory cap on H-1B visas, Homeland Security must take the necessary steps to maintain an accurate count of the number of aliens subject to the annual cap who are issued visas or otherwise provided nonimmigrant status by the Immigration and Nationality Act.[54] However, according to Homeland Security officials, the department's current processes do not allow them to determine precisely when approvals reach the number set by the cap. Instead, they stop accepting initial petitions for new H-1B workers that are subject to the cap when they estimate that the number of approved petitions is approaching the mandated limit. In fiscal year 2005, Homeland Security's Office of Inspector General found that USCIS exceeded the 65,000 cap limit by about 7,000 approved petitions and recommended the agency maintain more precise control over the number of H-1B visas issued.[55] Although the recommendation was closed by the Office of Inspector General in 2006, Homeland Security officials concede they still cannot precisely count, in an ongoing manner, petitions accepted under the cap despite several changes in how the agency accepts, monitors, controls, and forecasts receipts for submitted petitions subject to the cap. Further, officials noted that as long as the process of submitting and adjudicating H-1B petitions remains the same, they are unlikely to be able to provide a precise count of petitions accepted under the cap.

The capability to better track the cumulative H-1B workforce and petitions accepted under the annual cap may develop with the eventual completion of Homeland Security's program to modernize business processes and information systems, although challenges remain. Homeland Security's "Transformation Program" is a multiprogram, multiyear effort, ongoing since 2005, that includes a plan to implement an electronic I-129 petition, with a unique identifier for each H-1B worker. Using this identifier, Homeland Security would likely be able to share data with State and other external partners.[56] Homeland Security officials reported, for example, that they are currently working with agencies that include Justice and State to create a cross-reference table of agency identifiers for individuals applying for visas. Ultimately, the table would capture each record for the same person and employer from all partner agency programs, such that records for a specific individual can be merged under one unique person-centric identifier. When this occurs, it will be possible to identify who is in the United States at any one point in time under any and all visa programs. USCIS plans to develop internal guidance for the electronic I-129 petition over the next 2 years. However, according to previous GAO reports, Homeland Security's Office of Inspector General, and Homeland Security officials, the agency faces challenges finalizing and moving ahead with implementation of the program.[57]

Most Approvals for H-1B Workers Were for Workers from India or China and for Technology Positions

Between fiscal year 2000 and fiscal year 2009, the majority of approved H-1B workers (initial and extensions for both employers subject to the cap and cap-exempt employers) were born in Asia. Over the last decade, the top four countries of birth for approved H-1B workers were India, China, Canada, and the Philippines. Across all 10 years, about 64 percent of approved H-1B workers were born in these four countries, with the largest group from India (see fig. 9).

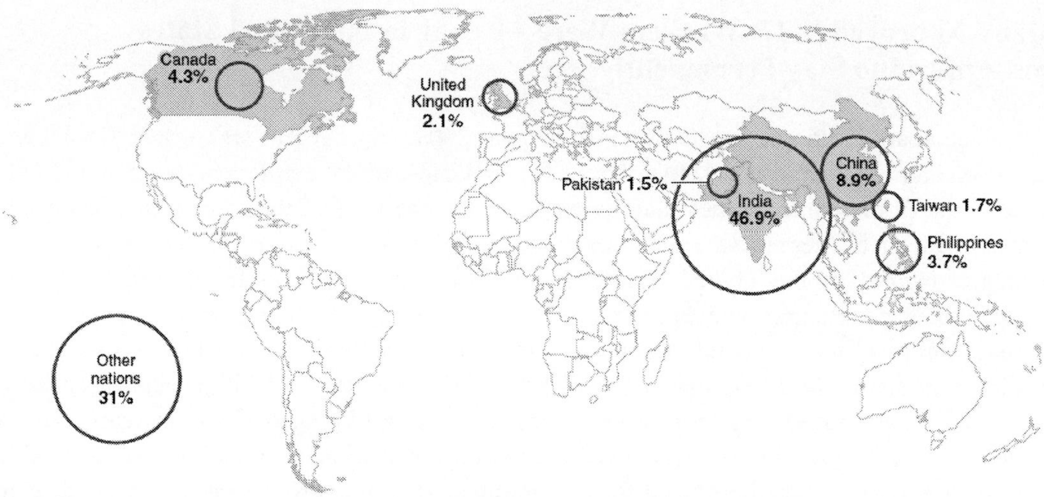

Source: GAO analysis of Homeland Security CLAIMS 3 data; National Atlas of the United States (base map).

[a] Includes both initial petitions and requests for visa extensions.

Figure 9. Country of Birth for Approved H-1B Workers, FY 2000–FY 2009[a].

Over the same period, more than 40 percent of approved H-1B workers (initial and extensions for both employers subject to the cap and cap-exempt employers) were approved to fill occupations in systems analysis and programming. The next-highest occupational category was college and university education, which represented about 7 percent of H-1B approvals, as shown in figure 10.

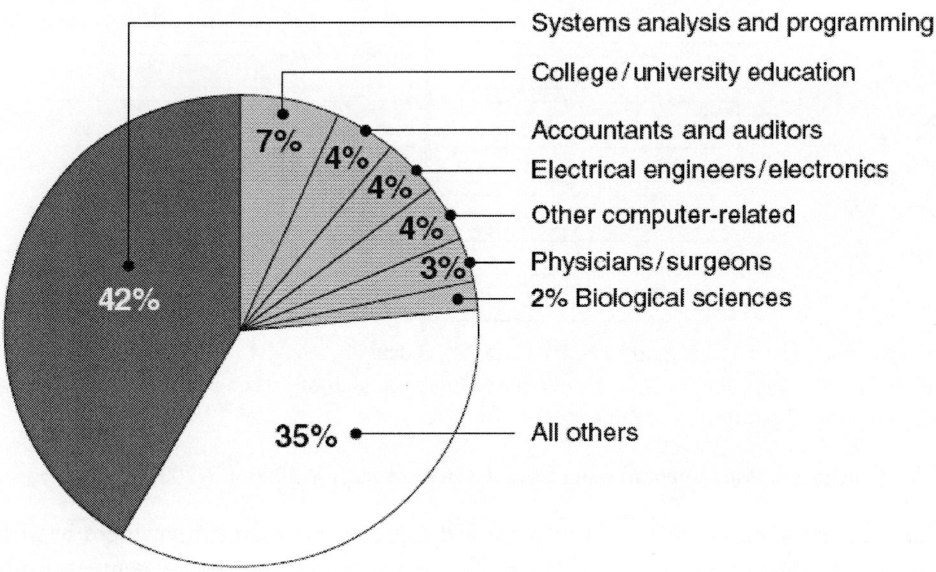

Source: GAO analysis of Homeland Security CLAIMS 3 data.

[a]Includes both initial petitions and requests for visa extensions.

Figure 10. Occupations Approved for H-1B Workers, FY 2000–FY 2009[a].

Many Approved H-1B Workers Were Already in the United States and Applied to Stay Permanently

As compared to fiscal year 2000, in fiscal year 2009, approved H-1B workers (initial and extensions for both employers subject to the cap and cap-exempt employers) were more likely to be living in the United States than living abroad at the time of their initial application, to have an advanced degree (master's, professional, or Ph.D.), and to have obtained their graduate degrees in the United States. From fiscal year 2000 to fiscal year 2009, the proportion of newly approved H-1B workers that were already living in the United States increased from 43 to 62 percent. Many of these workers are likely to have been on student or another visa status. In 2000, 40 percent of approved H-1B workers (initial and extensions) possessed an advanced degree (master's, professional, or Ph.D.), which increased to 59 percent by fiscal year 2009 (see fig. 11). One reason for this increase may be the H-1B Visa Reform Act of 2004, which allowed for an additional 20,000 approvals each year for foreign workers holding a master's degree or higher from an American institute of higher education.[58] Since then, the proportion of approved H-1B workers who graduated with a master's degree from an American institution of higher education increased from 29 to 36 percent of all approved workers—including initial petitions and visa extensions.[59]

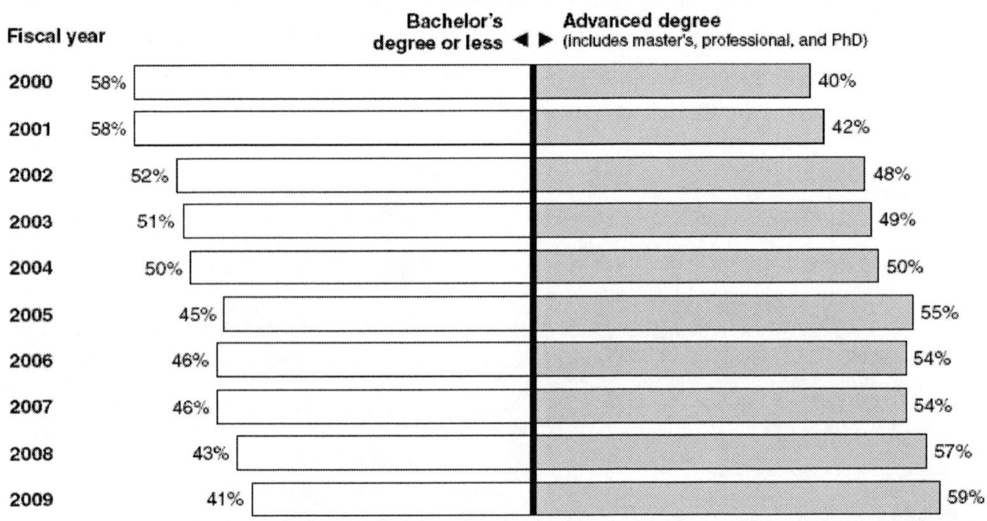

Source: GAO analysis of Homeland Security CLAIMS 3 data.
Note: Bars do not always sum to 100 percent due to our exclusion of missing or invalid data.
[a] Includes both initial petitions and requests for visa extensions.

Figure 11. Educational Attainment of Approved H-1B Workers, FY 2000–FY 2009[a].

These findings are consistent with previously discussed findings that there has been an increase in the number of approved H-1B workers receiving advanced degrees from U.S. universities, as well as those who are already residing in the United States at the time of H-1B visa approval. This in turn suggests that, in general, the approved H-1B population may include more recent graduates, who are younger and more highly educated, as compared to their U.S. citizen counterparts in similar occupations. In turn, the U.S. citizen population in similar occupations may include older, more experienced workers.

Finally, data on a cohort of approved H-1B workers whose petitions were submitted between January 1, 2004, and September 30, 2007, (including initial petitions from both employers subject to the cap and cap-exempt employers) indicate that a substantial proportion subsequently applied for permanent residence in the United States. Specifically, from a cohort of 311,847 approved H-1B petitions, we were able to obtain unique matches for 169,349 petitions from Homeland Security's US-VISIT data. Of these, GAO found that 56,454 of the individuals listed on these H-1B petitions had submitted a petition for permanent residence by 2010. Thus, at least 18 percent of the total cohort had applied for permanent residence by 2010.[60] Further, about half of those that applied had been approved for permanent residence by 2010, 45 percent were still pending, and just 3 percent had been denied.

THE IMPACT OF RAISING THE H-1B CAP ON THE U.S. WORKFORCE IS DIFFICULT TO FORECAST DUE TO COMPLEX ECONOMIC FACTORS

The Impact of Raising the Cap is Difficult to Estimate

In addition to lack of data on the total H-1B workforce previously discussed, the potential impact that raising the H-1B cap would have on the wages and employment of U.S. workers is difficult to estimate because of complex economic relationships. On the one hand, if the H-1B program successfully provides needed skills for the U.S. economy, economic theory suggests that the program should contribute to long-run economic growth, which is beneficial for all workers. For example, additional skilled labor could increase innovation and productivity, potentially leading to improved competitiveness of U.S. businesses, higher wages in aggregate, and lower prices on goods and services purchased by American consumers. On the other hand, certain groups of U.S. workers may experience lower wages and employment as a result of the inflow of H-1B workers. Furthermore, changes in the wages and employment of both U.S. workers and H-1B workers reflect both changes in demand for labor and changes in the supply of labor, making it difficult to determine the effect that changes in the number of H-1B workers would have on outcomes for U.S. workers.

Although demand for H-1B workers seemed to fluctuate in concert with broad economic indicators, relationships still cannot be inferred. As shown in figure 12, the number of submitted H-1B petitions has generally followed overall employment growth in the U.S. economy. This appears consistent with economic theory that suggests that businesses require additional labor during periods of economic growth, so employers will likely submit more H-1B petitions during these periods. At the same time, wage rates and employment levels for U.S. workers generally rise during periods of economic growth. Therefore, the number of H-1B petitions tends to rise when wages and employment for U.S. workers are rising (although the number of approvals is limited by the H-1B cap), and to fall when wages and employment for U.S. workers are falling. However, this relationship does not reveal what the wage rates and employment rates of U.S. workers would have been in the absence of H-1B workers.

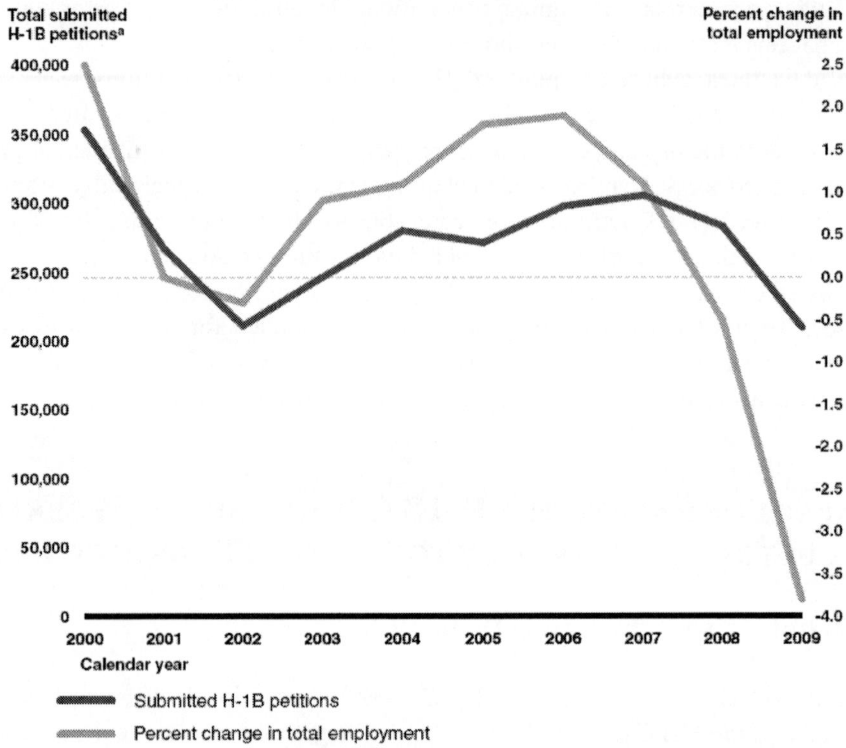

Source: GAO analysis of Homeland Security CLAIMS 3 data and CPS data.

[a] Total submitted H-1B petitions represent the number of petitions submitted in that calendar year. For example, 353,000 petitions were submitted in calendar year 2000. Percent change in total employment for a given year is the percent change in the number of workers employed between the previous calendar year and the current calendar year. Estimated change in total employment has 95 percent confidence intervals of within +/- 0.5 percentage points.

Figure 12. H-1B Submitted Petitions and Aggregate Employment Growth, 2000–2009.

Due to these complex economic relationships, coupled with limitations in data on the total H-1B workforce discussed previously, we did not attempt to forecast the impacts of prospective changes in the H-1B cap on the U.S. labor force.

Employment and Earnings Picture Was Mixed for Professions Absorbing H-1Bs

While GAO did not attempt to forecast the impacts of prospective changes in the H-1B cap, we examined 10 years of retrospective data on the employment, unemployment, and earnings of U.S. workers in the three occupations that absorbed the largest proportion of H-1B workers relative to the stock of U.S. workers in these occupations.[61] The three occupations with the highest number of H-1B approvals relative to the number of U.S. workers in that occupation were (1) systems analysts, programmers, and other computer-related workers;[62] (2) electrical and electronics engineers; and (3) college and university educators. For example, among systems analysts, programmers, and other computer-related workers aged 18 to 50, the number of approved H-1B petitions (initial and extensions) was 10 percent of the total stock of U.S. citizen workers in private sector jobs in this occupation in calendar year 2008.[63]

Our analysis of these three occupations generally revealed a mixed earnings and employment picture for U.S. workers in professions absorbing H-1Bs. (See appendix III for additional details.)

- With respect to median earnings, we found that U.S. workers in all three occupations, in every year, had significantly higher median earnings levels compared to all professional U.S. workers.
- With respect to real earnings growth, systems analysts, programmers, and and other computer-related workers had significantly higher real earnings growth[64] compared to all professional workers; in contrast, for electrical and electronics engineers, real earnings growth was not significantly different from that for professional workers, and for college and university educators, real earnings growth was relatively flat over the decade.
- Unemployment rates for both (1) systems analysts, programmers, and other computer-related workers and (2) electrical and electronics engineers were relatively cyclical; in contrast, the unemployment rate for college and university educators was somewhat less sensitive to business cycle fluctuations over the decade.
- Employment levels (i.e., the number of workers employed) for electrical and electronics engineers declined significantly over the decade; employment levels for systems analysts, programmers, and other computer-related workers were essentially unchanged; and employment levels for college and university educators grew significantly over the decade.

H-1B and U.S. Citizen Workers: Salary Differences

To examine more closely whether H-1B workers are being paid salaries that are comparable to U.S. workers, we examined data on salaries for the three occupations that absorbed the largest proportion of H-1B workers relative to the stock of U.S. workers in 2008,[65] and compared this to dataon the reported salaries listed by the employer on H-1B petitions.[66] A comparison of median annual salaries reveals that for systems analysts, programmers, and other computer-related workers—the largest of the three occupational categories we examined—H-1B workers tended to earn less than U.S. workers; however, some of the salary gap appears to be explained by differences in ages, which may reflect differences in the extent of their work experience.[67] As shown in table 1, which summarizes the median reported earnings of H-1B and U.S. workers by age and occupation, among systems analysts, programmers, and other computer-related workers, differences in median reported earnings between H-1B workers aged 20 to 29 and U.S. workers of the same age were not statistically significantly different, and the same was true for workers aged 30 to 39; however, H-1B workers aged 40 to 50 had median reported earnings that were significantly lower than the median earnings of U.S. workers in this occupation. Among electronics and electrical engineers, we did not find significant differences in median earnings of approved H-1B workers and U.S. workers, overall and within the age groups we examined. Among college and university educators, differences in reported earnings between H-1B workers and U.S. workers were not statistically significant except among younger age groups in which the H-1B workers had higher reported earnings than U.S. workers in the same age category; however, we could not account for all factors that might affect salary levels. (See the discussion “Limitations of Wage Comparisons” in appendix I for more information.) For all groups, differences in other factors, such as skill level, might explain some of the remaining salary differences; however, a lack of data on these factors precludes our analysis of them. In addition, differences in factors such as geographic location, size of firm, and industry, as well as level of education, which may also affect salary differences, are not controlled for here due to data limitations.[68] For example, if certain groups of workers are more heavily concentrated in high-cost parts of the country, this will be reflected in the median wage. (For additional analyses comparing U.S. workers with approved H-1B workers, see appendix II.)

In an attempt to better understand these results, we interviewed academic researchers and labor advocates who have studied the impact of H-1B workers on particular segments of the workforce. These experts and advocates provided examples of several specific segments of the workforce for which they believe the H-1B program has had negative impacts.

Because H-1B workers tend to be younger (with less potential work experience) than their U.S. counterparts who tend to be older (with more potential work experience), some labor advocates we spoke with argued that the H-1B program detrimentally impacts older IT professionals. Several researchers and labor advocates have stated that technology companies seek to replace older, American IT workers with cheaper, younger workers that are freshly supplied through the H-1B program in order to lower costs, and that IT companies have no incentive to retain and retrain older workers with the latest skills, since the H-1B program provides ready access to young workers with cutting-edge training. While companies could use any young, skilled workers to lower their labor costs in this manner, advocates argue that the H-1B program facilitates the practice of displacing older IT workers because it provides an inflow of new workers in IT fields that is much larger than would otherwise be available to U.S. employers. The analysis presented here does not provide a test of this theory because it does not identify what the wages of older U.S. IT professionals would have been in the absence of the H-1B program, nor does it account for the myriad factors affecting wage, for which we lack data.

Three researchers we spoke with expressed concern about the disincentives that U.S. students face in entering science, technology, engineering, and mathematics (STEM) fields.[69] For example, one disincentive is the duration of postdoctoral positions. Data show that since the 1960s, postdoctoral positions—which are generally exempt from the H-1B cap—have increased in length, with the largest increase in biological sciences.[70] One researcher posited that the increasing length of postdoctoral positions, especially in the biomedical fields, is due in part to the presence of large numbers of foreign nationals who are willing to work in these low-paid positions for many years. For foreign nationals, these postdoctoral positions may offer an entrée into the U.S. labor market, and the salaries may also compare well to the opportunities available in their home countries.

Table 1. Median Reported Salaries of Approved H-1B Workers and Estimated U.S. Worker Median Salaries in Selected Occupations, 2008

	Electrical/electronics engineering occupations			Systems analysis, programming, and other computer-related occupations			Occupations in college and university education		
Age Group	H-1B	U.S. workers	Significant difference	H-1B	U.S. workers	Significant difference	H-1B	U.S. workers	Significant difference
18- 50	$80,000	$80,000	no	$61,000	$70,000	yes	$48,000	$44,000	no
20 - 39[a]	80,000	75,000	no	60,100	65,000	yes	47,237	35,000	yes
20 - 29	73,000	[b]	[b]	60,000	58,000	no	42,000	30,000	yes
30 - 39	86,900	[b]	[b]	70,000	70,000	no	48,500	[b]	[b]
40 - 50	85,000	95,000	no	77,063	84,000	yes	51,905	52,500	no

Source: GAO analysis of U.S. self-reported earnings from Labor's CPS data and H-1B earnings reported by their prospective employers from USCIS CLAIMS 3 data.

Note: The CPS sample is restricted to U.S. citizens in full-time, private sector employment. Estimated median salaries for U.S. workers have 95 percent confidence intervals ranging from +/- 5 to +/- 50 percent of the estimate itself. When the difference between the estimated U.S. worker median is significantly different from the corresponding median salary for H-1B, it is noted in the table

[a] Tests for differences in medians are shown for the broader age group, 20 to 39 years, because we could not produce reliable estimates for the smaller age groups—i.e., for 20 to 29 years and 30 to 39 years—for all occupations, due to small sample size in CPS-based estimates.

[b] Indicates that sample size was too small to produce reliable CPS-based estimates.

Testimonial evidence also suggests that U.S. software programmers, particularly those seeking IT consulting jobs, may have been detrimentally affected by the significant presence of H-1B workers and, in particular, by the presence of certain staffing companies. One labor advocate we spoke with stated that staffing companies that farm out H-1B IT workers to other companies are abundant in the Northeast region of the country, and their presence has dramatically reduced the availability of jobs for U.S. software programmers in that region. Labor investigators we spoke with also noted the concentration of H-1Bs in the IT consulting industry, particularly in the Northeast region. These investigators noted that the bulk of the complaints they receive in this region pertain to staffing companies. In addition, Labor investigators told us that some staffing companies at times will pass an open position amongst themselves, rather than making a job opening known to the workforce at large. For example, if one staffing company is contacted with a request for a software programmer and does not have a worker with the appropriate skillset, this firm may— unbeknownst to the firm that is seeking the worker—"subcontract" the job out to a second staffing company who does have a worker with the appropriate skillset—and the first staffing company might take a cut of the wages received.

LIMITED AGENCY OVERSIGHT AND COORDINATION AND CHANGES TO THE H-1B PROGRAM HAVE WEAKENED U.S. WORKER PROTECTIONS

Responsibility for Worker Protection Is Limited and Dispersed among the Many Administering Agencies, and Hampered by Restrictions on Their Ability to Collaborate

Responsibility for the protection of workers with regard to the H-1B visa program is shared by four departments and their respective divisions. By virtue of their specific and often cordoned responsibilities, however, there is only nominal sharing of the kind of information that would allow for better employer screening or more active and targeted pursuit of program abuses. Once a visa-holder is employed, divisions within Labor, Homeland Security, and Justice may pursue enforcement of the H-1B program requirements in accordance with their broader responsibilities for enforcing labor or immigration laws. However, their work is largely complaint-driven, and information sharing among them, or with offices that must screen H-1B applications, is also limited. Table 2 summarizes agency oversight responsibilities and limitations, which are further elaborated in the following pages.

Limited and Dispersed Application Review

Labor's Employment and Training Administration

While Employment and Training reviews the LCA form submitted by a petitioning employer, this review is limited by law to looking for missing information and obvious inaccuracies.[71] For example, an employer may have failed to checkmark all the boxes for attesting to his or her willingness to comply with program requirements. While Labor's review catches some administrative errors made by applicants, it does not check the validity of the information on the LCA. Consequently, the review is not intended to identify potential employer violations such as work sites that do not exist or lack of compliance with the attestations made on the LCA. This review is primarily conducted electronically with officials reviewing the information flagged by the electronic system as problematic. Any greater scrutiny by Employment and Training is limited by law.

Table 2. Summary of Agency Oversight Responsibilities and Limitations for the H-1B Program

Agency division	Role	Limitations
Labor—Employment and Training Administration	Application review:Reviews employer LCA	Limited by statute to review only for missing information and obvious inaccuracies.
Homeland Security—U.S. Citizenship and Immigration Services	Application review:Reviews employee H-1B petition form (I-129) and decides if petition can be approved	Does not receive information from Labor's Employment and Training Administration or Wage andHour Division.
State—Bureau of Consular Affairs	Application review:Interviews prospective H-1B nonimmigrants with approved petitions and may issue visas to H-1B candidates living abroad	Limited ability for interviewers (consular officials) to question applications previously approved by Labor and Homeland Security.
Labor—Wage and Hour Division	Enforcement: Investigates complaints regarding compliance with program rules as to wages and working conditions	Limited by • prohibitions on officials initiating investigations based on information received from Labor or Homeland Security officials; • limited access to LCA database (iCERT); and • lack of subpoena authority for employer records.
Homeland Security—Directorate of Fraud Detection and National Security	Enforcement: Conducts random investigations of H-1B employers through site visits to verify information supplied in the LCA and I-129 petitions.	The Administrative Site Visit and Verification Program was initiated after a "Benefit Fraud and Compliance Assessment" (BFCA) found 21 percent fraud in H-1B program; however, Homeland Security is continuing toevaluate this program for effectiveness.
Justice—Office of Special Counsel	Enforcement: Investigates complaints (known as charges) related to acts of employment such as hiring and firing	Reluctance of workers to file complaints for fear of employer retaliation. Workers'lack of awareness of their employers'intention to hire H-1B workers. Limited agency information sharing.

Source: GAO review of agency information.

Homeland Security's U.S. Citizenship and Immigration Services

Adjudicators with USCIS conduct a review of both the employer's application and the foreign worker as a job candidate. Specifically, Homeland Security reviews two documents for consistency: the LCA submitted originally to Labor for review, and the I-129 petition, which is submitted by businesses to Homeland Security and generally contains correlating information.[72] In addition to reviewing for consistency, USCIS adjudicators explained that they take steps to verify the facts provided for both the employer and the prospective worker—for example, by requesting additional information from the employer. USCIS's adjudicators do not receive information regarding suspicious or problematic employers from Labor's Employment and Training Administration that Labor analysts may have become aware of during their review of the LCA because Labor does not have a formal mechanism for sharing such information with Homeland Security.

Department of State

State plays a role in the H-1B program by interviewing and potentially issuing visas to H-1B candidates living abroad, whose petitions were approved by Homeland Security. State conducts its own review of the H-1B petitioner and documentation pertaining to his or her employer by comparing information gleaned from interviews against basic information in the LCA and I-129 petition, such as the name of the petitioner and the foreign worker. However, official department guidance instructs consular officials not to question the petition approvals made by Homeland Security when making their decision on the visa application without having obtained new evidence.[73] State guidance stipulates that a petition can only be sent back when there has been a clear error committed in adjudicating the I-129 petition or new evidence is submitted that contradicts Homeland Security adjudicators' decisions. Officials noted that there is a high threshold for the identification of a clear error and this rationale is almost never used. State has, however, recommended 1,744 revocations in fiscal year 2009 based on new evidence. As a general rule, State consular officers treat information provided to and reviewed by Homeland Security on business establishments, relationships, and individual qualifications as bona fide.

Limited Enforcement

Labor's Wage and Hour Division

Labor's Wage and Hour investigates H-1B complaints primarily related to improper wage payments and failures to notify workers that a company intends to hire an H-1B worker. However, its ability to enforce worker protections with regard to the H-1B program is limited.[74] Although the Secretary of Labor has authority to initiate investigations, Wage and Hour reported that it had never initiated an investigation under this authority. Officials explained that they rarely proactively investigate companies for H-1B violations, and that they may generally only act on formal complaints.[75] Moreover, by law, investigations can only be initiated from information obtained from an aggrieved or credible party outside of Labor.[76] Further, Labor officials told us they have interpreted this restriction to include information from Homeland Security as well. As a result, Labor's Wage and Hour could not initiate a complaint based on any information it might receive from Homeland Security, such as information on potential abuses that Homeland Security might glean from its review of the

I-129 petition. In a prior report, GAO suggested that Congress remove these legal restrictions, but Congress has yet to take action.[77]

While the majority of complaints received by Labor have been reported by H-1B workers, very few complaints are filed. In 2009, only 664 out of 51,980 companies approved to hire new or extending H-1B workers had complaints against them. According to agency officials, H-1B workers are likely to be reluctant to file complaints against employers for fear that the company might be disbarred, which in turn could result in the complainant and fellow H-1B workers at the company losing their jobs and potentially having to leave the United States. Further, investigators told us that even after an H-1B worker files a complaint, the H-1B worker may not cooperate in the investigation for fear of similar repercussions. In these instances, investigators are sometimes unable to complete the investigation. The relatively small number of H-1Brelated complaints in 2009 nevertheless resulted in Labor requiring companies to pay over $10 million in unpaid wages to 1,202 workers and $739,929 in civil monetary penalties (see table 3).

Labor's ability to enforce worker protections under the program is also hampered by obstacles cited by officials at both headquarters and in Wage and Hour's Northeast Regional Office, which receives the greatest number of H-1B complaints:

First, with the introduction in June 2009 of the automated "iCERT" system maintained by Employment and Training, Wage and Hour stated that they can no longer access the database of LCAs. Prior access had allowed investigators to quickly assess the accuracy of the attestations made by an employer. Without this access, officials stated that they must request the LCA from the employer, which can increase the time and resources required to conduct an investigation. Employment and Training reported that improved access to the iCERT System is under development and planned for implementation in April 2011.

Second, Wage and Hour has limited ability to persuade employers to cooperate with investigations. The fine it can levy against employers for not cooperating is far less than the potential penalty for a finding of noncompliance with the terms of the program.[78] Investigators noted that when employers do not cooperate, it can take them months to obtain the requested paperwork, which essentially stalls the time-sensitive investigation.

Third, Wage and Hour lacks subpoena authority to obtain such records directly from the employer. In contrast, Wage and Hour, as well as Employment and Training, have subpoena power for other labor protection programs they administer, such as under the Fair Labor Standards Act and the Migrant and Seasonal Agricultural Worker Protection Act.[79] According to Wage and Hour officials, subpoena power increases cooperation from companies and is the most effective way to speed up investigations, since companies could face harsh penalties, such as debarment, for not cooperating. The Department of Justice also has subpoena power for its investigations related to the H-1B program.[80] Justice officials we spoke with noted that while they rarely have to invoke subpoena power in their investigations, generally employers are aware of the subpoena power and are therefore more likely to comply with Justice's requests for records.

Table 3. H-1B Complaints, Violations, Back Wages, and Fines Assessed by Labor's Wage and Hour Division, FY 2000–FY 2009

Fiscal year	Number of complaints received	Number of complaints resulting in investigations	Number of cases with violations[a]	Number of violations found	Amount due in back wages (in millions)	Number of employees due back wages	Civil monetary penalties assessed	Number of disbarments of H-1B employers
2000	123	117	54	375	$ 1.2	226	$ 21,000	3
2001	209	192	37	164	.6	135	17,750	7
2002	249	238	105	977	3.7	817	48,350	7
2003	158	148	121	711	4.0	550	128,890	19
2004	172	158	117	561	4.2	376	114,125	14
2005	184	173	90	733	5.1	593	86,100	17
2006	231	214	107	1,000	4.6	823	328,050	16
2007	299	291	133	1,026	6.4	657	324,325	13
2008	319	304	155	1,829	8.2	1162	362,750	17
2009	664	555	152	2,834	11.0	1202	739,929	13

Source: Labor's Wage and Hour.

[a]Cases with violations includes the number of cases in which Labor found the employer was in fact in violation of the program requirements. Each case may include multiple violations that were not originally included in the complaint, therefore making the number of cases with violations at times higher than the number of complaints.

Homeland Security's Directorate of Fraud Detection and National Security

In its capacity to investigate immigration fraud, FDNS has recently introduced some proactive enforcement for the H-1B program through several random investigations into temporary visa programs. Through a Benefit Fraud and Compliance Assessment (BFCA), Homeland Security examined 246 H-1B petitions for possible violations.[81] The BFCA found that 21 percent of H-1B petitions involved fraud or technical violations. Examples of fraud include cases in which businesses listed on the LCA and I-129 did not exist; educational degrees were found to be fraudulent; signatures were forged on supporting documents; and H-1B workers were performing duties or receiving payment significantly different from those described in the applications.

As a result of the high rate of fraud identified in the BFCA, Homeland Security launched what it calls its Administrative Site Visit and Verification Program—an ongoing initiative to visit work sites of H-1B-hiring companies considered to be at a higher risk for abusing the program, according to officials. During fiscal year 2010, USCIS oversaw 14,433 H-1B site inspections, which resulted in 1,176 adverse actions. Such actions can include the revocation or denial of benefits, and may involve referral of a case for criminal investigation.[82] FDNS is continuing to evaluate this initiative and refine the indicators it uses to identify groups of high-risk companies.

Department of Justice's Office of Special Counsel

Justice's Office of Special Counsel also conducts investigations; but its enforcement abilities are also limited. Justice's jurisdiction limits it to pursue charges related to unfair immigration-related employment practices, such as discriminatory hiring or firing.[83] For example, such charges generally allege that an H-1B worker was hired in place of a U.S. worker, or that a company is using discriminatory hiring practices that put U.S. workers at a disadvantage, such as explicitly advertising for an H-1B worker.

Justice receives and investigates few charges related to the H-1B program (at most 70 per year over the last 5 years with the number decreasing) and reported that their ability to enforce the law depends on the willingness and ability of U.S. workers to complain.[84] Justice officials explained that the low number of charges they receive is likely because U.S. workers are often unaware that an employer intends to or did hire an H-1B worker. For example, although employers are supposed to post a public statement declaring their intention to hire an H-1B worker, the statement might be posted in a lunch room where it may or may not be seen by affected employees. Further, Labor investigators reported that many of the companies they investigate do not comply with requirements to post notice. In contrast, Labor requires applicants for other temporary visa programs, such as the H-2A program, to display such postings on a centralized Web site that is managed by Labor.[85] Justice officials noted that the lack of a centralized Web site makes it difficult for U.S. workers to learn that U.S. employers are hiring H-1B workers and also for Justice to monitor the compliance of companies with antidiscrimination law, especially those operating offshore.

Justice informally shares information on a periodic basis with Labor and Homeland Security when it receives information about potential abuse that does not fall under its jurisdiction. However, there is no formal mechanism in place to exchange information with these other agencies, although officials explained that some attempts to arrange information-sharing agreements between Justice and these agencies have been made in the past. When Justice has referred cases that fell within Labor's jurisdiction, Justice officials told us they were not generally made aware of the outcomes of these referrals. Although Justice accepts referrals from other agencies, officials reported only receiving one referral from Labor related to the H-1B program.

Department of State

If or when State officials learn of an employer potentially violating program requirements, unlike other agencies, State may act as an aggrieved party on behalf of an H-1B worker and file a formal complaint with Wage and Hour regarding the business. For example, agency officials noted that during consular interviews with spouses of H-1B workers attempting to enter the United States, the consular official may uncover potential abuses by the H-1B worker's employer and will then file a complaint with Wage and Hour. However, such incidents are limited in number, with an average of 160 recommendations per year since 2005.

Lack of Accountability Provisions for Staffing Companies Also Hinders Enforcement

The laws governing the H-1B program do not include explicit provisions to hold employers that obtained the H-1B worker through a staffing company accountable to the program requirements that are applicable to the employer who applied for H-1B visas on behalf of foreign workers.[86] As previously noted, some staffing companies complete and submit to Labor an LCA as the employing company, but then contract the H-1B worker out to another employer. At times, that employer may contract the H-1B worker out again, creating multiple middlemen according to officials (see fig. 13). Regardless of where the H-1B worker is ultimately employed, Wage and Hour officials told us that only the staffing company, as the employer who has petitioned for the visa and made the attestations to comply, is technically accountable and ultimately liable for complying with program requirements. They explained that the contractual relationship itself does not transfer the obligations of the contractor for worker protection to any subsequent employers. Especially in instances in which multiple middlemen are involved, it is difficult to expect the staffing companies themselves to be accountable for the actions of an employer up to three or four employers removed.

Wage and Hour investigators reported that a large number of the complaints they receive were related to the activities of staffing companies. In fact, investigators from the Northeast region—the region that receives the highest number of H-1B complaints (see fig. 14)—said that nearly all of the complaints they receive involve staffing companies and that the number of complaints are growing. However, the precise number of complaints related to staffing companies is not known because Labor does not track this information in its complaint data. The most frequent type of violation resulting from a complaint is that the employer failed to pay the required wage rate. Other frequent violations identified as a result of complaints include the failure of the employer to post notice that they intend to hire an H-1B worker and the failure to comply with the attestations made in the LCA (see table 4).

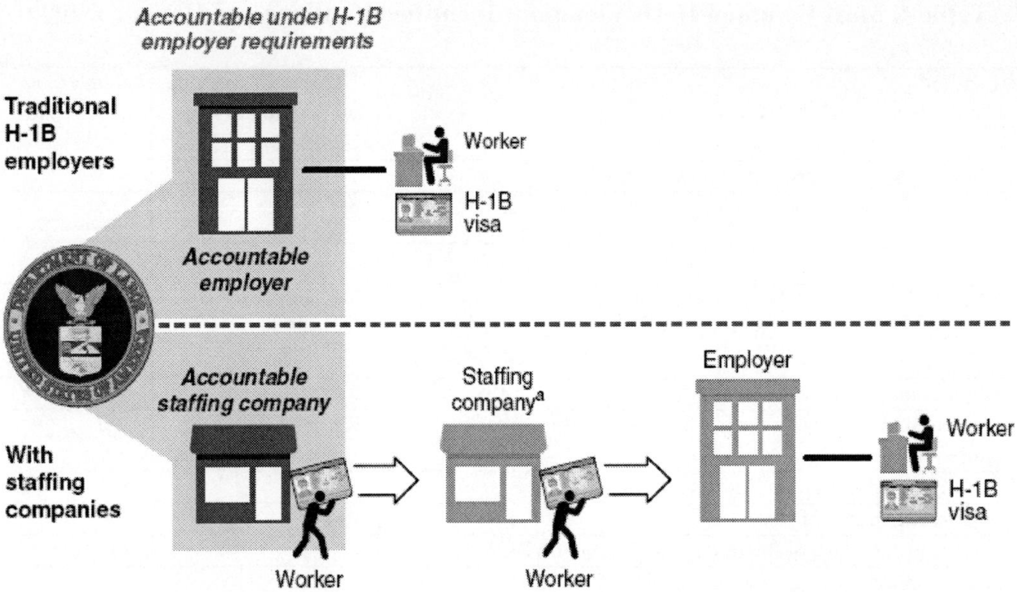

Source: GAO review of Labor information.
[a]In some cases there may be more than one staffing company involved in placing the H-1B worker.

Figure 13. Accountability for Types of Employers under the H-1B Program.

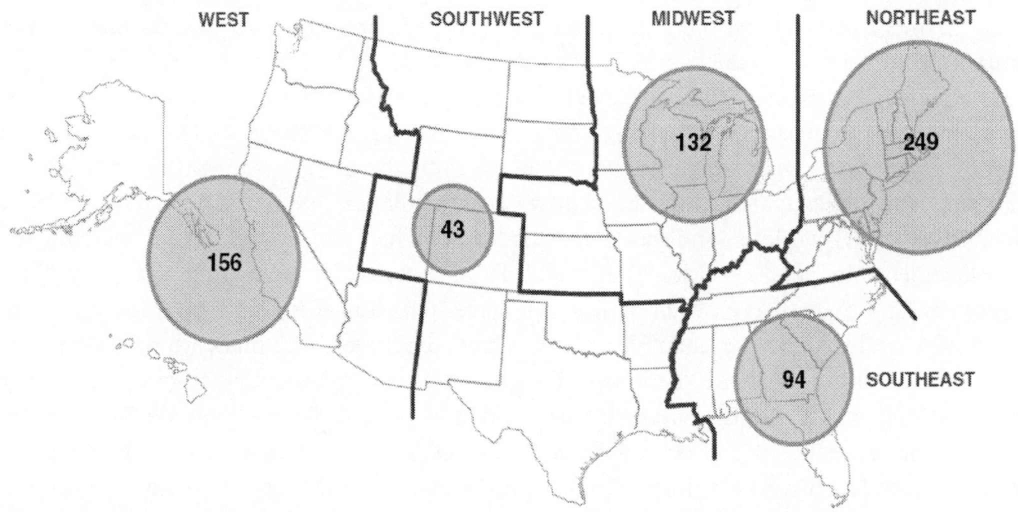

Source: GAO analysis of Labor Wage and Hour data; National Atlas of the United States (base map).
Note: This map reflects the number of complaints investigated, not the number of complaints received.

Figure 14. Wage and Hour H-1B Program Investigations by Region, FY 2006–FY 2009.

Table 4. Most Common H-1B Violations Identified by Wage and Hour, FY 2009

Violation[a]	Number of cases in which violations occurred	Number of occurrences
Failure to pay employee required wage rate	114	977
Failure to post notice of LCA filings for 10 days in two locations at each place of employment where H-1B will be employed	39	315
Failure to comply with the attestations made in the LCA	34	170
Required or accepted payment of the additional petition fee by employee	34	78
Failure to maintain documentation as required	28	80
Failure to make available for public examination any of the required records	23	290
Willfully failed to pay employee required wage rate	10	63
Misrepresented rate of pay on LCA	9	33
Misrepresented place of intended employment on LCA	6	24
Failure to provide H-1B worker copy of LCA	7	7

Source: Labor's Wage and Hour Division.

[a]These categories were determined by Labor's Wage and Hour Division officials. Because categories could not be aggregated by larger topics due to potential duplication, additional violations, such as misrepresenting facts on the LCA, may occur more frequently but are not reflected in this table.

Complaints received by Wage and Hour pertaining to staffing companies generally relate to the payment of H-1B workers, according to investigators. Officials told us that the most common complaint associated with staffing companies pertained to unpaid "benching"—when a staffing company does not have a job placement for the H-1B worker and does not pay them. In these instances, a staffing company sometimes asks the H-1B worker to conduct their own job search or to take an unpaid leave until the company identifies a client. For example, one investigator described how one employer maintained a house for its unemployed H-1B workers, and instructed them to conduct their own Internet searches for a job placement. In another case, Wage and Hour found that a staffing company forced employees to go on leave when it did not have jobs for them and boarded them in a guesthouse while they were unemployed. At times, employees are unaware of their right to receive payment during these "benched" time periods which, according to one complainant, lasted as long as 13 months. Investigators said that the problem of unpaid benching has become more severe with the economic downturn as staffing companies have fewer jobs in which to place H-1B workers. Instead, they may "stockpile" the workers in anticipation of an economic recovery.

In investigating complaints related to staffing companies, investigators often identify additional violations of the attestations on the LCA. For example, Labor officials noted that in 90 percent of their investigations related to staffing companies, the hiring company did not post notice of the filing of the LCA indicating the intention to hire an H-1B worker. In some instances, according to these officials, the subsequent employer may not even know that the contracted worker is an H-1B worker, much less be aware of any requirements associated with the visa—such as the requirement for employers to post notice of their filing of an LCA.

In addition, in some instances workers procured by staffing companies were either not working for the employer listed or not performing the duties described on the LCA.

Some attempts have been made to control the use of staffing companies in other visa programs and in the H-1B program. For example, the L-1 Visa Reform (Intracompany Transferee) Act of 2004 essentially barred staffing companies—whose main revenue source is providing labor-for-hire—from receiving L-1 visas.[87] However, according to experts we interviewed, some staffing companies avoided this legal restriction by differentiating themselves from staffing companies by describing themselves as "IT solutions" companies. In addition to providing labor-for-hire, such companies sell the development of a product, and therefore are not barred from the use of L-1 visas. Additionally, in January 2010, Homeland Security issued a memo on determining when there is a valid employer-employee relationship between a staffing company and an H-1B worker for whom it has obtained an H-1B visa.[88] Whether there is such a relationship depends largely on the right of a staffing company to control the manner and means by which the H-1B nonimmigrant works. However, officials indicated that it is too early to know if the memo has improved compliance with program requirements.[89]

Changes to Program Legislation Have Diluted Worker Protections

Changes to the H-1B program over time have weakened U.S. worker protections related to the (1) temporary nature of the program, (2) pool of H-1B workers eligible for H-1B status, and (3) cap.

Ability to Seek Permanent Residency While on Temporary Visa and Extension Periods

Since the 1990s, the law has allowed H-1B workers to pursue permanent residency in the United States and to remain in the country for an unlimited period of time while their permanent residency application is pending. The Immigration Act of 1990 removed the requirement that H-1B visa applicants have a residence in a foreign country that they had no intention of abandoning.[90] In addition, H-1B workers were able to apply for permanent status[91] and eventually to obtain an unlimited number of annual extensions as long as they file an LCA for permanent residency at least 1 year prior to submitting the final application for an extension of the H-1B visa.[92]

As a result of these legislative changes, the number of H-1B workers in the workforce has likely increased. As noted elsewhere in this report, many H-1B workers apply for green cards. In fact, among a cohort GAO reviewed, at least 18 percent applied for green cards within 6 years or less of the start date of their H-1B visas. Although the employment-based permanent residency applications take a number of years for a decision, the amount of time varies by home country, with approvals of employment-based permanent visas for skilled-worker categories taking the longest for citizens from China, India, and Mexico.[93] An H-1B worker from one of these countries could remain in the United States for over a decade before obtaining a green card.

Broadened Criteria for Worker Qualifications

Legislative changes have broadened the skill requirements for H-1B workers. The original H-visa program, established under the Immigration and Nationality Act in 1952, authorized visas for aliens with a residence in a foreign country that the alien had no intention of abandoning, who were of distinguished merit and ability, and were coming to the United States to perform temporary service of an exceptional nature requiring such merit and ability.[94] However, in 1990, besides removing the foreign residence requirement, the original language was replaced with language authorizing H-1B visas for aliens coming temporarily to the United States to perform services in a "specialty occupation."[95] A specialty occupation was defined as one that required a theoretical and practical application of a body of highly specialized knowledge, and at a minimum, a bachelor's or higher degree in the specific specialty (see app. V). This increased the pool of eligible workers to include a wider range of skill levels.

Labor's application data show that H-1B workers are often not paid wages associated with the highest skills in their fields. Specifically, these data show that over half (54 percent) of the workers with approved LCAs from June 2009 through July 2010 were categorized as entry-level positions and were paid at the lowest pay grades allowed under the prevailing wage levels (see table 5). This pay grade is designated for jobs needing a basic understanding of duties and the ability of the worker to perform routine tasks that require limited judgment. In comparison, 6 percent of approved applicants whose wages were reported on the LCA were paid within the top pay grade designated for workers that requires sufficient experience and a high level of independent judgment. However, such data do not, by themselves, indicate whether H-1B workers are generally less skilled than their U.S. counterparts, or whether they are younger or more likely to accept lower wages.

Table 5. Frequency of Wage Levels Reported on Approved LCAs, June 1, 2009–July 30, 2010

Wage level reported on LCA	Number of records	Percentage oftotal wagelevels reported
I: Entry Level (basic understanding of duties and perform routine tasks requiring limited judgment)	130,528	54%
II: Qualified (have good understanding of occupation and perform moderately complex tasks that require limited judgment)	69,806	29
III: Experienced (experienced with special skills or knowledge and sound understanding of occupation)	26,731	11
IV: Fully Competent (competent with sufficient experience and will require a high level of independent judgment)	14,617	6
Total reported	241,682	100%

Source: Labor's Employment and Training Administration.

In contrast to the H-1B visa program, temporary visa programs in other countries take steps to identify foreign workers with skills that are in short supply.[96] For example, Australia has a system in which applicants receive points for certain types of qualifications that are in short supply in the Australian economy. Those with the highest number of points are granted visas to enter. The United Kingdom uses a committee comprised of five independent economists to identify shortages in particular occupations. Canada has a pilot temporary program under way that also attempts to identify specific jobs where shortages exist and skills are needed.

The U.S. permanent visa program also does more to assure that the skills of the foreign worker are not readily available state-side by, in most cases, requiring the employer who sponsors the green card applicant to attest that it was not able to find a comparably skilled U.S. applicant.

Exemptions to the Cap and Alternative Visas

While providing employers greater access to foreign labor, exemptions to the H-1B cap and the existence of other visa programs for temporary workers have increased their numbers far beyond the cap. With universities, nonprofit organizations that conduct research, and governmental research organizations able to hire an unlimited number of H-1B workers through exemptions, many more H-1B workers have entered the United States each year than the annual numeric limit of 65,000 imposed by the cap. For example, 87,519 workers (initial and extensions) in 2009 were approved for visas to work for 6,034 cap-exempt companies. In addition, company executives reported that as an alternative to the H-1B visa, companies use the L-1 visa—which allows foreign workers to relocate to a company's U.S. office after having worked abroad for the company for at least 1 year. As previously noted, between 2000 and 2008, the number of foreign workers issued L-1 visas—which are not subject to a cap—has increased by more than 50 percent. As noted earlier, Homeland Security currently does not have the capability to determine the cumulative H-1B workforce, such that the effect on U.S. workers can be assessed. Whether or not Homeland Security's Transformation Program will address this problem remains to be seen.[97]

CONCLUSIONS

In creating the H-1B visa program, Congress sought to strike a difficult balance between satisfying the needs of a wide variety of businesses for high-skilled foreign labor while protecting access to jobs and appropriate compensation for U.S. workers. The initial temporary nature of the program and the annual cap were key tools to protect U.S. workers. Over its history, however, Congress has made numerous changes to the program, including broadening the eligibility requirements and allowing for exemptions to the cap and for H-1B workers to pursue long-term residency. The result is that, today, the number of H-1B workers approved to enter the United States each year greatly exceeds the numeric limit established by the cap, and the majority of applicants are categorized as entry-level. Moreover, a substantial proportion appears to remain in the country beyond the 6-year visa period in pursuit of permanent residency. Homeland Security, faced with challenges in administering a program managed in part by four different federal agencies, has difficulty tracking the cap and cannot readily determine how many H-1B workers are currently in the United States or how many stay after their visas expire. Lack of information on the total H-1B workforce makes it impossible to understand the long-term impact of the program and leaves the program vulnerable to fraud and abuse—a known issue in this program.

Restrictions on agencies' abilities to enforce program requirements and coordinate with one another widen the risk of fraud and abuse, and undermine efforts to enforce worker protections. Restrictions on sharing and leveraging information between and within federal agencies likely inhibit the pursuit of worker allegations of abuse and allow some labor abuses to go undetected. The involvement of staffing companies, whose share of H-1B workers is not precisely known but is likely not trivial, further weakens enforcement efforts because the end-user of the H-1B worker is not liable for complying with labor protection requirements.

At the same time, many members of the business community we interviewed cited their own frustrations with the ability of this program to serve their needs for high-skilled labor. The one-size-fits-all application process wastes business and government resources in compiling and reviewing paperwork on well-vetted companies with years of experience in the program. The lottery system does not permit companies to prioritize their candidates, and as a result, coveted H-1B slots may not be allocated to companies' top candidates. The annual application cycle hinders flexibility in hiring, prompting some companies to prematurely petition for candidates instead of holding out for better ones in years when the cap is hit early. Moreover, start-up companies, which some argue are the backbone of innovation in the United States, cannot use the H-1B visa for their employees until their company is fully established.

In an era when companies are competing in a global market for cutting-edge skills, the H-1B program plays an important role. As currently structured, however, the program may not be used to its full potential and may be detrimental in some cases. Some improvements can be made through executive actions by the agencies overseeing the program. However, balancing the needs of the economy for high-skilled foreign labor and protecting the employment and wages of current U.S. workers is a policy matter for Congress. Certainly there are no easy solutions, but data we present suggest that the program may continue to fall short and raise difficult policy questions. Such questions include the appropriateness of the current qualifications for H-1B workers, the use of H-1B visas as a bridge to permanent residence, the involvement of staffing companies in the H-1B program, and exemptions from the cap. As Congress considers immigration reform in consultation with diverse stakeholders and experts, and as Homeland Security moves forward with its modernization efforts, this is an opportune time for Congress to review the goals and purpose of the H-1B program and re-examine its key provisions.

MATTERS FOR CONGRESSIONAL CONSIDERATION

To ensure that the H-1B program continues to meet the needs of businesses in a global economy while maintaining a balance of protections for U.S. workers, Congress may wish to consider reviewing the merits and shortcomings of key program provisions and making appropriate changes as needed. Such a review may include, but would not necessarily be limited to

- the qualifications required for workers eligible under the H-1B program,
- exemptions from the cap,
- the appropriateness of H-1B hiring by staffing companies,

- the level of the cap, and
- the role the program should play in the U.S. immigration system in relationship to permanent residency.

To reduce duplication and fragmentation in the administration and oversight of the H-1B application process, consistent with past GAO matters for congressional consideration, consider eliminating the requirement that employers first submit a Labor Condition Application (LCA) to the Department of Labor for certification, and require instead that employers submit this application along with the I-129 application to the Department of Homeland Security's U.S. Citizenship and Immigration Services for review.

To improve the Department of Labor's ability to investigate and enforce employer compliance with H-1B program requirements, consider granting the department subpoena power to obtain employer records during investigations under the H-1B program.

To help ensure the full protection of H-1B workers employed through staffing companies, consider holding the employer where an H-1B visa holder performs work accountable for meeting program requirements to the same extent as the employer that submitted the LCA form.

RECOMMENDATIONS FOR EXECUTIVE ACTION

Based on our review, we are making four recommendations.

We are making the following two recommendations to the Secretary of Homeland Security:

To help ensure that the number of new H-1B workers who are subject to the cap—both entering the United States and changing to H-1B status within the United States—does not exceed the cap each year, U.S. Citizenship and Immigration Services should take steps to improve its tracking of the number of approved H-1B applications and the number of issued visas under the cap by fully leveraging the transformation effort currently under way, which involves the adoption of an electronic petition processing system that will be linked to the Department of State's tracking system. Such steps should ensure that linkages to the Department of State's tracking system will provide Homeland Security with timely access to data on visa issuances, and that mechanisms for tracking petitions and visas against the cap are incorporated into U.S. Citizenship and Immigration Services' business rules to be developed for the new electronic petition system.

To address business concerns without undermining program integrity, U.S. Citizenship and Immigration Services should, to the extent permitted by its existing statutory authority, explore options for increasing the flexibility of the application process for H-1B employers, such as

- allowing employers to rank their applications for visa candidates so that they can hire the best qualified worker for the jobs in highest need;
- distributing the applications granted under the annual cap in allotments throughout the year (e.g. quarterly); and

- establishing a system whereby businesses with a strong track-record of compliance with H-1B regulations may use a streamlined application process.

We are making the following two recommendations to the Secretary of Labor:

To improve the transparency and oversight of the posting requirement on the Labor Condition Application (LCA), as part of its current oversight role, the Employment and Training Administration should develop and maintain a centralized Web site, accessible to the public, where businesses must post notice of the intent to hire H-1B workers. Such notices should continue to specify the job category and worksite location noted on the LCA and required by statute on current noncentralized postings.

To improve the efficiency and effectiveness of its investigations of employer compliance with H-1B requirements, the Employment and Training Administration should provide Labor's Wage and Hour Division searchable access to the LCA database.

AGENCY COMMENTS AND OUR EVALUATION

The Departments of Homeland Security, Justice, Labor, and State were provided a draft of this report for review and comment. The Departments of Homeland Security and Justice provided written responses to one or more of our recommendations, which appear in appendixes VI and VII of this report. Labor and State did not provide a written response to our recommendations. In addition, Homeland Security, Justice, and Labor provided technical comments, which have been incorporated into the report where appropriate.

In brief, the Department of Justice expressed support for our recommendation that Labor develop and maintain a Web site where businesses post notice of their intent to hire H-1B workers. In addition, Justice offered two more recommendations that build on our findings regarding the lack of a labor market test for most H-1B employers and the limited use of its complaint process by U.S. workers.[98] However, Homeland Security did not agree with the two recommendations we made pertaining to Homeland Security's U.S. Citizenship and Immigration Services, nor did it agree with one matter for congressional consideration.

The recommendation in our draft report on improving H-1B cap management emphasized that Homeland Security should leverage its transformation effort by reaching an agreement with State to ensure that, by linking data systems, it would have real-time information on the number of visas approved under the cap. In response, Homeland Security cited as evidence of its intentions the work already under way to develop an electronic exchange of visa and immigration data with State. However, in our review of the department's memorandum of agreement and letter of intent with State that discuss such exchanges, we did not find specific references to improving cap management with State's visa data. Further, Homeland Security added that data to be exchanged with State may only slightly improve cap management because State's data (1) do not include individuals already in the United States who are seeking to change their visa status, and (2) will be too old to assist Homeland Security with cap management, since it is typically months after Homeland Security approves petitions that State issues visas to individuals residing outside of the United States.

We understand that, for individuals already residing in the United States, Homeland Security does not depend on State, but has its own data on changes in visa status for approved H-1B workers. We also acknowledge that for individuals residing outside of the United States, there is some lapse in time between Homeland Security's approval of an H-1B petition and State's issuance (or decision not to issue) a visa. Nevertheless, we maintain that possessing timely and accurate information on petitions and visas that count against the cap for all individuals—both within and outside the United States—could provide a more reliable basis for ongoing monitoring with respect to the annual visa cap. Improved tracking would in turn provide Homeland Security the information it needs to reduce the potential for exceeding the visa cap and ensure that, in high-demand years, only 65,000 visas are issued. In response to Homeland Security's comments, we clarified our recommendation with respect to the steps it should take, including the importance of incorporating better tracking mechanisms in the business rules to be developed for the new electronic petition system.

With regard to our recommendation that U.S. Citizenship and Immigration explore options for increasing the flexibility of the application process for H-1B employers within its statutory authority, Homeland Security raised several concerns about the feasibility of our suggested options and noted one initiative under way that may expedite the application process for employers. We continue to believe that additional efforts are warranted to more fully explore the potential benefits and costs of these options.

- Homeland Security said it believes that current law does not allow the department to exempt petitioners with track records of H-1B compliance from evidentiary requirements. However, we believe there may be additional opportunities to streamline the application process for businesses by not requiring them to resubmit evidence that they have already provided, without exempting petitioners from evidentiary requirements. Homeland Security noted its own initiative—the Validation Instrument for Business Enterprises (VIBE) system—is intended to reduce the need for petitioners to submit certain documentation by providing the department with the means to verify the petitioners' information through an independent source, but acknowledged in its technical comments that the system will not necessarily reduce the burden of providing supporting documentation for petitioners in the immediate future.
- Homeland Security noted that implementation of a beneficiary ranking process would be extremely complicated and resource intensive and would decrease flexibility for employers. We continue to believe that such obstacles could be surmountable through technology. For example, petitioner-level electronic accounts—as planned in the electronic petition system slated for 2012—could allow employers to manage, and possibly change, their rankings without necessarily decreasing their flexibility. Homeland Security also stated that implementing a quarterly cap allocation is neither warranted nor feasible. Again, we believe that distributing the annual cap in allotments throughout the year might be feasible with an electronic petition system. For example, quarterly allocations of visas could be administered by creating an electronic queue whereby petitions that were not selected in one lottery round would have priority in the next. An automated cap management system that combines electronic tracking and queuing might reduce, for federal managers themselves, the level of complexity involved in managing the program.

Homeland Security also expressed concern that a ranking system might encourage petitioners to over-submit petitions in an attempt to increase their chances of obtaining H-1B workers. The department is, nevertheless, considering a similar option that would allow petitioners to request visa slots prior to submitting an LCA. Whether or not petitioners would over-submit in response to either option is a matter that we believe should be further studied or tested. In summary, we believe that Homeland Security's ongoing Transformation Project—currently in its development phase— affords the opportunity to explore creative and thoughtful solutions to the challenges of administering the H-1B program. Such an examination could weigh the potential costs and risks associated with the options we outlined against their potential benefits in savings for taxpayers and petitioners—with the ultimate goal of supporting legitimate business needs while not compromising worker protections.

Homeland Security disagreed with our asking Congress to consider transferring the review of the LCA from Labor to U.S. Citizen and Immigration Services, citing internal lack of expertise in wage and labor determinations and Labor's role in enforcing labor violations. While we recognize Labor's expertise, Labor officials told us that, unless its legal authority is expanded to allow for verification of employer attestations, the Employment and Training Administration's review can only ensure that employers have completed the form's questions and check-box questionnaire and that there are no obvious inaccuracies. We maintain that such a limited review could be readily subsumed in Homeland Security's petition adjudication process because it too reviews the LCA. We are not recommending that Labor's enforcement role, carried out by its Wage and Hour Division, be transferred to Homeland Security. Further, we do not believe that Labor's enforcement efforts would be compromised by transferring the LCA approval process to Homeland Security, especially in light of challenges Wage and Hour faces with gaining access to LCA information from the Employment and Training Administration, as identified in this report.

We are sending copies of this report to the Secretaries of Homeland Security, Labor, and State, the Attorney General, appropriate congressional committees, and other interested parties. In addition, the report will be available at no charge on the GAO Web site at http://www.gao.gov.

If you or your staffs have any questions about this report, please contact me at (202) 512-7215 or sherrilla@gao.gov. Contact points for our Offices of Congressional Relations and Public Affairs may be found on the last page of this report. GAO staff who made major contributions to this report are listed in appendix VIII.

Andrew Sherrill
Director,
Education, Workforce, and Income Security

Appendix I: Objectives, Scope, and Methods

We conducted our work in response to a House report that accompanied the Consolidated Security, Disaster Assistance, and Continuing Appropriations Act of 2009. The House report directs GAO to examine the impact of the H-1B visa cap on the ability of domestic companies to develop modern technology and perform innovative scientific research and development (R&D), while ensuring U.S. workers are not unfairly displaced or otherwise disadvantaged by H-1B visa holders. To do this, in agreement with cognizant Hill staff, GAO addressed five objectives. Specifically, with respect to H-1B employers, we examined what is known about (1) their demand for H-1B workers and (2) how the H-1B cap affects their costs, R&D, and offshoring decisions. With respect to H-1B and U.S. workers, we examined what is known about (3) H-1B worker characteristics, (4) how raising the H-1B cap might affect employment and wages of U.S. workers, and (5) how well H-1B program requirements ensure that U.S. workers are not displaced or disadvantaged by the program.

This appendix provides a detailed account of the data sources used to answer these questions, the analyses we conducted, and any limitations we encountered. The appendix is organized into four sections. Section 1 describes the key information sources we used for the report. Section 2 describes our methods for comparing the characteristics and wages of U.S. workers with those of approved H-1B workers (which are presented in the report and in appendix II). Section 3 describes our methods for analyzing employment levels, unemployment rates, and wages of U.S. workers in those occupations with the highest concentration of approved H-1B workers. Section 4 describes our methods for analyzing the long-term immigration outcomes of a cohort of H-1B approved H-1B workers.

Section 1: Information Sources

Our information sources included electronic data from datasets administered by the Departments of Labor, Homeland Security, Justice, and State, and by private vendors. Details on the scope and purpose of these data are described below. For each of the datasets described above, we conducted a data reliability assessment of selected variables by conducting electronic data tests for completeness and accuracy, reviewing documentation on the dataset, interviewing knowledgeable officials about how the data are collected and maintained and their appropriate uses, or completing all of these. For the purposes of our analysis, we found the variables that we reported on from these datasets to be sufficiently reliable.[1]

In addition to electronic data, our information sources included interviews with a nonprobability sample of H-1B employers, site visits, and reviews of agency documentation and pertinent literature. Details on the scope and purpose of these information sources are also described below.

Department of Labor Data

Labor Condition Application Data

To obtain information on the characteristics of employers requesting H-1B workers and the positions they sought to fill over the past decade, we analyzed two administrative datasets containing information from the Labor Condition Application (LCA) filed by prospective H-1B employers to the Department of Labor (Labor).

First, we analyzed the Efile H-1B Disclosure Data managed by Labor's Employment and Training Administration (Employment and Training). These data included all the applications filed electronically from 2002 through 2009.[2] We analyzed the data from a total of 2,451,785 applications to determine (1) the number of unique companies that submitted applications each year; (2) the total number of H-1B workers these companies requested each year; (3) the number of applications that were certified or denied; and (4) the number of companies that were either H-1B dependent (i.e., those with 15 percent or more of their workforce comprised of H-1B workers) or willful violators.

Second, we obtained and analyzed more recent data on LCAs that were filed from June 2009 through July 2010, which were processed through Labor's new iCERT system. Unlike Labor's data from previous years, the iCERT data contained detailed information on the prospective H-1B worker's skill level, which is specified by the employer on the LCA. We received data including the skill level listed on 258,847 LCAs that were filed between June 2009 and July 2010. The iCERT data also contain a variable indicating whether the petitioning employer was H-1B dependent. We obtained and tabulated this variable for the top 150 H-1B hiring companies (which we defined as those requesting the highest number of H-1Bs in 2009).

Wage and Hour Complaint Data

To understand trends in H-1B complaints received by Labor's Wage and Hour Division (Wage and Hour) and their outcomes over time, we analyzed extracts from Wage and Hour's Investigative Support and Reporting Database. Specifically, for fiscal year 2000 to fiscal year 2009, we obtained the number of complaints received, the number of complaints resulting in investigations, the number of cases found to have violations, and the prevalence of specific types of violations. We also requested and received additional data from Wage and Hour on the outcomes of these investigations including the total back wages due to employees, the number of employees that were due to receive back wages, the total civil monetary penalties assessed to violators, and the number of disbarments of H-1B employers. To identify potential regional variations, for fiscal year 2006 to fiscal year 2009, we collected and reviewed the number and nature of complaints investigated by region. To more fully understand the extent and impact of the most common types of violations alleged in complaints that Wage and Hour investigated, for fiscal year 2009, we analyzed the number of cases involving each type of violation, the number of times each violation occurred,[3] and the number of employees impacted.

Current Population Survey Data

To determine the characteristics of U.S. workers in select occupations over the past decade, we analyzed Current Population Survey (CPS) data. The CPS Basic Monthly Survey—a survey of about 50,000 households that is conducted by the Bureau of Labor Statistics (BLS)—provides a comprehensive body of information on the employment and unemployment experience of the nation's population. The March Annual Social and Economic CPS supplement is one source of detailed information on income and work experience in the United States. We used both the basic monthly CPS survey data and published estimates based on these surveys over the past decade to produce annual estimates for the 10- year period. We used the March 2009 Annual Social and Economic supplement to produce some additional estimates in this report. A more complete description of the surveys, including sample design, estimation, and other methodology can be found in the CPS documentation prepared by Census and BLS.[4]

We used the March 2009 supplement data to produce estimates for U.S. citizens' longest held job in the previous year, highest degree attained, age, and wages.[5] For this analysis, we restricted the population to those U.S. citizens who were full-time wage and salary workers (excluding self-employed) aged 18 to 50 and working for private employers (excluding government). We estimated median salaries for this population by age and education level for three occupations of interest: (1) systems analysis, programming, and other computer-related occupations; (2) electrical/electronic engineering; and (3) college and university educators. The occupation and salary information used was for the longest held job in 2008. We compared these median estimates to median salaries reported on 2008 H-1B worker petitions for similar occupations and age groups.

We used CPS's basic monthly survey data to examine how the proportion of H-1B to U.S. citizen workers changed over the last decade for these same five occupations of interest. Specifically, for 2000 to 2009, we computed yearly averages from the 12 monthly CPS surveys from each of the years. For these estimates, we restricted the population to U.S. citizen full-time adult workers.[6] Although the occupational categories are the same as those used for the March 2009 supplement analysis, the occupation was for the job held by the U.S. worker the prior week. Additional details of this analysis are presented in Sections 2 and 3 of this appendix.

Because the CPS is a probability sample, based on random selections, the sample is only one of a large number of samples that might have been drawn. Since each sample could have provided different estimates, confidence in the precision of the particular sample's results is expressed as a 95 percent confidence interval. This is the interval that would contain the actual population value for 95 percent of the samples that could have been drawn. The 95 percent confidence intervals provided in this report were developed from standard error estimates that were either provided by BLS for the underlying estimate (for median weekly wages), or computed using formulas and methods described in CPS documentation.[7]

Consistent with the CPS documentation guidelines, we do not produce annual estimates from the basic monthly CPS data files for populations of less than 35,000, or estimates based on the March supplement data for populations of less than 75,000.

Department of Homeland Security Data

Data on H-1B Petitions Filed by Employers

To help analyze trends in demand for and characteristics of H-1B workers and employers over the last decade, we used administrative data collected by Department of Homeland Security's (Homeland Security) U.S. Citizenship and Immigration Services (USCIS) reflecting information supplied by prospective H-1B employers on the I-129 form, the form that is used to petition for an H-1B worker. These data, known as the Computer Linked Application Information Management System, Version 3.0 (CLAIMS 3) provide detailed information on the characteristics of prospective H-1B employers and workers. We used two versions of these data—CLAIMS 3 Mainframe and CLAIMS 3 Local Area Network (LAN)—because they contained different variables. Using the CLAIMS 3 Mainframe database from fiscal years 2000 through 2009, for each fiscal year we determined

- the number of H-1B initial petitions and extensions submitted by all employers, employers subject to the cap, and cap-exempt employers;

- the number of H-1B petitions approved or denied by Homeland Security, by initial petitions and extensions;
- the total number of companies and the total number of cap-exempt companies that submitted and had approved H-1B petitions, by initial petitions and extensions;
- the characteristics of companies that were approved by Homeland Security to hire H-1B workers, including their industry codes and the number of workers they requested; and
- the characteristics of workers that Homeland Security approved as H-1Bs, including whether or not the workers were residing in the United States at the time of application; their countries of birth, education level, age, rate of pay, occupation, industry, and the location of their prospective place of employment.[8]

Because the CLAIMS 3 Mainframe database does not distinguish or contain data on petitions subject to the master's cap, we also obtained and analyzed data from the CLAIMS 3 LAN database from fiscal years 2004 through 2009 to determine the number of approved H-1B petitions for workers who graduated with a master's degree or higher from an American institution of higher education.[9]

To understand how the number and demographic characteristics of approved H-1B workers compared to U.S. citizen workers over the last decade, we used USCIS's CLAIMS 3 Mainframe H-1B approval data for 2008[10] for five key occupations: (1) systems analysis, programming, and other computer-related occupations;[11] (2) electrical/electronic engineering; (3) college and university educators; (4) accountants, auditors, and related occupations; and (5) physicians and surgeons. These analyses are described in detail in Section 2.

Finally, we used CLAIMS 3 Mainframe data for fiscal year 2009 to identify the 150 employers with the highest number of approved H-1B petitions, and we collected additional data on these employers as described below in the "Data from Private Vendors" section.

Limitations of H-1B Petition Data

While the CLAIMS 3 data provided a variety of information on approved H-1B workers, these data had several limitations with respect to understanding demand for and characteristics of H-1B workers. Most importantly, they did not provide information on how many H-1B workers, whose petitions were approved, were actually working in the United States in any particular year. Therefore, although the CLAIMS 3 data are informative about approved H-1B petitions and about some characteristics of the workers listed on those petitions, these characteristics may not be indicative of the characteristics of all H-1B workers in a given year. For example:

- Of the H-1B petitions submitted in fiscal year 2008 and approved, we do not know the proportion that began work in 2008. Some may not have started work until 2009; others may not have started work at all.
- An individual H-1B worker could be represented in multiple petitions filed by different employers in the same year.
- An individual H-1B worker could be represented in multiple petitions filed by the same employer in the same year prior to March 2008.
- USCIS's CLAIMS 3 data can only provide information on the *flow* of new H-1B workers into the U.S. workforce, not about the stock of all H-1B workers in those

occupations. In other words, they can provide information on the number of H-1B workers whose petitions were submitted and approved for fiscal year 2008, but not on the number of H-1B workers that were actually employed in the United States in 2008.

Because of these uncertainties, we do not know how well the characteristics of approved H-1B workers whose petitions were submitted in any year would approximate the characteristics of the population of H-1B workers actually employed in that year. Further, because of these limitations we do not know the number of new H-1B workers actually entering the U.S. workforce in any given year.

United States Visitor and Immigrant Status Indicator Technology (US-VISIT) Data

To examine the long-term immigration outcomes for H-1B workers, we obtained data from Homeland Security's US-VISIT Arrival Departure Information System (ADIS) database, which were matched against H-1B petition data. US-VISIT data are collected on noncitizens at the point of entry into the United States and contain other immigration information, including the dates of entry into and exit from the country; the date a petition to convert to permanent residency was submitted (if one was submitted) and the status of that petition (approved, denied, or pending); the person's country of citizenship; and country from which their entry visa was issued. For a summary of the methods used and any limitations encountered in conducting data matches and related analysis, see Section 4 of this appendix.

Department of Justice Data

Complaint Data

To understand trends in the number of complaints (known as charges) that are filed with the Department of Justice (Justice) regarding the H-1B program over time, we obtained data on the number of H-1B-related charges Justice received from fiscal year 2006 through March 2010. Specifically, we analyzed information on all inactive cases,[12] including on whether the matter was Justice-initiated or complaint-driven, the number of charges per fiscal year, initial investigation and completionn dates, the alleged violation committed by the company cited in the charge, and the outcome of each charge. For cases that were resolved from fiscal year 2006 to March 2010, we analyzed summaries provided by Justice describing the nature and resolution of all cases on which Justice took action.

Department of State Data

Data on Visa Issuances

To determine the number of H-1B and L-1 visas issued from 2000 to 2009, we reviewed and compiled data on visa issuances published by the Department of State (State).

Data from Private Vendors

To learn more about the top 150 H-1B hiring companies in fiscal year 2009 (beyond the information available in agency administrative databases), we gathered additional information on these companies through Mergent Online and LexisNexis's Dossier databases. We used these databases toobtain information on country of incorporation, country of operations (location), primary North American Industry Classification System (NAICS), number of employees, net income, operating income, total assets, and business description for each company. For several companies for which neither database had available information or we wanted additional information (i.e., a more detailed business description), we downloaded and saved information from company Web sites.

Data Reliability

For each of the datasets described above, we conducted a data reliability assessment of selected variables by conducting electronic data tests for completeness and accuracy, reviewing documentation on the dataset, or interviewing knowledgeable officials about how the data are collected and maintained and their appropriate uses. For the purposes of our analysis, we found the variables that we reported on from these datasets to be sufficiently reliable. In several instances, we identified inconsistencies with the reporting of particular data fields. In these instances, we took steps to address these inconsistencies by using criteria to create decision rules. For example, a given H-1B employer might have reported different industry codes on their H-1B petition applications in a given year. When this occurred, except if a company had multiple industry codes listed the same number of times, we identified the industry that the employer most frequently listed on the petition. If more than one industry code appeared the same number of times, the company was double counted to reflect equally relevant industries. In other instances, when it was not possible to apply a reasonable decision rule, we did not include the data field in our analysis.

Interviews with H-1B Employers

To determine how the H-1B cap and program affects the costs, R&D, and offshoring decisions of firms doing business in the United States, we spoke to a nongeneralizable sample of 34 companies that employed H-1B workers in fiscal year 2008. For 31 of these companies, we conducted structured interviews with representatives of the company. For the remaining 3 companies, we spoke with a company representative in two separate focus groups.

Of the 31 firms with whom we conducted structured individual interviews, 22 were selected randomly from a stratified sample of all H-1B hiring firms in fiscal year 2008. The universe of H-1B hiring firms (excluding nonprofits and universities) was stratified into three groups according to the number of approved H-1B petitions. Anticipating a high refusal rate from companies we asked to participate in the structured interview, we over-sampled for each of these groups. Ultimately, of the 150 companies we contacted, 22 agreed to speak with us.[13] The following table summarizes the population of companies and the number of companies contacted.

Table 6. H-1B Employers Randomly Selected for Interview by GAO

Description	Population	Contacted	Participated
Large (100+ H-1B approvals)	185	50	5
Medium (10-99 H-1B approvals)	2,983	40	11
Small (1-9 H-1B approvals)	48,774	60	6
Total	51,942	150	22

Source: GAO.

The remaining firms with which we conducted additional structured interviews were selected by GAO based on referrals from industry contacts. Some of these firms were chosen because they were known leaders in key sectors of the economy, while others were chosen because they represented firms from sectors that were difficult to contact and whom we expected would not be well represented by the random sample (including one start-up company and one small H-1B-dependent staffing firm). Ultimately, we conducted structured individual interviews with 9 additional firms selected based on referrals from industry contacts, for a total of 31 individual interviews; and we conducted focus group interviews with 3 additional firms selected based on referrals from industry contacts. This selection of a total of 34 firms constitutes a nongeneralizable sample and cannot be used to make inferences beyond the specific firms selected.

The firms we spoke with were located throughout the country and reflected six industrial sectors and a range of sizes (from a few workers based in one location to thousands of workers positioned around the globe). Through these interviews, we spoke with key executives in a variety of technology-intensive industries, including information technology (IT); semiconductor manufacturing and other manufacturing and engineering firms; and pharmaceuticals and biotechnology. Regarding technology-intensive industries, we spoke with representatives of several large multinational companies, including four of the top U.S.-based H-1B employers (i.e., U.S.-based companies that were among the top 50 companies with the highest number of approved H-1B petitions), as well as several small and emerging technology companies who use H-1B workers for highly specialized positions. We also spoke with 10 IT services firms, including three large (meaning they employed at least 100 H-1B workers) foreign-owned H-1B staffing and outsourcing companies, and several smaller IT staffing and consulting firms. In addition, we spoke with companies in several other sectors, including two financial organizations, a health care provider, and a consumer retail firm.

To develop our structured interview questionnaire, we took several steps. First, we conducted two focus groups with H-1B employers and representatives of major industry organizations. In these focus groups, we tested preliminary versions of our interview questions, and used the discussion to revise the questions. We also conducted six tests of the structured interview with individual companies. The responses from the three companies that participated in our focus groups were not included in the tabulated results based on interviews with individual firms, because the structure of our individual firm interviews differed significantly from the structure of our focus groups. However, the responses from all six of our test interviews were included in our tabulated results of company interviews.

To analyze the data we collected from the company interviews, we conducted a content analysis of company responses. This analysis involved coding the interview responses and conducting frequency analyses of the topics and themes that were raised by the company representatives. Two analysts coded the responses. Any discrepancies in coding were discussed and resolved before finalizing the resulting data set.

During our interviews, employers and experts offered a number of suggestions for how the program could be improved. Although it was not possible to publish all of the suggestions, those that are mentioned in the report were chosen on the basis of the following factors: (1) frequency of suggestion, (2) feasibility, (3) potential for economic efficiency, and (4) corroboration with other information sources.

Site Visits, Interviews, and Review of Documentary Evidence

To understand the (1) H-1B certification, adjudication, and enforcement processes; (2) the responsibilities of each agency involved; (3) the effectiveness of the H-1B program's protections for U.S. workers; and (4) the reliability of the datasets we used, we conducted three site visits and conducted numerous interviews with agency officials, labor advocates, andacademics. To understand the processing of applications, we visited Labor's LCA processing center in Illinois and Homeland Security's I-129 processing center in California. We also conducted interviews with State's Kentucky Service Center, where I-129 petitions that have been approved by Homeland Security are entered into a State database that is accessible to consular offices around the world. To understand investigations related to approved H-1B visa holders, we visited Labor's Wage and Hour Division's Northeast Regional Office in Philadelphia, the regional office that had received the highest number of H-1B-related complaints in the country. In addition, we conducted interviews with officials from Labor, Homeland Security's USCIS and US-VISIT offices, State, and Justice with regard to their roles in all phases of the H-1B program. We also reviewed agency documentation and the laws and regulations related to the H-1B program.

To deepen our understanding of the role of the H-1B program for businesses in specific segments of the economy, and the impact of the H-1B program on U.S. workers, we interviewed a number of academics and business advocates. Specifically, we interviewed leading academics in the areas of business, economics, demography, international relations, and labor relations. To better understand the specific issues facing start-up companies and high-tech organizations, we conducted interviews with venture capital companies, and immigration law firms that work with start-up companies. To better understand the specific issues facing firms in the IT staffing and services industry, we interviewed industry advocacy organizations.

We also conducted an extensive review of the academic literature, which included articles and studies on the impact of migration on U.S. workers, trends in international business, and trends in the education of foreign students in science and technology fields.

Finally, to address all objectives, we reviewed relevant federal laws and regulations; news media articles, and the temporary immigration programs of several other countries that we selected based on our literature review and our discussions with experts.

Table 7 provides a summary of how the information sources described were used to answer each of the reporting objectives.

Section 2: Methods for Comparing U.S. and H-1B Workers

As part of our examination of the impact of the H-1B program on domestic employment, we used data from the 2009 March supplement of the CPS to estimate the number of U.S. citizen workers in 2008, their age distribution, and their education levels for five occupational categories[14] that received the most H-1B approvals in fiscal year 2009. Ideally we would have compared U.S. workers to actual H-1B workers; however, data on actual H-1B workers do not exist. The data we analyzed (CLAIMS 3), as explained above, pertain to prospective H-1B workers (those whose petitions were submitted in a given year and approved by Homeland Security).

To help ensure that we were comparing workers in the same occupational categories, we had to combine some occupational categories in the CPS to better match those in the CLAIMS 3 data, as shown in table 8.

Limitations of Wage Comparisons

In addition, we compared salaries of U.S. workers with those of H-1B workers, although this comparison had limitations. Specifically, we compared the CPS median salary estimates for the 2009 March supplement to median salary figures reported in CLAIMS 3 salary data for the approved H-1B workers whose petitions were submitted in 2008 for three of the occupations of interest overall and by age group. Although several of the comparisons we were able to make did show a statistically significant difference between the CLAIMS 3 H-1B workers' median salary and the "comparable" CPS estimate, these analyses have several limitations:

- Within each occupational group, there can be variation in the types of jobs and work performed. Our data do not account for these subtleties. Therefore, it is possible that H-1B workers may have been working in relatively more or less sophisticated jobs than U.S. workers within the same occupational group. For example, H-1B workers and U.S. workers in the occupation "college and university education" may have different fields of education and work in different types of institutions.
- The measures of median annual salaries for U.S. citizens could include bonuses, but the median annual salaries reported in the CLAIMS 3 database most likely do not. Neither median salary includes noncash benefits such as health insurance or pensions.
- CPS salary reported in the 2009 March supplement was for the longest held position actually worked in 2008, as reported by workers themselves (or knowledgeable members of their household). In contrast, the salaries reported in the CLAIMS 3 database are reported by prospective H-1B employers and reflect what the employer intends to pay the H-1B worker in fiscal year 2008 or fiscal year 2009, a time period covering October 1, 2007, through September 30, 2009.
- We identified patterns in the H-1B worker salary data that raise concerns about the validity of that data. Specifically, the frequency distributions we ran on the salaries of H-1B workers in the five key occupations showed that employers reported a number of very low and very high salaries for the "annual rate of pay" on the petition application. We had no basis for determining whether the high and low salaries were data entry errors, estimated payments for an employment period of more or less than a year, or were very high or low for some other reason. To minimize the influence of these outliers, we used median salary rather than mean.

Table 7. Summary of Information Sources by Objective

	Objective 1: Demand for H-1B workers and characteristics of H-1B employers	Objective 2: Impact of the H-1B cap and program on employers	Objective 3: Characteristics of approved H-1B workers	Objective 4: Employment and wages of the U.S. workforce in H-1B-intensive industries	Objective 5: Effectiveness ofprotections for U.S. workers
Department of Labor data					
LCA data	X				
Wage and Hour Division complaint data					X
CPS data			X	X	
Department of Homeland Security data					
H-1B employer petition data	X		X	X	
U.S-VISIT data			X		
Department of Justice complaint data					X
Department of State data on visa issuances	X				
Mergent Online data	X				
LexisNexis Dossier database	X				
Structured interviews with H-1B employers		X			
Site visits, interviews, and reviews of documentary evidence	X	X	X	X	X
Relevant laws and regulations	X	X	X	X	X

Source: GAO.

Table 8. Crosswalk from USCIS to Related CPS Occupation Codes

		Related CPSoccupations[a]			
USCISoccupations		2003-2009		2000-2002	
USCIS code(s)	USCIS occupational title	CPS codes	CPS occupational title	CPS codes	CPS occupational title
030 and 039	Systems analysis, programming, and other computer-related occupations[b]	1000, 1010, 1020, 1060, 1220	Computer scientists and systems analysts, computer programmers, database administrators, and operations research analysts	064, 229, 065	Computer systems analysts and scientists, computer programmers,operations and systems researchers and analysts
003	Electrical/electronic engineers	1410	Electrical and electronic engineers	055	Electrical and electronicengineers
160	Accountants, auditors, and related occupations	0800	Accountants and auditors	023	Accountants and auditors
090	Occupations in college and university education[c]	2200	Postsecondary teachers	113, 114, 115, 116, 117, 118, 119, 123, 124, 125, 126, 127, 128, 129, 133, 134, 135, 136, 137, 138, 139, 143, 144, 145, 146, 147, 148, 149, 153, 154	Categories 113-154, allof which appear here, are different types of "postsecondary teachers"
070	Physicians and Surgeons	3060	Physicians and surgeons	084	Physicians

Source: Basic Monthly CPS, 2009, and USCIS.

[a] Related CPS codes and titles changed in 2003.

[b] See footnote 14 for details on how "other computer-related occupations" was defined.

[c] H-1B workers at universities may be employed in positions other than teaching.

In light of these limitations, caution should be used in interpreting differences found in comparing estimated 2008 median U.S. citizen worker salaries and the median salaries for H-1B worker petitions submitted in 2008.

Section 3: Analysis of Employment and Wages of U.S. Workforce

To determine how raising the H-1B cap might affect the employment and wages of U.S. workers, we examined labor market indicators (employment levels, unemployment rates, and usual weekly earnings) of U.S. workers in three occupations approved to receive the largest proportion of approved H-1B petitions relative to the total U.S. workforce in those occupations: (1) systems analysis, programming, and other computer-related occupations; (2) electrical and electronics engineers; and (3) college and university education. For this analysis, we relied on three sets of published CPS estimates of annual averages based on data collected through CPS basic monthly surveys: (1) median weekly earnings (at last week's primary job) of full-time wage and salary workers by detailed occupation and sex, 2000 to 2009 annual averages; (2) employed persons by detailed occupation and sex, annual averages 2000 to 2009; and (3) unemployment levels and rates by detailed occupation, 2000 to 2009 annual averages. These data were provided to us by staff at BLS.

In addition to presenting estimates of the employment levels, unemployment rates, and median usual weekly earnings for each occupational group, we also calculated and presented estimates of the change over the decade in the unemployment rate and median usual weekly wage for each occupational group, and the growth rate relative to year 2000 for the employment level for each occupational group.[15]

In order to better understand trends identified in our analysis and the specific issues facing workers in segments of the economy that may not be apparent from national labor force statistics, we also spoke with several labor advocates who work with and advocate for computer scientists and computer programmers, as well as academic researchers who do research on the U.S. science, engineering, and technology workforce.

Section 4: Analysis of Long-Term Immigration Outcomes of H-1B Workers

To examine the long-term immigration outcomes of H-1B workers, GAO obtained data from Homeland Security's US-VISIT ADIS database. The ADIS data provided was based on matching ADIS data with 302,550 records from Homeland Security's CLAIMS 3 database[16] submitted by GAO to US-VISIT for this purpose. The CLAIMS 3 records used for matching consisted of approved initial H-1B petitions that were valid to start work in H-1B status between January 1, 2004, and September 30, 2007.

Matched Data Received from US-VISIT

US-VISIT matched the submitted records by first name, last name, and date of birth to the ADIS data system. US-VISIT's matching returned a total of 5,091,369 event records from the ADIS system, containing information about 375,641 persons in the ADIS system. These event records, which US-VISIT provided GAO, contained data on the following events for foreign nationals: entry into the country; exit from the country; petition to convert to permanent residence status (I-485); and status of petition to convert to permanent residence (approved, denied, or pending.) Each event record has an associated event date. US-VISIT also provided the following identifying information: ADIS person identifier, first name, last name, date of birth, country of citizenship, country of issuance, I-94 number, and CLAIMS 3 receipt number, where available.

How GAO Determined Reliable Matches

GAO took a number of steps to identify reliable matches between CLAIMS 3 and ADIS data. We determined that the match was reliable if at least one of the following three conditions held: (1) the ADIS person had an H-1B visa status at some point during their history; (2) the CLAIMS 3 receipt number in the CLAIMS 3 data matched at least one of the CLAIMS 3 receipt numbers recorded in the ADIS system; (3) the I-94 number recorded with the petitioners' I-129 form matched at least one of the I-94 numbers on file in the ADIS system. In the case of one-to-many and manyto-many matches, we selected the match that met criteria 2 or 3 over criteria 1. We determined that 169,349 records met these criteria.

There are various reasons why a visa might not be used or a beneficiary might not be in the ADIS system for an approved H-1B petition. For example, an H-1B visa might not be used for an approved petition when the employer decides not to offer the beneficiary the job; the beneficiary decides not to accept the job; or the beneficiary obtains a different U.S. visa status, such as through marriage, student visas, or other work visas.[17] An H-1B visa might be used, but the beneficiary would not be in the ADIS system for several reasons. First, the ADIS system became fully operational in January 2004; those who were already in the United States at the time they submitted their H-1B petition (such as students enrolled in U.S. universities) and did not enter or exit the country after January 2004 may not have been entered in the ADIS system. In addition, some beneficiaries who entered the United States by land may have entered the country without going through an official border station where they submit an I-94 form. Finally, a beneficiary's record may not be in the ADIS system due to data quality problems. For example, if an H-1B beneficiary changed their name through marriage and subsequently had an I-485 submitted on their behalf, US-VISIT may at times be unable to link the I-485 submission to the H-1B beneficiary due to the name change.

We conducted this performance audit from May 2009 through January 2011 in accordance with generally accepted government auditing standards. Those standards require that we plan and perform the audit to obtain sufficient, appropriate evidence to provide a reasonable basis for our findings and conclusions based on our audit objectives. We believe that the evidence obtained provides a reasonable basis for our findings and conclusions based on our audit objectives.

Appendix II: Characteristics of U.S. and H-1B Workers in Five Occupational Groups

This appendix provides additional analyses of the characteristics of U.S. and approved H-1B workers in five occupational groups between 2000 and 2009.

For H-1B-Heavy Occupations, the Proportion of H-1B-Approved Workers Generally Decreased over Time

For five occupational groups with large numbers of approved H-1B workers over the last decade, we compared newly approved H-1B workers[1] with the stock of U.S. citizen workers in those occupations and found that the relative number and proportion of newly approved H-1B workers varied over the decade for all five occupations, but decreased overall. The five occupations we examined and that represent occupations with the highest concentration of newly approved H-1B workers included systems analysts, programmers, and other computer-related workers; electrical and electronics engineers; (3) accountants and auditors; (4) college and university educators; and (5) physicians and surgeons.

Despite some fluctuations over time, the overall number of newly approved petitions for H-1B workers across these five occupational groups declined from 137,371 in 2000 to 44,946 in 2009, and the proportion relative to estimates of U.S. citizen workers fell from about 2.5 percent to less than 1 percent between 2000 and 2009. For specific occupations, as shown in figure 15, the highest proportion of newly approved H-1B workers as compared to U.S. citizen workers was in the systems analysis, programming, and other computer-related occupations, averaging about 3 percent across the decade, while the lowest proportion was in the accounting occupations and physicians and surgeons occupations, averaging less than 1 percent. Further, for electrical and electronics engineering and systems analysis, programming, and other computer-related occupations, the declines in the proportion of newly approved H-1B workers as compared to U.S. citizen workers seem to coincide with the economic downturn of 2002.

We did not examine potential reasons behind this relative decline in the proportion of H-1B workers over time; however, fluctuations in the economy and H-1B cap were likely contributing factors.

For H-1B-Heavy Occupations, Approved H-1B Workers Were Younger and More Educated Relative to U.S. Citizen Workers

In 2008, approved H-1B workers (initial and extensions) were generally younger and more educated as compared to their U.S. citizen counterparts in similar occupations, although this varied by the particular occupation (see fig. 16).[2]

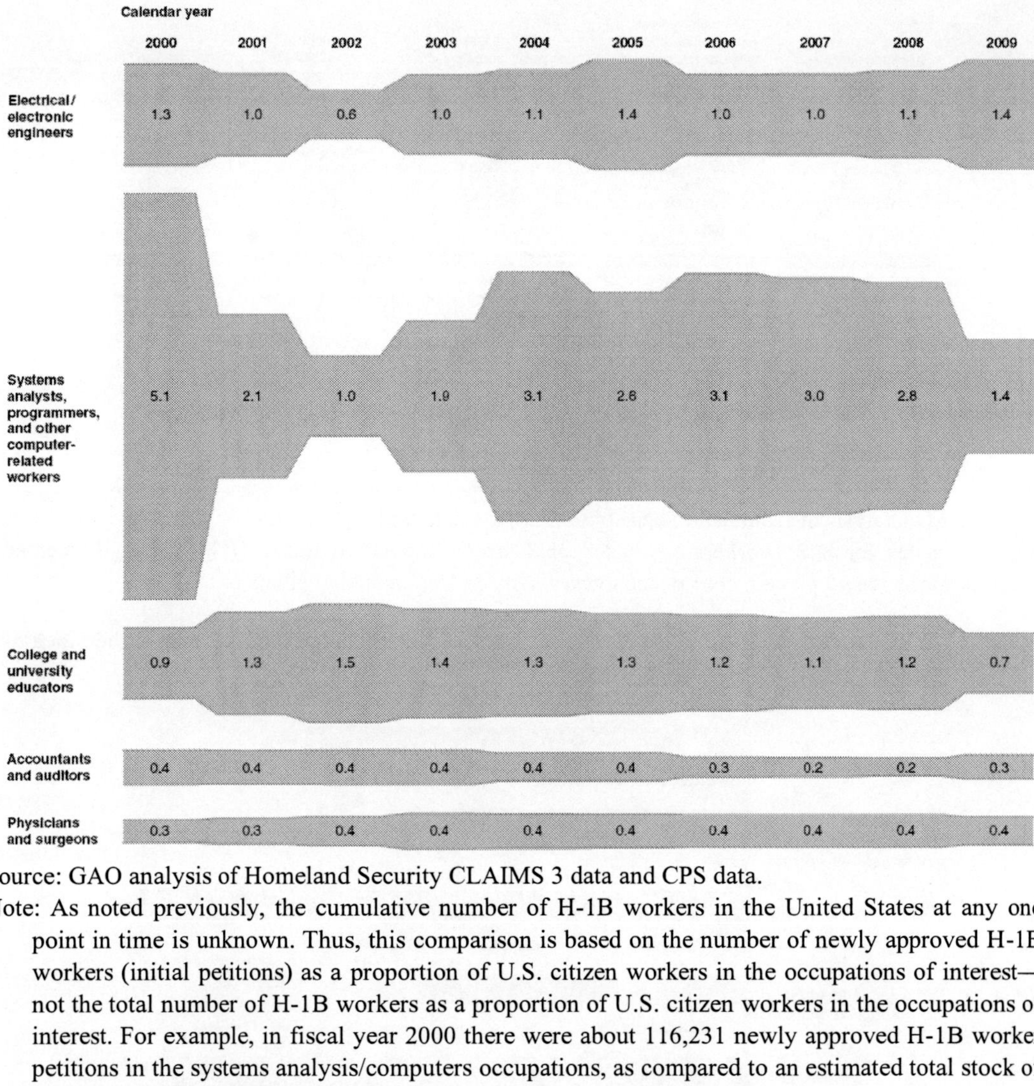

Source: GAO analysis of Homeland Security CLAIMS 3 data and CPS data.

Note: As noted previously, the cumulative number of H-1B workers in the United States at any one point in time is unknown. Thus, this comparison is based on the number of newly approved H-1B workers (initial petitions) as a proportion of U.S. citizen workers in the occupations of interest—not the total number of H-1B workers as a proportion of U.S. citizen workers in the occupations of interest. For example, in fiscal year 2000 there were about 116,231 newly approved H-1B worker petitions in the systems analysis/computers occupations, as compared to an estimated total stock of 2,290,612 U.S. citizen workers. Estimated percents displayed in this figure have 95 percent confidence intervals that are within +/- 0.25 percentage points of the estimate itself.

Figure 15. Flow of Newly Approved H-1B Worker Petitions as a Proportion of the Estimated Total Stock of U.S. Citizen Workers by Occupation, 2000–2009.

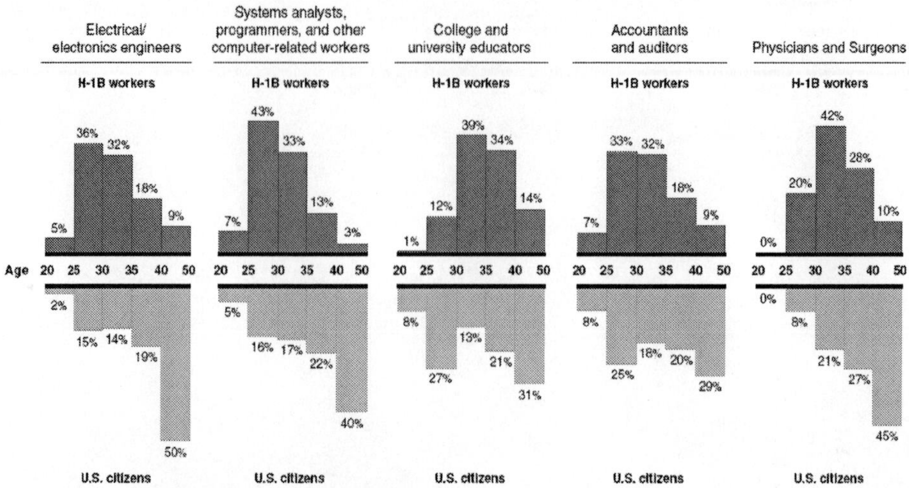

Source: GAO analysis of Homeland Security CLAIMS 3 data and CPS data.

Note: Estimates for U.S. workers are based on Current Population Survey (CPS) data. Percentage estimates have 95 percent confidence intervals of +/- 13 percentage points or less.

Figure 16. Age of Approved H-1B Workers (Initial and Extensions) and Estimated Age of the Stock of U.S. Citizen Workers in Select Occupations, 2008.

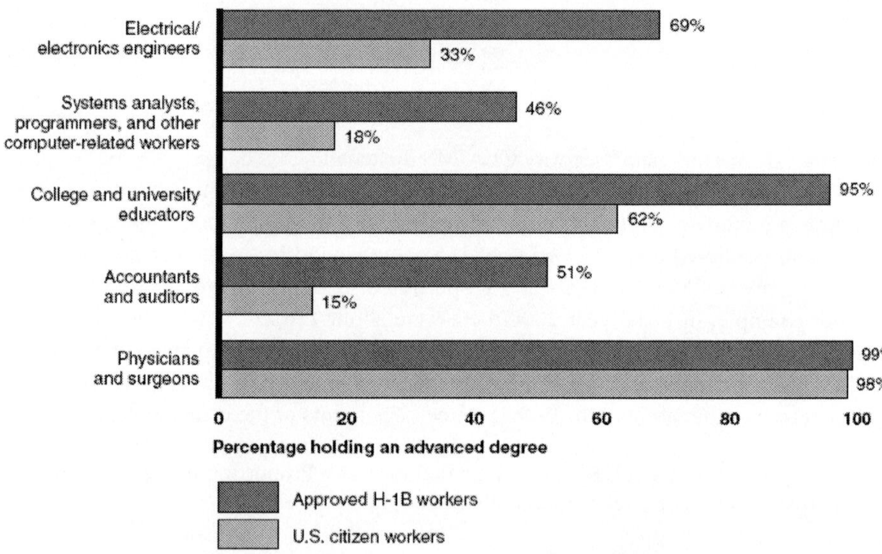

Source: GAO analysis of Homeland Security CLAIMS 3 data and CPS data.

Note: Estimates for H-1B workers are based on approved petitions. Estimates for U.S. workers are based on CPS data. CPS percentage estimates for electrical engineering, electronics, and related occupations and for university and college education have 95 percent confidence intervals of within +/- 12 percentage points of the estimate itself. CPS percentage estimates for other occupations shown have 95 percent confidence intervals of within +/- 4 percentage points of the estimate itself. Estimates are for the population of U.S. citizen workers, aged 18 to 50, in full-time private employment (excluding those working in government and the self-employed).

Figure 17. Proportion of Approved H-1B Workers (Initial and Extensions) and Estimated U.S. Citizen Workers with Advanced Degrees in Select Occupations, 2008.

In these five occupations, we generally found that a higher percentage of approved H-1B workers had earned an advanced graduate degree (including master's, Ph.D., or professional degree) than U.S. citizen workers, as shown in figure 17. Across the five occupations, 56 percent of approved H-1B workers had graduate degrees, as compared to an estimated 29 percent of the total stock of U.S. citizen workers.[3] For this comparison, all U.S. citizen estimates are for the population of U.S. citizens aged 18 to 50 years old in private, full-time employment, excluding those in government employment and the self-employed.

APPENDIX III: LABOR FORCE TRENDS FOR U.S. WORKERS IN SELECTED OCCUPATIONS

This appendix presents analyses of median earnings growth, unemployment rates, and employment levels for the three occupations with the highest proportion of approved petitions for H-1B workers over the past decade.

A Retrospective View Shows a Mixed Employment and Earnings Picture for Professions Absorbing H-1Bs

To shed light on the U.S. workforce most likely to have been affected by the H-1B program over the past decade, we reviewed 10 years of data on the employment, unemployment, and earnings of U.S. workers in the three occupations[1] with the largest proportion of approved H-1B petitions relative to the stock of U.S. workers over the past decade. We found that U.S. workers in all three occupations, in every year, had significantly higher median earnings levels compared to U.S. workers in all professional occupations. We also found that one of the three occupations—systems analysts and computer programmers—had significantly higher earnings growth compared to all professional U.S. workers. However, unemployment rates were cyclical for two groups and employment levels varied among the three groups (i.e., declining for electrical and electronics engineers, growing for college and university educators, and remaining essentially unchanged among systems analysts and computer programmers).

Earnings and Earnings Growth among Selected Occupations

Real earnings growth among systems analysts, programmers, and other computer-related U.S. workers was relatively strong over the decade—12 percent—and was significantly larger than real earnings growth among all professional workers over the decade, which was about 4 percent. Among electrical and electronics engineers, real earnings growth was about 8 percent over the decade; however, the difference between this increase and that of all professional workers was not statistically significant. Among college educators, real earnings did not grow significantly over the decade. As can be seen in figure 18, in every year over the past decade all three occupations had median weekly earnings levels that were significantly higher than the median earnings among all professional workers. However, real earnings growth among college and university educators was essentially flat over the decade.

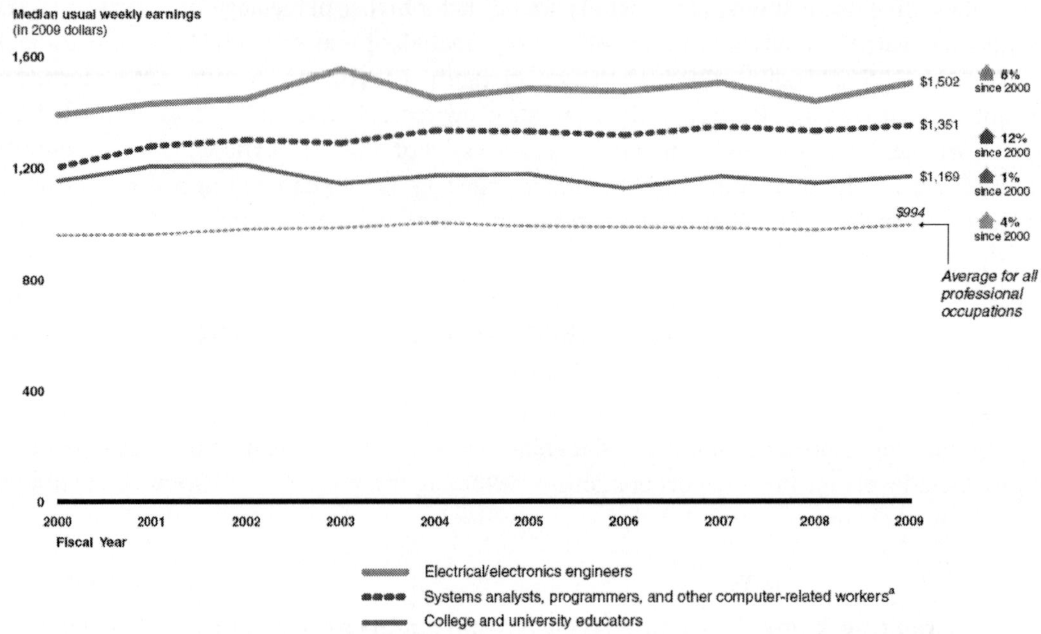

Source: GAO analysis of data from the CPS provided by the Bureau of Labor Statistics.

[a]The occupation "systems analysis, programming, and other computer-related workers" includes five CPS occupational groups: (1) computer scientists and systems analysts; (2) computer programmers; (3) computer software engineers; (4) database administrators; and (5) operations research analysts. The central tendency for wage shown here is a weighted average of the median wage for each of these five occupations. Estimated median earnings have 95 percent confidence intervals within +/- 1 percent of the estimate itself for all professional occupations; within +/-3 percent for systems analysis, programmers, and other computer-related occupations; within +/- 11 percent for electrical and electronics engineers; and within +/- 6 percent for college and university educators.

Figure 18. Median Usual Weekly Earnings in Constant 2009 Dollars among U.S. Workers in Occupations with Large Numbers of H-1B Petitions, 2000–2009.

Rates of Unemployment among Selected Occupations

Unemployment rates among (1) electrical and electronics engineers and (2) system analysts, programmers, and other computer-related workers showed greater cyclical variation than did the unemployment rate for all U.S. workers in professional occupations. In contrast, the unemployment rate among college and university educators was somewhat less sensitive to business cycle fluctuations, and in most years was close to or lower than the unemployment rate for all professional occupations (see fig. 19).

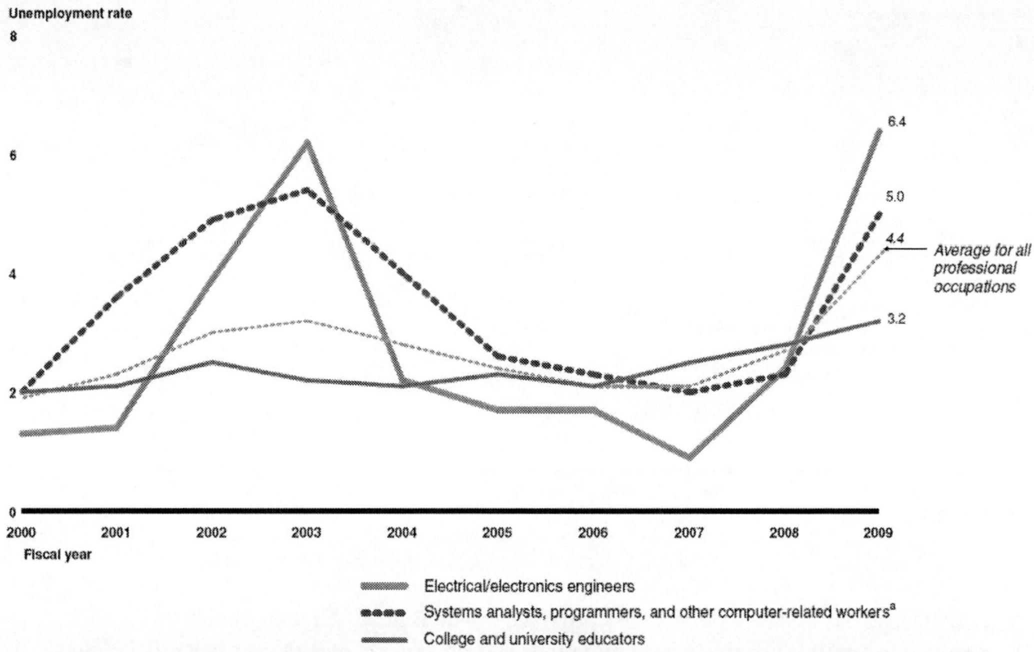

Source: GAO analysis of data from the CPS provided by the Bureau of Labor Statistics.

[a] The occupation "systems analysis, programming, and other computer-related workers" includes five CPS occupational groups: (1) computer scientists and systems analysts; (2) computer programmers; (3) computer software engineers; (4) database administrators; and (5) operations research analysts. Estimated unemployment rates have 95 percent confidence intervals within +/- 0.3 percentage points for all professional occupations; within +/-1.2 percentage points for systems analysis, programmers, and other computer-related occupations; within +/- 3 percentage points for electrical and electronics engineers; and within +/- 1.1 percentage points for college and university educators.

Figure 19. Unemployment Rate among U.S. Workers in Occupations with Large Numbers of H-1B Petitions, 2000–2009.

Employment in Selected Occupations

Employment among electrical and electronics engineers declined by 29 percent over the decade, and there was no significant change in the level of employment among systems analysts, programmers, and other computer-related workers. In contrast, employment grew by 15 percent among all professional occupations over the past decade. Employment among college and university educators grew by 26 percent over the decade (see fig. 20).

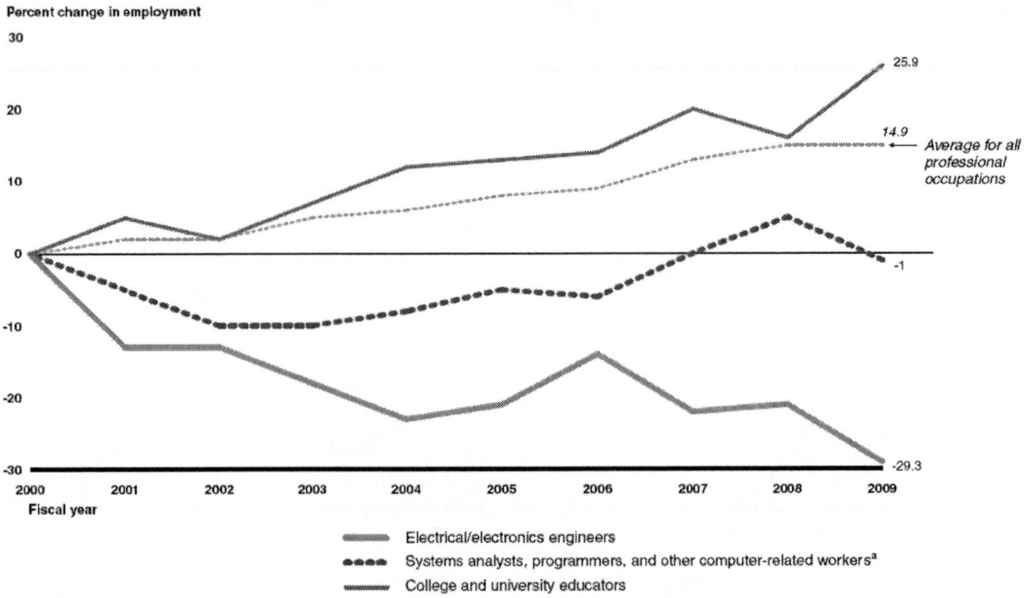

Source: GAO analysis of data from the CPS provided by the Bureau of Labor Statistics.

[a] The occupation "systems analysis, programming, and other computer-related workers" includes five CPS occupational groups: (1) computer scientists and systems analysts; (2) computer programmers; (3) computer software engineers; (4) database administrators; and (5) operations research analysts. Estimated percent changes in employment relative to 2000 have 95 percent confidence intervals within +/- 2 percentage points for all professional occupations; within +/- 7 percentage points for systems analysis, programmers and other computer-related occupations; within +/- 15 percentage points for electrical and electronics engineers and for college and university educators.

Figure 20. Percent Change in U.S. Worker Employment Since 2000 in Occupations with Large Numbers of H-1B Petitions, 2000–2009.

Appendix IV: Characteristics of H-1B Employers

This appendix provides additional analyses of H-1B employers in fiscal year 2000 through fiscal year 2009 and more detailed analyses of the top 150 H-1B hiring companies in fiscal year 2009.

Many Employers Approved for H-1B Workers Were in Scientific, Professional, and Technical Services

Over a third of employers approved to hire H-1B workers between fiscal year 2000 and fiscal year 2009 were employers that provided scientific, professional, or technical services (see fig. 21). For example, in fiscal year 2009, at least 38 percent of employers approved to hire one or more H-1B workers indicated that they were in one industry—the professional, scientific, and technical services industry. Services within this industry include legal services; accounting, bookkeeping, and payroll services; architectural, engineering, and specialized design services; computer services; consulting services; and research services. Also in fiscal year 2009, the manufacturing, health care and social assistance, educational services, and finance and insurance sectors received the next-highest share of one or more H-1B approvals—that is, 11, 10, 7, and 6 percent of companies approved to hire H-1B workers, respectively.

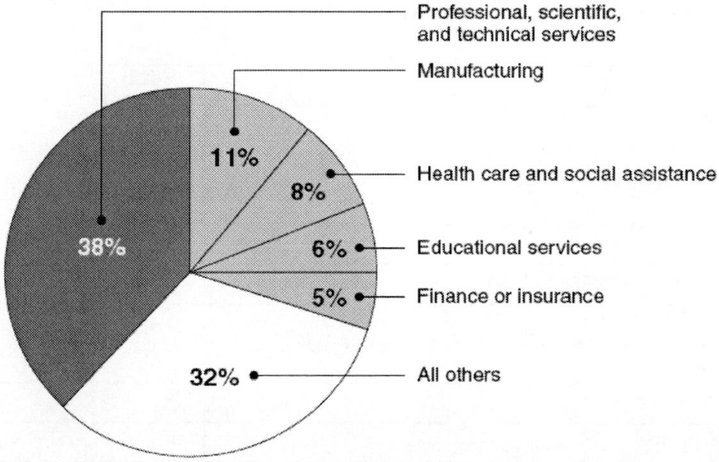

Source: GAO analysis of Homeland Security CLAIMS 3 data.

Figure 21. Industries of Employers Approved to Hire H-1B Workers, FY 2000–FY 2009.

Many Employers Approved for H-1B Workers Were Located in High-Technology Corridors

While H-1B hiring employers were located throughout the continental United States in fiscal year 2009, they tended to be concentrated in several high-technology pockets of the country such as Silicon Valley, Southern California, and the Tri-State area of New York, New Jersey, and Connecticut (see fig. 22).

The Vast Majority of Top 150 H-1B Employers Operated in the United States

For the 150 employers with the largest number of approved petitions in fiscal year 2009 (representing 26 percent of all approvals in fiscal year 2009), and for which we were able to obtain additional publicly available information (133 employers), we found that the majority of employers operated in the United States, although 7 operated in India and 2 in the United Kingdom.

GAO also reviewed data from Labor's LCAs on the top 150 employers of H-1Bs in fiscal year 2009, including whether the employer is H-1Bdependent; whether the employer is a willful violator; and the number of petitions requested at each of the four possible skill levels. As indicated in table 9, among the 150 companies for which Labor provided data, 24 were H-1B dependent, and 9 of which were also deemed "willful violators." The remaining 126 firms were neither H-1B dependent nor willful violators. In addition, on average, these firms indicated that they would pay workers at the prevailing wage for skill-level one 52 percent of the time; the prevailing wage for skill-level two 30 percent of the time; the prevailing wage for skill-level three 12 percent of the time; and the prevailing wage for skill-level four 6 percent of the time.

Table 9. Select Characteristics of the Top 150 H-1B Employers, FY 2009

Characteristic[a]	Total
Publiclytraded	66
Private	68
Missing	16
Subsidiaries	58
Incorporated in a Foreign Country	7
Location of employer	
USA	123
India	7
United Kingdom	2
Missing	18
H-1B Dependent	24
Willful Violators	9
Proportion of time employers, on average, will payprevailingwage at each skill level	
Skill level one	52%
Skill level two	30%
Skill level three	12%
Skill level four	6%
Number of employees[b]	
Median	16,151
10,000 or fewer	48
Over 10,000	80
Over 100,000	12
Over 200,000	8
Over 500,000	1

Source: GAO analysis of Mergent Online and LexisNexis's Dossier databases and Labor data.

[a]Due to missing data on some characteristics, the data presented does not always represent 150 companies.

[b]For the 128 employers for which information on the number of employees was available, the dates associated with the employer counts for employees ranged from December 2004 to June 2010, although most dates were in fiscal year 2009.

Source: GAO analysis of Homeland Security CLAIMS 3 data; National Atlas of the United States (base map).

Figure 22. Location of Cities with High Numbers of Approved H-1B Petitions, FY 2009.

Many of the Top 150 H-1B Employers Were in the Manufacturing or Educational Services Industry

Regarding industry, we found that, similar to the universe of all H-1B hiring employers, most of the top H-1B employers were in the professional, technical, and scientific services industry, although many were also in the manufacturing industry or the educational services industry.[1] While the top 150 H-1B-hiring employers spanned a range of industries, these employers were distinctly concentrated in a few, more specific industry groups, including electronic computer manufacturing; software publishing; custom computer programming services (firms that write, modify, and test software for clients); computer systems design services; and colleges, universities, and professional schools.

In terms of the type of employers, a relatively large number (44 of the 150 employers) were universities, compared to 6 percent of H-1B hiring employers in fiscal year 2009. We also found that at least 33 employers could be categorized as information technology (IT) services—those that either provide staff or full project teams to other companies for IT projects (see table 10).[2]

Table 10. Characteristics of the Top 150 H-1B Employers, FY 2009

Characteristic[a]	Total
Industry[b]	
Professional, scientific, technical services	33
Custom computer programming services	*12*
Computer systemsdesign services	*8*
Other	*13*
Manufacturing	33
Electronic computer manufacturing	*6*
Other	*27*
Educational services	28
Characteristica	Total
Colleges, universities, and professional schools	*23*
Other	*5*
Information services	13
Software publishing	*5*
Other	*8*
Finance and insurance	10
Health care and social assistance	8
Other industry	6
Missing	19
Type of employer[b]	
Institutions of higher education	44
Financial institutions	13
IT services	33

Source: GAO analysis of Mergent Online and LexisNexis's Dossier databases.

[a]Due to missing data on some characteristics, the data presented do not always represent 150 companies.

[b]The industry numbers are based on the North American Industry Classification System codes, and the types of employers are based on GAO's analysis of company descriptions.

APPENDIX V: SELECTED H-1B PROGRAM LAWS

This appendix provides a chronological list of major laws and descriptions of certain key provisions related to the H-1B program. Laws identified may contain additional provisions related to the H-1B program not described here, and there may be additional laws not included here that have made various changes in the H-1B program. This is not intended to be an exhaustive summary of all laws and provisions related to the H-1B program.

Selected laws	Description of key provisions
Immigration and Nationality Act, ch. 447, §§ 101(a)(15)(H) and 214(c), 66 Stat. 163, 168and189-90 (1952).	• Authorized H-1B visas for aliens with a residence in a foreign country that the alien had no intention of abandoning, who were of distinguished merit and ability, and were coming to the United States to perform temporary service of an exceptional nature requiring such merit and ability.
Immigration Reform and Control Act of 1986, Pub. L. No. 99-603, § 102, 100 Stat. 3359, 3474-80.	• Makes it an unfair immigration-related employment practice for most employers to discriminate against any individual (other than an unauthorized alien) with respect to hiring, recruitment, firing, or referral for fee because of such individual's origin or citizenship status. States that it is not an unfair immigration-related employment practice to hire a U.S. citizen or national over an equally qualified alien. • Requires that complaints of violations be filed with the Special Counsel for Immigration-Related Unfair Employment Practices (established by the act) within the Department of Justice. • Authorizes the Special Counsel to (1) investigate complaints and determine (within 120 days) whether to bring such complaints before a specially trained administrative law judge and (2) initiate investigations and complaints. Permits private actions if the Special Counsel does not file a complaint withinsuch 120-day period.
Immigration Act of 1990, Pub. L. No. 101-649, § 205, 104 Stat. 4978, 5019-22.	• Removed requirement that alien have a residence in a foreign country and no intention of abandoning it, and revised statute to authorize H-1B visas for aliens coming temporarily to the U.S. to perform services in a "specialty occupation," which was defined as one that requires, at a minimum, theoretical and practical application of a body of highly specialized knowledge and the attainment of a bachelor's or higher degree in the specific specialty (or its equivalent). • Established the LCA process, to be administered by Labor, that requires employers to make certain attestations.[a] • Limited the number of H-1B visas that could be issued during a fiscal year to 65,000 beginning in fiscal year 1992. • Limited the period of authorized admission as an H-1B nonimmigrant to 6 years. • Established "dual intent" provision, under which H-1B visa holders could alsopursue permanent residency. • Assigned responsibility to Labor to enforce program rules by investigating complaints made by H-1B workers or their representatives against employers, and by making referrals to Justice and imposing civil monetary penalties where it finds a failure by the employer to meet certain required conditions or the misrepresentation of material fact.
Immigration Technical Corrections Act of 1991, Pub. L. No. 102-232, tit. III, § 303(a)(7)(B)(iii), 102 Stat. 1742, 1747.	• Restricted Labor to reviewing LCAs only for completeness and obvious inaccuracies. • Required Labor, if an LCA is complete and has no obvious inaccuracies, to certify it within 7 days
American Competitiveness and Workforce Improvement Act of 1998, Pub. L. No. 105-277, div. C, tit. IV, §§ 411-418, 112 Stat. 2681-641, 2681-642 – 2681-657.	• Temporarily raised the cap on H-1B visas for fiscal years 1999 to 2001 to a high of 115,000; returned the cap to 65,000 for the following years. • Defined "H-1B-dependent employer" as employer that has • 25 or fewer full-time equivalent employees in the U.S. and employs more than seven H-1B nonimmigrants; • 26 to 50 full-time equivalent employees in the U.S. and employs more than 12 H-1B nonimmigrants; or • At least 51 full-time equivalent employees in the U.S., of whom at least 15 percent are H-1B nonimmigrants. • Required H-1B-dependent employers and those that committed a willful failure or misrepresentation during the 5 years preceding filing of an LCA[b]to include additional attestations. • Provided that H-1B-dependent employers and such willful violators are notrequired to make these additional attestations with respect to H-1B nonimmigrants receiving annual wages of at least $60,000 or those with a master's or higher degree (or its equivalent) in a specialty related to the job. • Required that H-1B workers waiting for final adjudication of their requests forpermanent residence status be given 1-year extensions of their H-1B visas until their requests have been adjudicated. • Provided Labor increased authority to investigate and enforce program compliance and assess civil monetary penalties against employers found to be in violation of certain program requirements. • Required that steps be taken to maintain accurate count of the number of aliens issued H-1B or other nonimmigrant visas.[c]

(Continued)

Selected laws	Description of key provisions
American Competitiveness in the Twenty-first Century Act of 2000, Pub. L. No. 106-313, §§ 102-106, 114 Stat. 1251, 1251-55.	• Temporarily raised the cap on H-1B visas for fiscal years 2001 to 2003 to 195,000; cap returned to 65,000 for the following years. • Exempts an alien from the H-1B cap if he or she is employed (or has received an offer of employment) at • an institution of higher education or its related or affiliated nonprofit entity; • a nonprofit research organization; or • a governmental research organization. • Created increased portability of H-1B visas by authorizing H-1B workers to accept new employment upon the filing by the prospective employer of a new petition on his or her behalf. The H-1B worker's employment authorization may be extended until the petition is adjudicated.
United States-Chile Free Trade Agreement Implementation Act, Pub. L. No. 108-77, § 402(b)(2)(B), 117 Stat. 909, 940 (2003) and the United States-Singapore Free Trade Agreement Implementation Act, Pub. L. No. 108-78, § 402(1), 117 Stat. 948, 970-71.	• Created a new nonimmigrant classification available each fiscal year to up to1,400 professionals from Chile and 5,400 professionals from Singapore, known as H-1B1. These H-1B1 visas count against the H-1B cap.
H-1B Visa Reform Act of 2004, Pub. L. No. 108-447, div. J, tit. IV, subtit. B, §§ 422, 424 and 425(a) 118Stat. 3353, 3353-56.	• Provided Labor increased authority to initiate investigations in cases where the Secretary personally certifies there is reasonable cause and approves the investigation. Information providing the basis for the investigation must originate outside Labor unless it was lawfully obtained in the course of another Labor investigation. In addition, receipt of information submitted to Justice or Labor to secure employment of an H-1B worker cannot provide the basis for such investigation. • Exempted the first 20,000 petitions received for individuals who have earneda master's degree or higher from a U.S. institution of higher education. • Raised the fee imposed on most employers when filing an H-1B visa petitionto $750 or $1,500 and imposed an additional fraud prevention and detection fee of $500.
Pub. L. No 111-230.	• Increased the fees by $2,000 for petitions filed between August 13, 2010, and October 1, 2014, if the petitioner has 50 or more employees in the U.S. and more than fifty percent of those U.S. employees are in H-1B or L nonimmigrant status.

Source: GAO.

[a] Required attestations were as follows: (1) employer will pay H-1B workers the employer's actual wage for the position or the prevailing wage in the area, whichever is higher; (2) employer will provide working conditions for H-1B employees that will not adversely affect the working conditions of workers similarly employed; (3) no strike or lockout exists in the course of a labor dispute in the occupational classification at the place of employment; and (4) the employer has provided notice that it is filing an LCA application to the bargaining representative (if any) of its employees in the occupational classification and area for which aliens are sought, or if there is no bargaining representative, by posting notice of the filing in conspicuous locations at the place of employment.

[b] Additional attestations include the following: (1) employer did not and will not displace a U.S. worker it employs within 90 days before and 90 days after filing any visa petition supported by the LCA; (2) employer will not place the nonimmigrant with any other employer where he or she performs duties at a worksite owned, operated, or controlled by that other employer and there are indicia of an employment relationship between the nonimmigrant and other employer unless it has inquired whether the other employer has displaced or intends to displace one of its U.S. workers within 90 days before or 90 days after the placement; and (3) employer has taken good faith steps, prior to filing the LCA, to recruit in the United States using procedures that meet industrywide standards and offering compensation at least as great as that required to be offered to H-1B nonimmigrants, U.S. workers for the job and has offered it to any U.S. worker who applies and is equally or better qualified for it.

[c] This responsibility was originally assigned to the Attorney General but was later transferred to Homeland Security. Pub. L. No. 109-13, div. B, tit. IV, § 406, 119 Stat. 32

APPENDIX VI: COMMENTS FROM THE DEPARTMENT OF HOMELAND SECURITY

U.S. Department of Homeland Security
Washington, DC 20528

Homeland Security

November 30, 2010

Andrew Sherrill
Director
Education, Workforce, and
Income Security Issues
441 G Street, NW
U.S. Government Accountability Office
Washington, DC 20548

Dear Mr. Sherrill:

RE: GAO-11-26, Draft GAO Report: H-1B Visa Program: Reforms Are Needed to Minimize the Risks and Costs of Current Program, (130916)

Thank you for the opportunity to review and comment on the Government Accountability Office (GAO) draft report entitled, "H-1B Visa Program: Reforms Are Needed to Minimize the Risks and Costs of Current Program." The Department of Homeland Security (DHS) appreciates the opportunity to review and respond to the Government Accountability Office (GAO) subject report.

To ensure that the number of new H-1B workers who are not cap-exempt and who seek to enter the United States each year does not exceed the statutory cap, GAO recommends that the Secretary of Homeland Security direct U.S. Citizenship and Immigration Services (USCIS) to take the following steps:

Recommendation 1: To improve its tracking of the number of approved H-1B applications and the number of issued visas under the cap by fully leveraging the transformation effort currently underway, which involves the adoption of an electronic petition processing system that will be linked to the Department of State's tracking system. Homeland Security should consider entering into a Memorandum of Understanding with the Department of State, or modifying their existing agreement, to ensure that by linking electronic data systems, both agencies will have real-time information on the number of visas that have been approved under the cap.

Response: Non-concur. USCIS has been working within DHS, and collaborating with the Department of State (DOS), to establish an appropriate data exchange framework, including the Consular Consolidated Database (CCD), that would support retrieval of case data. The existing data-sharing Memorandum of Understanding (MOU) between DHS and DOS is sufficient without modification. However, USCIS and the DOS Bureau of Consular Affairs did draft and sign a more specific Letter of Intent (LOI) to establish electronic visa, immigration, and citizenship data exchanges. This LOI complies with the existing MOU and documents the intent to continue the existing data-sharing relationship and establish electronic visa, immigration, and citizenship data exchanges through the USCIS Transformation Program, the DOS Global Visa System, Global Citizenship Services, and Consular Case Management Service projects.

Even if electronic data sharing is established, it will still be difficult to maintain an exact count of petitions for visa issuance while timely adjudicating petitions. USCIS believes that implementing this recommendation may only slightly improve cap management. First, DOS visa data will not include individuals already in the United States seeking to change their nonimmigrant status. Second, most real-time visa data will be too old for cap management use. While most non-exempt petitions are filed and approved between April and September, it is typically months later when DOS issues the relating visas. For example, USCIS received more than enough petitions in the first few days of each filing season to meet the FY08 and FY09 caps. Those petitions requested October 1 employment start dates. USCIS held the random selection process in April and receipted and approved the petitions shortly thereafter. The approved beneficiaries needing nonimmigrant visas did not appear at the consulates to obtain the H-1B visa until months later. By that time, most H-1B cap petitions had already been adjudicated.

Recommendation 2: To ensure business concerns without undermining program integrity, USCIS should to the extent permitted by its statutory authority, explore options for increasing the flexibility of the application process for H-1B employers, such as:

- Allowing employers to rank their applications for visa candidates so that they can hire the best qualified worker for the jobs in highest need;
- Distributing the applications granted under the annual cap in allotments throughout the year (e.g. quarterly); and
- Establishing a system whereby businesses with a strong track-record of compliance with H-1B regulations may use a streamlined application process.

Response: Non-concur. USCIS does not believe that the recommendation to allow employers to rank beneficiaries is feasible. Such a practice would lead to an extremely complicated cap management process. Allowing for ranking of beneficiaries would also require complex file intake and adjudication processes. These processes would be time-consuming and resource-intensive. It would actually decrease flexibility for employers because employers would have to submit a list of ranked petitions at the beginning of the cap season and could not later add beneficiaries or change rankings. Finally, as USCIS stated in previous meetings with GAO, the implementation of a beneficiary ranking process could create significant vulnerabilities as it might encourage petitioners to submit additional petitions for individuals they have no intention of hiring in an attempt to increase the chances of obtaining a cap number for a particular individual.

USCIS also does not believe that quarterly cap allocation is warranted or feasible for the H-1B program. H-1B specialty occupations are not as affected by seasonal demands as the H-2B classification. Furthermore, maintaining an accurate quarterly cap would be even more complex and problematic than maintaining the annual cap. Under quarterly allotment, petitions could be filed beginning in April, July, October, and January. It is possible that beginning in October, caps for the first, second, and third quarters could all be open at the same time, thereby tripling the complexity of cap management.

USCIS does not believe that current law allows us to exempt petitioners with track records of H-1B compliance from evidentiary requirements. However, the Agency is developing our Validation Instrument for Business Enterprises (VIBE) system. VIBE is an adjudicative tool that will provide officers with the means to verify through an independent information provider the petitioner's business information. In September 2009, USCIS awarded Dun & Bradstreet the contract to serve as the independent information provider. Once USCIS fully implements VIBE, we anticipate that it will reduce the need for petitioners to submit duplicative paper documentation to establish their current level of business operations. This will, in turn and over time, reduce the number of Requests for Evidence (RFEs) USCIS issues to otherwise eligible petitioners.

Draft Matters for Congressional Consideration 2: To reduce duplication and fragmentation in the administration and oversight of the H-1B application process, consistent with past GAO matters for congressional consideration, consider eliminating the requirement that employers first submit a Labor Condition Application (LCA) to the Department of Labor (DOL) for certification, and require instead that employers submit this application along with the I-129 application to the Department of Homeland Security's U.S. Citizenship and Immigration Services for review.

Response: Non-concur. USCIS does not believe that eliminating the requirement for employers to first submit an LCA to DOL is either desirable or practicable. The LCA is an attestation of standards to which the employer must adhere. By completing and signing the LCA, the employer:

- Agrees to several issues regarding an employer's responsibilities, including the wages, benefits, and working conditions provided to U.S. workers and the nonimmigrant workers; and
- States that at the time of filing there is no strike or lockout in the course of a labor dispute at the place of employment.

USCIS reviews the H-1B petition, the certified LCA, and the petitioner's supporting evidence to determine if:

- The job meets the requirements of a specialty occupation;
- The qualifications of the prospective H-1B worker meet the statutory and regulatory requirements; and
- The content of the certified LCA corresponds with the petition under review.

USCIS does not re-adjudicate the DOL's determinations on the LCA; it relies on DOL's expertise to make these findings. USCIS does not believe that it has the necessary expertise to make wage and labor determinations. Moreover, it is DOL, not USCIS, that has the authority to enforce any violations of the LCA.

Thank you for the opportunity to comment on this Draft Report. We look forward to working with you on future Homeland Security issues.

Sincerely,

Jerald E. Levine
Director
Departmental Audit Liaison Office

APPENDIX VII: COMMENTS FROM THE DEPARTMENT OF JUSTICE

U.S. Department of Justice

Civil Rights Division

Office of Special Counsel for Immigration-Related Unfair Employment Practices - NYA
950 Pennsylvania Ave, NW
Washington, DC 20530
Main (202) 616-5594
Fax (202) 616-5509

November 23, 2010

Andrew Sherrill
Director, Education, Workforce, and Income Security Issues
U.S. Government Accountability Office
441 G Street, N.W.
Washington, D.C. 20548

Dear Mr. Sherrill,

Thank you for the opportunity to review the final draft of the Government Accountability Office (GAO) report, *H1-B Visa Program: Reforms are Needed to Minimize the Risks and Costs of Current Program*. The report was reviewed by the Department of Justice, Civil Rights Division, Office of Special Counsel for Immigration Related Unfair Employment Practices (OSC), which participated in the GAO review. This letter constitutes the Department's formal comments. I request that the GAO include this letter in the final report.

<u>GAO Recommendation that the Department of Labor Develop and Maintain a Centralized Website, Accessible to the Public, Where Businesses Must Post Notice of Their Intent to Hire H-1B Workers</u>

The Department of Justice supports this recommendation, and believes the website would help U.S. workers determine if they have been impermissibly replaced by H-1B visa holders and identify employers who may be engaged in a pattern or practice of discrimination against U.S. workers.

<u>Before Seeking to Hire an H-1B Visa Holder, all Employers Should be Required to "Test" the Labor Market to Determine Whether Qualified U.S. Workers Are Available and to Hire any Equally or Better Qualified U.S. Workers Who Apply</u>

The Department of Justice notes that only a small number of employers are currently required to "test" the labor market for qualified U.S. workers prior to seeking an H1-B visa and to hire any equally or better qualified U.S. workers who apply for the job.[1] At present, an

[1] Specifically, prior to applying for an H-1B non-immigrant visa, such employers must attest that they have made a good faith effort to recruit U.S. workers using procedures that meet industry-wide standards, and that they will offer the job for which they are seeking H-1B non-immigrants to all U.S. workers who apply and have qualifications equal to or better than the H-1B non-immigrants sought.

employer is subject to this requirement only if the employer is submitting a labor condition application (LCA) to employ an H-1B non-immigrant who earns less than $60,000 annually and does not possess a master's or other higher degree, and the employer is either a H-1B dependent entity[2] or a willful violator.[3]

Although this issue is mentioned in the draft report, the GAO does not propose any recommendations to address this deficit. To ensure that U.S. workers are not disadvantaged by the H-1B program, the Department of Justice believes that that all employers be required to provide attestations that they have first "tested" the labor market and hired any equally or better qualified U.S. workers when they submit an LCA to employ an H-1B non-immigrant.

The Department of Labor Should Display Information about Worker Protections and OSC's Contact Information on all H1-B Educational Material and the Centralized Database for H1-B Postings

The Department of Justice believes that greater awareness about the anti-discrimination provision of the Immigration and Nationality Act, 8 U.S.C. § 1324b, and OSC's enforcement of worker protections against citizenship status discrimination, will help ensure that U.S. workers who may have been discriminated in favor of H1-B visa holders are able to vindicate their rights. Therefore, it recommends that the Department of Labor display information about worker protections available under the anti-discrimination provision and OSC's worker hotline number on all H1-B educational material and on the centralized database for H1-B postings, if the database is implemented.

The extensive efforts that your staff has put into this report and the opportunity to work with the GAO on these important issues are appreciated.

Sincerely,

Leon Rodriguez by CB

Leon Rodriguez
Chief of Staff

[2] Pursuant to 20 C.F.R. 655.736(a)(1), an H-1B dependent employer is determined by calculating the number of full-time employees relative to the number of H-1B visa holders employed. Depending on the total numbers of employees, a company will be deemed H-1B dependent if it has between 15% and 28% H-1B visa holders on staff.

[3] A willful violator is an employer that meets all of the following standards:

(i) A finding of violation by the employer is entered in either of the following two types of enforcement proceedings:
(A) A Department of Labor proceeding under section 212(n)(2) of the INA (8 U.S.C. 1182(n)(2)(C)); or
(B) A Department of Justice proceeding under section 212(n)(5) of the INA (8 U.S.C. 1182(n)(5)).

(ii) The Department of Labor and/or Department of Justice finds that the employer has committed either a willful failure or a misrepresentation of a material fact during the five-year period preceding the filing of the LCA; and

(iii) The findings of the agencies are entered on or after October 21, 1998. 20 CFR §655.736.

End Notes

[1] Immigration Act of 1990, Pub. L. No. 101-649, § 205, 104 Stat. 4978, 5019-22 (codified at 8 U.S.C. § 1101(a)(15)(H)(i)(b).

[2] H.R. Rpt. No. 110-862 at 132-133.

[3] Offshoring generally refers to the practice, by either U.S. companies or government entities, of replacing goods or services produced domestically with imported goods or services. See GAO, *International Trade: Current Government Data Provide Limited Insight into Offshoring of*

Services, GAO-04-932 (Washington, D.C.: Sept. 22, 2004) and *Offshoring of Services: An Overview of the Issues*, GAO-06-5 (Washington, D.C.: Nov. 28, 2005).

[4] Data on employer applications for H-1B visas that were submitted to the Department of Labor prior to fiscal year 2002 were not readily available.

[5] Twenty-two companies were randomly selected from the 51,942 H-1B employers that received approved petitions in fiscal year 2008. An additional 12 H-1B hiring firms were selected based on referrals from industry contacts, because they were known leaders in key sectors of the economy, and other factors. See appendix I for more details.

[6] 8 U.S.C. § 1184(i). Fashion models of distinguished merit and ability also qualify for H-1B visas and do not need to meet the definition of specialty occupation. This report will focus solely on the specialty workers.

[7] Pub. L. No. 105-277, tit. IV, § 411, 112 Stat. 2681, 2681-642.

[8] Pub. L. No. 106-313, § 102, 114 Stat. 1251, 1251.

[9] §103, 114 Stat. 1252.

[10] Pub. L. No. 108-447, div. J, tit. IV, subtit. B, § 425(a), 118 Stat. 2809, 3356.

[11] United States-Chile Free Trade Agreement Implementation Act, Pub. L. No. 108-77, § 402(a)(2)(B), 117 Stat. 909, 940 (2003), and United States-Singapore Free Trade Agreement Implementation Act, Pub. L. No. 108-78, § 402(2), 117 Stat. 948, 970-71 (2003).

[12] Other changes to the program have occurred. For example, the 2000 legislation increased "visa portability" for H-1B workers, permitting them to change employers within their 6- year time period (sequential employment) once the new employer files an H-1B petition on their behalf. AC21, § 105, 114 Stat. 1253.

[13] AC21 § 106(a) and (b), 114 Stat. 1253-54.

[14] The identification card that proves permanent resident status of an alien in the United States, a U.S. Permanent Resident Card, is commonly referred to as a "green card." It serves as proof that its holder, a lawful permanent resident, has permission to reside and work in the United States.

[15] Homeland Security is required to take necessary steps to maintain an accurate count of the number of aliens subject to the H-1B cap who are issued visas. 8 U.S.C. § 1184 notes.

[16] The Secretary of Labor may also initiate an investigation of any H-1B employer if the Secretary of Labor has reasonable cause to believe that the employer is not in compliance with the program. 8 U.S.C. § 1182(n)(2)(G). However, the authority is limited in that the Secretary of Labor must certify that reasonable cause exists and that the investigation was initiated for reasons other than Labor's review of the employer's application for completeness and obvious inaccuracies.

[17] U.S. workers (and others on their behalf) may file a complaint, known as a charge, to the Department of Justice's Office of Special Counsel for Immigration Related Unfair Employment Practices, which will pursue discrimination charges alleging that an employer has given certain preferential treatment in hiring an H-1B worker. 8 U.S.C. § 1324b(b) and (c). Any aggrieved person or organization may also file a complaint with Labor against an employer. When Labor's Wage and Hour Division finds the employer out of compliance with H-1B program requirements, it can assess fines and impose remedies such as payment of back wages to H-1B workers and disqualification from the program, depending on the specific violations, for from 1 to 3 years.

[18] By statute, Labor is required to conduct its review within 7 days and may only review applications for omissions and obvious inaccuracies. 8 U.S.C. § 1182(n)(1)(G)(ii) and 20 CFR 655.730(b). It has no statutory authority to verify the authenticity of the information.

[19] 8 U.S.C. § 1182(n)(1)(A)-(D).

[20] 8 U.S.C. § 1182(n)(1)(E)(ii). H-1B-dependent employers are those with 25 or fewer total employees and more than 7 H-1B employees, 26 to 50 total employees and more than 12 H-1B employees, or with at least 51 total employees and at least 15 percent of them H-1B employees. 8 U.S.C. § 1182(n)(3)(A). H-1B-dependent employers are exempt from this requirement with respect to

employees to whom they pay at least $60,000 per year, as well as employees with a master's degree or higher in a specialty related to their H-1B employment. 8 U.S.C. § 1182(n)(3)(B).

[21] H-1B employers are exempt from this requirement with respect to certain high-priority employees under 8 U.S.C. § 1153(b)(1).

[22] 8 U.S.C. § 1101(a)(15)(H)(ii)(a).

[23] 8 U.S.C. 1101(a)(15)(H)(ii)(b).

[24] 20 C.F.R. §§ 655.1-655.119 (2009).

[25] Each submitted petition is for one H-1B worker. Thus, the number of petitions submitted to Homeland Security can be used as a proxy for the number of workers requested. However, this proxy has several limitations, which are detailed in appendix I.

[26] Initial petitions for new H-1B workers are counted against an annual cap (currently 65,000 for regular petitions and 20,000 since 2005 for petitions for those with graduate degrees from a U.S. institution of higher education), unless they are submitted by cap-exempt employers. Cap-exempt employers are universities, and nonprofit, or governmental research organizations. 8 U.S.C. § 1184(g)(5).

[27] Reported numbers only reflect petitions entered into Homeland Security's Computer Linked Application Management System, Version 3 (CLAIMS 3) data system—processed by Homeland Security. At any point in a given year, when Homeland Security determines that submitted initial petitions that are subject to the cap will likely exceed the cap, the agency stops accepting these petitions, and does not enter them into its data system. For initial petitions that are subject to the cap and are submitted on the last day, Homeland Security holds a "lottery" to determine which to accept under the cap. Initial petitions that are subject to the cap and are not selected via the lottery are not entered into Homeland Security's data system, CLAIMS 3. For fiscal year 2008 and fiscal year 2009, the cap was reached very early in the filing season, after which requests subject to the cap were not entered into CLAIMS 3 or processed by Homeland Security. As a result, it is likely that the number of processed initial petitions subject to the cap is highly underestimated in these years.

[28] This is true only for regular petitions not subject to the master's cap. In years in which the master's cap is reached first, after processed petitions subject to the master's cap exceed the 20,000 master's cap, Homeland Security adds unprocessed master's petitions into the universe of regular cap cases; therefore, in these years some master's petitions have two chances of being selected for processing. Homeland Security does not track the number of processed petitions that were eligible for the master's cap, but were ultimately counted against the regular cap.

[29] Continuing petitions, known as extensions, are not limited by and do not count against the annual cap with one exception—if the H-1B worker was initially approved to work for an employer that is not subject to the cap and the worker changes to an employer that is subject to the cap.

[30] Our petition and employer-level analysis of petitions for H-1B workers processed by Homeland Security used data from its CLAIMS 3 Mainframe database, which does not allow us to determine which petitions for H-1B workers were subject to the master's cap. Homeland Security's CLAIMS 3 LAN database does track information related to H-1B workers graduating with a master's degree or higher from an American institution of higher education, but these two data systems are not linked.

[31] All employer-based analyses were restricted to petitions with valid Employer Identification Numbers. About 220,000 of 2.8 million petitions were excluded from our analysis due to missing or invalid Employer Identification Numbers.

[32] L-1 visas are issued to intracompany transferees who work for an international firm or corporation in executive and managerial positions or have specialized product knowledge. 8 U.S.C. § 1101(a)(15)(L). L-1 visa holders can stay in the United States for up to 5 or 7 years, depending on the type of services provided. 8 U.S.C. §1184(c)(2).

[33] As noted earlier, Homeland Security does not enter petitions that are subject to the cap and submitted after the cap is reached into its data system, CLAIMS 3. Because our analysis is based on requests entered into its data system, we cannot determine approval rates for all submitted petitions.

[34] LCA data for these years do not allow for these two categories to be analyzed separately.

[35] Such employers are also referred to as third-party contractors or placing employers. Employers at which staffing companies place H-1B workers are referred to as placement employers.

[36] For additional information on H-1B employers, please refer to appendix IV.

[37] This selection of 31 firms constitutes a nongeneralizable sample and cannot be used to make inferences beyond the specific 31 firms selected. We also spoke with 3 additional companies as part of focus groups we conducted, consisting of H-1B employers and industry associations. See appendix I for more information on our focus groups and individual interviews.

[38] We defined "large" firms as those with 1,000 or more employees in the United States, and "small" firms as those with fewer than 500 employees in the United States. Multinational firms are defined as those who indicated that they have branches or affiliates outside of the United States.

[39] The median reported combined legal and filing fee cost was $3,820.

[40] This increase can be attributed, at least in part, to changes in the law. For example, in 2005, Homeland Security was required to begin collecting an additional $500 fee to be used for fraud prevention and detection purposes. In addition, recent legislation established an additional fee of $2,000 for petitions filed through September 30, 2014, for petitioners with 50 or more employees in the United States and more than 50 percent of those U.S. employees on H-1B or L visas. Act of August 13, 2010, Pub. L. No. 111-230, § 402(b), 123 Stat. 2485, 2487. [41] Academic research has also identified some of these factors as important drivers in private sector decisions about the location of R&D. See for example, Ashok Bardhan and Dwight Jaffee, "Globalization of R&D: offshoring innovative activity to emerging economies" in *Global Outsourcing and Offshoring: An Integrated Approach to Theory and Corporate Strategy*, Farok Contractor, Vikas Kumar, Sumit Kundu and Torben Pedersen, Eds. (Cambridge University Press, November 2010).

[42] As noted earlier, personnel from IT services firms we spoke with describe their firms using different terms, including staffing firms, solutions firms, and consulting firms. According to industry representatives, a pure IT staffing firm (or "labor augmentation" firm) simply provides workers with the expertise necessary to staff a project, while an "IT solutions" firm takes responsibility for the deliverable product.

[43] According to an industry organization representing the IT services industry, outsourcing firms that offshore work typically call themselves IT solutions firms in order to differentiate themselves from staffing firms. Others view them as a different business model—that is, one that uses onshore staff to provide access to a large, less expensive offshore labor force. An example might be an offshore outsourcing firm that takes over an IT help desk department, and uses its onshore component (staffed by H-1B workers) to establish relationships with and manage projects for the client company in the United States, while using the offshore component to staff the help desk. As such, several of the IT services firms we contacted that conducted offshore outsourcing could be considered a hybrid between an IT staffing and a solutions firm, at times providing IT staff to work at client sites, at times offshoring IT work to their overseas component, and at times providing both onshore and offshore work for a client.

[44] The January 8, 2010, memorandum by Associate Director Donald Neufeld (commonly referred to as the "Neufeld Memo"). For more information on this memo, see our discussion of the fifth objective.

[45] 20 C.F.R. § 214.2(h)(4)(ii) (2009). This requirement, according to one executive at a staffing firm we spoke with, was not necessarily enforced in the past.

[46] An H-1B visa transfer can be submitted at any point throughout the year, may not be subject to the cap, and—according to firm officials we spoke with—is typically processed much more quickly than a petition for an initial H-1B visa. Some said they were able to satisfy Homeland Security that

they have a client contract in place before submitting the H-1B transfer petition because the client could meet the potential employee (unlike for foreign nationals applying for initial H-1B visas) and therefore was more willing to write the contract. Also, petitions for H-1B transfers could be submitted throughout the year, allowing staffing firms to submit the petitions at the time they were arranging the work contract with the client company. Like petitions for initial H-1B visas, H-1B transfer petitions involve firms submitting LCAs prior to requesting the transfer.

[47] One staffing firm reported that another important source of employees is the spouses of current H-1B visa holders, who can petition for a change in visa status to H-1B once they are offered a job.

[48] For a discussion of IT services firms that conduct offshore outsourcing and employ large numbers of H-1B workers, see Ron Hira, "U.S. immigration regulations and India's information technology industry," *Technological Forecasting and Social Change*, vol. 71, issue 8 (October 2004): 837-854.

[49] Some researchers have noted that while many of the large offshore outsourcing firms started out in the "lower end" of the IT services market (for example, business process outsourcing, quality assurance, and design verification), some of these firms now offer engineering services and R&D services to their clients, and are seeking to expand the "higher value" portion of their business. For example, see Rafiq Dossani, "A Decade After Y2K: Has Indian IT Emerged?," in *Re-examining the Service Revolution*, D. Brexnitz and J. Zysman, Eds. (Yale University Press, forthcoming in 2011); and Ron Hira, "The Globalization of Research, Development, and Innovation," in *Manufacturing a Better Future for America*, Richard McCormack, Editor (Washington, D.C.: Alliance for American Manufacturing, 2009).

[50] GAO, *H-1B Foreign Workers: Better Controls Needed to Help Employers and Protect Workers*, HEHS-00-157 (Washington, D.C.: Sept. 7, 2000).

[51] For example, the Start-Up Visa Act, introduced by Senators Kerry and Lugar (S. 3029) and Representatives Maloney and Watson (H.R. 5193) in the 111th Congress was an effort to expand the E-B5 visa to immigrant entrepreneurs who, among other things, have investment capital available from a sponsoring U.S. venture capital or angel investor of at least $100,000 in an equity financing of not less than $250,000. The E-B5 visas are authorized under 8 U.S.C. §1153(b)(5) and generally are available currently to investors with at least $1,000,000 of personal capital available to invest in the United States. However, some parties we spoke with noted that it would be useful to have a venture backing requirement with a relatively low threshold so that the visa would be available to early-stage innovators.

[52] 8 U.S.C. § 1184 note.

[53] Attempts have been made to estimate the number of H-1B workers residing in the United States, but challenges to doing so include statutory changes in the numeric cap and inability to track H-1B workers after they enter the country.

[54] 8 U.S.C. § 1184(g).

[55] Specifically, the OIG recommended the agency count visas issued and changes from another visa type to an H-1B until they reach the cap limit. See Department of Homeland Security, Office of Inspector General, *USCIS Approval of H-1B Petitions Exceeded 65,000 Cap in Fiscal Year 2005*, OIG-05-49 (September 2005).

[56] According to Homeland Security Officials, I-129 form modifications are included in the USCIS Transformation Program's overall form redesign initiative. Homeland Security anticipates accepting electronic I-129 applications as a part of the Transformation Program's Increment 1 Release B, which is scheduled to begin deployment in 2012.

[57] See GAO, *Homeland Security: Despite Progress, DHS Continues to Be Challenged in Managing its Multi-Billion Dollar Annual Investment in Large-Scale Information Technology Systems*, GAO-09-1002T (Washington, D.C.: Sept. 15, 2009).

[58] Pub. L. No. 108-447, div. J, tit. IV, subtit. B, § 425(a), 118 Stat. 2809, 3356.

[59] According to Homeland Security officials, the agency first began tracking petitions submitted under the master's cap in fiscal year 2006.

[60] We could not analyze the remaining petitions in the cohort because we could not obtain a unique match for the individual listed in the petition between the data in CLAIMS 3 and the US-VISIT system. More information about the US-VISIT data and how GAO matched the data is available in appendix I.

[61] From the five occupations that absorbed the largest numbers of H-1B approvals, we selected the three occupations that absorbed the largest proportion of H-1B approvals relative to the stock of U.S. workers in that occupation in 2008. We made this comparison by comparing data on U.S. workers from the March 2009 CPS, which asks about employment and earnings from calendar year 2008, to H-1B petitions (both initial and continuing) submitted in calendar year 2008.

[62] In order to compare the CPS U.S. workforce occupations to the H-1B beneficiary occupations, we combined some occupational categories in both CLAIMS 3 and CPS to better align the CPS and USCIS data. The occupation "systems analysis, programming, and other computer-related occupations" includes five CPS occupational groups: (1) computer scientists and systems analysts; (2) computer programmers; (3) computer software engineers; (4) database administrators; and (5) operations research analysts. In CLAIMS 3, the occupation "systems analysis, programming, and other computer-related occupations" includes two occupational groups: (1) occupations in systems analysis and programming and (2) other computer-related occupations—database administrators, database design analysts, and microcomputer support specialists. See appendix I for more details.

[63] H-1B petitions in this occupation are approximately 10 percent of the total number of U.S. workers aged 18 to 50 years old, in the private sector, in this occupation. Note that if U.S. workers in the government sector and self-employed workers are included, H-1B petitions would then be approximately 9 percent of the total number of U.S. workers in this age group and occupation.

[64] Real earnings are adjusted for inflation and indexed to 2009 dollars.

[65] As noted earlier, because of differences in the occupational categories in CLAIMS 3 and CPS data on U.S. workers, five of the occupational categories for U.S. workers are grouped together. Computer programmers, computer scientists and systems analysts, computer software engineers, computer support specialists, and operation research analysts are grouped into the category "systems analysis, programming, and other computer-related occupations."

[66] Table 1 restricts the analysis to U.S. workers in full-time, private sector employment. Including self-employed and government workers increases the estimated number of U.S. workers in each occupation, with the largest increase in college and university educators. Including government workers and the self-employed does not qualitatively change most of the results presented in table 1, with the following exceptions: for the occupation "systems analysts, programmers, and other computer-related occupations," there is no longer a statistically significant difference between the wages of H-1B workers and U.S. workers, in the age categories 20 to 39 or 40 to 50. For the occupation "college and university educators," when government and self-employed workers are included in the analysis, there is a statistically significant difference between the wages of H-1B workers and U.S. workers in the age category 40 to 50, with the median U.S. worker earning about $10,000 more than the median H-1B worker.

[67] See appendix II for the age distributions of approved H-1B workers and U.S. citizens in these occupations, which show that H-1B workers in (1) systems analysis, programming, and other computer-related occupations and (2) electrical and electronics engineers were generally younger than their U.S.-citizen counterparts.

[68] GAO did not present analysis of wage rates by occupation within different geographic areas or within education levels because of small sample size constraints in the analysis of CPS data.

[69] Using National Science Foundation data, the Congressional Research Service reports that the percentage of doctorates in the sciences that were earned by foreign students on temporary visas rose from 23 percent in 1997 to 32 percent in 2006, and the percentage of doctorates in engineering

that were earned by foreign students on temporary visas rose from 41 percent in 1997 to 59 percent in 2006. Further, in 2007, 57 percent of postdoctoral students in the biological sciences were foreigners on temporary visas.

[70] According to a National Academy of Sciences study, the average length of postdoctoral positions in the biological sciences increased from an average of 24 months for cohorts graduating prior to 1965 to an average of 46 months for cohorts graduating in the early 1990s.

[71] 8 U.S.C. § 1182(n)(1)(G)(ii).

[72] The LCA form requires additional information to the I-129 regarding the prevailing wage source and check boxes for attestations to U.S. worker protections.

[73] State's guidance for consular officers specifically states: "Consular officers do not have the authority to question the approval of H petitions without specific evidence, unavailable to Homeland Security at the time of petition approval, that the beneficiary may not be entitled to status. Disagreement with DHS's interpretation of the law or the facts, however, is not sufficient reason to ask DHS to reconsider its approval of the petition."

[74] Specifically, Wage and Hour Division can only initiate H-1B-related investigations as a result of one of four circumstances: (1) Wage and Hour receives a complaint from an aggrieved person or organization; (2) Wage and Hour receives specific, credible information from a knowledgeable source (other than an aggrieved party) that an employer willfully failed to meet certain LCA conditions, engaged in a pattern or practice of failures to meet such conditions, or committed substantial failure to meet such conditions that affects multiple employees; (3) Wage and Hour conducts random investigations of employers who (within the last five years) were found by the Secretary of Labor to be willful violators of the H-1B program provisions; (4) the Secretary of Labor personally certifies that there is reasonable cause to believe that an employer is in violation and then approves commencement of an investigation. 8 U.S.C. §§ 1182(n)(2).

[75] While Wage and Hour annually conducts approximately a half dozen random investigations into H-1B employers identified as willful violators, these investigations concern employers already identified as problematic and at maximum have included seven investigations per fiscal year with none in 2009. Wage and Hour does not conduct proactive or random investigations of H-1B employers that are in good standing.

[76] 8 U.S.C. § 1182(n)(2)(ii) and (iii).

[77] GAO, *H-1B Visa Program: Labor Could Improve Its Oversight and Increase Information Sharing with Homeland Security*, GAO-06-720 (Washington, D.C.: June 22, 2006).

[78] The maximum fine Wage and Hour can levy for noncompliance in investigations is $1,000. [79]29 U.S.C. §§ 161 and 1862(b)

[80] 8 U.S.C. § 1324b(f)(2).

[81] The USCIS H-1B Benefit Fraud and Compliance Assessment, published in September 2008, specifically reviewed 246 of the 96,827 approved, denied, or pending I-129 petitions filed between October 1, 2005, and March 31, 2006.

[82] According to officials, cases referred for criminal investigation may include examples such as fraud conspiracies, cases involving individuals from special interest countries, and attorney or document preparer fraud.

[83] 8 U.S.C. § 1324b(a)(1).

[84] Although Justice investigates few H-1B cases, in its technical comments, Justice indicated that H-1B cases sometimes represented a significant percent of investigations (i.e., 29, 14 and 10 percent of cases in 2006, 2007 and 2009, respectively).

[85] H-2A job postings from the last 30 days are made public by Labor at http://icert.doleta.gov/.

[86]If an employer-employee relationship exists between a staffing company and an H-1B worker, the staffing company may submit an LCA and is thus statutorily bound by program requirements.

[87] Pub. L. No. 108-447, div. J, tit. IV, subtit. A, § 412, 118 Stat. 2809, 3351 - 52 (codified at 8 U.S.C. § 1184(c)(2)(F).

[88] This memo is commonly referred to as the "Neufeld Memo."

[89] On February 18, 2010, USCIS's Office of Public Engagement hosted a collaboration session in connection with the Neufeld Memo. At that session, which was attended by approximately 40 stakeholders in person and more than 600 via telephone, various concerns about the memorandum were raised.

[90] Pub. L. No. 101-649, § 205(e)(1), 104 Stat. 4978, 5022.

[91] Pub. L. No. 101-649, § 205(b)(2), 104 Stat. 4978, 5020. This was known as the dual intent provision because the H-1B visa is temporary but the worker's intent is to become a permanent resident.

[92] AC21 § 106(a) and (b), 114 Stat. 1253-54 and AC21§104(c). Such annual extensions are available when 365 or more days have elapsed since the H-1B worker submits an LCA for permanent status. The initial H-1B extension application is submitted 3 years after the initial application is approved and extends the temporary program limit to 6 years. Thus, the practical effect is that an H-1B worker seeking to remain in the United States while waiting for a green card must apply for the green card prior to their fifth year as an H-1B worker.

[93] Permanent visa classes include employment-based preferences, family-sponsored, and diversity immigrant categories, with only employment-based preferences being used as comparison in this report.

[94] Ch. 477, § 101(a)(15)(H)(i), 66 Stat. 163, 166.

[95] Pub. L. No. 101-649, § 205(c), 104 Stat. 4978, 5021.

[96] We did not conduct an independent legal analysis of foreign laws. Rather, we relied upon secondary source materials.

[97] 20 C.F.R. § 656.17(g) (2009)

[98] Specifically, Justice recommended that (1) before seeking to hire an H-1B visa holder, all employers should be required to "test" the labor market to determine whether qualified U.S. workers are available and to hire any equally or better qualified U.S. workers who apply, and (2) the Department of Labor should display information about worker protections and the Office of Special Counsel's contact information on all H-1B educational material and the centralized database for H-1B postings. See appendix VII for Justice's comments.

End Notes for Appendix I

[1] In several instances, we identified inconsistencies with the reporting of particular data fields. In these instances, we took steps to address these inconsistencies using criteria to create decision rules. For example, a given H-1B employer might have reported different industry codes on their H-1B petition applications in a given year. When this occurred, we used the industry code that the employer most frequently listed on its petitions. In other instances, when it was not possible to apply a decision rule, we did not include the data in our analysis.

[2] Prior to 2002, these data are not available electronically.

[3] For each case, a violation can occur multiple times.

[4] See BLS, *Technical Paper 66: Design and Methodology - Current Population Survey and Current Population Survey, 2009 Annual Social and Economic (ASEC) Supplement.* Electronic versions are available at http://www.census.gov/prod/2006pubs/tp-66.pdf and http://www.census.gov/apsd/techdoc/cps/cpsmar09.pdf.

[5] The most recently available March supplement is from 2009, which asks about earnings and education for the past year (2008).

[6] For this population, we did not exclude government workers and self-employed workers.

[7] For estimates based on the 2009 March supplement CPS survey, standard errors are described in appendix G of http://www.census.gov/apsd/techdoc/cps/cpsmar10.pdf. For estimates based on

averages on basic monthly CPS surveys, standard error computation is described in the BLS Employment and Earnings publications (see http://www.bls.gov/opub/ee/empearn200912.pdf).

[8] We did not include H-B3 (fashion models) in these analyses, but included all other types of approved H-1B workers.

[9] According to Homeland Security officials, this variable was not available in the CLAIMS 3 Mainframe data and was only available from fiscal year 2006 onward because, prior to that year, this information was not tracked.

[10] In order to compare characteristics of H-1B workers to U.S. citizen workers by occupation, we matched data from Homeland Security's CLAIMS 3 database with information from CPS's March supplemental data. We used the most recently available March supplement (i.e., from 2009), which asks about earnings and education for the past year (2008). We selected 2008 CLAIMS 3 data to most closely match the CPS data time frames. See Section 2 for more details on this analysis.

[11] The occupational categories for "systems analysis and programming" and "other computer-related occupations" were combined into one category for the purposes of this analysis. "Other computer-related occupations" includes database administrators, database design analysts, and microcomputer support specialists. See Section 2 for additional details on the occupational codes.

[12] Due to the sensitivity of Justice's ongoing investigations, we were only provided information on cases which were no longer active.

[13] The high refusal rate was consistent with a past GAO review of the H-1B program, which endeavored to speak with private businesses about their experiences with the program (see GAO, *H-1B Foreign Workers: Better Tracking Needed to Help Determine H-1B Program's Effects on U.S. Workforce*, GAO-03-883 (Washington, D.C.: Sept. 10, 2003).

[14] The occupation "systems analysis, programming, and other computer-related occupations" includes five CPS occupational groups: (1) computer scientists and systems analysts; (2) computer programmers; (3) computer software engineers; (4) database administrators; and (5) operations research analysts. In CLAIMS 3, the occupation "systems analysis, programming, and other computer-related occupations" includes two occupational groups: (1) occupations in systems analysis and programming and (2) other computer-related occupations—database administrators, database design analysts, and microcomputer support specialists.

[15] In order to calculate the median usual weekly earnings for the combined category of "systems analysis, programming, and other computer-related occupations" we calculated the weighted average of the median usual weekly earnings for each of the occupational groups, using the number of full-time wage and salary workers employed in each detailed occupation as the weight.

[16] See our discussion of the CLAIMS 3 data above.

[17] H-1B petitioners are permitted to apply for other visas while their H-1B visa status is open.

End Notes for Appendix II

[1] For this comparison, we included H-1B workers whose initial petitions were submitted each specific calendar year and were approved as of October 2009. Calendar year 2009 only includes data up through October.

[2] In order to compare characteristics of H-1B workers to U.S. citizen workers by occupation, we compared data from Homeland Security's CLAIMS 3 database with information from CPS's March supplemental data. The most recently available March supplement is from 2009, which asks about earnings and education for the past year. We selected 2008 CLAIMS 3 data to most closely match the CPS data time frames. The occupation "systems analysis, programming, and other computer-related occupations" includes five CPS occupational groups: (1) computer scientists and systems analysts; (2) computer programmers; (3) computer software engineers; (4) database administrators; and (5) operations research analysts. In CLAIMS 3, the occupation "systems

analysis, programming, and other computer-related occupations" includes two occupational groups: (1) occupations in systems analysis and programming and (2) other computer-related occupations—database administrators, database design analysts, and microcomputer support specialists.

[3] Graduate degree category includes degrees that are master's, Ph.D., or professional.

End Notes for Appendix III

[1] In order to compare the CPS U.S. workforce occupations to the H-1B beneficiary occupations, we combined some occupational categories in both CLAIMS 3 and CPS to better align the CPS and CLAIMS 3 data. The occupation "systems analysis, programming, and selected other computer-related occupations" includes five CPS occupational groups: (1) computer scientists and systems analysts; (2) computer programmers; (3) computer software engineers, (4) database administrators; and (5) operations research analysts. In CLAIMS 3, the occupation "systems analysis, programming, and selected other computer-related occupations" includes two occupational groups: (1) occupations in systems analysis and programming and (2) other computer-related occupations—database administrators, database design analysts, and microcomputer support specialists.

In: U.S. Visa Policies, Programs and Considerations
Editor: Aaron R. Miller
ISBN: 978-1-61470-333-4

Chapter 8

H-2B Visa Program: Closed Civil and Criminal Cases Illustrate Instances of H-2B Workers Being Targets of Fraud and Abuse*

United States Government Accountability Office

Why GAO Did this Study

The H-2B visa program assists U.S. employers anticipating a shortage of domestic nonagricultural workers by permitting them to hire nonimmigrant foreign workers temporarily. The program is overseen by several agencies, including the Department of Labor (Labor), the Department of Homeland Security's United States Citizenship and Immigration Services (USCIS), and the Department of State. Employers often hire labor recruiters or other intermediaries to assist with the process of obtaining labor certifications and finding foreign workers. GAO was asked to determine if there were examples of recruiters and employers engaging in illegal or fraudulent activity within the H-2B visa program.

GAO reviewed recent closed civil and criminal court cases involving H-2B workers, obtained data from Labor and USCIS on H-2B visas issued in fiscal years 2008 and 2009 and in first 6 months of fiscal year 2010, and interviewed advocacy groups that represent H-2B workers in litigation. In addition, GAO made undercover calls and site visits to recruiters, posing as H-2B employers and foreign H-2B workers and asked a series of questions related to legal requirements of the program. GAO also visited several H-2B housing and work site locations. Case studies and results of tests and site visits cannot be projected to the entire population of H-2B employers and recruiters.

* This is an edited, reformatted and augmented version of a United States Government Accountability Office publication, Report to the Chairman, Committee on Education and Labor, House of Representatives, GAO-10-1053, dated September 2010.

What GAO Found

GAO reviewed 10 closed cases over the last 5 years that involved H-2B employers and recruiters that violated various labor laws or settled allegations of violations outside of court. These 10 cases involved diverse employers in different industries with employees in 29 states with violations in areas such as employers failing to pay promised wages, overtime, or both; employers charging H-2B workers exorbitant fees; and employers and recruiters submitting fraudulent documentation to government officials. For example, in one case H-2B workers became indebted to their employer through a series of arbitrary charges. The employer then forced workers to take second jobs at local fast food restaurants to pay these debts. The table below provides a summary of cases where H-2B workers rights were violated.

Industry, location	Details
Hotel – South Dakota	• Hotel owners forced H-2B workers to work in substandard conditions, confiscated workers' passports, and threatened workers that they would be sent home in a "box" if they disobeyed orders. • In 2008, the couple was found guilty on nine counts, including conspiracy, holding people in peonage, making false statements, and visa fraud.
Construction and foreign contract labor firm - Louisiana	• Workers from India paid at least $20,000 for H-2B visas to enter the United States but were never employed by the construction company. • The construction company owner pled guilty to conspiracy, and the other conspirators were found guilty of 1 count of conspiracy, 14 counts of encouraging and inducing illegal immigration, and 1 count of money laundering.
Labor broker, hospitality employers, and immigration attorney - Virginia	• Conspirators fraudulently obtained H-2B certification from Labor for over 3,800 individuals, leased workers to undisclosed businesses not listed on the visa petitions, defrauded the government of $7.4 million in payroll taxes never remitted to the Internal Revenue Service. • The conspirators pled guilty to charges including conspiracy, visa fraud, and tax evasion charges that were linked to an international organized crime ring.

Source: GAO analysis of court files.

GAO personnel found that most recruiters they called or visited posing as prospective H-2B employers and workers did not encourage our undercover agents to violate program rules. Of the 18 recruiters in multiple states we contacted, 15 appropriately did not offer any advice on violating H-2B program rules. However, during three calls, H-2B recruiters did provide suggestions on how to circumvent program rules, such as providing "good excuses" to help "weed out" prospective U.S. workers or recouping costs through "off-the-book" transactions to avoid restrictions on pay deductions. Additionally, GAO found that H-2B workers contacted during the site visits to their housing locations were generally pleased with their living and working conditions. However, at one location the H-2B workers were afraid to speak with outside individuals for fear of retaliation from their employer.

September 30, 2010
The Honorable George Miller
Chairman
Committee on Education and Labor
House of Representatives

Dear Mr. Chairman:

With the United States continuing to attract tens of thousands of foreign nationals each year who seek legal employment, the H-2B visa program is intended to benefit both American employers and foreign workers. Employers anticipating a shortage of American nonagricultural workers may hire nonimmigrant foreign workers[1] to fill temporary labor needs though the H-2B visa program. Employers often hire labor recruiters[2] or other intermediaries to help find foreign workers and obtain the required labor certifications. The workers come from a diverse set of countries and work in a range of industries, most often construction, landscaping, manufacturing, hospitality service, and food processing. Several federal agencies oversee the program, including the Department of Labor (Labor), the Department of Homeland Security's United States Citizenship and Immigration Services (USCIS), and the Department of State (State).

Several recent convictions have shown that some employers and recruiters may be abusing the foreign workers in the program. In addition, some employers may violate program rules by subverting program regulations requiring that employers first attempt to hire U.S. workers. You asked us to determine if there were examples of recruiters and employers that were engaging in illegal or fraudulent activity within the H-2B visa program. Specifically, we (1) reviewed recent closed civil and criminal court cases of fraudulent, illegal, and abusive activity by recruiters and employers participating in the H-2B program and (2) conducted undercover tests of employer and recruiter practices.

To identify court cases of recent fraud and abuse within the H-2B program, we researched court documentation involving violations of the H-2B program in the last 5 years that resulted in a criminal conviction, civil or administrative liability, or significant financial settlement. We reviewed a nonrepresentative selection of 10 closed cases, from leads provided by advocacy groups and our own research, associated with workers employed in 29 states and various industries to illustrate the types of abuse and fraud that occurred in the H-2B program, but we cannot generalize these findings to the program.

To examine methods used by H-2B employers and recruiters, we reviewed recent civil and criminal cases involving H-2B workers; obtained data from Labor and USCIS on H-2B visas issued in fiscal years 2008 and 2009 and in the first 6 months of fiscal year 2010; and interviewed advocacy groups that represent H-2B workers in litigation. We conducted undercover calls to 18 U.S.-based H-2B recruiters and staffing agencies. These recruiters were selected from leads provided by advocacy groups and our own research. Using scenarios based on recent court cases and program requirements, we posed as potential employers and foreign workers to assess whether selected recruiters would advocate violating program laws and regulations. We also made undercover site visits to two selected recruiters that we had previously contacted by phone. Finally, we conducted site visits of H-2B worker housing locations to identify instances of substandard housing accommodations or other forms of abuse and the mistreatment of H-2B workers. These sites were selected from leads provided by advocacy groups and our own research. Case studies, site visits, and results of proactive testing cannot be projected to the entire population of H-2B employers and recruiters.

We conducted the work for this investigation from April 2010 through September 2010 in accordance with the standards prescribed by the Council of Inspectors General for Integrity and Efficiency. Additional details on our scope and methodology are included in appendix I.

BACKGROUND

The Immigration and Nationality Act allows foreign nationals to enter the United States to perform temporary labor if unemployed individuals capable of performing the work cannot be found in the United States. Labor and USCIS are responsible for reviewing employers' applications for H-2B workers, and State is responsible for issuing visas to workers. Under the program, employers in industries with a onetime occurrence, peak load, seasonal, or intermittent needs can supplement their domestic workforces with H-2B workers. The temporary work must be for full-time employment and the employer's need for the workers must generally be less than a year. The H-2B classification may be extended for qualifying employment in 1-year increments up to a total of 3 years. Up to 66,000 H-2B visas can be issued each fiscal year.

Prospective H-2B employers must apply to Labor for a temporary labor certification attesting that American workers capable of performing the work are not available and that the employment of foreign workers will not adversely affect the wages and working conditions of similarly employed American workers. The H-2B program requires the employer to attest to Labor that it will offer a wage that equals or exceeds the highest of the prevailing wage, the applicable federal minimum wage, the state minimum wage, or the local minimum wage to the H-2B worker. The employer also must agree to offer terms and working conditions typical to U.S. workers in the same geographical area;[3] not use H-2B workers to replace striking workers; comply with all federal, state, and local labor, health, and safety laws; and detail and clarify all paycheck deductions in the job offer and ensure that all deductions are reasonable. The employer must also not place any workers outside the area listed on the Labor application without first obtaining a new certification and must notify Labor and USCIS if an H-2B worker quits before the end of the term of employment. In addition, the employer agrees to forbid any recruiter from seeking or receiving payment from H-2B workers, except for costs that are the responsibility of the worker.[4] Moreover, the employer agrees not to seek or receive payment of any kind from the H-2B workers related to labor certification.

COURT CASES REVEAL UNFAIR WAGES, EXCESSIVE FEES, AND FRAUDULENT DOCUMENTATION IN THE H-2B PROGRAM

The 10 cases that we reviewed demonstrate fraud and abuse committed by recruiters and employers participating in the H-2B visa program and operating in 29 states. Though the cases include a diverse group of employers in different industries, our review of these 10 cases showed violations in areas such as unfair wages for employees, excessive fees charged to employees, and fraudulent documentation submitted to federal agencies to circumvent program rules.

Employers Failed to Pay the Prevailing Hourly Wage or Overtime

In 6 of the 10 cases we reviewed, there were allegations that employers did not pay their H-2B employees the established hourly wage, overtime, or both. For example, a carnival operator in New York paid employees by the week regardless of the number of hours worked. Working up to 80 hours a week, the employees averaged less than $5.00 an hour—far less than the $8.00 to $12.20 promised. In another case, H-2B employees alleged that an Arkansas-based forestry corporation did not pay overtime wages despite work weeks regularly exceeding 40 hours.

Employers Charged H-2B Workers Excessive Fees

In 6 of the 10 cases we reviewed, employers charged their H-2B workers fees that were for the benefit of the employer or charged excessive fees that brought employees' wages below the hourly federal minimum wage. These charges included visa processing fees far above actual costs, rent in overcrowded apartments that drastically exceeded market value, and transportation charges subject to arbitrary "late fees." Workers left the United States in greater debt than when they arrived. In one case, these fees reduced employees' paychecks to as little as $48 for a 2-week period. A total of 4 of these cases resulted in a criminal conviction, including civil or administrative liability, and the remaining 2 cases resulted in a significant financial settlement.

Employers and Recruiters Submitted Fraudulent Documentation

In 8 of the 10 cases we reviewed, employers were alleged to have submitted fraudulent documentation to Labor, USCIS, and State to either exploit their H-2B employees or hire more employees than needed. Employers and recruiters misclassified employee duties on Labor certification applications to pay lower prevailing wages; used shell companies to file fraudulent labor certification applications for unneeded employees, then leased the additional employees to businesses not on the visa petitions; and preferentially hired H-2B employees over American workers in violation of federal law. A total of 5 of these cases resulted in a criminal conviction, including civil or administrative liability, and the remaining 3 cases resulted in a significant financial settlement. There is no law or program requirement that prohibits companies from being awarded federal contracts even if they have been found to have violated H-2B immigration laws. Several of these employers continued to receive H-2B certifications and money from federal contracts while in litigation, after reaching a settlement as a result of litigation, or after being found guilty of various charges.

Table 1 summarizes the 10 cases in which H-2B employers and recruiters committed visa fraud or exploited their H-2B workers.

Table 1. Summary of Court Cases

Case	Location	Defendants	Case details	Outcome
1.	Arizona, Delaware, Maryland, New Jersey, New York, Pennsylvania, and Virginia	Temporary employment recruiting agency	• The agency conspired with client businesses to return employed illegal aliens to native countries, and then fraudulently obtain H-2B visas to bring the employees back. • The agency submitted falsified documents to Labor, State, and USCIS using names from a Mexico phone book and fictitious biographical information to serve as placeholders, so that additional H-2B visas were on hand in case client businesses needed to hire additional alien workers. • The agency coached the employees to lie to U.S. immigration officials during visa application interviews and about their previous presence in the United States. • Federal criminal suit was filed in 2009.	• In 2009, all parties involved (the owner, his wife, his sister, and an unrelated office manager) pled guilty. The owner's sister was sentenced to 3 years of probation, 200 hours of community service a year for 3 years, and a $50,000 fine. The office manager and the owner's wife received 5 years of probation. Additionally, his wife received 200 hours of community service a year for 5 years and a $2,000 fine, while the office manager received 250 hours of community service a year for 5 years and a $20,000 fine. The owner passed away while awaiting sentencing.
2	New York	Carnival operator	• In 2008, New York's Office of Attorney General (OAG) began to investigate this company after receiving complaints from H-2B workers about wages and substandard housing. The OAG alleged that the company: • discriminated against 54 Mexican H-2B employees by not paying the salary promised; • housed employees in overcrowded, cockroach- and bedbug-infested trailers with unsanitary restrooms; • did not provide safety equipment or proper attire; • verbally harassed employees; and • paid $275 to $350 a week regardless of hours (employees earned an average of $5.00 an hour but were promised $8.00 an hour and $12.20 an hour for overtime).	• In 2009, the carnival operator settled with the OAG and did not admit liability, but agreed to pay $325,000 in restitution and damages to the employees. • The employer agreed to submit to an independent monitor to ensure, among other things, compliance with minimum wage and overtime law and provide equal treatment and sanitary housing to employees.

Case	Location	Defendants	Case details	Outcome
3	South Dakota	Hotel	• The employer forced nine employees to work in substandard conditions and placed them in servitudea at their hotel. • The employer offered employees $6.05 an hour but actually paid $3.00 per room and required that each room be cleaned for an hour. • The employer did not pay overtime. • The employer charged nine employees $1,200 each in visa processing fees, despite actual fees totaling $1,200 for all nine workers. • The employer charged seven employees $1,050 a month for an apartment they shared, though it normally rented for $375. • The employer forced employees to pay arbitrary charges, leading them to take second jobs at local fast food restaurants to pay these debts. • The employer isolated the workers from the community and threatened physical abuse. • The employer confiscated the employees' passports and threatened deportation in a "box" if they disobeyed orders. • Federal criminal suit was filed in 2007.	• In 2008, the couple who owned the hotel was found guilty on nine counts, including conspiracy, holding people in peonage,b making false statements, and visa fraud. • The husband was sentenced to 50 months in jail, while his wife received 36 months in jail. Each received a $15,000 fine.
4.	Virginia	Landscaping company	• A labor union filed a complaint with the Department of Justice alleging that the employer discriminated against U.S. workers by preferentially hiring H-2B employees in violation of federal law. • The company obtained certifications for over 2,500 H-2B workers from Labor since 2007.	• A settlement agreement was reached on May 11, 2010, in which the employer did not admit liability but agreed to modify its hiring policy and personnel practices and provide full back pay of $11,173 to a U.S. citizen who was denied a job.

(Continued)

Case	Location	Defendants	Case details	Outcome
5	Arkansas	Forestry company	• A class action was filed against the company alleging violations of the Fair Labor Standards Act and Migrant and Seasonal Agricultural Worker Protection Act. The plaintiffs alleged that the company: • failed to pay over 2,200 workers the prevailing wage or overtime for 6 years by exploiting their inability to speak English and their lack of understanding U.S. laws; f• orced 7-day work weeks and frequent overtime without breaks; • violated the Migrant and Seasonal Agricultural Worker Protection Act by failing to reimburse the workers for expenses they incurred and making unlawful withholdings and deductions from wages; and • forced workers to move to another work site but deducted living expenses from their paychecks for both locations.	• During litigation, the company was held in contempt of court three times for intimidating workers who expressed interest in joining the lawsuit. • The company entered into a settlement agreement in which it did not admit liability but agreed to pay $2.75 million in February 2010 after workers sued to recover unreimbursed expenses for obtaining H-2B visas. • The company continues to receive active labor certifications from Labor to recruit H-2B workers since the settlement. • The company obtained certifications for over 1,900 H-2B workers from Labor since 2007. • The company received over $200,000 from federal contracts during litigation. Page 7 GAO-10-1053 H-2B Visa Program

Case	Location	Defendants	Case details	Outcome
6.	Louisiana	Construction company and foreign contract labor firm	• The company obtained $1.8 million from a fraudulent H-2B visa conspiracy to bring 87 Indian nationals into the United States illegally. • The company submitted fraudulent H2B documentation to federal agencies allegedly seeking workers from India. • The company charged at least $20,000 for H-2B visas but never employed the Indian nationals. • Representatives of the firm traveled to India to assist the Indian nationals with the application process and corresponded with the U.S. Consulate on behalf of the workers. • These conspirators were indicted on federal criminal charges in 2008.	• In 2009, the construction company owner pled guilty to conspiracy and was sentenced 3 years probation and 6 months home confinement. • In 2009, the other conspirators were found guilty of 1 count of conspiracy, 14 counts of encouraging and inducing illegal immigration, and 1 count of money laundering and sentenced to 41 months imprisonment.
7.	Virginia	Labor broker, hospitality employers, and immigration attorney	• The conspiracy fraudulently obtained H-2B certification from Labor for over 3,800 individuals. • The conspirators obtained certifications for more workers than needed, leasing the additional workers to undisclosed hotels or businesses not listed on the visa petitions. • The conspirators generated over $35 million in gross income by establishing a permanent foreign labor pool for jobs normally filled by Americans. • The conspirators defrauded the government of $7.4 million in payroll taxes never remitted to the Internal Revenue Service. • The businesses charged H-2B workers exorbitant fees for visa-related services and excessive rent for unsanitary, overcrowded houses. • The conspiracy started in 2003 and was terminated in 2009 when federal criminal charges were filed.	• Nineteen suspects pled guilty to several charges including conspiracy, visa fraud, and tax evasion charges that were linked to an international organized crime ring. • Some individuals convicted in the conspiracy received probation, home confinement with electronic monitoring, or federal prison sentences. • Suspects were sentenced from October 2009 through February 2010. Page 8 GAO-10-1053 H-2B Visa Program

(Continued)

Case	Location	Defendants	Case details	Outcome
8.	Florida	Hospitality labor broker	• Company representatives posed as executives from other legitimate businesses to fraudulently obtain H-2B certifications from Labor. • The company coerced workers to sign contracts agreeing to lower pay than originally promised. • The company charged up to 16 workers rent to live together in a twobedroom house. • The company paid as little as $48 for 2 weeks of work because of excessive paycheck deductions, including fees for not cleaning housing accommodations and arriving late for transportation to work sites. • Investigative documents indicate that the conspiracy started in 1999 and continued until 2007, when federal criminal charges were filed.	• The court referred to the treatment of these workers as "legal slavery." • All four executive officers received federal prison sentences and joint $1 million dollar asset forfeiture. • Final sentencing for defendants occurred in 2008.
9.	Pennsylvania	Landscaping company and labor broker	• A federal civil suit was filed in 2007 alleging that the company did the following: • Requested more H-2B workers than needed to lease them to other businesses via a recruitment firm at a premium rate; • Misclassified employee duties on Labor certification applications to pay lower wages to H-2B workers; • Required foreign workers to pay preemployment bonds guaranteeing that they would work for the entire season or forfeit the bond to company, in order to secure H-2B positions. Workers stated that the bonds were not refunded after terms of employment ended; • Forced workers to pay excessive rent to live in employer-owned, substandard housing; and • Fired workers who complained or threatened the company with breach of contract.	• In 2009, the court approved a settlement that required the employer to pay H-2B workers over $20,000 and submit documentation verifying adherence to Fair Labor Standards Act and H2B regulations in future employment practices.

Case	Location	Defendants	Case details	Outcome
10.	Colorado, Connecticut, Delaware, Indiana, Maryland, Massachusetts, Minnesota, Missouri, New Jersey, New York, Ohio, Pennsylvania, Texas, Virginia, and Wisconsin	Landscaping company	• A federal class action civil suit was filed in 2005, representing H-2B workers employed by the company from 2002 to 2005. • The plaintiffs alleged that the employer made excessive deductions from paychecks, often resulting in workers receiving less than minimum wage. • H-2B workers sought relief under the Fair Labor Standards Act for minimum wage and overtime violations, breach of contract, and wrongful termination.	• The company paid a $600,000 settlement to workers in 2008, the largest amount at that time. • In 2008, the court ruled that H-2B travel costs, visa expenses, and employee fees primarily benefited the employer and could not be deducted from paychecks. • Since 2008, the firm has been awarded over $35,000 in federal contracts, and has applied for certifications for over 8,000 employees.

Source: GAO analysis of court records, federal contract data, and Labor data.

[a] A condition of compulsory service in which the victim is compelled to perform labor or services against the victim's will for the benefit of another person through, among other things, the use of force, threats of force, restraint, or use or threat of coercion through law or the legal process.

[b] A condition in which the victim is forced to perform labor against the victim's will to pay off a debt.

In Undercover Tests, Most Recruiters Did Not Encourage H-2B Visa Fraud but Some Offered to Help Violate Laws and Regulations

Of the 18 recruiters in multiple states we contacted, 15 H-2B recruiters did not encourage our undercover agents posing as prospective H-2B employers and employees to violate H-2B program rules. Most recruiters told our fictitious employers that they would have to pay H-2B employees the appropriate prevailing wage, as well as advertise job openings in local markets before seeking H-2B certifications. Most recruiters also informed our fictitious employers that they would not be able to profit from fees charged to H-2B employees for expenses such as rent or travel. In addition, one recruiter correctly told our fictitious prospective H-2B employee that she would have to return to her home country before applying for H-2B worker status.

However, in three cases recruiters offered advice on violating or evading program rules. A Texas recruiter suggested that we discourage American workers from accepting our landscaping job openings by having applicants run around the shop carrying a 50-pound bag to determine they were fit for the work. The recruiter also suggested conducting interviews before 7 a.m. and requiring drug testing prior to the interview as means to "weed out" qualified American applicants. In addition, the recruiter suggested that our current American landscape workers be fired "for cause" or induced to quit months before filing a petition for H-2B workers to avoid arousing suspicion by Labor. Furthermore, the recruiter made comments about recouping employer costs through "off-the-book" transactions for rent to avoid caps on payroll deductions. A recruiter in New York offered to provide "good excuses" to help "weed out" prospective U.S. workers who applied for our housekeeping jobs.

We also found that recruiters we visited did not offer our undercover agents assistance in violating the rules of the H-2B program. A recruiter in Kentucky told us that it usually petitions Labor for more workers than needed in case the employer has to hire one or two U.S. workers. This allows the employer to still be able to obtain the amount of H-2B workers it was seeking. However, the recruiter suggested that interest in these positions is usually limited because of low wages. Additionally, the recruiter suggested that U.S. workers would only apply for our jobs so that they could continue to receive unemployment benefits. We selected two recruiters located in Texas and New York that we had contacted during our undercover phone calls, posed as prospective H-2B employers willing to pay a retainer fee, and sought their assistance to help us obtain H-2B workers and violate the rules of the program. These recruiters refused to offer assistance in violating the program rules or to accept our retainer fee.

Our site visits to H-2B employee housing revealed that most of the workers we spoke with felt they had adequate housing, pay, and working conditions, though we did find some occurrences that were suspicious. H-2B employees at a circus in West Virginia with prior allegations of wage abuse and exorbitant recruitment fees stated that their employer provided adequate meals, transportation, and living accommodations that were not deducted from their salaries. The accommodations consisted of 6 to 7 employees living in one travel trailer. When our undercover agents asked to enter the trailer, the workers were adamant that no one was allowed inside without their employer's consent. We also visited known housing locations for H-2B seafood processing employees in North Carolina. The employees told our investigators that they were afraid to speak with outside individuals for fear of retaliation from the employer. One employee said that another employee had recently been fired and sent back to their home country for reporting a burglary at their housing location to the police. Again, we were not allowed inside the employees' housing.

As agreed with your office, unless you publicly announce the contents of this report earlier, we plan no further distribution until 30 days from the report date. At that time, we will send copies to interested congressional committees, the Secretary of Labor, the Secretary of Homeland Security, and other interested parties. The report also will be available at no charge on the GAO Web site at http://www.gao.gov.

If you or your staff have any questions about this report, please contact me at (202) 512-6722 or kutzg@gao.gov. Contact points for our Offices of Congressional Relations and Public Affairs may be found on the last page of this report.

Sincerely yours,

Gregory D. Kutz
Managing Director
Forensic Audits and Special Investigations

Appendix I: Scope and Methodology

To identify court cases of illegal or fraudulent activity within the H-2B visa program, we researched court documentation involving violations of the H-2B program in the last 5 years that resulted in a criminal conviction, civil or administrative liability, or significant financial settlement. To illustrate cases of fraudulent, illegal, and abusive activity in the H-2B program, we identified 10 closed cases for detailed audit and investigation. The 10 cases were selected from leads provided by advocacy groups and our own research based on criteria that provided indications of fraud and abuse. For example, to investigate methods used by H-2B employers and recruiters, we reviewed recent civil and criminal cases involving H-2B workers; obtained data from the Department of Labor (Labor)[1] and the Department of Homeland Security's United States Citizenship and Immigration Services[2] on H-2B visas issued; and interviewed representatives of advocacy groups that represent H-2B workers in litigation. The cases were associated with workers employed in 29 states and various industries to illustrate a broad range of abuse or fraud occurring in the H-2B program.

To illustrate potential fraudulent recruiting methods utilized by H-2B recruiters, we conducted undercover calls to 18 U.S.-based H-2B recruiters and staffing agencies. These recruiters were selected from leads provided by advocacy groups and our own research. Using scenarios based on recent court cases and program requirements, we posed as potential employers and foreign workers to assess whether selected recruiters would advocate violating program laws and regulations. We also made undercover site visits to two selected recruiters that we had previously contacted by phone call.

To identify potential instances of abuse, we conducted site visits of H-2B worker housing locations to identify instances of substandard housing accommodations or other forms of exploitation and the mistreatment of H-2B workers. These locations were selected from leads provided by advocacy groups and our own research. Case studies, site visits, and results of proactive testing cannot be projected to the entire population of H-2B employers and recruiters.

We conducted the work for this investigation from April 2010 through September 2010 in accordance with the standards prescribed by the Council of Inspectors General for Integrity and Efficiency.

End Notes

[1] An H-2B worker is defined as a foreign nonimmigrant worker employed by a U.S. employer to perform temporary nonagricultural labor or services. 8 U.S.C § 1101(a)(15)(H)(ii)(b).

[2] A recruiter is an individual or company hired by U.S. businesses to identify and hire foreign workers for employment under the H-2B visa program.

[3] H-2B workers are covered by the Fair Labor Standards Act (FLSA). FLSA establishes minimum wage, overtime pay, recordkeeping, and youth employment standards affecting employees in the private sector and in federal, state, and local governments.

[4] According to Labor regulations, acceptable fees that are the responsibility of H-2B workers include passport or visa fees or reimbursement for the lesser of the actual cost or fair market value of transportation abroad.

End Notes for Appendix I

[1] Total number of records extracted may be understated because of the variation of each employer or representative name entered into the Labor database.

[2] The data cover fiscal years 2008 and 2009 and the first 6 months of fiscal year 2010.

INDEX

#

9/11, 23, 26, 32, 36, 43, 44, 45, 47, 64, 75, 99
9/11 Commission, 23, 32, 36, 43, 44, 47, 64, 75

A

abuse, 87, 149, 177, 183, 184, 231, 232, 240, 241
access, 10, 20, 21, 25, 30, 32, 33, 35, 37, 43, 45, 70, 79, 81, 143, 156, 157, 159, 160, 161, 162, 170, 173, 175, 183, 185, 186, 188, 222
accommodations, 231, 238, 240, 241
accounting, 89, 95, 202, 208
accreditation, 46
active centers, 107
adequate housing, 240
adjustment, 5, 29, 89, 91
administrative support, 118
administrators, 199, 206, 207, 208, 224, 227, 228
advocacy, 2, 146, 196, 229, 231, 241
Afghanistan, 109
Africa, 50, 52, 54, 92, 93
African National Congress, 24
age, 3, 7, 11, 24, 25, 32, 36, 55, 90, 169, 171, 191, 192, 196, 197, 224
agencies, viii, 20, 21, 25, 30, 33, 34, 36, 39, 72, 100, 119, 121, 123, 125, 127, 128, 132, 141, 143, 163, 164, 177, 178, 183, 184, 229, 231, 233, 237, 241
AIDS, 24
airports, 22, 64, 66, 71, 75
Alaska, 94
Albania, 52, 53
Algeria, 53
alien smuggling, 25
annual rate, 197
appropriations, 37, 38, 39, 46, 47, 109
Appropriations Act, 38, 39, 46, 47, 73, 84, 87, 101
Argentina, 53, 63, 77, 79, 81, 102
Armenia, 53, 102
arrest, 123, 128
arrests, 57
Asia, 50, 54, 92, 93, 164
Asian countries, 98
assessment, 43, 121, 132, 189, 194
assets, 46, 47, 80, 194
asylum, 16, 28, 51, 62, 77
audit, 116, 146, 201, 241
Austria, 77, 81, 82, 102
authenticity, 220
authorities, 3, 24, 25, 31, 32, 37, 81, 87, 118
authority, 4, 11, 12, 13, 16, 22, 23, 24, 25, 26, 30, 31, 32, 34, 35, 37, 40, 41, 42, 44, 61, 62, 64, 71, 72, 73, 75, 77, 82, 116, 118, 127, 128, 129, 139, 173, 174, 175, 188, 213, 214, 220, 225
awareness, 118, 173

B

Bangladesh, 52, 53, 54
bank financing, 105
bargaining, 214
base, 105, 133, 165, 179, 211
behaviors, 99
Belarus, 53
Belgium, 63, 77, 81, 102
beneficiaries, 201
benefits, viii, 25, 68, 69, 83, 84, 85, 104, 110, 177, 197, 240
biological sciences, 170, 225
biotechnology, 195
blood, 11
board members, 107
Bolivia, 102

bonds, 238
bonuses, 197
border control, 80
border crossing, 8
border security, 40, 43, 68, 119, 139
Bosnia, 102
brain, 98
brain drain, 98
breakdown, 77, 92
Bulgaria, 52, 53, 80
Bureau of Customs and Border Protection, 3, 82
Bureau of Labor Statistics, 144, 146, 190, 206, 207, 208
business costs, 158
business cycle, 169, 206
business model, 156, 222
business processes, 164
business travelers, 11
businesses, 79, 89, 91, 92, 95, 97, 106, 161, 162, 167, 174, 177, 183, 184, 186, 187, 196, 227, 230, 233, 234, 237, 238, 242

C

cables, 118
Cairo, 35
Cameroon, 53
candidate recruitment, 157
candidates, 13, 142, 157, 158, 161, 173, 174, 184, 185
Caribbean, 52, 54
cash, 128
category a, 7, 108, 109, 186
category d, 106
CDC, 11
Census, 190
certification, 1, 2, 4, 10, 14, 17, 19, 33, 72, 81, 149, 160, 185, 196, 230, 232, 233, 237, 238
Chad, v, 23, 24, 47, 77, 79, 83
chain of command, 31, 118, 125
challenges, viii, 113, 114, 115, 124, 129, 133, 136, 141, 143, 164, 183, 188, 223
chancroid, 11
children, 7, 15, 51, 55, 59, 86, 107, 110
Chile, 102, 109, 147, 214
China, 35, 54, 58, 92, 93, 99, 102, 107, 108, 143, 164, 181
cholera, 11
circus, 240
citizens, viii, 22, 31, 69, 76, 77, 78, 80, 83, 84, 106, 111, 112, 146, 171, 181, 191, 197, 205, 224
citizenship, 1, 4, 10, 15, 22, 25, 33, 78, 81, 90, 108, 193, 201, 213
City, 105
classes, 28, 31, 35, 85, 90, 106, 116, 126, 226
classification, 34, 149, 214, 232
cleaning, 238
clients, 160, 161, 211, 223
climate, 139
Coast Guard, 128
coding, 195
coercion, 239
collaboration, 118, 125, 126, 136, 160, 226
collateral, 128
colleges, 211
Colombia, 102
commerce, viii, 40, 61, 67, 69, 84, 90
commercial, 32, 65, 86
communication, 120
communist countries, 51
communities, 21, 33, 120, 162
community, 20, 67, 184, 234, 235
community service, 234
comparative advantage, 110
compensation, 31, 183, 214
competition, 21, 96, 159
competitiveness, 110, 167
complement, 35, 37, 97
complexity, 187
compliance, 72, 75, 148, 161, 162, 173, 177, 181, 185, 186, 187, 213, 220, 234
computation, 162, 227
computer, 133, 148, 168, 169, 171, 191, 192, 199, 200, 202, 205, 206, 207, 208, 209, 211, 212, 224, 227, 228
computer software, 206, 207, 208, 224, 227, 228
computer systems, 133, 211
conference, 101
confinement, 237
Congo, 11, 102
Congress, viii, 1, 2, 7, 10, 14, 15, 22, 23, 24, 26, 27, 30, 32, 35, 36, 37, 38, 39, 43, 44, 45, 46, 47, 49, 50, 52, 56, 57, 59, 61, 64, 66, 70, 71, 72, 73, 74, 75, 78, 79, 83, 84, 85, 101, 111, 120, 134, 135, 141, 144, 160, 162, 175, 183, 184, 188, 223
consent, 240
Consolidated Appropriations Act, 24
Consolidated Security, Disaster Assistance, and Continuing Appropriations Act of 2009, 188
conspiracy, 230, 235, 237, 238
construction, 99, 105, 107, 230, 231, 237
Consular Affairs, vii, 3, 5, 6, 7, 8, 9, 17, 18, 19, 20, 21, 24, 25, 27, 28, 29, 31, 33, 37, 38, 39, 40, 41, 42, 58, 93, 127, 130, 136, 173
consulting, 35, 172, 195, 209, 222
consumers, 110, 167

consumption, 98
content analysis, 195
controversial, 69
controversies, 24
convention, 80, 111
convergence, 109
conviction, 231, 233, 241
cooperation, 64, 72, 75, 175
coordination, 40, 46, 100, 118, 120, 125
correlation, 92
corruption, 120
cost, 37, 38, 51, 67, 76, 98, 105, 136, 157, 159, 170, 222, 242
cost saving, 67
Costa Rica, 102
counterbalance, 58
counterterrorism, 35, 37, 43, 64, 75, 114, 121, 122
country of origin, 98, 139
covering, 35, 197
credit market, 98
creditors, 77
crimes, 12, 18, 25, 127
criminal activity, 2, 25, 119
criminal acts, 12
criminal investigations, 124, 129
criminals, 30, 68, 72
Croatia, 70, 102
Cuba, 53
culture, 159
currency, 77, 98
curriculum, 136
customers, 156
Customs and Border Protection, vii, 7, 27, 28, 65, 78, 79, 119, 139
Customs and Border Protection (CBP), vii, 3, 27, 65, 82
cycles, 158
Cyprus, 80
Czech Republic, 77, 78, 80, 102

D

dairy industry, 105
danger, 76, 130
data collection, 133
data set, 195
database, 3, 20, 21, 33, 35, 45, 65, 70, 79, 81, 119, 121, 122, 139, 163, 173, 175, 186, 191, 192, 193, 194, 196, 197, 198, 199, 200, 206, 207, 208, 221, 224, 226, 227, 228, 242
debts, 230, 235
decision makers, 132
decision-making process, 120
defendants, 238
demographic characteristics, 192
demography, 196
denial, 2, 17, 18, 31, 116, 121, 123, 162, 177
Denmark, 77, 81, 82, 101
Department of Agriculture, 23, 44
Department of Health and Human Services, 23, 44
Department of Homeland Security, viii, ix, 3, 28, 36, 39, 42, 43, 44, 46, 47, 49, 51, 52, 53, 59, 61, 66, 77, 78, 79, 80, 81, 82, 83, 84, 86, 87, 88, 95, 101, 113, 114, 115, 136, 137, 139, 142, 143, 144, 146, 185, 191, 198, 215, 223, 229, 231, 241
Department of Justice, vii, 3, 15, 23, 27, 28, 77, 79, 87, 144, 146, 175, 177, 186, 193, 198, 213, 218, 220, 235
Department of Labor, viii, 4, 23, 29, 44, 143, 144, 145, 146, 185, 189, 198, 220, 226, 229, 231, 241
Departments of State (DOS), vii, 27
depth, 35, 132
derivatives, 87, 88
detectable, 43
detection, 44, 130, 214, 222
detection techniques, 130
detention, 128
devaluation, 77
developed countries, 84, 97, 110
DHS, v, vii, viii, 3, 21, 26, 27, 28, 31, 32, 33, 35, 36, 37, 38, 39, 40, 41, 42, 45, 46, 47, 51, 54, 55, 56, 57, 61, 62, 64, 65, 66, 68, 69, 70, 71, 72, 75, 76, 78, 79, 80, 81, 82, 83, 84, 86, 87, 88, 89, 93, 95, 109, 111, 113, 114, 115, 116, 117, 118, 119, 120, 122, 123, 125, 126, 127, 128, 130, 133, 134, 135, 136, 139, 223, 225
diplomacy, 40
direct investment, 84, 99, 105
disability, 74
disclosure, 88, 89, 156
discrimination, 220
diseases, 10, 11
distribution, 44, 50, 52, 54, 55, 84, 87, 98, 106, 135, 196, 241
District of Columbia, 94
diversity, vii, 5, 29, 49, 50, 51, 52, 53, 54, 55, 56, 57, 58, 106, 226
documentary evidence, 198
DOJ, vii, 3, 26, 27, 28, 40, 41, 77, 79
DOL, 14, 23, 44
domestic investment, 110
dominance, 58
draft, 15, 18, 19, 20, 134, 135, 186
drug testing, 240
due process, 40, 45

E

earnings, 3, 107, 146, 168, 169, 171, 200, 205, 206, 224, 226, 227
earnings data, 146
economic activity, 85, 86, 99, 106
economic crisis, 77
economic downturn, viii, 83, 84, 180, 202
economic efficiency, 195
economic growth, 67, 68, 83, 97, 98, 107, 167
economic indicator, 167
economic losses, 142
economic performance, 99
economic relations, 97, 143, 167, 168
economic theory, 96, 97, 98, 99, 167
economics, 196
education, 14, 49, 51, 54, 147, 161, 163, 166, 191, 192, 196, 197, 204, 224, 226, 227
educational services, 209, 211
educators, 168, 169, 170, 191, 192, 202, 205, 206, 207, 208, 224
Egypt, 35, 52, 53
El Salvador, 51
eligibility criteria, 4
e-mail, 116
embassy, 114, 126, 132
emergency, 11, 22, 24, 61, 62, 63, 77
employees, 35, 46, 57, 86, 108, 118, 125, 128, 136, 139, 149, 158, 176, 177, 180, 184, 190, 194, 210, 213, 214, 220, 221, 222, 223, 225, 230, 232, 233, 234, 235, 239, 240, 242
employers, viii, 14, 141, 142, 143, 145, 146, 148, 149, 150, 151, 152, 153, 155, 156, 157, 158, 160, 161, 162, 164, 165, 166, 167, 170, 171, 173, 174, 175, 176, 177, 178, 180, 183, 185, 186, 187, 188, 189, 190, 191, 192, 195, 197, 198, 208, 209, 210, 211, 212, 213, 214, 220, 221, 222, 225, 226, 229, 230, 231, 232, 233, 237, 240, 241, 242
employment, vii, viii, 4, 12, 13, 14, 21, 26, 49, 50, 57, 83, 84, 85, 86, 87, 90, 97, 98, 99, 101, 105, 106, 107, 109, 110, 111, 139, 143, 145, 146, 148, 149, 167, 168, 169, 171, 173, 177, 180, 181, 184, 189, 190, 192, 196, 197, 200, 204, 205, 207, 208, 213, 214, 220, 221, 224, 226, 231, 232, 234, 238, 242
employment growth, 167
employment levels, 167, 169, 189, 200, 205
employment opportunities, viii, 83, 84, 110
employment relationship, 214
enforcement, 30, 34, 35, 37, 40, 41, 42, 64, 75, 119, 120, 122, 139, 143, 148, 160, 172, 177, 184, 188, 196
engineering, 160, 170, 171, 191, 192, 195, 200, 202, 204, 208, 223, 224
entrepreneurs, 85, 86, 106, 110, 159, 162, 223
environment, 35
equipment, 234
equity, 223
espionage, 25
Estonia, 77, 78, 80, 102
EU, 69, 80
Europe, 50, 51, 52, 54, 69, 92, 93
European Commission, 82
European Union, 80
evidence, 57, 69, 97, 116, 119, 134, 146, 149, 157, 160, 161, 172, 174, 186, 187, 201, 225
examinations, 4, 11, 33
exclusion, vii, 1, 2, 4, 5, 9, 10, 12, 13, 15, 17, 21, 24, 25, 41, 51, 58, 62, 69, 166
executive branch, 46, 70
Executive Office for Immigration Review (EOIR), vii, 3, 15, 23, 27, 28
exercise, 22, 31
expertise, 35, 37, 88, 131, 188, 222
exploitation, 100, 129, 241
exports, 99, 109
extracts, 190
extradition, 72

F

facilitators, 43
Fair Labor Standards Act, 175, 236, 238, 239, 242
fairness, 56
faith, 149, 214
families, 40
family members, 7, 20, 57
fanaticism, 36
farmers, 105
fast food, 230, 235
FBI, 21, 22, 33, 34, 68, 79
FDI, 84, 86, 97, 98, 107, 110
fear, 173, 175, 230, 241
Federal Bureau of Investigation, 22, 34, 80, 119
federal government, 14, 105, 139
Federal Government, 121, 139
federal law, 146, 147, 196, 233, 235
Federal Register, 23, 58, 66, 77, 78, 79
financial, 3, 12, 20, 77, 86, 92, 96, 99, 101, 105, 130, 159, 195, 231, 233, 241
financial data, 20
financial incentives, 130
fingerprints, 32
Finland, 77, 81, 82, 102

fiscal year 2009, 124, 129, 146, 152, 153, 156, 157, 164, 166, 174, 190, 192, 193, 196, 197, 208, 209, 210, 211, 221
flexibility, 141, 184, 185, 187
flight, 25, 36, 65, 78, 110, 115
FLSA, 242
fluctuations, 98, 154, 169, 202, 206
focus groups, 194, 195, 222
food, 231
force, 13, 111, 239
Ford, 68, 79, 136
foreign direct investment, 83, 86, 97, 110
foreign investment, 86, 97, 99, 100, 104, 105, 109
foreign language, 108, 130
foreign nationals, vii, 1, 2, 3, 7, 9, 10, 11, 12, 14, 15, 20, 21, 22, 24, 25, 33, 40, 50, 52, 57, 58, 62, 64, 67, 71, 74, 75, 81, 84, 92, 95, 98, 106, 110, 111, 145, 159, 160, 170, 201, 223, 231, 232
foreign policy, 13, 31, 34, 36, 41
foreign-born population, 59
formula, 49, 52, 54, 63, 108
France, 22, 29, 53, 75, 77, 81, 82, 102
fraud, 15, 25, 32, 35, 44, 50, 57, 68, 100, 118, 119, 125, 127, 129, 130, 139, 143, 146, 149, 162, 173, 177, 183, 184, 214, 222, 225, 230, 231, 232, 233, 235, 237, 241
fraudulent activity, ix, 229, 231, 241
free trade, 93, 94, 109, 147
frequency distribution, 197
funding, 38, 39, 40, 51, 119
funds, 13, 38, 99, 100, 105, 106, 107, 111, 120

G

GDP, 99
genocide, 25
Georgia, 94, 102, 131
Germany, 22, 29, 52, 53, 77, 81, 82, 102
global economy, 184
gonorrhea, 11
goods and services, 99, 167
governments, 36, 40, 43, 99
grades, 182
graduate students, 110
grants, 16
granuloma inguinale, 11
Greece, 69, 77, 80, 81
group work, 105
growth, 8, 21, 67, 79, 85, 89, 91, 97, 98, 99, 110, 159, 167, 169, 200, 205
growth rate, 99, 200
Guatemala, 51
guidance, viii, 11, 88, 113, 114, 115, 117, 124, 125, 126, 128, 133, 134, 135, 164, 174, 225
guidelines, 107, 125, 191
guilty, 230, 233, 234, 235, 237

H

H-2B visa program, viii, 229, 231, 232, 241, 242
Hawaii, 94
health, 1, 4, 9, 10, 11, 14, 20, 23, 24, 33, 44, 51, 79, 81, 195, 197, 209, 232
Health and Human Services, 11
health care, 14, 195, 209
health insurance, 197
HHS, 11, 23, 24, 44
high school, 49, 51, 54
higher education, 147, 148, 166, 192, 212, 214, 221
hiring, 143, 146, 154, 156, 158, 159, 160, 161, 162, 173, 177, 180, 184, 190, 193, 194, 208, 209, 211, 213, 220, 235
history, 1, 4, 9, 12, 33, 51, 71, 79, 81, 119, 183, 201
HIV, 10, 11, 24
HIV/AIDS, 10, 24
homeland security, 31, 36, 39, 40, 41, 121, 130
Homeland Security (DHS), vii, 3, 27, 28, 51, 61, 82, 83, 95, 115, 136
Homeland Security Act, 24, 25, 27, 28, 31, 36, 39, 41, 45, 77, 115, 117, 124, 126, 127, 128, 130, 134, 136, 139
Honduras, 103
Hong Kong, 35, 93, 95, 109, 110
hospitality, 230, 231, 237
host, 35, 97, 110, 120, 122, 124, 130, 131
hotel, 235
hotels, 89, 237
hourly wage, 233
House, 24, 38, 39, 41, 42, 44, 46, 47, 56, 59, 79, 101, 145, 188, 229, 231
House of Representatives, 24, 145, 229, 231
housing, 158, 229, 230, 231, 234, 238, 240, 241
human, 12, 57, 98, 105, 106, 126, 128
human capital, 98, 105, 106
human right, 128
human rights, 128
Hungary, 70, 80
Hurricane Katrina, 101
husband, 235
hybrid, 222

I

Iceland, 77, 81, 82

identification, 66, 80, 130, 174, 220
identity, 22, 32, 66
illegal aliens, 234
immigrant visas, vii, 5, 6, 24, 49, 50, 84, 85, 86, 87, 98
immigrants, vii, 1, 3, 5, 8, 13, 14, 28, 37, 40, 49, 50, 52, 53, 54, 55, 56, 57, 58, 71, 84, 85, 87, 95, 100, 105, 106, 107, 110
immigration, vii, 1, 2, 3, 4, 10, 12, 15, 18, 19, 21, 23, 25, 26, 27, 28, 30, 31, 32, 33, 35, 37, 38, 40, 41, 42, 43, 44, 45, 47, 49, 50, 54, 57, 58, 59, 63, 65, 66, 68, 71, 74, 76, 77, 79, 81, 91, 101, 109, 116, 119, 126, 131, 144, 146, 158, 161, 162, 172, 177, 184, 185, 186, 189, 193, 196, 200, 213, 223, 230, 233, 234, 237
Immigration Act, vii, 10, 16, 30, 45, 49, 50, 73, 84, 85, 86, 91, 181, 213, 219
Immigration and Customs Enforcement (ICE), vii, viii, 27, 28, 46, 47, 82, 113, 115
Immigration and Nationality Act, vii, 1, 3, 10, 23, 24, 28, 30, 44, 49, 50, 62, 85, 86, 91, 107, 108, 116, 164, 181, 213, 232
immunity, 12, 79
Impact Assessment, 80
imprisonment, 24, 237
improvements, 20, 32, 133, 184
inadmissible, 1, 2, 3, 11, 13, 15, 16, 17, 20, 25, 30, 66, 79
incarceration, 24
income, 10, 13, 14, 20, 91, 111, 190, 194, 237
income tax, 111
India, 54, 58, 92, 93, 107, 143, 156, 164, 181, 209, 210, 223, 230, 237
individuals, viii, 15, 22, 34, 44, 65, 68, 77, 79, 80, 86, 88, 89, 109, 111, 113, 119, 128, 143, 147, 148, 164, 167, 186, 187, 214, 225, 230, 237, 241
Indonesia, 53
industrial sectors, 146, 195
industries, 99, 105, 110, 158, 159, 160, 194, 195, 198, 211, 230, 231, 232, 241
industry, 67, 78, 99, 105, 108, 111, 146, 154, 161, 170, 172, 192, 194, 195, 196, 208, 211, 212, 220, 222, 223, 226
infection, 11
inferences, 195, 222
inflation, 99, 224
influenza, 11
influenza virus, 11
information sharing, viii, 61, 64, 68, 70, 75, 172, 173
information technology, 144, 156, 195, 211, 223
infrastructure, 158
injections, 104
INS, 32, 39, 40, 41, 42, 59, 73, 82, 86, 87, 100, 111
inspections, 10, 30, 40, 66, 79, 177
inspectors, 7, 22, 23, 29, 43, 44, 45, 51, 65, 68, 79
institutions, 146, 147, 197, 212
integration, 35
integrity, 63, 185
intelligence, 21, 22, 33, 34, 36, 37, 40, 43, 76, 120, 122, 132
intelligence gathering, 40
Intelligence Reform and Terrorism Prevention Act, 7, 32, 44, 75
interface, 79
interim regulations, 7
intermediaries, ix, 229, 231
Internal Revenue Service, 3, 230, 237
international migration, 84
international relations, 196
international trade, 91
intrinsic value, 91
investment, 84, 85, 86, 87, 88, 89, 91, 92, 95, 96, 97, 98, 99, 100, 101, 105, 106, 107, 108, 110, 111, 131, 223
investment capital, 223
investments, 83, 84, 86, 87, 91, 95, 97, 98, 99, 100, 101, 104, 105, 106, 108, 110, 111
investors, viii, 6, 83, 84, 85, 86, 87, 88, 89, 90, 92, 95, 96, 97, 98, 99, 100, 101, 104, 105, 106, 107, 108, 109, 110, 111, 223
Iowa, 94
Iran, 53, 103
Iraq, 69, 109
Ireland, 50, 51, 52, 53, 58, 77, 81, 82, 103
Islamabad, 35
Israel, 53, 70, 72
issues, 7, 23, 27, 28, 39, 42, 44, 47, 56, 59, 81, 84, 101, 118, 119, 127, 148, 161, 186, 196, 200
Italy, 22, 29, 75, 77, 81, 82, 103

J

Japan, 22, 29, 53, 77, 81, 82, 92, 93, 98, 99, 103, 110
job creation, 85, 86, 104, 107
job performance, 158
joint ventures, 108
Jordan, 103
Judiciary Committee, 41, 44, 68, 79, 86, 101
jurisdiction, 35, 116, 118, 127, 128, 129, 143, 177

K

Kenya, 52, 53
Korea, 103

L

labor force, 84, 97, 168, 200, 222
labor market, 14, 20, 21, 40, 149, 186, 200, 226
labor markets, 40
labor relations, 196
landscape, 240
language skills, 131
languages, 130
Latin America, 50
Latvia, 70, 77, 78, 80, 103
law enforcement, 21, 22, 32, 33, 34, 35, 37, 40, 43, 61, 62, 63, 64, 65, 72, 75, 77, 79, 81, 114, 119, 120, 121, 122, 123, 125, 126, 129, 131, 133, 135, 139
laws, vii, 1, 2, 10, 24, 30, 31, 43, 63, 66, 73, 77, 109, 116, 147, 172, 178, 196, 198, 212, 213, 214, 226, 230, 231, 232, 233, 236, 241
laws and regulations, 196, 198, 231, 241
lawyers, 159
lead, 28, 36, 106
leadership, 37
Leahy, 36, 46
learning, 160
legal permanent resident (LPR) investors, viii, 83, 84
legislation, 25, 30, 36, 44, 59, 66, 72, 73, 86, 87, 101, 109, 115, 117, 147, 220, 222
legislative proposals, 2
leprosy, 11
level of education, 170
Liberia, 53, 103
light, 2, 27, 34, 36, 188, 200, 205
limited liability, 84
Lithuania, 53, 70, 77, 78, 80
litigation, 229, 231, 233, 236, 241
living conditions, 139
loans, 77, 105
lobbying, 101
local conditions, 120
local government, 25, 242
logistics, 162
Louisiana, 94, 230, 237
lower prices, 167
lymphogranuloma venereum, 11

M

Macedonia, 103
magnitude, 159
majority, 67, 89, 90, 92, 97, 110, 150, 159, 164, 175, 183, 209
management, 95, 115, 121, 123, 186, 187
manufacturing, 89, 159, 195, 209, 211, 212, 231
marketplace, 143
marriage, 4, 33, 201
Maryland, 89, 94, 234, 239
materials, 226
mathematics, 170
matter, 43, 141, 158, 184, 186, 188, 193
meat, 105
media, 23, 43, 88, 196
median, 169, 171, 191, 197, 200, 205, 206, 222, 224, 227
Medicaid, 10, 24
medical, 11, 77, 139
membership, 10, 69, 79, 92
memorandums of understanding, 114
mental disorder, 11
merchandise, 91
methodology, 119, 190, 232
Mexico, 8, 54, 58, 94, 103, 181, 234
migrants, 84, 98
migration, viii, 49, 50, 58, 84, 96, 97, 98, 99, 110, 196
military, 13, 15, 44, 46, 109
minimum wage, 232, 233, 234, 239, 242
mission, 37, 40, 46, 80, 114, 115, 121, 123, 125, 126, 130, 134, 136
Missouri, 94, 239
misuse, 50, 57
models, 97, 110, 220, 227
modernization, 143, 144, 184
modifications, 160, 223
money laundering, 12, 230, 237
Montana, 94
Morocco, 35, 52, 53
motels, 89
motivation, 99
multinational companies, 159, 195
multinational corporations, 109
multinational firms, 158
multiplier, 99, 101, 105, 110
multiplier effect, 99, 105, 110
murder, 12

N

national income, 110
national origin, 50
national security, 7, 10, 18, 20, 40, 41, 43, 50, 57, 68, 119, 121, 123, 133, 135
nationality, 30, 31, 37, 66, 80, 91, 92, 93, 108, 116
NCTC, 22, 34, 36
Nepal, 53, 54
Netherlands, 77, 81, 82, 103

New Zealand, 22, 29, 77, 81, 82, 95
Nigeria, 27, 28, 36, 52, 53
noncitizens, 28, 193
nonprofit organizations, 183
North America, 52, 54, 92, 93, 145, 193, 212
Northern Ireland, 49, 52
Northwest Airlines, 2, 27, 28, 36, 115
Norway, 77, 82, 103

O

Obama, 38, 39, 80
Obama Administration, 39
obstacles, 175, 187
occupational groups, 202, 206, 207, 208, 224, 227, 228
Oceania, 92, 93
officials, viii, 13, 21, 27, 28, 33, 34, 35, 36, 37, 43, 65, 69, 80, 87, 101, 104, 113, 114, 115, 118, 119, 122, 123, 124, 125, 126, 127, 128, 129, 130, 131, 132, 133, 134, 135, 136, 137, 141, 146, 151, 154, 159, 162, 163, 164, 173, 174, 175, 177, 178, 180, 181, 188, 189, 194, 196, 222, 224, 225, 227, 230, 234
oil, 105
oil spill, 105
Oklahoma, 94
open markets, 95
operations, viii, 38, 43, 67, 90, 91, 109, 113, 114, 115, 117, 118, 120, 121, 124, 126, 128, 129, 130, 134, 135, 141, 156, 159, 193, 199, 206, 207, 208, 224, 227, 228
operations research, 199, 206, 207, 208, 224, 227, 228
opportunities, 40, 43, 99, 130, 131, 139, 158, 170, 187
Organization for Economic Cooperation and Development, 92
outsourcing, 159, 160, 195, 222, 223
overlap, 58, 129
oversight, 143, 172, 185, 186
overtime, 230, 233, 234, 235, 236, 239, 242
ownership, 91, 108

P

Pakistan, 35, 53, 103
Paraguay, 103
parity, 87
parole, 23, 44, 73, 77
participants, 6, 29, 71
pathways, 57, 88
Patriot Act, 74
payroll, 208, 230, 237, 240
penalties, 148, 175, 176, 190, 213
per capita income, 97
permission, 25, 77, 220
permit, 7, 34, 42, 161, 162, 184
Peru, 53
pharmaceutical, 159, 161
pharmaceuticals, 195
Philadelphia, 101, 105, 106, 111, 196
Philippines, 35, 54, 58, 103, 164
photographs, 21, 33
physical abuse, 235
physicians, 11, 14, 192, 202
plants, 105
playing, 28, 36
pleasure, viii, 61, 62, 67
Poland, 53, 62, 69, 70, 80
polarization, 98
police, 77, 241
policy, vii, viii, 1, 2, 3, 9, 13, 14, 23, 25, 27, 28, 30, 31, 41, 42, 43, 44, 56, 58, 83, 84, 97, 100, 111, 115, 116, 143, 162, 184, 235
policy options, viii, 83, 84
policymakers, 28, 36
population, 54, 55, 92, 107, 163, 166, 190, 191, 193, 194, 204, 205, 226, 229, 232, 242
port of entry, 11, 22, 28, 29, 30, 61, 63, 65, 75
portability, 214, 220
Portugal, 77, 82
potential benefits, 110, 187, 188
poverty, 14, 20, 77
poverty line, 14, 20
preferential treatment, 220
preparation, 127
President, 22, 38, 41, 43, 46, 47, 70, 79, 82, 111, 112
President Obama, 70
prevention, 118, 214, 222
primary data, 133
principles, 119
probability, 191
productivity growth, 110
professionals, 108, 170, 214
profit, 100, 240
program features, 157
programming, 165, 171, 191, 192, 199, 200, 202, 206, 207, 208, 211, 212, 224, 227, 228
project, 157, 159, 161, 211, 222
property rights, 95
proportionality, 91
protection, 40, 139, 172, 175, 178, 184, 185
public health, 5, 11, 24, 40, 62
public interest, 82

public safety, 25, 40, 121, 133, 135
public support, 69
publishing, 159, 211, 212
Puerto Rico, 94

Q

qualifications, 91, 143, 149, 150, 161, 174, 182, 184
quality assurance, 223
quartile, 132
query, 65, 163
questioning, 39
questionnaire, 188, 195

R

race, 74
real estate, 89
recession, 77
reciprocity, 31, 36, 40, 69, 80
recognition, 57, 85
recommendations, 32, 36, 41, 43, 44, 47, 113, 115, 121, 122, 123, 141, 178, 185, 186
recovery, 180
recruiting, 241
reform, 2, 57, 144, 184
Reform, 10, 16, 21, 25, 26, 30, 34, 40, 42, 45, 46, 50, 72, 73, 74, 77, 147, 166, 181, 213, 214
reforms, 36, 59
refugee status, 28
refugees, 3, 11, 14, 28, 40, 106
regulations, 4, 8, 11, 27, 31, 41, 42, 62, 86, 91, 99, 100, 105, 107, 110, 111, 116, 139, 146, 186, 196, 223, 231, 238, 242
reimburse, 236
relatives, 78, 106
reliability, 124, 135, 189, 194, 196
relief, 3, 13, 15, 28, 239
rent, 233, 237, 238, 240
repair, 107
requirements, viii, 3, 7, 10, 22, 23, 25, 29, 31, 32, 44, 61, 62, 64, 68, 69, 72, 73, 75, 76, 82, 85, 87, 88, 90, 92, 95, 96, 105, 107, 108, 109, 111, 141, 143, 145, 148, 156, 172, 176, 177, 178, 180, 181, 183, 184, 185, 186, 187, 189, 213, 220, 225, 229, 231, 241
research institutions, 142
researchers, 14, 160, 161, 170, 199, 200, 223
resistance, 75
resolution, 84, 118, 119, 125, 127, 157, 193
resources, 20, 35, 36, 68, 100, 105, 135, 158, 175, 184
response, viii, 10, 50, 95, 115, 121, 135, 141, 142, 160, 161, 186, 187, 188
restaurants, 230, 235
restitution, 234
restrictions, 62, 95, 97, 99, 175, 230
retail, 195
retaliation, 173, 230, 241
revenue, 181
rights, 149, 230
rings, 57
risk, 11, 22, 35, 38, 39, 64, 67, 68, 75, 86, 91, 107, 110, 113, 114, 119, 120, 131, 132, 133, 134, 161, 162, 177, 184
risk profile, 35
risks, viii, 25, 57, 68, 70, 83, 84, 110, 119, 188
Romania, 53, 62, 80
roots, 108
rules, 16, 51, 69, 77, 80, 91, 92, 101, 108, 109, 148, 162, 173, 185, 187, 194, 213, 226, 230, 231, 233, 240
rural areas, 107
Russia, 53

S

safety, 34, 68, 133, 232, 234
sample design, 190
SARS, 11
Saudi Arabia, 32, 35, 40, 115, 116, 120, 128, 130
savings, 98, 188
Schengen Agreement, 80
school, 139, 211, 212
science, 145, 161, 170, 196, 200
scope, 31, 125, 128, 146, 189, 232
seafood, 240
Secretary of Homeland Security, 11, 13, 22, 24, 25, 26, 31, 32, 47, 62, 63, 77, 115, 116, 118, 127, 128, 134, 139, 185, 241
secure communication, 22, 34
security, viii, 1, 4, 7, 9, 22, 25, 28, 31, 32, 33, 35, 36, 37, 38, 39, 40, 41, 44, 51, 56, 57, 59, 61, 62, 63, 64, 65, 68, 70, 71, 75, 76, 77, 81, 83, 84, 113, 114, 115, 116, 117, 118, 119, 120, 124, 125, 126, 127, 128, 129, 132, 133, 134, 135, 139
seed, viii, 49, 50, 58
seizure, 123
self-employed, 191, 204, 205, 224, 226
self-study, 131
semiconductor, 159, 195
Senate, 26, 30, 36, 41, 42, 44, 45, 46, 47, 56, 68, 78, 79, 86, 101, 111, 113, 115, 145
sensitivity, 227
sentencing, 234, 238

services, 37, 38, 40, 41, 91, 107, 156, 157, 159, 160, 182, 195, 196, 208, 211, 212, 213, 219, 221, 222, 223, 237, 239, 242
severe acute respiratory syndrome, 11
sex, 74, 200
short supply, 182
shortage, viii, 145, 229, 231
showing, 96, 99, 152
sibling, 4, 29
Silicon Valley, 159, 162, 209
Singapore, 77, 82, 103, 109, 147, 214, 220
skilled workers, 154, 170
slavery, 238
Slovakia, 70, 77, 78, 80
small firms, 142, 158, 162
smallpox, 11
smuggling, 126, 128
social network, 99
social security, 14
software, 57, 159, 161, 172, 211
solidarity, 69
solution, 66, 79, 104
South America, 11, 92, 93
South Dakota, 94, 101, 104, 105, 111, 230, 235
South Korea, 77, 78, 80, 92, 93, 99
Spain, 77, 82, 104
specialists, 44, 224, 227, 228
specific knowledge, 28, 37, 40
specifications, 3, 49, 52
spillover effects, 105
Sri Lanka, 104
SSA, 25
stabilization, 101
staff members, 100
staffing, 28, 37, 40, 123, 133, 134, 135, 143, 144, 156, 157, 159, 160, 172, 178, 179, 180, 181, 184, 185, 195, 196, 222, 223, 225, 231, 241
stakeholders, 144, 184, 226
standard error, 191, 226
standard of living, 97
standardization, 80
statistics, 83, 95, 200
statutes, 15, 30
statutory authority, 25, 73, 185, 187, 220
steel, 99
storage, 79, 99
structure, 105, 195
subpoena, 173, 175, 185
substitutes, 97
substitution, 25
Sudan, 53
supervision, 46, 108
supervisors, 32
survival, 159
Sweden, 77, 82, 104
Switzerland, 22, 29, 77, 82, 104
syphilis, 11

T

tactics, 122
Taiwan, 62, 93, 98, 99, 102
talent, 162
target, 44, 111, 145
tax evasion, 230, 237
taxes, 230, 237
taxpayers, 188
teachers, 199
teams, 211
technical assistance, 76
technical comments, 134, 186, 187, 225
techniques, 32, 126, 130, 131
technological advances, 95
technologies, 44
technology, 32, 106, 110, 142, 143, 145, 154, 158, 162, 170, 187, 189, 195, 196, 200, 209
telephone, 78, 116, 226
tension, 125, 127, 129
tensions, 37, 114
terrorism, 18, 20, 24, 36, 57, 68, 69, 129, 130, 139
terrorist activities, 13, 25
terrorist attacks, vii, 1, 2, 7, 8, 9, 10, 30, 36, 43, 115
terrorist organization, 10, 13, 24, 44
terrorist watchlist, 122
terrorists, viii, 21, 34, 36, 37, 40, 43, 50, 61, 68, 129
testing, 66, 232, 242
Thailand, 104
The Homeland Security Act, 26, 31, 82, 116, 139
theft, 63, 74, 76
threats, 35, 114, 116, 118, 119, 121, 122, 126, 132, 239
time frame, 83, 227
time periods, 180
Title I, 10, 15
Title II, 15
Title IV, 10
Togo, 53, 104
torture, 12
tourism, viii, 36, 40, 61, 67, 69, 79
tracks, 21, 33, 122, 135, 163
trade, 36, 40, 79, 85, 90, 91, 95, 97, 98, 99, 101, 108, 109, 110
trade agreement, 101
trade liberalization, 97
trafficking, 12, 57

training, 10, 13, 15, 31, 32, 35, 44, 49, 51, 54, 105, 113, 114, 116, 118, 122, 123, 124, 126, 130, 131, 134, 136, 139, 158, 170
transactions, 230, 240
transformation, 101, 105, 185, 186
transparency, 186
transportation, 39, 43, 233, 238, 240, 242
transportation security, 39
Transportation Security Administration, 128
Treasury, 32, 65, 79, 115, 119, 139
treaties, 85, 90, 108
treatment, 69, 77, 80, 147, 234, 238
Trinidad, 104
tuberculosis, 11, 24
Turkey, 52, 53, 54, 104
turnover, 124, 136

U

U.S. Citizenship and Immigrant Services (USCIS), vii, 27
U.S. Department of Commerce, 99, 110
U.S. Department of Labor, 14
U.S. economy, 85, 167
U.S. immigration law, 64, 71, 75
U.S. immigration policy, vii, 1, 2, 58, 162
U.S. labor market, 149, 159, 170
Ukraine, 52, 53
unemployed individuals, 232
unemployment rate, 107, 169, 189, 200, 205, 206, 207
United Kingdom, 77, 82, 95, 104, 182, 209, 210
United Nations, 110
universe, 194, 211, 221
universities, 142, 159, 166, 183, 194, 199, 201, 211, 212, 221
university education, 165, 171, 197, 199, 200
Uruguay, 63, 77, 82
USA Patriot Act, 40, 74
USDA, 23, 44
Uzbekistan, 53

V

variables, 98, 132, 189, 191, 194
variations, 190
vehicles, 79
Venezuela, 35
venture capital, 146, 158, 162, 196, 223
vessels, 79
veto, 108
violence, 13
viral hemorrhagic fever, 11
visa issuances, vii, 1, 2, 27, 28, 31, 36, 37, 40, 41, 42, 44, 77, 92, 146, 185, 193, 198
Visa Security Program, v, vii, viii, 27, 28, 35, 38, 39, 46, 47, 113, 115, 116, 117, 119, 120, 121, 122, 124, 128, 129, 130, 133, 134, 136, 139
Visa Waiver Program, v, 22, 23, 26, 29, 44, 45, 61, 72, 78, 79, 80, 81
visa waiver program (VWP), viii, 61, 62
vote, 25
voters, 80

W

wage differentials, 98, 99
wage level, 182
wage payments, 174
wage rate, 167, 178, 180, 224
wages, 14, 84, 109, 143, 145, 146, 159, 162, 167, 170, 172, 173, 175, 176, 182, 184, 189, 190, 191, 198, 200, 213, 220, 224, 230, 232, 233, 234, 236, 238, 240
waiver, viii, 7, 11, 12, 14, 15, 16, 22, 23, 24, 25, 26, 61, 62, 64, 71, 73, 75, 78, 79, 80, 81, 82
war, 72, 77
War on Terror, 80
Washington, 46, 79, 80, 94, 109, 110, 115, 119, 130, 133, 136, 137, 139, 220, 223, 225, 227
watershed, 9
web, 62
welfare, 36, 40, 63, 76
workforce, 97, 143, 145, 156, 159, 163, 164, 167, 168, 170, 172, 181, 183, 190, 192, 193, 198, 200, 205, 224, 228
working conditions, 14, 149, 173, 214, 230, 232, 240
workload, 68, 121, 128
World Bank, 110
World Trade Center, 10, 21, 34
World War I, 15, 30
worldwide, 81, 86, 92, 106, 128, 131, 132, 137

X

x-rays, 11

Y

Yale University, 223
yellow fever, 11
Yemen, 39
yield, 99
young women, 57